A GRAMMAR OF
MISHNAIC HEBREW

A GRAMMAR OF
MISHNAIC HEBREW

BY

M. H. SEGAL, M.A.

OXFORD
AT THE CLARENDON PRESS

Oxford University Press, Amen House, London E.C.4

GLASGOW NEW YORK TORONTO MELBOURNE WELLINGTON
BOMBAY CALCUTTA MADRAS KARACHI KUALA LUMPUR
CAPE TOWN IBADAN NAIROBI ACCRA

FIRST EDITION 1927
REPRINTED LITHOGRAPHICALLY
IN GREAT BRITAIN
AT THE UNIVERSITY PRESS, OXFORD
FROM CORRECTED SHEETS OF THE FIRST EDITION
1958

PREFACE

THIS little book has been written with a twofold object : first, to provide students of early Rabbinic literature with a fairly complete grammar of the dialect of that literature ; and, secondly, to demonstrate the organic connexion of this Mishnaic dialect with Biblical Hebrew, and its relative independence of contemporary Aramaic, at least in the field of grammar. A good deal of material belonging to comparative grammar has, therefore, been introduced, and constant reference is made to the standard authority in the English language on the grammar of Biblical Hebrew, viz. Dr. Cowley's edition of *Gesenius-Kautzsch's Hebrew Grammar*. As that work is most familiar to English readers, I have followed it, as far as possible, in the arrangement and terminology of the present work.

The examples illustrating grammatical rules have been drawn mainly from the Mishna and, to a smaller extent, from the *Baraitot* and other Hebrew elements of the Babylonian Talmud, because these works are the most accessible to ordinary students. Other less accessible works, like the Tosefta, the Jerusalem Talmud, and the *Midrashim*, have been drawn upon only occasionally. The English renderings of the examples have been made as literal as possible, in order to exhibit clearly the construction and phraseology of the original.

As is well known, the text of Rabbinic works is in a neglected condition, and readings are often uncertain. In citations from the Mishna I have taken care to give only examples of which the reading is established as fairly correct by agreement between the Palestinian text of Lowe and the Babylonian texts of the current editions of the Mishna, and of the Mishna embodied in the Babylonian Talmud. I have refrained from troubling the reader with variant readings which serve no grammatical purpose. Occasionally, however, differences of reading have been indicated where they have a bearing on the grammar of the dialect.

It has not been found practicable to accompany the work with a general index. In order to facilitate reference to its contents, the Table of Contents has been made as detailed as necessary.

I desire to acknowledge my indebtedness to Professor Albrecht's excellent little book, *Neuhebräische Grammatik*, which has furnished me with numerous examples, and has thus lightened my labours in the preparation of this work.

I have also to record with gratitude the interest taken in the publication of this work by that good friend of all English students of Rabbinics, the late Dr. Israel Abrahams, ל״ז.

My friends Mr. Herbert Loewe, of Exeter College, Oxford, and Canon Danby, of Jerusalem, have read the proofs, and have otherwise helped me with corrections and suggestions. If the work be found free from typographical errors, it will be due chiefly to their help combined with the skill and vigilance of the readers of the Clarendon Press.

M. H. SEGAL.

THE HEBREW UNIVERSITY,
JERUSALEM.
September, 1926.

NOTE TO THE NEW IMPRESSION

IN this new impression a number of misprints and other errors have been corrected, but otherwise the book has been left unchanged.

Readers familiar with modern Hebrew who may wish to pursue further the grammatical study of Mishnaic Hebrew are recommended to consult the author's דקדוק לשון המשנה (Tel Aviv, 1936), which provides a fuller and more detailed treatment of the subject.

M. H. S.

THE HEBREW UNIVERSITY,
JERUSALEM.
January, 1957.

CONTENTS

INTRODUCTION

PART I

PHONOLOGY AND ORTHOGRAPHY

I. EVIDENCE FOR THE PRONUNCIATION

(*a*) **External.**

(*b*) **Internal.**

II. THE VOWELS

III. THE CONSONANTS

1. **Gutturals.**

2. Palatals.

3. Dentals.

4. Labials.

5. Sibilants.

6. Sonants.

7. Semi-Vowels.

8. ת, פ, כ, ד, ג, ב.

9. Other Consonantal Changes.

PART II

. MORPHOLOGY

I. THE PRONOUN

1. The Personal Pronoun.

2. The Demonstrative Pronoun.

3. Relative Pronoun.

II. THE VERB

A. General Survey.

1. LEXICAL.

CONTENTS

B. The Stems.

1. The Simple Stem.

CONTENTS

3. The Causative Stem.

C. The Tenses.

D. Weak Verbs.

(1) Guttural Verbs.

(6) Verbs ע״ע.

(7) Verbs ל״א.

(8) Verbs ל״ה.

(9) Verbs with Pronominal Suffixes.

III. THE NOUN

1. General Survey.

2. Formation of Nouns.

(1) *Nouns derived from the Simple Stem.*

CONTENTS

PART III

SYNTAX

I. THE VERB

1. Tenses and Moods.

(4) THE INFINITIVE.

2. The Government of the Verb.

(1) *Subordination of Noun to Verb as Accusative.*

(2) *Subordination of Noun to Verb by a Preposition.*

II. THE NOUN

1. Determination of the Gender.

2. Use of the Article.

3. Expression of the Genitive.

III. THE PRONOUN

1. The Personal Pronoun.

2. Possessive Pronoun.

3. Demonstrative Pronoun.

4. Interrogative Pronoun.

5. Relative Pronoun. The Use of ־שֶׁ.

6. Expression of the Reflexive and Reciprocal.

7. Expression of the Indefinite.

IV. SENTENCES AND CLAUSES

1. Nominative Absolute.

2. Agreement between Subject and Predicate.

3. Sentences expressing an Oath or a Vow.

4. Interrogative Sentences.

5. Desiderative Sentences.

6. Negative Sentences.

7. Relative Clauses.

8. Circumstantial Clauses.

12. Comparative Clauses.

13. Disjunctive Clauses.

14. Adversative, Exceptive, and Restrictive Clauses.

15. Temporal Clauses.

CONTENTS

16. Final Clauses.

17. Consecutive Clauses.

ABBREVIATIONS

Tractates of the Mishna, Tosefta, and the Talmuds :—

Ab.	אָבוֹת (iv)		Makš.	מַכְשִׁירִין (vi)
ʻAr.	עֲרָכִין (v)		Mid.	מִדּוֹת (v)
ʻAZ.	עֲבוֹדָהזָרָה (iv)		Miq.	מִקְוָאוֹת (vi)
Be.	בֵּיצָה (ii)		Meg.	מְגִלָּה (ii)
Bik.	בִּכּוּרִים (i)		Meʻil.	מְעִילָה (v)
Bek.	בְּכוֹרוֹת (v)		Men.	מְנָחוֹת (v)
Ber.	בְּרָכוֹת (i)		MQ.	מוֹעֵד קָטָן (ii)
BB.	בָּבָא בַּתְרָא (iv)		MŠ.	מַעֲשֵׂר שֵׁנִי (i)
BM.	בָּבָא מְצִיעָא (iv)		Naz.	נָזִיר (iii)
BQ.	בָּבָא קַמָּא (iv)		Nid.	נִדָּה (vi)
Da.	דְּמַאי (i)		Ned.	נְדָרִים (iii)
ʻEd.	עֲדִיּוֹת (iv)		Oh.	אֲהָלוֹת (vi)
ʻEr.	עֵרוּבִין (ii)		ʻOr.	עָרְלָה (i)
Giṭ.	גִּטִּין (iii)		Pa.	פָּרָה (vi)
Ho.	הוֹרָיוֹת (iv)		Pe.	פֵּאָה (i)
Ḥag.	חֲגִיגָה (ii)		Pes.	פְּסָחִים (ii)
Ḥal.	חַלָּה (i)		Qid.	קִידּוּשִׁין (iii)
Ḥul.	חֻלִּין (v)		Qin.	קִנִּים (v)
Kel.	כֵּלִים (vi)		RH.	רֹאשׁ הַשָּׁנָה (ii)
Kil.	כִּלְאַיִם (i)		San.	סַנְהֶדְרִין (iv)
Ker.	כְּרִיתוֹת (v)		So.	סוֹטָה (iii)
Ket.	כְּתוּבּוֹת (iii)		Suk.	סוּכָּה (ii)
Maʻa.	מַעֲשְׂרוֹת (i)		Šab.	שַׁבָּת (ii)
Mak.	מַכּוֹת (v		Šebi.	שְׁבִיעִית (i)

Šebu.	שְׁבוּעוֹת (iv)		ṬY.	טְבוּל יוֹם (vi)
Šeq.	שְׁקָלִים (ii)		'Uq.	עוּקְצִין (vi)
Ta'a.	תַּעֲנִית (ii)		Ya.	יָדַיִם (vi)
Tam.	תָּמִיד (v)		Yo.	יוֹמָא (ii)
Tem.	תְּמוּרָה (v)		Yeb.	יְבָמוֹת (iii)
Ter.	תְּרוּמוֹת (i)		Zab.	זָבִים (vi)
Ṭoh.	טָהֳרוֹת (vi)		Zeb.	זְבָחִים (v)

NOTE.—The figures after the tractates indicate the Order (סֵדֶר), or part of the Mishna, in which these tractates are found.

In citations from the Mishna, Tosefta, and the Jerusalem Talmud roman numerals indicate the chapter and arabic numerals the section or הֲלָכָה, thus: Ber. iii. 5. Citations from the Tosefta are marked by *t.* before the name of the tractate. Citations from the Jerusalem Talmud are marked by *j.* before the name of the tractate. In citations from the Babylonian Talmud, the folio is indicated by arabic numerals and the page or column by *a, b* thus : San. 75 b.

L.	The Mishnah on which the Palestinian Talmud rests, ed. by W. H. Lowe, Cambridge, 1883.
Ab. deRN.	אָבוֹת דְּרַבִּי נָתָן
Gen. R.	בְּרֵאשִׁית רַבָּה
Ex. R.	שְׁמוֹת רַבָּה
Lev. R.	וַיִּקְרָא רַבָּה
Num. R.	בְּמִדְבָּר רַבָּה
Lam. R.	אֵיכָה רַבָּתִי
Qoh. R.	קֹהֶלֶת רַבָּה
Mekil.	מְכִילְתָּא
Singer	*The Authorised Daily Prayer Book*, ed. Singer.
BDB.	*Hebrew and English Lexicon of the O. T.*, ed. Brown, Driver, and Briggs, Oxford, 1906.

Ges.-K.	Gesenius-Kautzsch's *Hebrew Grammar*, ed. A. E. Cowley, Oxford.
JQR.	*Jewish Quarterly Review.*
MGWJ.	*Monatschrift für die Geschichte u. Wissenschaft d. Judentums.*
ZAW.	*Zeitschrift für die Alttestamentliche Wissenschaft.*
ZDMG.	*Zeitschrift d. deutschen morgenländischen Gesellschaft.*
Aram.	Aramaic.
BH	Biblical Hebrew.
MH	Mishnaic Hebrew.
Gr.	Greek.
Lat.	Latin.

LITERATURE

A. Geiger, *Lehr- u. Lesebuch zur Sprache der Mischnah*, Breslau, 1845.

L. Dukes, *Die Sprache der Mischna*, Esslingen, 1846.

J. H. Weiss, משפט לשון המשנה, Wien, 1867.

C. Siegfried & H. Strack, *Lehrbuch d. neuhebräischen Sprache*, 1884.

L. Metmann, *Dië hebräische Sprache*, Jersualem (no date).

K. Albrecht, *Neuhebräische Grammatik auf Grund d. Mišna*, München, 1913.

F. Hillel, *Die Nominalbildung in der Mischnah*, 1891.

H. Sachs, *Die Partikeln der Mischna*, 1897.

M. H. Segal, Mišnaic Hebrew and its relation to Biblical Hebrew and to Aramaic, *JQR.* (Old Series), vol. XX, pp. 647–737, and separately, Oxford, 1909.

Siegfried, *Zur Lehre von dem zus. gesetzten Satze im Neuhebr.*, Kohut, Semitic Studies, pp. 543 ff.

Albrecht, שֶׁ in der Mišna, *ZAW.*, 1911, pp. 205 ff.

J. Barth, *Die Nominalbildung in den semit. Sprachen*, 1894.

S. Stein, *Das Verbum in der Mischnasprache*, 1888.

A. Kohut, *Aruch Completum*, Wien, 1878–92.

J. Levy, *Neuhebr. Wörterbuch*, 1876–89.

M. Jastrow, *Dictionary of the Talmud*, 1886–1903.

S. Krauss, *Griechische u. Lateinische Lehnwörter im Talmud*, 1898–9.

ADDENDA

Sect. 2, note 2. So *Midrash Tehillim* (ed. Buber), ix. 3 : שנו חכמים
בלשון המשנה. The term is also frequent among medieval
writers, e. g. Rashi on Gen. xl. 11. Menaḥem b. Saruq uses
לשון משנה in contrast to לשון עברית, i. e. BH, cf. מחברת (ed.
Filipowsky), p. 9. Abraham de Balmis uses it in contrast to
לשון מקרא, cf. מקנה אברהם, ch. iv, Sect. פעלת.

Sect. 25, p. 18. Qid. iv. 1 is cited in Hebrew in Yᵉb. 85 a ; cf.
Grätz, *Geschichte*[4], iii. 711. That the *Kᵉtuba* was originally
in Hebrew is shown by its Hebrew name (for the form cf.
§ 229 below, and Stade, *Heb. Gram.*, § 204 b. The Aram.
כתובתא is a Hebraism). Cf. also its Gr. equivalent συγγραφή,
Tobit vii. 14, and Grätz, *ibid.* 706.

Sect. 63. Krauss's suggestion (*ZDMG.*, 1919, 732) that ברבי
should be pointed בְּרִבִּי, בִּיר +רַבִּי is improbable. It would have
been spelt *plene*, בירבי.

Sect. 126. Another example of Puʻal is found in Pᵉsiqta R. ix.
(ed. Friedmann, p. 33 a) : נוּצָּחְתִּי, to prevail.

Sect. 134. A quadriliteral form of Nithpaʻel is found in מִתְנַוְנֶה,
fem. מִתְנַוְנָה to fail, decay, BQ 91 a ; So. iii. 5 ; Ḥul. 57 b ;
also יִתְעַלֵּפֶּה to swoon, Šab. 9 b ; Ḥul. 3 b. Cf. Kohut, vi. 209,
and Ibn Ganaḥ, *Riqma*, 81, who explains it as an intensive.

Sect. 149. סרגל. Cf., however, Perles, *Festschrift für A. Schwarz*,
303, and Krauss, *ibid.*, 575.

Sect. 150. שלהב. Cf., however, Barth, *Etymologische Studien*, 49.

Sect. 168. יתווחרו. Cf. Ginzberg, *Festschrift für A. Schwarz*,
348.

Sect. 187. Cf. Barth's note in Petuchowsky's *Mischnajjot* (Berlin, 1922), iii. 89.

Sect. 191. Add מְסַתְוֹנֶן, מְסַתְוֹנֶנֶת to strain, refine, Pᵉsiq. R. 58 a.

Sect. 211. הרצתי. Cf. Fränkel, *ZAW.*, xix, 181.

Sect. 269. בורקי, ברקאי. Cf. also Ginzberg, *Journal of Jewish Lore* (Cincinnati, 1919), 202 f.

Sect. 282, p. 127. סממנים. Cf. Nöldeke, *Syr. Gram.* 74. The form may, perhaps, be a double plural, cf. Brockelmann, *Grundriss*, i. 451; also Bauer-Leander, *Histor. Gram. d. hebr. Sprache*, §§ 146, 160.

Sect. 298, n. 1. With pronominal suffixes the form דִּי alone is used, as in BH, thus: דִּיִּי Bᵉr. 24 b; דְּיָךְ j. San. vii. 1; דִּיוֹ BQ 18 b; דָּיָהּ Bᵉr. 9 b; דַּיֵּינוּ 16 a; דַּיֵּיכֶם j. Šᵉbi. iv. 3; דַּיִּין (masc.) Šab. 31 b; דַּיִּין (fem.) Nid. i. 1.

Sect. 302. The use in Jewish Aram. of אַף עַל, אֵלוּ, אֲפִילוּ, אֲבָל פִּי כֵן, and הוֹאִיל is borrowed from MH, cf. Levias, *Gram. of Aram. idiom contained in the Babyl. Talmud*, § 182. Cf. also Gen. R. 91: אֲבָל, לְשׁוֹן דְּרוֹמִי הוּא אֲבָל בְּרַם is a southern expression for ברם verily. The Aram. ברם is also found in MH, e. g. Šab. 13 b.

Sect. 304. On הרי and ארי cf. also Barth, *Jahresbericht d. Rabb.-Seminars zu Berlin*, 1909–10, 27 ll.

Sect. 335. Cf. further כָּל שֶׁהוּבָא בְחַמִּין = כָּל שֶׁבָּא בְחַמִּין everything which has been put into hot water, Šab. xxii. 2. Similarly we find the active infin. used with a passive significance: צָרִיךְ אַתָּה לְנַדּוֹת thou shouldst be excommunicated, Ta'an. iii. 12; הָיָה בֵּיתוֹ לִבְנוֹת גְּדֵרוֹ לִסְגּוֹר שָׂדֵהוּ לִקְצוֹר if his house had to be built, his wall to be closed in, his field to be harvested, Nᵉd. iv. 7; cf. § 348.

Sect. 392. Cf. also זוֹנָה שֶׁבַּזּוֹנוֹת the worst of harlots, j. Šab. viii. 3; חָסִיד שֶׁבַּחֲסִידִים the greatest saint, j. Kᵉt. i. 8.

Sect. **402.** שמין. Cf. in a medieval text: שמין זהוב ⅛ of a gold dinar, Mann, *The Jews in Egypt and Palestine*, ii. 188. The editor's correction is unnecessary.

Sect. **431.** Cf. Frankel, מבוא הירושלמי, 10 a.

Sect. **435.** Cf. Be. 3 b; Zeb. 72 a, where a distinction is drawn between כָּל שֶׁדִּרְבּוּ לִימָנוֹת and אֶת שֶׁדִּרְבּוּ לִימָנוֹת 'Or. iii. 6, the first being definite and the second indefinite.

Sect. **437.** כלום. Cf. also Schulthess, *Gram. d. christ.-paläst. Aram.*, § 65, 2. אחד also serves to express an indefinite subject: א״ל אֶחָד שֶׁאֵינוֹ נֶאֱמָן עַל הַמַּעַשְׂרוֹת some one, who was not to be trusted about tithes, said to him, Dam. iv. 1. 6; Ta'a. ii. 5; מַעֲשֶׂה בְּאֶחָד it happened of some one, Yeb. xvi. 4; עָמַד אֶחָד some one arose, Ket. xiii. 2.

Sect. **449.** On כל אדם קורין cf. Frankel, דרכי המשנה (Warsaw, 1923), 273.

Sect. **502.** On אחד . . . ואחד. So also with plur. nouns in the masc.: אֶחָד כֵּלִים גְּדוֹלִים וְאֶחָד כֵּלִים קְטַנִּים whether large vessels or small vessels, Miq. iv. 1; fem.: אֶחָד בְּתוּלוֹת וְאֶחָד בְּעוּלוֹת אֶחָד גְּרוּשׁוֹת וְאֶחָד אַלְמָנוֹת whether virgins or married women, divorced women or widows, Yeb. iv. 10; אֶחָד חֲקִירוֹת וְאֶחָד בְּדִיקוֹת whether cross-examinations as to circumstances or as to time and place, San. v. 2; sometimes, however, אחת is found with the fem.: אַחַת גְּדוֹלָה וְאַחַת קְטַנָּה Suk. i. 11. בֵּין . . . בֵּין is also found before nominal forms, but without -שֶׁ: בֵּין לַחִים בֵּין יְבֵשִׁים whether moist or dry, Šab. iv. 1.

Sect. **503.** אבל may also introduce a co-ordinated noun clause: נוֹטְלִים אֲבָל לֹא מַחֲזִירִים hot but not cooked; חַמִּים אֲבָל לֹא תַבְשִׁיל (L ולא) one may remove but not put back, Šab. iii. 1.

Sect. **504.** So אֶלָּא שֶׁבַּמְּדִינָה but in the province, &c., in contrast to the Temple, Tam. vii. 2. Cf. also Ginzberg, *Journal of Jewish Lore*, 1919, 279.

INTRODUCTION

1. THE Hebrew language has been used for the expression of human thought, whether in speech alone, or in writing alone, or in both speech and writing, for some 3000 years. Its history may be roughly divided into four periods: (1) Biblical Hebrew (BH), from the earliest times to the end of the Biblical period, say about 200 B.C.E.; (2) Mišnaic Hebrew (MH), from about 400–300 B.C.E.[1] to about 400 C.E.; (3) Medieval Hebrew, from the redaction of the Babylonian Talmud, about 500 C.E., to 1700; (4) and Modern Hebrew, from the beginning of the eighteenth century to this day. The revival of Jewish life in Palestine through Zionism has brought with it a new efflorescence of Hebrew both as a literary medium and as a spoken tongue.

2. The present work is devoted to a study of the grammatical characteristics of the Hebrew language of the second period. We designate the Hebrew of that period ‘Mišnaic Hebrew’[2] from the Mishna and its allied literature which form the sole literary remains that have come down to us in that particular idiom.

The name Mišnaic Hebrew is to be preferred to the name ‘New Hebrew’, by which the idiom is commonly known; for it serves to mark off this idiom both from the Hebrew of the first period, and also from the Hebrew of the third and fourth periods.

---

[1] The first period overlaps the second period, as BH continued to be used as a literary idiom long after the rise of MH. Cf. § 17.

[2] לְשׁוֹן הַמִּשְׁנָה, as in the late superscription to Ab. vi. 1. Cf. also Num. R. 1.

The term 'New Hebrew', on the other hand, distinguishes our
idiom from BH only, but ignores the later phases through which
the Hebrew language passed after the Talmudic age, or confuses
these important phases with the particular idiom of the second
period.

3. In earlier Mišnaic literature no distinction is drawn between
BH and MH. The two idioms are known as לְשׁוֹן הַקֹּדֶשׁ, the Holy
Tongue, as contrasted with other languages, which are described
as לְשׁוֹן חוֹל, the common tongue. Thus, in So. vii. 1 ff. it is laid
down that certain prescribed religious formulae may be recited
בְּכָל לָשׁוֹן, which is interpreted as לְשׁוֹן חוֹל (Ber. 40 b; cf. also
Šab. 40 b), and other formulae may be recited only בִּלְשׁוֹן הַקֹּדֶשׁ.
These latter include passages from Scripture, like מִקְרָא בִכּוּרִים
(Deut. xxvi. 3 b–10 a), חֲלִיצָה (xxv. 9 b), בְּרָכוֹת וּקְלָלוֹת (ib.
xxvii. 15–26), which had to be recited in the actual words of
Scripture, i. e. in BH. But they also include בְּרָכוֹת כֹּהֵן גָּדוֹל,
which were composed in MH (So. vii. 7; cf. the commen-
taries, *ad loc.*), and the address of the כֹּהֵן מְשׁוּחַ מִלְחָמָה (Deut.
xx. 3–4) which was amplified in MH (ib. So. viii. 1 f.). Cf. also:
הָיָה ר׳ מֵאִיר אוֹמֵר כָּל הַדָּר בְּאֶרֶץ יִשְׂרָאֵל וְקוֹרֵא קְרִיאַת שְׁמַע שַׁחֲרִית וְעַרְבִּית
וּמְדַבֵּר בִּלְשׁוֹן הַקֹּדֶשׁ הֲרֵי הוּא בֶן עוֹלָם הַבָּא:—R. Meir (*c.* 175 C.E.) used
to say: 'Whoever dwells in the Land of Israel, and reads the
Šema'[1] morning and evening, and speaks the Holy tongue, lo he
belongs to the world to come,' Sifre, Deut. xxxii. 43; where
certainly ordinary MH must be meant, like that used by R. Meir
himself in this dictum. Again, מִכָּאן אָמְרוּ כְּשֶׁהַתִּינוֹק מַתְחִיל לְדַבֵּר
אָבִיו מְדַבֵּר עִמּוֹ בִּלְשׁוֹן הַקֹּדֶשׁ וּמְלַמְּדוֹ תוֹרָה:—Hence they said: When
a child begins to speak, his father speaks with him in the Holy
tongue, and teaches him Torah, ib. Deut. xi. 19: אָמַר רַבִּי בְּאֶרֶץ
יִשְׂרָאֵל לְשׁוֹן סוּרְסִי לָמָּה אוֹ לְשׁוֹן הַקֹּדֶשׁ אוֹ לָשׁוֹן יְוָנִית:—Rabbi (200 C.E.)
said: in the Land of Israel why the Sursi (Syrian) tongue?

---

[1] Deut. vi. 4; Singer, p. 40 f.

Either the Holy tongue, or the Greek tongue, So. 49 b ; BQ 83 a ;

—: אָמַר רַב יוֹסֵף בְּבָבֶל לְשׁוֹן אֲרָמִי לָמָּה אוֹ לְשׁוֹן הַקֹּדֶשׁ אוֹ לְשׁוֹן פַּרְסִי

R. Joseph (c. 350 c. e.) said: In Babylon, why the Aramean tongue ?
Either the Holy tongue, or the Persian tongue, ib., where again
MH must be meant, the language used by the speakers themselves

Thus, also, BH is called עִבְרִית, as opposed to תַּרְגּוּם, the
Aramaic portions of Daniel and Ezra, Ya. iv. 5 (תַּרְגּוּם שֶׁכְּתָבוֹ
לְשׁוֹן, לְשׁוֹן רוֹמִי contrasted with or ;(עִבְרִית וְעִבְרִית שֶׁכְּתָבוֹ תַּרְגּוּם
עַרְבִי, לְשׁוֹן אֲרָמִי, Sifre, Deut. xxxiii. 26 ; or with עֵילָמִית, Elamite,
and גִּיפְטִית, Egyptian, Šab. 115 a ; Meg. 18 a ; but so is MH called
עִבְרִית, as contrasted with יְוָנִית, Giṭ. ix. 8 ; and עִבְרִי, j. Meg. i. 11.

A distinction between BH and MH is found only in later
times, when MH had ceased to be used outside the learned circles
in the schools. Thus, R. Joḥanan (c. 275 c.e.) objects to the use
in a *halaka* of the expression מְסָכוֹ, which he calls לְשׁוֹן תּוֹרָה, and
insists on the use of מְזָגוֹ, which he describes as לְשׁוֹן חֲכָמִים,
'AZ. 58 b. Similarly the same teacher demands the use of רְחֵלוֹת
(—לְשׁוֹן חֲכָמִים), in the Mishna, Ḥul. xi. 1, instead of רְחֵלִים
(—לְשׁוֹן תּוֹרָה), Ḥul. 137 b.[1]

4. The literary monuments of MH consist of the record of the
teaching and sayings of the *Tannaim* and *Amoraim*,[2] as preserved
in early rabbinic literature. These may be classified as follows:

(i) Tannaitic, in the following works which are exclusively in
MH: Mishna, Tosefta,[3] Abot deR. Nathan, Masiktot Qeṭannot,

---

[1] So in Aram. : לִישָׁנָא דְאוֹרַיְיתָא, contrasted with לִישָׁנָא דְרַבָּנָן, Qid. 2 b.

[2] תַּנָּאִים, a Hebraized Aram. form of the MH שׁוֹנִים, repeaters (of the
traditional law)—the Teachers of the Mišnaic period, as contrasted with
אֱמוֹרָאִים, expositors (of the Mishna)—the Teachers of the post-Mišnaic, or
Talmudic period.

[3] The Mishna is found in two chief recensions, (i) a Palestinian text, as
given in the Jerusalem Talmud, and in the text edited by Lowe (L.). To this
recension belongs also the text found in codex Kauffmann (K); see Krauss,

Mᵉkilta, Sifra, Sifre, Seder 'Olam, and the *Baraitot,*[1] scattered over
the Palestinian and Babylonian Talmuds.   We must also include in
this class the sayings of the Tannaim, as reported by the Amoraim
in the two Talmuds and in the Aggadic Midrashim.   In these
works, though they are partly composed in Aram., the Tannaim
are, as a rule, made to speak in MH, even in ordinary conversations, and with women and children : cf. for example, 'Er. 53 b
(ר׳ יוֹסֵי הַגְּלִילִי , ר׳ יְהוֹשֻׁעַ בֶּן חֲנַנְיָא), Nᵉd. 62 a, 66 b.

(ii) Amoraic.   The teaching and sayings of the Amoraim, as
recorded in the two Talmuds and in the Aggadic Midrashim.

The earlier Amoraim, especially in Palestine, used MH very
frequently, though they are often found to speak in Aram.   But
even the later Amoraim, and even in Babylon, used MH exclusively for the following purposes : statements of the formulated
halaka[2]; homiletical expositions of the Scriptures[3]; parables (מָשָׁל),

---

MGWJ., li, pp. 54 ff.   (ii) a Babylonian text, as given in the Babylonian Talmud
of the Mishna.   With this the text found in current editions usually, but not
always, agrees; cf. Frankel, דרכי המשנה (2nd ed., Warsaw, 1923), pp. 231 ff.
Similarly the text of the Tosefta is found in a Palestinian recension, as
represented by the edition of Zuckermandel (Passewalk, 1877–82), and a
Babylonian text found in the current editions printed with the Alfasi.   On
these and other works named, cf. the respective articles in the *Jewish
Encyclopaedia*; Schechter, Hastings' *Dictionary of the Bible*, Extra Volume,
pp. 57 ff ; Strack, *Einleitung in d. Talmud.*

[1] בְּרַיְתָא, Aram. for MH (מִשְׁנָה חִיצוֹנָה), the external Mishna, viz. the
halakot not included by Rabbi in his standard Mishna.

[2] Even in popular addresses.   Cf. the confusion by a popular audience in
Babylon of the phrase, used by R. Matna (fourth cent. C. E.) in an address,
מַיִם שֶׁלָּנוּ ' water *kept over night*' and '*our* water ', Pᵉs. 42 a.   This confusion
could only have arisen in MH, and not in Aram., which would have used
different words for these two ideas, viz. דְּבִיתוּ and דִּילָנָא ; cf. Rashi, *ad loc.,*
and also Wijnkoop, *JQR.*, vol. xv (1903), p. 29.   Further the confusion by
a popular audience in Palestine in the time of Rabbi of מֵי בֵיצִים and
מֵי בְצָעִים (= בִּצִּים = בִּצּוֹת), San. 5 b.   Contrast, however, the different
account in j. Šᵉbi. vi, 1 ; Giṭ. 1, 2.

[3] The evidence can be found on almost every page of both Talmuds, and

even in the middle of an Aram. conversation (cf. e.g. BQ 60b; Ta'a. 5b); and prayer (cf. Ber. 17a, 55b, 60a, b; Ket. 8b). The frame-work of the Talmuds is in Aram. So also the discussions about the *Halaka*, and the ordinary conversations of the Amoraim are in Aram. Tales and traditions about the Tannaim and past ages in general, are usually in MH, sometimes interspersed with later Aram. additions (cf. e.g. Ber. 27b; BM 59b, &c.).

5. The differences between BH and MH are obvious and striking. They extend to grammar, vocabulary, and general style of expression. Some grammatical forms which are common in BH either have become rare, or have disappeared altogether in MH. Again, certain forms which are rare in BH have become the normal type in MH. Then as to vocabulary, we meet in MH large numbers of words which are rare or unknown in BH, but are common in Aram. Again, many words that are common in BH are absent in MH. Many BH words are used in MH in a changed connotation, usually as in Aram. Moreover, MH contains a large number of technical words and phrases which are unknown in BH. It has also borrowed a large number of names of objects from the Greek and Latin, which further help to detract from its Hebraic character. Finally, the diction of MH is quite unlike the ordinary BH style. Many familiar BH constructions are entirely absent in MH, whilst new constructions and usages have arisen in MH which are often similar to those known in Aram. or identical with them.

6. The similarities between MH and Aram., combined with the fact that MH has come down to us in works produced by the schools of the learned at a time when Aram. was used as a common vernacular among the Jews, have led many scholars to

also in the earlier Aggadic Midrashim. Cf., for example, the use of MH and Aram. in *halaka* in the first pages of BM, and in *Aggada* in the first pages of Ber.

the view that MH was merely a Hebraized Aram., artificially created by the Schoolmen, like the Latin of the Middle Ages, and that it never had an independent existence as a natural medium of ordinary speech in the daily life of the Jews. This view rests, however, on a misconception of the whole character of MH. Far from being an artificial scholastic jargon, MH is essentially a popular and colloquial dialect. Its extensive literature does not consist of books composed by literary men in their study. It is rather a record of sayings, oral teaching, and discussions of men of the people on a variety of subjects, embracing, practically, all the manifold activities in the daily life of an organized civilized society. Its vocabulary and its grammar both bear the stamp of colloquial usage and popular development. Apart from the technical phraseology of the specialized *halaka*, not a single trace can be discovered in it of that artificiality with which it has been credited.

7. As to the alleged dependence of MH on Aram., a careful examination of the grammar and vocabulary of MH as presented in the following pages will show that, while Aram. has undoubtedly influenced MH in many directions, it would be an exaggeration to describe this influence as a dependence of MH on Aram. In its morphology, MH is absolutely independent of Aram., and largely also in its syntax. In its main characteristics, the grammar of MH is practically identical with the grammar of BH. Where it differs from BH grammar, the genesis of the difference can generally be traced back to an older stage in the language, out of which the new forms developed in a natural way. Forms that deviate from the regular type of BH are usually found in BH in isolated cases as grammatical irregularities. It is nearly always possible to trace the connexion of a MH form with a BH proto-type, at least in later BH literature. If such forms in MH and late BH happen also to be found in Aram., they are usually also found in other Semitic languages, especially in a late stage of

development. They are thus not Aramaisms, but grammatical phenomena common to the whole, or to a portion, of the Semitic family. On the other hand, MH has also a considerable number of forms which are quite unknown in Aram., and which could not have arisen if MH had been the artificial creation of men whose natural language was Aram.

8. It is chiefly in the sphere of syntax, particularly in the use of the tenses, the expression of the genitive, and the construction of the dependent clause, that MH deviates most from BH, and comes nearest to Aram. But this is due to the fact that, whereas BH is a highly poetical literary language, MH, like Aram., is a simple homely idiom, with no pretence whatever to poetical or picturesque expression. The refined, but often ambiguous, constructions of the poetical prose of BH could not have survived in the daily speech of the people throughout those centuries of violent changes which followed upon the golden age of BH literature. Refinement of expression had to be sacrificed to clearness and usefulness. Thus, popular Hebrew of daily use must have freed itself from the conventionalized literary forms of BH at a comparatively early date, if it ever had been subject to them at all. The simplification of Hebrew syntax in speech was in time reflected also in literature. It is possible to trace this gradual process of simplification in the later books of the Hebrew Bible, until we reach the severe plainness and baldness of MH. No doubt, Aram. exercised a powerful influence in that direction. But the tendency was inherent in Hebrew itself, and if left alone Hebrew would have developed on somewhat similar lines, though perhaps not so rapidly as it actually did under Aram. influence.

9. The evidence of MH grammar is strongly supported by MH vocabulary. It is true that MH has a large number of words which are common in Aram. But, on the other hand, it can also show a considerable number of words which are not found in Aram.

As is to be expected of two closely related dialects living side by side, MH borrowed extensively from Aram., but so did Aram., especially Jewish Aram., borrow extensively from MH, particularly in the sphere of religion and the higher life.[1] The presence of so many Aram. words and expressions in MH can affect its genuine Hebraic character as little as, for example, the numerical preponderance of the Latin element in the English dictionary can affect the genuine Teutonic character of the English language; or, let it be said, as little as the presence in Aram. itself of so many Hebrew and other foreign words and phrases can affect the Aramean character of the old language of Syria and Mesopotamia.

10. Moreover, a detailed examination and analysis of the MH vocabulary, such as is given below for the verb (§§ 83–102), reveals the fact that the Aram. influence on the MH vocabulary has been exaggerated in the same way as the Aram. influence on the MH grammar. It has been the fashion among writers on the subject to brand as an Aramaism any infrequent Hebrew word which happens to be found more or less frequently in the Aram. dialects. Most of these 'Aramaisms' are as native in Hebrew as they are in Aram. Many of them are also found in other Semitic languages. The lists given below show that of the 300 new verbs in MH only some 25 verbs can be described as undoubtedly genuine Aram. loan-words. The other so-called Aram. verbs are either ordinary Semitic words (§ 95), or are common to both Hebrew and Aram. (§ 94).

11. Further, the lists given there also show a group of over fifty verbs which are common to BH and to Aram. of the Mišnaic period, and yet are not found in MH (§ 84). If MH was merely a Hebraized Aram., or an artificial mixture of Aram. and BH, why did it not appropriate those verbs which belonged to

[1] Even the Christian dialect of Palestinian Aram. borrowed freely from MH; cf. Nöldeke, *ZDMG.*, xxii, pp. 513, 522.

both the elements of which it is said to have been composed?
Again, the lists show a group of over thirty verbs of undoubted
Semitic origin which are peculiar to MH, and which are not found
even in Aram. (§ 93). How is one to explain the origin of these
verbs, if MH was but an artificial mongrel, made up of BH
and Aram.?

12. The same phenomenon appears in the other parts of the
MH vocabulary. Thus, in the particles we have only a dozen
or so loan-words from Aram., against a considerable number of
new formations and adaptations from old Hebrew words and
expressions (§§ 294, 300, 302, 304). The numerals are practically
all identical with BH, and free from Aramaisms (§§ 394 ff.). So
also the pronoun exhibits some interesting new formations, but is
practically free from Aram. influences (§§ 66–81). In the noun,
MH has borrowed much from Aram.; but it has also borrowed
much from Greek, Latin, and other sources. On the other hand,
the substance of the MH noun rests on the BH noun, not only
in its grammatical, but also in its lexical character. Furthermore,
as in the case of the verb, MH has preserved a considerable
number of old Hebrew nouns not found in BH or in Aram., and,
in addition, has coined from Hebrew roots many new names for
objects and ideas produced by the changed conditions of life
(cf. §§ 217 ff., and the nouns enumerated in ' Formation of Nouns ',
§§ 220 ff.).

13. It is clear from the facts presented by its grammar and
vocabulary that MH had an independent existence as a natural
living speech, growing, developing, and changing in accordance
with its own genius, and in conformity with the laws which govern
the life of all languages in general, and the Semitic languages
in particular. It was greatly influenced by Aram., its close
neighbour and rival, but it was not submerged by Aram. till after
some centuries, when political factors made it impossible for MH

to continue as a living speech. The home of MH was Palestine.
So long as the Jewish people retained some sort of national
existence in Palestine, MH continued to be the language of at least
a section of the Jewish people living in Palestine. As Jewish life
in Palestine gradually decayed, and eventually suffered total
extinction, so MH was banished step by step from everyday life,
and eventually, towards the end of the Mišnaic period, became
confined to the learned in the schools and academies. With the
ruin of these schools in Palestine, MH disappeared altogether
from its native home, but continued to exist side by side with
Aram. in the Jewish academies of Babylon, whither it had been
carried by the Palestinian immigrants. When, in their turn, the
Babylonian academies also decayed, towards the end of the
Talmudic period, the last remnant of MH died out. The dialect
continued a more or less fitful and precarious existence as a literary
medium, until it passed into the new literary dialect of Medieval
Hebrew.

14. We may now attempt to define more precisely the relation
of MH to BH. In defining this relation we have to recapitulate
the lexical and grammatical characteristics of MH, already briefly
outlined above.

The bulk of the MH vocabulary is found in BH. This applies
especially to the most necessary words, such as pronouns, numerals,
particles, and the most common verbs and nouns. But a considerable number of BH words have been lost in MH, particularly
words that were rare in BH, and used only in poetry, even though
these were common and prosaic words in Aram. (cf. for verbs,
§§ 84 ff.). On the other hand, MH shows a considerable number
of words of undoubted Hebrew origin, which are not found in BH.
This may, indeed, be due to a mere accident, in view of the
scanty and fragmentary remains of BH literature. Nevertheless,
the possession by MH of Hebrew words not known in BH

establishes the important fact that MH was not derived from BH, but that it drew its lexical material from a source much wider than the literature of the Hebrew Bible. What was that source? Was it a literary source, more extensive than the Hebrew Bible, containing, in addition to the Bible, books discarded when the Canon of Scripture was fixed, and now lost, but familiar to the creators of MH (assuming again that MH was an artificial creation of the Rabbis)? This is hardly probable. For if those lost books were of such merit and value, that the Rabbis thought them worthy of the closest and most intimate study, and became familiar with their vocabulary as with the vocabulary of the books of the Bible themselves, then those books would not have been excluded from the Canon as of no value, or as of heterodox tendencies. It is much more reasonable to assume that the MH vocabulary was in the main drawn not from a literary source, but from the actual Hebrew speech of daily life which preceded the Mišnaic period, and which, of course, possessed many Hebrew words that did not find their way into the books of the Bible. If this assumption be correct, MH is the direct lineal descendant of the spoken Hebrew of the Biblical period, as distinguished from the literary Hebrew of the Biblical period preserved in the Hebrew Scriptures.

This explains also why MH has not preserved the poetical words and expressions of BH. These words and expressions were not used at all, or only rarely, in the colloquial Hebrew of Biblical times, which was the ancestor of MH. This also explains the homely and severely prosaic chracter of MH. It was a purely colloquial, one might say a vulgar idiom, directly descended from an older colloquial or vulgar idiom.[1]

---

[1] We use the term 'vulgar' in its original sense of popular. The explanation that the usual prosaic baldness of MH is due to the technical character of the *halaka* leaves out the extensive *haggada* which, though not technical, is yet

15. This view of the origin of MH affords also a satisfactory explanation of the grammatical characteristics of the dialect. As has already been stated above, MH agrees in the main with BH grammar. Its various differences from BH consist chiefly of BH irregularities which have become the regular type in MH. On examination these will be found to be colloquial and popular variations from the standardized literary idiom. Cf. below the discussion on the pronouns אֲנוּ, § 68 ; הַלָּלוּ, הַלָּה, § 73 ; שֶׁ־, § 78 ; the Nithpa'el, § 131 ; the consecutive tenses, § 157, &c. Some of these variations are probably due to differences of dialect in the Hebrew spoken in different parts of Palestine. Traces of the existence of dialects, especially in Northern Palestine, are found even in BH.[1] The concentration of all Jewish life in Palestine in and around Jerusalem, which began towards the end of the Judean monarchy, and which lasted throughout the period of the second Temple, must have introduced those dialectal variations into the speech of Jerusalem. From the spoken vernacular these irregularities found their way also into the literary dialect of the time. Hence the phenomenon that from the days of Jeremiah onwards, BH begins to show, in constantly increasing numbers, forms and expressions which are the normal type in MH, and many of which are also found in Aram.

16. It is not possible to trace the rise and development of MH, owing to the lack of early literary monuments in the dialect. The earlier *halaka* still shows a free and picturesque mode of expression, cf. מוּכַּת עֵץ, Ket. i. 6 ; לֹא מִפִּיהָ אָנוּ חַיִּין, נִסְתַּחֲפָה שָׂדֶךָ, הִנִּיחַ מָעוֹתָיו, ix. 2 ; כּוֹשֵׁל שֶׁבָּהֶן, שׁוֹחֶה בָעֲצִיצוֹ, iii. 5 ; דְּרוּסַת אִישׁ, 7 ; פָּשַׁט לוֹ אֶת הָרֶגֶל, 3 ; הַבָּנִים יִשְׁאֲלוּ עַל הַפְּתָחִים, עַל קֶרֶן הַצְּבִי, xiii. 2 ;

similar in its diction to the *halaka*. That the *halaka* was sometimes capable of picturesque expression, is shown by the examples cited in § 16.

[1] Cf. below, § 78 ; Stade, *Heb. Gr.*, pp. 11–14 ; Bergsträsser, *ZAW.*, xix, pp. 41 ff. ; Sznejder, pp. 27 ff.

יְפְרַח בָּאֲוִיר, 7 ; אֶשֵׁב עַד שֶׁיָּלְבִּין רֹאשִׁי, 5 ; also BQ. i. 1, &c. Also the descriptive passages in Yo. i. 5, 7, &c. ; Suk. iv. 4, 5 ; v. 4, &c. ; Ta'a. iii. 5 ; So. i. 4, 6 f. ; ix. 15 ; Men. x. 3 f. ; Tam. i. 1 f. ; Neg. xii. 5 f. ; Pa. iii. 1 f., &c. Contrast also the picturesque tale of Simon the Just, t. Naz. iv. 7 ; Naz. 4 b, with the style later developed in such tales (מעשיות). A characteristic specimen of the early historical tale is found in Qid. 66 a (§ 126, n.). No doubt many of the Palestinian apocryphal and apocalyptic books must have been composed in a similar style, as can be seen from the Hebrew fragments of such compositions that have come down to us.

17. But, nevertheless, BH, with a MH colouring, continued to be the principal literary medium long after it had died out as a living speech, as is shown by the later books of BH. There can be no doubt that the authors of Chronicles, Esther, Ecclesiastes, Daniel, Sirach, and the Psalms of Solomon did not use BH in their ordinary everyday life. BH was to them only a literary and artificial medium of expression which they had acquired in the schools from the study of the old sacred literature. That is why they sometimes show awkwardness in handling the old Hebrew idiom, and difficulty in expressing their thoughts with clearness and exactness. That is also why they often lapse into usages and expressions which remind us of MH or of Aram. What language did the authors of those late BH books speak in their daily life? Or, in other words, what was the language of ordinary life of educated native Jews in Jerusalem and Judea in the period from 400 B.C.E. to 150 C.E.? The evidence presented by MH and its literature leaves no doubt that that language was MH. Of course, those educated Judeans also understood Aram., and used it even in writing, but only occasionally, and not habitually—in the same way as the educated Boer in South Africa sometimes uses English, or as the Flamand in Belgium may often use French.

18. Thus, for a number of generations, the Judean Jews

remained Hebrews in their language, using the classical dialect—
BH—for literary purposes, and the popular dialect—MH—as
a medium of speech in their ordinary daily life, in the school,
in the Temple and the Synagogue. Gradually, however, the influx
into Jerusalem of Aram.-speaking Jews from the Eastern Diaspora,
and also from Galilee, Transjordania, and Syria, established Aram.
as a native tongue in Jerusalem. The native Jews then became
bi-lingual, using both Aram. and MH indiscriminately in ordinary
life, but MH exclusively in the school, and for religious purposes.
Eventually, Aram. gained the upper hand, and MH, like BH,
became a לְשׁוֹן הַקֹּדֶשׁ, a purely religious language; then, finally,
at the end of the Mišnaic period it was reduced to a לְשׁוֹן חֲכָמִים
(§§ 3, 13).

19. It is possible to indicate only approximately the probable
dates of these linguistic changes. The rise of MH may be
assigned to the period associated by tradition with the 'Men of
the Great Synagogue'. The saying reported of them is already
in pure MH (Ab. i. 1). They are also reputed to have been
the authors of the oldest portions of the Jewish liturgy, which
are likewise couched in MH (cf. Bᵉr. 33 a). That period may
approximately be identified with the end of the Persian rule and
the beginning of the Greek rule in Palestine, say 400–300 B. C. E.
The BH books of the period all show distinct traces of MH,
viz. Chronicles, Canticles, Esther, and especially Qohelet and
Sirach, and also Daniel.[1]

20. MH seems to have attained the height of its power during
the rise of the Hasmonean dynasty.[2] Its decline as a spoken
language seems to have begun with the fall of that dynasty and

---

[1] Driver, *Introduction to Lit. of OT.*⁹, pp. 474 f., 484 f., 539 f.

[2] Cf. Graetz, *Geschichte d. Juden*⁴, III, i, pp. 81–2; Klausner, *Origin of
Mishnaic Hb.*, Scripta Universit. Hierosol., Orientalia atque Judaica I,
Art. IX.

the reign of Herod. The destruction of many of the native
families in the bloody wars which accompanied the coming of the
Romans and the establishment of the Herodians (whose original
language was probably Aram.); the closer connexion between
Jerusalem and the Aram. Jewries of Syria and the Eastern Diaspora
which followed on the incorporation of Palestine in the Roman
Empire; and the settlement of those Aram.-speaking Jews in
Jerusalem, all tended to spread the use of Aram. at the expense
of MH. But MH still remained a popular speech, as is testified
by numerous passages in its literature. Thus, e.g., the Jewish
damsels at their dances in the vineyards sing to the young men
in MH (Ta'a. iv. 8); the taunt-song against the tyranny of the
powerful priests is in MH (Pes. 57 a; t. Men. xiii. 21); popular
vows are in MH (Ned. i. 1, &c.).[1]

21. Finally, the destruction of Jewish life in Judea after the
defeat of Bar Kokba (135 c.e.), and the establishment of the new
Jewish centre in the Aram.-speaking Galilee, seem to have led to
the disappearance of MH as a popular tongue. In that age we
find R. Meir pleading for the preservation of MH speech at least
among the pious, just as he pleads against the emigration from
the Holy Land, which then prevailed in consequence of the Roman
oppression. The Aramaization of the Jews in Palestine was
completed one generation later, when Rabbi complains of the
exclusive use of Aram. in the Land of Israel (cf. § 3).[2]

---

[1] Cf. בנדרים הלך אחר לשון בני אדם, Ned. 30 b, 51 b and Rashi, *ad loc.*

[2] Nevertheless, Rabbi's words prove that MH was still thought of as
a language of everyday life. So two generations later than Rabbi, R. Jonathan
of Beit Jibrin says : אַרְבַּע לְשׁוֹנוֹת נָאֶה לְעוֹלָם שֶׁיִשְׁתַּמְּשׁוּ בָּהֶם לַעַז לְזֶמֶר
רוֹמִי לִקְרָב סוּרְסִי לְאֵילְיָא עִבְרִי לְדִיבּוּר:—There are four tongues good for the
world to make use of : the Foreign (= Greek) for song, the Roman for war,
Sursi (= Syriac) for lamentation, and Hebrew for (ordinary) speech, j. Meg. iv. 4.
So R. Joseph's saying (§ 3) proves that MH was known as a spoken language
in Babylon in the fourth century c. e.

22. Before concluding this sketch, we may refer briefly to the evidence advanced for the view that Aram. was the exclusive language of the Jews in Judea during our period.[1] This evidence consists in the use of Aram. in Ezra and Daniel, and in *Megillat Ta'anit*; the use in the Synagogue of an Aram. translation (Targum) of the Scriptures; the use of Aram. in legal documents, like *K^etuba* (marriage settlement), *Get* (bill of divorcement), &c.; the use of Aram. in inscriptions in the Temple; the reported Aram. sayings of some Rabbis in the Mishna and Tosefta, and of Jesus in the Gospels; the existence of Aram. proper names, and of Aram. words in Josephus.

The most that this evidence can prove is that during our period Aram. was understood and used in Palestine, a fact which nobody denies. It cannot, however, prove that Aram. was the exclusive vernacular of all Jews of that period. For against these remains of Palestinian Aram., there is the vast MH literature, including the MH liturgy; there is, further, MH itself, with all its popular and original elements, to prove that during our period Jews in Judea spoke MH.

23. It must be remembered that Jerusalem was more than merely a Judean city. It was the metropolis of a world-wide Jewry. Beside the native Judean majority, there were in Jerusalem also important colonies of Aram.- and Greek-speaking Jews, especially in Roman times. In addition to the Aram.-speaking residents, vast numbers of Aram.-speaking Jews visited the Holy City for the celebration of the Festivals of the Temple. It is not, therefore, surprising that there were Aram. inscriptions in the Temple, just as there were also Greek inscriptions (Šeq. vi. 5; iii. 2); that there were numerous Aram. proper names, just as there were numerous Greek proper names; that the Synagogue used an Aram. Targum for the benefit of unlettered Galilean and Oriental

---

[1] The evidence is collected by G. Dalman, *The Words of Jesus*, pp. 1-13.

Jews, or that the calendar of the *Megillat Ta'anit* (completed
c. 70 C. E.), intended as it was for all classes of Jews, should
have been composed in Aram.; or that certain legal documents
of common and universal use should have been in Aram.
Against the few isolated sayings of Hillel (a Babylonian!), and
some other Rabbis, there are numerous sayings by the same
Rabbis in MH.[1]   So also Josephus cites Hebrew words in
addition to Aram. (cf. *Antiquities*, iii. 7 ; x. 6).   With regard to
the language of Jesus, it is admitted that in the Roman period,
and perhaps earlier, Aram. was the vernacular of the native Galilean
Jews.   But even in Galilee, MH was understood and spoken,
at least by the educated classes.

24. The Aram. chapters in Ezra and Daniel, dealing as they do
with Babylonian and Persian subjects, may have been the work
of Jews of the Eastern Diaspora.   This seems very probable, at
least, with regard to the Aram. in Ezra.   A Jerusalem Jew would
not have said לִירוּשְׁלֶם . . . אֲזַלוּ (iv. 23), but אֲתוֹ . . . לִירוּשְׁלֶם.
Again, a Jerusalem Jew would not have described the Temple
repeatedly as בֵּית אֱלָהָא דִּי בִּירוּשְׁלֶם (iv. 24 ; v. 2, 16; vi. 12, 18).

25. The same may be said of Aram. legal documents.   It is
possible that the formulae of the *Kᵉtuba*, *Get.*, &c., originated
in Babylonia, and their Aram. was retained also by MH-speaking
Jews, in order to give these documents the recognition of the
Persian authority.[2]   On the other hand, legal documents of
undoubted Judean origin were composed in MH.   So the *Prosbol*,
instituted by Hillel (Šᵉbi. x. 4), the קִיּוּם שְׁטָר (confirmation of
a bill that has become illegible, BB x. 6), and scrolls of genealogy

---

[1] Note the express remark of the narrator : וּבִלְשׁוֹן אֲרָמִית אָמְרָן וּבלשׁון
אֲרָמִית שְׁמָעָן ;—he said (he heard) them in the Aram. tongue, t. So. xiii. 4–6,
as if the use of Aram. by Samuel the Little (died *c.* 70 C. E.) and Simeon the
Just called for a special explanation.

[2] Cf. Cowley, *Aram. Papyri*, p. 119.   For early *Kᵉtubot* in Aram. ibid.,
pp. 44, 54, 131.

(Yᵉb. iv. 13. In Qid. iv. 1 we have an extract of such a document in Aram., with, however, several Aramaized Hebrew terms:
גְּרֵי, אֲסוּפִי, &c. This Mishna is attributed to the Babylonian Hillel,
Yᵉb. 37 a). So also a special condition in the Judean Kᵉtuba is
cited in MH, as contrasted with the Jerusalem and Galilean Kᵉtubot,
which followed the established legal formula, and are cited in
Aram. (Kᵉt. iv. 12). Other special conditions in the Kᵉtuba are
also given in MH (ib. ix. 1, 5). So the Geṭ of divorcement and
of manumission are cited in MH (Giṭ. ix. 1, 3).

26. The view has also been expressed [1] that the usual language
in the Temple was Aram., and that it was only in the last few
years of its existence that the Pharisees replaced the Aram. in the
Temple by MH. This view is based chiefly on the report that
on two occasions High Priests heard in the Temple *Bath Qol*
speaking Aram. But, surely, the evidence of such an isolated
legendary report cannot outweigh the evidence of innumerable
passages in MH literature which prove that the Temple ritual was
carried on in MH. No doubt, the Babylonian priests (Mᵉn. xi. 7)
may have spoken Aram. in the Temple, as elsewhere; but it is
incredible that in the Temple of all places, with all its reverence
for tradition, Hebrew would have been banished in favour of
a new and un-Jewish tongue. Hebrew has remained the exclusive
language of the Synagogue to this very day. Even if we had not
the evidence of Rabbinic tradition, we should conclude that such
was also the case in the ancient Temple.

27. Further, there is no evidence whatever that the use of
Hebrew or Aram. was a subject of controversy between the
Pharisees and the Sadducees. Nor is there any reason to believe
that the Sadducees preferred Aram. to MH. On the contrary,
one would be inclined to infer from their exclusive, aristocratic

---

[1] Büchler, *Die Priester u. d. Cultus*, pp. 60 ff. The account of the Bat Qol
is found in So. 33 a; t. So. xiii. 4–6.

character, and from their conservative political tendencies, that
the Sadducees would have favoured the use of the old national
language, rather than the foreign *patois* of the unlettered populace.
The sayings of the Sadducees are all reported in MH, cf. Ya. iv. 6–8;
Mᵉn. 65 b, &c.; and a conversation between a Sadducee High
Priest and his father, Yo. 19 b.

28. In conclusion, we must refer briefly to the linguistic trustworthiness of the Mišnaic tradition, which has been called into
question by some writers.[1] Its trustworthiness is established
by the old rule, older than the age of Hillel, that a tradition—
which, of course, was handed down by word of mouth—must
be repeated in the exact words of the master from whom it had
been learnt: חַיָּב אָדָם לוֹמַר בִּלְשׁוֹן רַבּוֹ. This rule was strictly
observed throughout the Mišnaic and Talmudic periods (cf. 'Ed. i. 3,
with the commentaries; Bᵉr. 47 a; Bᵉk. 5 a), and was, in fact, the
basis of the authority of the Oral Law. So careful were the Rabbis
in the observance of this rule that they often reproduced even
the mannerisms and the personal peculiarities of the Masters from
whom they had received a particular tradition, or *halaka*. This
rule makes it certain that, at least in most cases, the sayings of
the Rabbis have been handed down in the language in which
they had originally been expressed. There were, of course,
exceptions, as when heathens are made to speak in MH (Ša. 31 a;
Ta'a. 18 a, b); but, nevertheless, the rule was strictly observed
in all *halakot*, and also in Aggadic and other sayings which are
reported as the *ipsissima verba* of the speakers. This linguistic
faithfulness of the tradition is proved by the preservation of a
number of sayings in Aram. (e. g. 'Ed. viii. 4; Ab. i. 13; v. 22,
23, &c.), and by the preservation of the text of *Megillat Ta'anit*
in Aram., though the exposition of the text is given in MH.[2]

---

[1] M. Friedmann, *Onkelos u. Akylas*, pp. 86 ff.; Dalman, op. cit., p. 8.

[2] Cf. Ta'a. 17 b, 18 b; Mᵉn. 65 a, and the special edition, Neubauer,
Medieval Jewish Chronicles, ii, pp. 3 ff.

These Aram. traditions were not translated into MH, but were left in their original language. It follows, therefore, that MH sayings were originally spoken in MH. A striking illustration of the care which the Rabbis took to reproduce the actual language of their predecessors is afforded by the interchange between Aram. and MH in narrative passages. Thus, we often find narratives in MH which contain conversations in Aram. (e.g. So. 48 b; Ša. 31 a, &c.). Again, we find, even more frequently, narratives in Aram. in which the persons of the story are made to speak in MH (e. g. Pes. 3 b; BM 83 b, 84 b, &c.). This change of language between the narrator and the persons introduced into his story is clearly due to a deliberate effort on the part of the narrator to reproduce the original speech of the persons he is reporting, whether MH or Aram.[1]

---

[1] Cf. also Ben Jehudah, עד אימתי דברו עברית, pp. 77 ff.; Sznejder, p. 54 (כב).

PART I

PHONOLOGY AND ORTHOGRAPHY

I. PRONUNCIATION

The evidence for the pronunciation of MH may be grouped under two heads:

29. (*a*) **External**:

(1) *The transcription of Greek and Latin words in MH.*[1]

(2) *The transcription of Hebrew words in Greek and Latin, viz. in Origen's Hexapla and in Jerome's writings.*[2]

This evidence has to be qualified by the consideration of the inequalities which exist between the Hebrew and the Greek and Latin alphabets, and their respective inability to express adequately each other's peculiar sounds. Thus, for example, MH was unable to transcribe correctly the Greek and Latin vowels. Similarly, Greek and Latin were unable to express the Hebrew sibilants, the Hebrew gutturals, and the variation in the sound of the letters, ב, ג, ד, כ, פ, ת.

(3) *The traditional pronunciation preserved among the Jews.*

30. This is a valuable witness, representing as it does a living and uninterrupted tradition reaching back to the time when MH was still a living speech. The value of this tradition is, however, discounted by the considerable differences in pronunciation which

---

[1] Cf. Krauss, *Lehnwörter*, i, §§ 1 ff., and, more briefly, Albrecht, §§ 5, 7-9, 10.

[2] Cf. Siegfried, *ZAW.*, iv, pp. 35 ff.

exist between the Jews of different countries.[1] Some of these differences are, no doubt, original, and go back to dialectal variations in Hebrew itself as spoken in different parts of Palestine. Others are the result of the influence of the various vernaculars spoken by the Jews in the Diaspora. Moreover, many errors must have crept into the traditional pronunciation. This tradition is, therefore, not to be trusted when it disagrees with the established rules of grammar.

31. (4) *The punctuation, complete or partial, found in some MSS. of the Mishna, and other MH works.*[2]

This is even less trustworthy than the living pronunciation. There never was an authoritative system of punctuation for the Mishna, as for the Hebrew Bible. The scribes were often ignorant, and never consistent. At best the punctuation in the MSS. can only serve as evidence of the pronunciation current in the time and the locality of the particular scribes.

(*b*) **Internal:**

(1) *The method of vocalization by vowel letters.*

32. This is helpful, but insufficient and often misleading, in view of the inadequacy of the few vowel letters to represent what must have been a fairly complicated vowel system. Thus ו represents no less than seven distinct vowel-sounds ($ó$, $ō$, $ŏ$, $^o\overline{\cdot\cdot}$; $ú$, $ū$, $ŭ$), י represents six distinct sounds ($í$, $ī$, $ĭ$; $é$, $ē$, $ĕ$). Cf. below, § 39.

33. (2) *The mutation of consonants.*

The interchange between various consonantal sounds affords evidence as to the relationship between these sounds, their similarities, and their differences. Cf. below, §§ 42, 44, &c.

---

[1] On the various systems of pronunciation among Jews cf. A. Z. Idelsohn, *MGWJ.*, vol. lvii 527 ff., 697 ff.; M. B. Sznejder, תּוֹרַת הַלָּשׁוֹן, pp. 117 ff.

[2] This punctuation, as also the whole of the MS. material of MH, still awaits special investigation.

(3) *Information in MH literature.*

34. The literature contains a few scattered notices which shed some light on contemporary pronunciation, particularly the guttural letters. Cf. below, § 41.

35. (4) *The analogy of BH, as represented by the Massoretic Text of the Hebrew Scriptures.*

This is undoubtedly the most valuable witness for the correct pronunciation of MH. The gradual fixing of the present text of the Hebrew Scriptures took place in the MH period. The men responsible for that text spoke MH, and the living MH speech must have been reflected to a considerable extent in the form given to the Authorized Text, especially in the vowels.

II. THE VOWELS

1. Vowel Changes.

36. In the absence of a trustworthy system of punctuation in MH, it is not possible to determine with any certainty the character and value of the MH vowels, or to ascertain what modifications they had undergone in comparison with the BH vowels. The spelling gives us no help. The three vowel letters א, י, ו, corresponding to the three Semitic vowels, *a, i, u*, are used to represent a large variety of modifications of these three vowels, both short and long, simple and composite. On the whole, it may be assumed, for the reason given in the last section, that the MH vowel system is identical with the latest form of the BH vowels, as represented in our consonantal texts of the Hebrew Bible, and in the system of punctuation elaborated in later centuries by the Massoretic Schools. No doubt, there must have been also a strong Aram. influence on the pronunciation of the MH vowels, but with our present knowledge of the subject, it is impossible to say

what that influence was. Moreover, this Aram. influence would
have been operative also on the contemporary pronunciation of the
BH vowels, if not to the same extent. The various sources of
external evidence enumerated above in (*a*) have, unfortunately,
not yet been investigated and compared. But it may safely be
said that that evidence would not materially modify this statement.

37. A vowel change which has no parallel in BH is found
in the change of *ē* into *ū* in two nouns: אֵם mother, becomes
אוּם in the derived significance of 'the matrix of a female, and of
a millstone', Ṭoh. ix. 8, and then 'bulk', 'substance', Neg. i. 5;[1]
and שֵׁם name, becomes שׁוּם in the derived sense of 'subject',
chiefly in later texts, and with the preposition מִן = מִשּׁוּם because,
Pea i. 3. So also with other prepositions, e.g. עַל שׁוּם Pes. x. 5, &c.
But this latter is most probably an Aramaism due to the scribes.[2]
Palestinian texts show also a change of *ă* into *ŭ*, as רַצְעָן — רוּצְעָן;
קֻרְדָּם — קוּרְדּוֹם, cf. § 267. This vowel change is common in
Palestinian Jewish Aram.

---

[1] L reads here אֵם. So Lev. R. 14 = matrix. In the original sense of
'mother' אוּם is found only once, j. Yeb. xi. 1. The change is due to
assimilation with the labial *m*. Cf. the Assyr. *ummu*, and the Arab. اُمّ.
This form is not found in Aram.

[2] L has usually שֵׁם, even with prepositions when other texts have שׁוּם.
[So cod. K, Krauss, *MGWJ.*, li, p. 452.] With the preposition לְ, it is almost
always לְשֵׁם in all texts. L, however, has sometimes לְשׁוּם by the side of
לְשֵׁם, e.g. Zeb. i. 2, 3. Cf. Assyr. *šumu*. Jewish Aram. has both שֵׁם and
שׁוּם. Syr. only ܫܡܐ. See König, *Lehrgebäude*, i. 2, p. 512. See further,
Weiss, מל״ה׳מ, pp. 14–15; Bacher, *Aelteste Terminologie*, p. 118; *Terminologie d. Amoräer*, p. 218. Albrecht's suggestion (§ 6) that שׁוּם is an
artificial modification to distinguish this meaning of שֵׁם from its use for the
Divine name is disproved by the great frequency of the use of שֵׁם in a secular
sense. Moreover, the use of this form שׁוּם belongs to a later stage in MH,
when the Deity was described by other terms, such as הקב״ה, הַמָּקוֹם, &c.

2. The Spelling of Vowels.

38. The vowels are represented in MH by vowel letters much more frequently than in BH. The vowel letters are, as in BH, א, ה, ו, and י.

א. The א is used as in BH to represent *â* and *ā*: רָאשֵׁי heads, RH iii. 1, &c.; אֶלָּא but, Ber. i. 2; כָּאן here, ibid. i. 4;[1] at the end of a word in foreign feminine nouns: טַבְלָא *tabula*, MQ iii. 7; הֶגְמוֹנְיָא ἡγεμονία, Giṭ. i. 1. This is an Aramaism which is also found in BH.[2] א is found also after other vowels whenever it belongs to the root, קוֹרֵא, יֹאכַל, לֹא, אִלְמָלֵא if not, Ab. iii. 2. After *ā*, *ă*, when followed by ו, or in some texts by י, to indicate that the ו or י are consonants: לָאו not, Ber. i. 1; בַּנַּאי a builder, Kel. xiv. 3; גוֹבַאי locusts, Ber. vi. 3; זַכַּאי innocent, San. iii. 6; רַשַּׁאי permitted, Ber. i. 7.[3]

ה. The ה is found as a vowel letter only at the end of a word. Its use is exactly the same as in BH.

39. ו. The ו represents not only *û* and *ô*, but also *ŭ*, *ŭ*, and *ō*, *ŏ*, *o*ָ: מְקוּבָּל accepted, Ber. v. 5; לִקַּט gathered, Pea v. 1; כּוֹבֶד heaviness, Ber. v. 1; גָּבְהָן their height, רָחְבָּן their breadth, עוּבְיָין their thickness, 'Er. i. 6; עוֹמְרֵי sheaves, Pea vi. 1; עוֹמָרִים, vi. 5; חֻמָשִׁים fifths, Ter. vi. 4.[4]

---

[1] L. has always כן, cf. below, § 295.

[2] Cf. Ges.-K., § 80 h. L., however, retains a final ה also in such foreign words. Cf. also in native words: צְנְעָא, L צינעה, privacy; P^{es}. i, 3 קַיְמָא; L. קיימה, existence, Y^eb. iv. 1, שְׁמָא (§ 302), &c. מהוהא Kel. xxiv. 17; Ṭ̣oh. ix. 9 (ed. מהוהה) has א at the end, owing to the presence of the ה twice before in the same word. Cf. נמהה, Kel. xxvii. 12.

[3] Cf. the plural forms זַכָּאִין, רַשָּׁאִים below, § 282. L. has usually יי for אי. See below, § 56.

[4] L has חמשים עמרים. So elsewhere L. has the defective spelling, e. g. כתלו for ed. כותלו, BB ii. 4, &c. So cod. K, Krauss, *MGWJ.*, li, p. 325; but see below, § 282.

Similarly, the ׳ is found also after *ĭ*, *ē*, and *ĕ*, e. g. מִידָּה measure, B^{er}. ix. 7 ; כִּוֵּן he directed, ii. 1 ; עֲבֵירָה transgression, i. 3 ; חֲבֵירְתָּהּ her companion, Šab. xi. 5.

Sometimes ׳ follows *ā* before ו to indicate the consonantal character of ו : עַכְשָׁיו, עָנָיו, B^{er}. 6 b, on the analogy of such forms as דְּבָרָיו, בָּנָיו. Some Pal. texts have even לָיו for לָאו.

It must be added that this method of spelling is not always applied consistently, and that it often differs from text to text. But as a rule, the full spelling is more common than the defective spelling, particularly when the consonants might be read in more than one way.[1]

For the rendering in MH of Greek and Latin vowels, cf. Krauss, *Lehnwörter*, i, § 23 ff. (for MH and Aram.), Albrecht, § 7.

III. THE CONSONANTS

40. What has been said above on the pronunciation of the MH vowels is also true to a very high degree of the MH consonants. The pronunciation of the consonants was, on the whole, the same as in BH at the time of the Massoretic redaction of the Scriptures. The evidence of the other sources is, however, fuller in the case of the consonants than the vowels. In what follows we shall briefly summarize this evidence, and also tabulate the various mutations among the consonants.

1. The Gutturals א, ה, ח, ע.

41. The various BH gutturals were still distinguished in MH as late as the fourth century c. e. Thus we find later Amoraim discussing whether certain words in the Mishna should be pro-

---

[1] Cf. also below in verbs, §§ 122, 126 ; and in the plural of nouns, § 282. For isolated cases in BH, cf. Ges.-K., § 90. The full spelling is also usual in Medieval Hebrew ; cf. ספר חסידים § תתפ״ו; Güdemann, התורה והחיים, i, p. 153.

nounced with א or ע: גְּמִיאָה or גְּמִיעָה sipping, Šab. viii. 1 ; גַּרְאִינִין
or גַּרְעִינִין kernels, vii. 4 ; אוּמְמוֹת or עוּמְמוֹת dim, Pes. 75 b; מָאמְצִין
or מְעַמְצִין shutting the eyes, Šab. xxiii. 5 (Šab. 75 a); מְאַבְּרִין or
מְעַבְּרִין extend, 'Er. v. 1; אֲכוּזוֹ or עֲכוּזוֹ[1] buttock, Bek. vi. 6 ('Er. 53 a, b);
אֵידֵיהֶן or עֵידֵיהֶן heathen festivals ('AZ. 2 a). This can only refer
to the pronunciation and not to the spelling in a written text, and
proves that there was yet a distinction in the sound of א and ע.
But this distinction was not universal. Thus we are told in
a *Baraita* (beginning of the third century, Meg. 24 b) that people
of certain localities, including Beth Shean and Haifa, could not
distinguish between א and ע. The same is said of the school
of R. Eliezer b. Jacob (end of second century, Ber. 32 a), and of
the Galileans who are held up to ridicule for their slovenliness in
speech, particularly in the pronunciation of the gutturals ('Er. 53 b).
They, together with certain others, could not distinguish between
any of the gutturals. Thus, חַרְדָל mustard, they pronounced הַרְדַל,
and וְחִכִּיתִי לַה' (Isa. viii. 17) they read וְהִכֵּתִי, which was tantamount
to blasphemy (Meg., loc. cit.).[2]

Jerome still heard a distinction in the various gutturals, though
in his transcription, as also in that of Origen, the differentiation
between the hard and the soft ח, the hard and the soft ע, was not
copied from living speech, but rather from the older transcription
of the LXX. (But note the mutation of ח and כ, § 43).

42. *Transcription from the Greek and Latin.*

א equals the Gk. *spiritus lenis*: אַוֵּיר ἀήρ, Šab. xi. 3 ; אַפְרוֹדִיטִי
= 'Ἀφροδίτη, 'AZ. iii. 4. א represents the Lat. initial vowel, like
אִיטַלְקִי *italicus*, Šebi. i. 2 ; but also initial H: אַדְרְיָאנִי Hadrianic,
'AZ. ii. 3; and initial V: אֶסְפַּסְיָנוֹס Vespasian, So. ix. 14.

---

[1] Or עבוזו; cf. Kohut, *Aruch.*, i. 74; iv. 157 ff.
[2] Cf. also j. Ber. ii. 4, viii. 6 ; j. 'Er. v. 1 ; j. 'AZ. i. 2 ; Gen. R. 26;
Lam. R. ii. 2. See Dalman, *Gram. d. jüd.-Pal. Aram².*, p. 57 f. ; Berliner,
Beiträge z. heb. Gram. in Talmud, p. 15 ff.; Frankel, מבוא הירוש, 49 a.

ה represents the Gk. *spiritus asper*: הֶגְמוֹנְיָא ἡγεμονία, Giṭ. i. 1; הֵילֵינִי Ἑλένη, Yo. iii. 10; rarely also the *spiritus lenis*: הֶדְיוֹט ἰδιώτης, Yo. vii. 5; הַכְלֵסִים ἄχυλος, Ter. xi. 4.

ח equals *spiritus asper* in חִילָק ἁλικός (a kind of salt fish), 'AZ. ii. 6; also sometimes χ: חַלִיקוּפְּרִי Χαλκοπάρειος, Makš. i. 3.

ע seems to represent the *spiritus lenis* in עָמִיל ἄμυλον, Pes. iii. 1 (but some texts have אמיל, אמל).

Mutation of the Gutturals.

43. א and ה. As a rule, Palestinian texts prefer initial א, and Babylonian texts ה: הֵיכָן, L.: אֵיכָן where, 'Er. x. 15 [1]; הַגָּדוֹת, L.: אַגָּדוֹת *Aggadot*, Ned. iv. 3. Conversely, אוֹגֶן, L.: הוֹגֶן [2] rim, 'Er. viii. 6; Kel. xxv. 6; אוֹנָאָה, L.: הוֹנָאָה wrong, BM iv. 3; אֵילָך further, Ber. i. 2, and הֵילָך, Pes. vii. 13; הַזְהָרָה = אַזְהָרָה forewarning, Pes. iii. 1. Cf. below, §§ 249, 295.

א and ע: אוּפָּד and עוּפָּד, L., valuation, San. iv. 5; אִירוֹנִיּוֹת, L., עִירוֹנִיּוֹת urban, 'Ed. ii. 5; כָּאוֹר, BQ ix. 4, and כָּעוֹר, 'Ar. iii. 1, ugly; יִתְאַכֵּל, L., יִתְעַכֵּל to be digested, Ber. viii. 7. Cf. above, § 41.

ה and ח: הָרִיעַ, L., חָרִיעַ bastard saffron, Kil. ii. 8; חִידוּק = הִידוּק sticking,[3] Kel. iii. 5; מוֹהֶל, L., מוֹחֶל secretion,[4] Miq. vii. 4; מהה to be shabby, worn, Kel. xxvii. 12 = BH מחה.

ח and כ: לְכְלוּךְ soiling,[5] Miq. ix. 4 = לְחְלוּחַ, from לַח wet. This shows that there was also a hard pronunciation of the ח, as in earlier BH.

---

[1] Cf BH הֵיךְ (Dan. x. 17; 1 Chron. xiii. 12) with אֵיךְ (2 Sam. vi. 9).

[2] Cf. BH אֲגָנוֹת (Exod. xxiv. 6).

[3] As in Aram. Cf. Kohut, iii, pp. 185 f., 349 a.

[4] Cf. BH מָהוּל (Isa. i. 22). See Kohut, v, p. 109.

[5] Cf. Kohut, v, pp. 31, 40 f.

2. The Palatals ג, כ, ק.

Transcription from Greek and Latin.

44. ג transcribes the Gk. γ, and the Lat. *g* : גַּמָּא γαμμα, Mid. iii. 1 :
גִּינוּסְיָא γενέσια, 'AZ. i. 3 ; אַנְטִיגְנוֹס 'Αντίγονος, Ab. i. 3 ; גְּרָדוֹן *gradus*,
'AZ. i. 7. ג may, perhaps, also represent the Gk. κ in גִּימוֹן, Šab. v. 4,
κημός. Combined with ז, ג represents ξ in גְּזוֹזְטְרָא ἐξώστρα, BB iii. 8.
L., however, has here and elsewhere כְּצוֹצְרָה.

So Jerome renders ג by *g*. He does not distinguish the dagheshed
ג from the raphe ג̄, most probably because the Lat. alphabet possessed
no equivalents for these finer sound distinctions.

כ represents Gk. χ : כִּי the letter χ, Mᵉn. vi. 3 ; also Gk. κ :
כּוֹכְלָיָיר κοχλιάριον ; כּוֹכְלָת κοχλίας, Šab. vi. 3. Also in combination
with ס, the Gk. ξ : אַכְסַדְרָה ἐξέδρα, 'Er. viii. 4 ; אַכְסַנְיָא ξενία (with
prosthetic א, cf. below, § 64), Dam. iii. 1.

Jerome renders כ by *ch*. He does not distinguish between כ
and ג, for the reason stated above.

ק represents the Gk. κ : קוֹלְמוֹס κάλαμος, Šab. i. 3 ; דְּרָקוֹן δράκων,
'AZ. iii. 3 ; rarely χ : אֶסְקָרִיטִין ἐσχαρίτης, Ḥa. i. 4. Together with
ס, it renders also the Gk. ξ at the end of a word : פִּנְקָס πίναξ,
Ab. iii. 6.

ק transcribes the Lat. *c* : קַלֶנְדָּם *Calendae*, 'AZ. i. 3 ; קַסְדָּא *cassis*,
Šab. vi. 2. Combined with ו, it renders *qu* : קוּסְטוֹר *quaestor*,
Bᵉk. v. 3 (L. Babylonian texts have קַסְטוֹר or קַסְדּוֹר).

So Jerome transcribes ק by *c*.

Mutation of the Palatals.

45. ג and כ : מזג to dilute, mix, Dam. vii. 2, BH מסך. Cf
'AZ. 54 b, cited above, § 3. בגר to be of age, Kᵉt. iii. 8, BH בכר.
Cf. also גְּזוֹזְטְרָא, L. כְּצוֹצְרָה, cited above, § 44.

ג and ק : מְקָרְדִין to scrape, 'Ed. iii. 12, BH גרד ; קַפֵּחַ very tall,
Bᵉk. vii. 6, BH גֻּבֵּחַ.

כ and ק: קְרָסֵם to cut, nibble, Pea ii. 7, BH כְּרְסֵם; קִפֵּל to double, fold, Šab. ii. 3, BH כפל.

For the mutation between כ and ה, cf. above, § 42.

3. The Dentals ד, ט, ת.

46. ד represents Gk. δ: דְיָתֵיקִי διαθήκη, MQ iii. 3; דְּרָקוֹן δράκων, 'AZ. iii. 3. Also sometimes τ: פְּרוֹזְדּוֹר προστάς, Ab. iv. 16. Lat. *d*: דִּינָר *denarius*, Men. xiii. 4; פּוּנְדָה *funda*, Ber. ix. 5.

Jerome also renders ד by *d*, whether aspirate or soft (ד, ד).

ט represents Gk. τ: טְפוֹס τύπος, Dam. v. 3, 5; לִיטְרָה λίτρα, Ter. iv. 10; but also sometimes θ: אַסְטְנֵיס ἀσθενής, Ber. ii. 6; אַבְטִינָס Εὔθυνος, Yo. i. 5. Rarely δ: קַפּוֹטְקְיָא (L. קפוד), Καππαδοκία, Ket. xiii. 10.

Lat. *t*: טַבְלָה *tabula*, אַסְקוּטְלָה *scutella*, MQ iii. 7. So Jerome renders ט by *t*.

ת represents the Gk. θ: תֵּיק θήκη, Šab. xvi. 1; תּוֹרְמוֹס θέρμος, Kil. i. 3; אֲפוֹתֵיק ἀποθήκη, 'AZ. ii. 7. Lat. *th*: קְלָתָה *calathus*, Bik. iii. 8. So Jerome renders ת by *th*.

Mutation of Dentals.

47. ד and ט: דְּמוּעַ mixed, Ter. v. 6, and נטמע, Ket. 14 b; טְפוֹס, Dam. v. 4, and דְּפוּס, in citation of Bab. Talmud, BM 56 a, and elsewhere.

ד and ז: זלף to pour, drip, Pa. vi. 2, BH; דלף, אֶשְׁדְּרָה spinal cord, Ḥul. iii. 2, L. שִׁיזְרָה.

ט and ת: טעה to err, Ber. ii. 3, BH תעה; perhaps טֶבֶל untithed, Dam. vii. 5, BH תֶּבֶל[1]. For mutation between ט, ס, צ, cf. below, §51.

4. The Labials ב, פ.

48. ב, whether dageshed or raphe, represents Gk. β: בִּימוֹס or (L.) בּוֹמוֹס βωμός, 'AZ. iii. 7, Yo. viii. 6; בּוּלְמוֹס βούλιμος, קוּבְיָא

---

[1] Cf. Barth, *Etymol. Stud.*, p. 37.

κυβεία, San. iii. 3. Rarely through mutation also π: בַּרְדְּלֵס πάρδαλις, BQ i. 4 (some texts have פרד'); אַבְטוֹלְמוֹס Πτολεμαῖος, 'Er. iii. 4; and even φ: דּוּלְבְקִי δελφική, 'AZ. v. 5 (in some texts more correctly דלפקי).

Further, ב represents υ in ευ: אַבְטִינָס Εὔθυνος, Yo. i. 5; לִבְקֶן λευκόν, Beκ. vii. 6; אָבִיתוֹם (L., other texts have ו: אַוְתִיוֹם) εὐθέως, Nid. ii. 2. ב represents Lat. b: בָּסִילְקִי basilica, 'AZ. i. 7; טַבְלָה tabula, MQ iii. 7; לִבְלָר libellarius, Pea ii. 6; but also υ: בִּיבָּרִין vivarium, Šab. xiii. 5.

Jerome always transcribes ב by b, whether dageshed or raphe, never by v.

פ represents Gk. π: פּוּלְמוֹס πόλεμος, So. ix. 14; פַּרְצוּף πρόσωπον, Yeb. xvi. 3. The Gk. φ: פְּיָלֵי φιάλη, So. ii. 2; אַפְרוֹדִיטֵי 'Αφροδίτη, 'AZ. iii. 4.

With ס the Gk. ψ: אַפְסוֹנְיָא ὀψωνία, San. ii. 4; פְּסַכְתֵּר ψυκτήρ, 'Er. x. 15; לַפְסָן λαμψάνη, Kil. i. 5.

The Lat. p: מַפָּה mappa, Ber. viii. 3; קַפֶּנְדְּרְיָא (via) compendiaria. 'AZ. v. 4; נָפּוּץ (L. נַפּוּם) napus, Kil. i. 5.

Lat. f: פְּלָיְטוֹן foliatum, Šab. vi. 2, viii. 2; אֲפוּנְדָה funda, Ber. ix. 5. Perhaps also b in סַפְסָל subsellium, Šab. xxiii. 5.[1]

In LXX, פ is always transcribed by φ, never by π, except פסח, and foreign names. So Jerome transcribes it always by ph, never by f, or p. He expressly states that only פ in אַפַּדְנוֹ (Dan. xi. 45) equals Lat. p.

49. Mutation between ב and פ.

בקע to split, break, Ta'a. 15 b, BH בקע; עָפֵשׁ to be mouldy, Pes. 7a, BH עָבֵשׁ; קַפֵּח, Beκ. vii. 6, BH גָּבֵּח; אָבִיק outlet, Miq. vi. 10, perhaps BH אָפִיק; בַּכְבָּב arched, hollow vessel, Kel. ii. 3, from BH כָּפַף: הֶפְקֵר = הֶבְקֵר, in Pal. texts, ownerless property, Pea vi. 1.

For the mutation between ב and ו, cf. below, § 57.

---

[1] Jastrow, *Dictionary*, s. v. derives it from סֶפֶל.

5. The Sibilants ס, שׁ, שׂ, ז, צ.

50. MH has preserved the distinction between the three similar sibilants, ס, שׁ, שׂ. Thus שׂ is preserved in a considerable number of words: שָׂחָה (to swim), שָׂדֶה, שָׂכַר, שֶׂבַע, עָשָׂר, עָשָׂה, נָשָׂא, בָּשָׂר, בְּשָׂמִים, שָׂרַף, שַׂק, שָׂנֵא, שָׂמַח, שְׂמֹאל, שָׂכָר, שֵׂכֶל, שִׂים, שָׂחַק, &c. But many words that have שׂ in BH are regularly spelt in MH with ס, no doubt owing to a change of sound, due probably to Aram. influence, from שׂ to ס. Thus, the following which have שׂ in BH are spelt in MH with ס: סָבַר, סָב, חָרַס, הִסְתַּכֵּל, הֵפִיק, אֶרֶס, פָּרַס, עֶרֶס, סֶרֶט, סָרַג, סָפַק, סַבִּין, סִיד, סָחַט, סָדַר, &c., &c. Sometimes the texts waver: מְעוּפָּה—מְעוּשָּׂה, Giṭ. ix. 9. סָרַף—שָׂרַף, 'Or. i. 7;

Jerome, however, mentions only the distinction between ס (*samech*) and שׂ (*sin*). Perhaps his ear was not able to mark the finer distinction between the very similar sounds of שׂ and ס. He represents these sounds, as well as צ (*sade*) by *s*, owing, no doubt, to the poverty of the Latin alphabet in sibilants. Similarly, LXX transcribes these four sibilants by σ.

51.   *Transcription from Greek and Latin.*

ס is very common for Gk. σ: סִיטוֹן σιτώνης, Dam. ii. 4; אִסְטָסִיס στάσις, San. xii. 5; לְסָטִים λῃστής, Pᵉs. iii. 7. With בּ and פ for ξ, cf. above, § 44. With בּ for ψ, cf. above, § 48.

So also for the Lat. *s*: אֶסְדָּה *esseda*, Bᵉr. iv. 6; בָּסִילִיקֵי *basilica*, AZ. i. 7; קוּפְסָה *capsa*, Kel. xvi. 7.

ז represents Gk. ζ: זוֹם ζωμός, Pᵉs. iii. 1; אוֹרֶז ὄρυζα, Pea viii. 3. But also σ: פְּרוֹזְבּוֹל προσβολή, Šᵉbi. x. 3, 4; פְּרוֹזְדּוֹר προστάς, Ab. iv. 16;[1] אַטְלִיז κατάλυσις,[2] Tᵉm. iii. 5. Also, perhaps, ξ: חֲזִינָה ἀξίνη, Kel. xiv. 2; כָּרוֹז κήρυξ, Šᵉq. v. 1.[3]

Jerome transcribes ז by *z*.

---

[1] Cf. Krauss, ii, p. 484.   [2] Also קַטְלִיזָא, 'AZ. 40 b.

[3] These are doubtful. כָּרוֹז may be a Semitic word; cf. the Lexicons.

צ represents sometimes Gk. σ: מַרְצוּף μάρσυπος, Šab. viii. 5;
פַּרְצוּף πρόσωπον, Yᵉb. xvi. 3; אֶצְטָדִין στάδιον, BQ iv. 4; אִצְטְלִית
στολή, Yo. vii. 1; כְּצוֹצְרָה ἐξώστρα (L. for גּוּזְוְטְרָא in Bab. texts,
cf. above, § 44), Mid. ii. 5. Also Lat. s in קַצְרָה castra, ʿAr. ix. 6;
נָפוּץ (also נַפּוּם) napus, Kil. i. 5.

52. *Mutation of Sibilants.*

ס and שׁ: כָּבַשׁ to tread, press, and כָּבֵס to tread, wash (BH);
דָּבַס to tread, Syr. ܕܒܫ.[1]

ס and ז: מָזַג and מָסַךְ (cf. above, § 44).[2]

ס and ט: קִרְסֵם (§ 45) and קִרְטֵם to pluck, lop, Maʿa. iii. 3.

ס and צ: יָרַס to crush, ʿUq. ii. 5, BH רִצֵץ; צְלָעוֹת rocks, BH
סֶלַע, Šebi. v. 4; סִיב fibre, ʿUq. iii. 3, and צִיב tassel, Ḥul. ix. 1.[3]

צ and ט: קוֹרֶט particle, drop, ʿAZ. ii. 6, BH. קָרַץ.

6. The Sonants ל, מ, נ, ר.

53. ל represents Gk. λ, Lat. *l*: לִסְטִים λῃστής, Pes. iii. 7; לִבְלָר
libellarius, Pea ii. 6. By mutation, also ρ, *r*: אֶסְכָּרָה ἐσχάρα, Pes.
vii. 2; פַּלְהֶדְרִין πάρεδροι, Yo. i. 1; מַרְגָּלִית *margarita*, Ab. vi. 9;
מַרְקוּלִיס *Mercurius*, ʿAZ. iv. 1.

מ represents Gk. μ, Lat. *m*: מַרְצוּף μάρσυπος, Šab. viii. 5; מַפָּה
mappa, Bᵉr. viii. 3. מ is sometimes assimilated with the following
consonant: לַפְסָן λαμψάνη, Kil. i. 5; קַפַּנְדַּרְיָא (*via*) *compendiaria*,
ʿAZ. v. 4.

נ represents Gk. ν, Lat. *n*: אַנְטִיגְנוֹס ʾΑντίγονος, Ab. i. 3; נָפוּץ
napus, Kil. i. 3. It is also found for μ, *m* before a labial: אַנְפּוֹרְיָא
ἐμπορία (L. אמ׳), BM ii. 1; אַנְפִּלְיָא *impilia*, Yᵉb. xii. 1.

---

[1] Albrecht's suggestion (§ 4 e) that מִדְרָס may be an artificial form to
distinguish it from מִדְרָשׁ Midrash, is altogether improbable. The verb דרס
is extremely common in various connotations; cf. Kohut, iii, pp. 156–60.

[2] Cf. the transcription of Gr. σ (= ס) by ז, above, § 51.

[3] Cf. also the transcription of Gr. σ, Lat. s by צ, above, § 51.

ר. The evidence of Jewish tradition and the pointing of the MSS.[1] show that ר was pronounced as a guttural, as in BH, causing the same vowel changes as the regular gutturals. But it was also pronounced as a lingual, as is shown by its mutation with ל, as above, and below § 54.

It represents Gk. ρ, Lat. *r* : דְּרָקוֹן δράκων, ʿAZ. iii. 3 ; דִּינָר *denarius*, Ab. vi. 9.

Mutation of the Sonants.

54. ל and ר : הִשְׁתַּדֵּל to strive, Ab. ii. 5, Aram. אֶשְׁתַּדַּר, Dan. vi. 15; שַׁלְשֶׁלֶת chain, Kel. xiv. 3, BH שַׁרְשְׁרֵת [2]; גַּלְעִינָה kernel, ʿUq. ii. 2, Ter. xi. 5 ; נִתְאַרְמְלָה = נִתְאַלְמְלָה = נִתְאַלְמְנָה (L.) to be widowed, Ket. ii. 1.

מ and נ : רֵיקָן empty, Pes. v. 6, BH רֵיקָם ; הֵן for הֵם ; the plural ending ין— for ים— ; the pronominal suffix for the 3rd masc. pl. ן for ם. (Cf. below, §§ 70, 281.)

7. Semi-vowels ו, י.

55. ו. While still retaining its semi-vocal character, ו appears to have been hardened into a real consonant. Hence, it is more frequent in MH as an initial letter than in BH. Thus, וִידּוּי confession, San. vi. 7 ; וַדַּאי certain, Yo. viii. 8 ; וָלָד child (BH), MŠ. iii. 9 ; וַעַד assembly, Ab. i. 4 ; וֶסֶת habit, Nid. i. 1 ; וָרִיד jugular vein, Ḥul. ii. 4 ; וָתִיק active, Ber. 9 b. In verbs : וִיתֵּר to be plentiful, San. xi. 5, &c. (Cf. below, § 168.)

The consonantal character of ו is also shown by its mutation with soft ב (בֿ), cf. below, § 57.

In transcriptions the ו sometimes represents Lat. *v* : וִילוֹן *Velum*, Neg. xi. 11. Perhaps also the Aeolic Digamma : וֶסֶת ἔθος, Nid. i. 1 ;

---

[1] e.g. עֵירַה, L., ʿAZ. v. 10.

[2] These may, however, belong to two different roots : שׁלל = שׁלה to draw, and שׁרר to be firm, hence שְׁרוֹת rings, Isa. iii. 19 ; Šab. v. 1.

אַוֵּיר *ἀήρ*, Šab. xi. 3. ו is also found in the place of the Hiatus: אַסְטְוָה¹ *στοά*, Pes. i. 5.

Jerome renders ו by *u*.

56. י seems to have been pronounced very much like א (*spiritus lenis*). This explains its frequent mutation with א. However, it never transcribes a Greek or Latin initial vowel, for which א is used, cf. above, § 42. But י is regularly used to represent the first of the two vowels in the Hiatus: אַנְפּוֹרְיָא *ἐμπορία*, BM ii. 1; אַפְסוֹנְיָא *ὀψωνία*, San. ii. 4; קוּבְיָא *κυβεία*, iii. 3; פָּלְיָטוֹן *foliatum*, Šab. vi. 3; אוֹלְיָרִין *olearius*, Ṭoh. vii. 8; פָּנְדְּיוֹן *dupondius*, Pea viii. 7.

Jerome transcribes י by *i*.

57. When consonants, ו, י are often written twice, to prevent their being mistaken for vowel letters: וַוֶּרד rose, Šebi. vii. 6; נִתְכַּוֵּן to intend, Ter. iv. 4; פַּרְוֹור outskirts, Ḥal. iv. 11; חַיָּיט tailor, Šab. i. 3; נְיָיר paper, viii. 2. So in Pal. texts: בַּיְּי, Kel. xiv. 3; גוֹבַיְי, Ber. vi. 3; כְּדָיְי worthy, i. 7, for בַּנַּאי, גוֹבַאי, כְּדָאי, cf. above, § 38, foot-note.

Mutations.

58. ו and ב: גִּוֵּל disfigure, So. i. 7, BH נָבֵל; עַנְוֹה barley crop, Pea. vii. 7 (L. ענבה), i. 2, cf. BH עָנָב²; לְכָלֵב = לָלֵב *Lulab* = לוּלָב to sprout; פַּרְבָּר outskirts, BH פַּרְוֹור.³

י and א: מְבוֹי, BH מָבוֹא, entrance, alley, 'Er. i. 1; שֵׁיר, BH שְׁאָר, remainder, Zeb. v. 1; נוֹי beauty, 'AZ. iii. 4, for נוֹא, from נָאֶה. Cf. also the textual variants: הוֹרָאָה and הוֹדָיָיה thanksgiving, Ber. ix. 4; חֲצָאי from חֲצִי half, 'Ed. iii. 1; בְּלָאוֹת and בְּלִיוֹת old garments, Yeb. ix. 3, from בְּלִי, &c. Cf. also the interchange between the third radical of the verbs ל״א and ל״ה.⁴

---

¹ So L. and some other texts. Others, again, especially Bab. texts, have אִצְטַמְבָּה, אַסְטַמְבָּה. Cf. Kohut, i, pp. 166 f. Also סְטָיוֹ or סְטָיוֹ, Suk. 51 b.

² Cf. the commentaries, especially Maimonides, ad. loc.

³ Cf. אַסְטְמָבָּה—אַסְטְוָה, above, § 55 note, and בִּיבָרִין—*vivarium*, above, § 48.

⁴ However, this interchange between י and א, never occurs, as in Aram., at the beginning of a word; cf. Dalman, pp. 97-8.

8. The Letters ב, ג, ד, כ, פ, ת.

59. The BH distinction between the hard and the soft sounds
of these letters (*dagesh* and *raphe*) existed also in MH. This is
proved by many considerations. Thus, all the various Jewish
systems of pronunciation have preserved this distinction. It is also
supported by the transcriptions of Greek and Latin words, and by
the sound mutations in MH.

Thus, ב represents β, *b* (= בּ), and also *v, v* (= בֿ), § 47. It
interchanges with ו (= בֿ), § 57.

ג interchanges with ק = גּ, § 44, and also with ח (= גֿ), § 42.

ד represents δ, *d*, and also τ, § 45. It interchanges with ט (= דּ),
and also with ז (= דֿ), § 46.

כ represents κ, *c* (= כּ), and also χ, *ch* (= כֿ), § 43. It interchanges with ק (= כּ), and also with ח (= כֿ), §§ 44, 42.

פ represents π, *p* (= פּ), and also φ, *f* (= פֿ), § 47.

ת represents θ, *th* (= תֿ), § 45. It interchanges with ט (= תּ), § 46.

60. The difference in the *dagesh* and *raphe* sounds was not,
however, so marked as in some of the modern Jewish pronuncia-
tions. This is proved by the dictum in a late Baraita (Bᵉr. 15 b),
that in reading the Šemaʿ (Singer, pp. 40 f.) a pause must be
introduced between the enunciation of עֵשֶׂב and the following בְּשָׂדְךָ
(Deut. xi. 5), between הַכָּנָף and פְּתִיל (Num. xv. 38), so as not to
produce an assimilation of the final letters of one word with the
initial letters of the following word (שֶׁיִּתֵּן רֶיוַח בֵּין הַדְּבֵקִים).

9. Other Consonantal Changes.

61. Transposition (*Metathesis*). זָקַר to fling (נִזְקָרִין), Yo. 38 b
= זָרַק; עָלַב to insult, Yo. 23 a = לעב, j. So. 19 a, 2 Chron. xxxvi. 16
(Hiphʻil); מַלְגֵּו large fork, Šab. 92 b, t. ib. ix. 10 [1] = מַזְלֵג ; מַרְזֵב spout,
BB iii. 8, from זָרַב = רָזַב (= זוב) to flow [2]; עָמֵץ to close the eyes, Šab.

---

[1] שְׁנַיִם אוֹחֲזִין בְּמַלְגֵּז וְלוֹנְזִין. So in the Mishna in Bab. Talmud, Šab. 122 b
(xvii. 1).

[2] Cf. זְרִיבָה, a flowing, j. San. xi. 7. See Kohut, iii, p. 319, and *BDB.*,
p. 279.

xxiii. 5 = עָצַם ; קְטְרֵג to accuse, j. Šab. 5 b, from קַטִּיגוֹר (= κατήγορος),
Ab. iv. 11. Perhaps also רָמַז to wink, Git. v. 7, רָזַם (Job xv. 12).
Probably also הֲרֵי aspect, nature of a case, BQ i. 1 = אֲרֵי = רְאֵי,
BQ 4 a, &c.[1]

62. Rejection. (*a*) *Aphaeresis.* In addition to the rejection of
initial weak consonants when without vowels in verbs פ״י, נ״פ, &c.,
as in BH (cf. below, §§ 165, 169 ; Ges.-K., § 19 h), MH shows
aphaeresis also in a few other cases, viz. with the gutturals א, ח, ע, ה
(as preformatives), and preformative מ :

גִּיס brother-in-law, San. iii. 4 = אָגִיס, as in L. and j. ib. iii. 7 ;
לְעָזָר, לִיעֶזֶר, in Pal. texts, for אֶלְעָזָר, אֱלִיעֶזֶר.

ח : פִּיר a pit, Kᵉt. 79 b, Nᵉd. 89 b = חָפִיר ; שִׁיפָה mat, Makš. v. 8
= חֲשִׁיפָה[2] ; סְחוּס = סָחוּס = חַסְחוּס cartilege, Bᵉk. vi. 1 (cf. L.).

ע : שׁוּנִית cliff, Oh. xviii. 6 = עֲשׁוּנִית, Mᵉkil. on Exod. xv. 5.[3]

ה : פָּרֵת cutting off = הַפָּרֵת (cf. below, § 115).

מ : מוּעָט small = מְמוּעָט ; חוּתָּךְ cut off = מְחוּתָּךְ (cf. § 129).

Further, לִידָה birth, Kᵉt. iv. 3 = יְלִידָה (cf. below, § 228). קִיחָה
leather thong, Kel. xvi. 4 ; taking, Qid. 2 a = לְקִיחָה (cf. below, § 228).

63. (*b*) *Syncope.* MH shows the same cases of elision of a consonant in the middle of a word, as appear in BH (Ges.-K. § 19 k).
In addition syncope takes place in a number of compounds, e. g.
אֶלְמָלֵא if not = לֹא + אִם + אִלּוּ, Ab. iii. 2 ; its equivalent in Pal. texts :
אִילּוּלֵא = לוּלֵי + אִם ; בְּרַבִּי (or בְּרַבִּי) = (?) בְּרֵבִי = בֶּן + רַבִּי, Pea ii. 4 ; כִּיצַד how

---

[1] הֲרֵי cannot be a contraction of הֲרְאֵי (Levy i. 493 b), since it is in the
construct state. Bacher's view (*Aelteste Terminologie*, pp. 46–8), that הֲרֵי
is an interjection (= וַהֲרֵי) is improbable. הֲרֵי is synonymous with רְאֵי.
The two expressions are used in different types of texts with exactly the same
significance.

[2] דוּת = חֲדוּת cistern, cited by Albrecht (§ 9 a), rests upon a scribal error.
With two exceptions (t. Oh. xii. 6), it is always הֲדוּת (also in plur. הֲדוּתִיוֹת
t. BB iii. 1), and should be הַחֲדוּת = הַהֲדוּת, as in Syr. and Arab. ; cf.
Kohut, iii. 32.

[3] Cf. the comment of Weiss, ad loc. (p. 46), and also Kohut, viii, p. 116 f.

צַד+זֶה+כְּאִי=, as often written in the Halakic Midrashim: כַּלֵּךְ get away = כַּלֵּה+וְלֵךְ, t. Ter. i. 1; San. 67 b (cf. Rashi, ad loc.); עַכְשָׁיו now, 'AZ. i. 1, a compound of uncertain composition (cf. below, § 296); the elision of א in אֲנִי, when joined as an enclitic, especially to participles, e. g. הֲרֵינִי behold I = אֲנִי + הֲרֵי; חוֹשְׁשֵׁנִי I fear me, חוֹשֵׁשׁ+אֲנִי (cf. below, § 341, and foot-note).

Further examples of syncope of א are found in יִשָּׁבֵב=יִשְׁבְּאָב, as in L. and BH, Ḥul. ii. 4, and in the popular זִיבָה = וְאֵבָה she wolf, j. Šeq. v. 1.

64. (c) *Apocope*. The rejection of a final letter is found in אִי not = אֵין, before words beginning with א; so כֵּן = כֵּי (cf. below, § 298); אִי = אִם if. Probably also הַלָּה that one = הַלָּז (cf. below, § 73). In proper names, יוֹסֵי (or Pal. יוֹסָה) = יוֹסֵף, Ab. i. 41; שַׁמַּאי = שִׁמְעָיָה, ib. i. 10.[1]

For elision of consonants in foreign words, cf. Krauss, LW i. §§ 214 ff.; Albrecht, § 9 b.

65. Augmentation. As in BH, an א is sometimes prefixed to a word: אֶגוּדָל thumb, Yo. ii. 1 = גוּדָל (L., cf. גּוּדְלֵי רַגְלָיו, Šab. 151 b); אֲגַף wing, Neg. xiv. 1 = גַּף (cf. BH); אַכְרוֹב cabbage, 'Or. iii. 7. 'Uq. ii. 7 (L., and elsewhere in Pal. texts) = כְּרוֹב, Ter. x. 11.

The prosthetic א is especially frequent in the transcription of foreign words beginning with two or more consonants: אִסְטָסִיס = στάσις, San. xii. 5; אַסְפְּלָנִית = σπληνίον, Šab. xix. 2; אַכְסַנְיָא = ξένος, Dam. iii. 1; אַסְקוּטְלָא *scutella*, MQ iii. 7. So also before one consonant: אִלְפָּס = λοπάς, Šab. iii. 5; אֲפוּנְדָּה = *funda*, ib. x. 3. Cf. Krauss, §§ 261 ff.; Albrecht, § 10.

Insertion of ר: חַרְטוֹם beak, Ṭoh. i. 2 = חוֹטָם nose, Kel. xxvi. 4 (cf. below, § 274), and in the formation of Quadriliterals, below § 107.

66. *Softening* of a sound, owing to dissimilation, is found in לְבַלְבֵּב = לִבְלֵב לִילְב (cf. above, § 58); שְׁפוֹפֶרֶת tube, Šab. ii. 4 = שְׁפַרְפֶּרֶת (cf. below, § 245).

---

[1] Cf. BH, 1 Chr. ii. 28, &c. So יֵשׁוּ, Jesus, for יֵשׁוּעַ. Cf. J. Klausner, ישו הנוצרי, p. 237. These forms are, probably, caritatives.

PART II

MORPHOLOGY

I. THE PRONOUN

1. The Personal Pronoun.

67. (1) The 1st pers. sing. is אֲנִי. אָנֹכִי is found only in quotations from the Bible, or in direct allusions to Biblical passages.[1] The disuse of אָנֹכִי dates already from BH times. Thus אנכי is not found in the later or popular BH books, like Canticles, Lamentations, Haggai, Zachariah i–viii, Ezra, Esther, and Qohelet; and only once in Ezekiel, Daniel, Nehemiah, and Chronicles.[2] So also Aram. (with the exception of the Zinjirli dialect),[3] Arabic and Ethiopic have forms corresponding to אֲנִי only, while Assyrian, Moabite, and Phoenician use forms corresponding to אנכי only. In earlier Hebrew alone are the two forms found existing side by side, but אֲנִי, being the shorter of the two, gradually came to be employed more frequently, especially in colloquial speech, until the longer form disappeared entirely from common use.

68. The plural is always אֲנוּ.[4] This form occurs, as is well

---

[1] e.g. San. vi. 2 ; Šab. 105 a.   [2] Cf. *BDB.*, p. 59 and reff.

[3] Cf. G. A. Cooke, *N. Sem. Inscr.*, Nos. 61, l. 1, אנך ; 62, l. 19, אנכי ; but 63, l. 20, אנה. For the origin and mutual relation of אני and אנכי cf. Stade, *Heb. Gr.*, p. 135, and Barth, *Pronominalbildung*, pp. 3–4.

[4] אֲנַחְנוּ occurs in the early portions of the Liturgy, cf. S. Singer, *The Authorized Daily Prayer Book*, pp. 4, 51, &c. So in Pes. x. 5, but L. has אנו. אנחנו is also found exceptionally in an ordinary passage, Ket. x. 2, but here also L. has אנו.

known, only once in BH, and then only in the Kᵉtib (Jer. xlii. 6),
which is rather remarkable, since the Kᵉtib generally represents
a more archaic type of language. אֲנוּ seems to be a popular
formation from אֲנִי, on the analogy of the plural forms of the
pronominal suffixes קְטָלֵנוּ, קְטָלָנוּ, or of מִמֶּנּוּ, מִמֶּנִּי; cf. also the
verbal plurals קְטָלוּ, יִקְטְלוּ, &c. From the colloquial language
the form crept into the Book of Jeremiah, but was struck out
by the Massoretes as a vulgarism.

All other Semitic languages have forms corresponding to אֲנַחְנוּ.
So especially the Aram. dialects, אנחנן, נחנא, אנחנא, and in the
latest and most debased dialects אנן, with the syncope of the inaudible
guttural.[1]

69. (2) In the 2nd pers. אַתָּה is used for the masc., and אַתְּ for
the fem., as in BH. אַתְּ for the masc. is exceedingly rare in the
earlier MH literature, and may always be due to scribal errors.
It is, however, frequent in texts of a later date, particularly of
Palestinian origin, and in the Haggadic Midrashim. This use must
be considered an Aramaism (but sporadically also in BH).

The plural is אַתֶּם for the masc. Of the fem. plural, אַתֵּן, no
example occurs in our literature. The form אַתֶּם is also found
for the fem.: t. BB viii. 19: נִיוָנְתֶּם אַתֶּם . . . נִשֵּׂאתֶם אַתֶּם.

70. (3) The 3rd pers. has הוּא for the masc., and הִיא for the
fem. The plur. is הֵם, הֵן respectively. הֵמָּה is found only in
Biblical quotations (Ab. vi. 2).

The forms אַתֵּן for the 2nd masc. plur., and especially הֵן for the
3rd masc. plur., are also found, but they are merely due to a
phonetic change common in MH (cf. above, § 54). They may,
however, be also due to the influence of Aram., in which these
pronouns end in ן.

---

[1] Barth (op. cit., p. 6 (e)), holds that אנן is formed from אנא by the
addition of the plur. suff. ן, like אנו from אני.

71. *The Pronominal Suffixes.* The pronominal suffixes are in MH the same as in BH. The 3rd plur. masc. has, however, also here ן for ם. But often the reading is not certain, and varies from text to text. There are also examples of the masc. form used for the fem., e.g. מִכֶּם, אַחַת, כּוּלְּכֶם, כּוּלָּם, T^{er}. viii. 11, 12; לָהֶם, Ḥal. i. 7.

2. The Demonstrative Pronoun.

72. (1) Singular זֶה masc., זוֹ fem., plur. אֵלּוּ.

The form זוֹ for זֹאת occurs in BH in Hos. vii. 16; in the cycle of North Israelitish stories in the Book of Kings (זֹה, 2 Ki. vi. 19), both of which exhibit a number of dialectal peculiarities; also, in Ezekiel (זֹה, xl. 45), in a late psalm (זוֹ, Ps. cxxxii. 12), and six times in Qohelet.

It is, therefore, very probable that the shorter form זֹה, or זוֹ, existed from early times as a dialectal form in the northern speech, from which it gradually spread to the south, and in the course of time supplanted the longer form זֹאת.

The plur. אֵלּוּ for BH אֵלֶּה occurs also in Sirach (אֵילוּ, li. 24). The change of the second vowel may have been due to an unconscious desire to indicate more clearly the plural character of the word. The vowel chosen is the same as in אָנוּ, discussed above, § 67.

73. (2) BH has also preserved the demonstrative use of the pronoun of the 3rd pers., הוּא, הִיא, הֵם, הֵן; חֲמוֹרְךָ הוּא that ass of thine, opposed to חֲמוֹרְךָ זֶה, BB v. 2; so often הֲרֵי הוּא, הֲרֵי הִיא, הֲרֵי הֵם. More commonly with the article, as in BH הָהֵם, הַהִיא, הַהוּא.

74. (3) The stronger BH demonstrative הַלָּזֶה is found only in the shortened form הַלָּז (Judges vi. 20) for the masc., Ṭoh. vi. 5, 8. Fem. הַלֵּזוּ, Y^eb. xiii. 7; t. ib. v. 4; xiii. 6.[1]

---

[1] But L. has הַלָּז. So in BH הַלָּז is also found for the fem., 2 Kings iv. 25.

This form הַלָּז is further shortened to הַלָּה by the apocope of ז.[1]
It is only used substantively, MŠ. iii. 2; San. viii 2, &c. In
Yeb. iii. 5, ʿEd. iv. 9, הַלָּה stands also for the fem. וְהַלָּה תֵצֵא מִשּׁוּם
אֲחוֹת אִשָּׁה and that one goes forth[2] as a wife's sister.

The plur. of הַלָּה, הַלָּז is הַלָּלוּ, evidently a contraction of הַל + אֵלּוּ;
מוּמִין הַלָּלוּ these defects, Ket. vii. 8, and frequently.

75. (4) The emphatic particle אֵת is also used as a demonstrative,
either alone or with pronominal suffixes, e. g. אֵת שֶׁלִּפְנֵי הַמִּטָּה וְאֵת
שֶׁלְּאַחַר הַמִּטָּה those before the bier and those behind the bier, Bᵉr.
iii. 1; אוֹתָהּ הַחַלָּה וְאוֹתוֹ הַסֵּדֶר that loaf and that order, Mᵉn. ii. 2.

76. (5) *The Article.* In the form and use of the Article, MH
agrees with BH. See further in the Syntax (§§ 373–78).

3. The Relative Pronoun.

77. The relative is in MH everywhere שֶׁ. אֲשֶׁר occurs only
in quotations (Pe. ii. 2 from Isa. vii. 25; So. ix. 5 from Deut. xxi. 3,
&c.), and in early liturgical language, which is conceived in an
elevated and semi-Biblical strain; thus, in the Passover Haggadah,
אֲשֶׁר גְּאָלָנוּ, Pes. x. 61; in the Evening Service, אֲשֶׁר בִּדְבָרוֹ (Singer,
p. 96); and often in Benedictions, אֲשֶׁר קִדְּשָׁנוּ (ib. pp. 4, 134, 210, &c.);
אֲשֶׁר נָתַן (pp. 5, 68); אֲשֶׁר יָצַר (pp. 4, 299); אֲשֶׁר בָּרָא (pp. 280, 299);
and a few more. Elsewhere שֶׁ is used: שֶׁבְּכָל (p. 51), שֶׁיָּדַעְנוּ,
(p. 239), and in Benedictions, Bᵉr. vi. 3; vii. 3; ix. 1 ff.; Singer,
pp. 5 f., 276, 290, 291, &c.

78. In BH the form occurs twice in the Song of Deborah
(שַׁקַּמְתִּי), a North Israelitish production; three times in the story of
Gideon, a North Israelitish hero; once in the North Israelitish

---

[1] Cf. above, § 64. Barth, however, holds that הַלָּה is the original form
which was later strengthened by the addition of זה, op. cit., pp. 78, 105 f.

[2] i. e. הַחוּצָה, Deut. xxv. 5. L. has וְהַלָּז. So ʿAr. ix. 4 edd. have הַלָּה,
but L. has הַלָּז.

section of the Book of Kings ; exclusively, except in the late superscription, in the collection of popular songs known as Canticles,
which probably originated in Northern Israel ; sporadically in the
later BH books, and very frequently in Qohelet (cf. Ges.-K., § 36).
Now, whatever the relation of the two forms to each other,[1]
there can be no doubt that שֶׁ is as old as אֲשֶׁר, if not older. Its
confinement in the earlier books of the Bible to North Israelitish
documents would prove that its use must have been common in
the colloquial speech of Northern Palestine, under the influence,
to some extent at least, of the Phoenician אשׁ,[2] שׁ, the Assyrian *ša*,
and, perhaps, also the Aram. זִי, דִי. The scarcity of its occurrence
even in these documents must be explained by the assumption
that it was regarded as a vulgarism which the literary language
had to avoid. Its use gradually extended to Southern Palestine,
and being the shorter and more pliable form, it must in the course
of time have entirely supplanted the longer אֲשֶׁר in the language
of the common people, and from this it descended directly to MH.
But the literary prejudice against it seems to have remained even
after BH had ceased to be a living speech. Hence its non-
occurrence in Esther, its scarcity in Chronicles, and the anxiety
to avoid it which is displayed by a studious imitator of the ancients
like Sirach, and even by such an independent mind as the author
of Qohelet.[3]

4. The Possessive Pronoun.

79. Possession is very frequently expressed in MH by the
combination of the relative שֶׁ with the preposition לְ. In older
texts this combination is still attached to the noun which it governs,

---

[1] Cf. Barth, op. cit., pp. 162–4 ; Bergsträsser, *ZAW.*, xix, pp. 41 ff.

[2] Cf. Schröder, *Phœniz. Sprache*, § 65 and foot-note.

[3] Note such awkward and inconsistent expressions as בְּשֶׁל אֲשֶׁר יַעֲמוֹל
(= Aram. . . . בְּדִיל דִּי), viii. 17 ; מִבְּלִי אֲשֶׁר לֹא יִמְצָא, iii. 11, &c.

e. g. שְׁלַוָּבְחִין, Zᵉb. v. 1.[1]   Gradually שֶׁל־ was detached from the noun by the scribes, and now appears as an independent particle שֶׁל. So especially with pronominal suffixes שֶׁלִּי, שֶׁלָּךְ, &c., which have become regular possessive pronouns. Cf. Ab. v. 10 ; BM i. 5, &c.   See further in the Syntax, §§ 406–9.

5. The Interrogative Pronoun.

80. (1) מָה, מִי, as in BH.

(2) By prefixing the interrogative particle אֵי to the demonstrative זֶה, זוּ, a new interrogative pronoun has been formed, אֵיזֶה, fem. אֵיזוֹ which? This is often strengthened by the enclitic הוּא, הִיא, הוּא, with which it is often written as one word, and the final א omitted : אֵיזֶהוּ, Zᵉb. v. 1 ; אֵיזוֹהִי, Kel. xvii. 6. In the older texts, however, the three components are still kept separate : אֵי זֶה הִיא, אֵי זֶה הוּא, cf. L., loc. cit.

Prepositions are attached to אֵי : בְּאֵיזֶה, בְּאֵיזוֹ, San. v. 1 ; מֵאֵיזֶה, Ab. vi. 9.   Contrast BH אֵי מִזֶּה, 2 Sam. xv. 2, Jonah i. 8 ; אֵי לָזֹאת, Jer. v. 2.

81. The plural of אֵיזֶה, אֵיזוֹ, אֵיזוּ is אֵי אֵלּוּ, which is found only once in MH literature, viz. Naz. 6 b· (אֵי אֵלּוּ הֵן יָמִים ·. · .). Elsewhere it is contracted to אֵילוּ, spelt אֵלּוּ through the ignorance of the scribes, who confused it with the demonstr. plur. אֵלּוּ.[2] This confusion may account for the scarcity of this form in our literature. Perhaps the Rabbis, who had a passion for lucidity and precision, deliberately avoided it for fear of this confusion with the demonstr.

Exx.: אֵלּוּ מְצִיאוֹת שֶׁלּוֹ וְאֵלּוּ (L.) וָאִלּוּ חַיָּיב לְהַכְרִיז Which things when found are his [the finder's], and which is he bound to proclaim?[3] BM ii. 1 ; וְרוֹאִים אֵלּוּ הָאֲבָנִים הָרְאוּיוֹת לְהִשְׁתַּבֵּר They

---

[1] Cf. Krauss, *MGWJ.*, li, p. 56.

[2] This confusion is found even in modern scholars, e. g. Albrecht, § 30 a.

[3] Cf. the parallel expressions : אֵיזֶהוּ נֶשֶׁךְ וְאֵיזֶהוּ תַּרְבִּית? אֵיזֶהוּ נֶשֶׁךְ · · · , ib. v. 1 ; אֵיזֶהוּ תָּם וְאֵיזֶהוּ מוּעָד?, BQ ii. 4, &c. So, perhaps, also elsewhere,

consider which are the stones that are likely to have been broken,
ib. x. 1; טָעָה וְאֵין יָדוּעַ אֵלּוּ שֶׁהָפְכוּ וְאֵלּוּ שֶׁקֵּדְמוּ If he made a mistake
and it is not known which had changed and which had advanced?
t. Neg. ii. 7; בְּאֵלּוּ מַשְׁקִין אָמְרוּ In the case of which fluids have
they said it? Makš. iii. 2; ¹ בְּאֵילוּ נְדָרִים אָמְרוּ In the case of which
vows have they said it? t. Ket. vii. 8 || Ket. 72 b; בְּאֵילוּ בְּנֵי מֵעַיִם
אָמְרוּ In the case of which intestines have they said it? t. Ḥul.
iii. 15 || Ḥul. 56 b; בְּאֵילוּ פָנִים בָּאִים לִפְנֵי הַמָּקוֹם With what face will
they come before the Almighty? Pesiqta, § 25; עַל אֵלּוּ עֳמָרִים נֶחְלָקוּ
Over which sheaves did they dispute? t. Pe. iii. 2. So probably
also עַל אֵלּוּ מוּמִים שׁוֹחֲטִין אֶת הַבְּכוֹר Over which blemishes may one
slay the first-born animal? Bek. vi. 1; לְאֵילוּ נַאֲמִין Whom shall
we believe? Pesiqta Rab., p. 138 b.

82. We can trace clearly in BH the development of this new
interrogative. In אֵי זֶה בֵּית הָרֹאֶה, 1 Sam. ix. 18, the emphasis
is on אֵי (= אַיֵּה), while זֶה serves merely as an enclitic particle
to give directness to the question, and the proper answer to the
question would be הִנֵּה, or פֹּה בֵּית הָרֹאֶה. Gradually, however,
the emphasis was shifted from אֵי to זֶה, as in אֵי זֶה הַדֶּרֶךְ נַעֲלֶה,
2 Kings iii. 8, Which way shall we go up?, as is shown by the
answer, דֶּרֶךְ מִדְבַּר אֱדוֹם, 2 Chron. xviii. 23. These two usages
existed side by side, until, finally, the older usage disappeared, and
אֵיזֶה ceased to be an interrogative of place, and became a pure
interrogative pronoun or adjective. So in Qoh. ii. 3, and, especially,
in xi. 6, where it stands before a verb, אֵי זֶה יִכְשָׁר, and is used
exactly as in MH.²

e.g. Pea i. 1; BB. iii. 7. The interrogative style is exceedingly common
in MH.
¹ Cf. the parallel expression : בְּאֵיזֶה מַקְדֵּחַ אָמְרוּ ?, Oh. ii. 3, &c.
² See further the writer's remarks, *JQR.*, xx (1908), p. 661 f.

II. THE VERB

A. General Survey.

In all Semitic speech the verb forms the backbone of the language. A detailed study of the MH verb may, therefore, help us to a correct estimate of the character of the MH idiom, and of its relation to BH. In what follows we shall review the MH verb both from the lexical and the grammatical side.

1. LEXICAL.

83. Of the 1,350 verbs which are found in the Lexicon of BH MH has lost 250 verbs, and gained 300 new verbs. The majority of these lost verbs will be found on examination to consist of rare and poetical expressions which from an early date may have been confined to literature, or to certain dialects, and were rarely, or never, used in the normal language of every-day speech. A smaller, but still considerable number of verbs (over 50) consists of common and prosaic BH words which, for some reason, were lost in MH, and replaced by other equivalent verbs. A third group is of special interest: it consists of about 50 verbs which are common to both BH and Aram., but yet have not been preserved in MH, a fact which tells against the theory that MH is but an artificial conglomeration of BH and Aram.

In what follows will be found a classified list of BH verbs lost in MH.

(A) *BH Verbs not found in MH.*

84. (1) Rare or poetical expressions:[1] אזן weigh, אנש, אנק, אפף, בחל, בלג, בלק, בתק, גהה, גהר, גור stir up strife, דוץ, דכה,

---

[1] In this group have been entered verbs that cannot be included in any of the following groups. Groups (2), (4), (5), and (6) also contain numerous rare and poetical forms. The English equivalents have been given only where they are necessary for the identification of the verb. For the meaning of the other verbs in these lists, the reader is referred to the Dictionaries. For the purpose of this survey, Aram. verbs found in BH are regarded as BH verbs.

‏זרם, זור‎ press down, ‏זור‎ be loathsome, ‏זבד, הדך, הדה, דלח‎,
‏חנן‎ be ‏חמק‎ be ruthless, ‏חמץ‎ be red, ‏חטם‎, ‏חול‎ be strong,
‏יקש, יפח, ידד, יגה, יגב, טמה, חרת‎ engrave, ‏חרש, חפף‎, loathsome,
tear ‏מלח‎ ‏מאר, לאט, כשה, כסם‎ (Hiph'il), ‏כבר, כאה, ישם‎, shoot, ‏ירא‎
‏נסס, נחין, נוש, נון, נהה, נהב, נבב, נאר, נאק‎ flap, ‏מרא‎ ‏מלל, מלץ‎, away,
weigh, ‏סלה‎ make light, ‏סלה, סלא, נתע, נתם, נקע, נצא‎, be sick,
turn aside, ‏עטף‎ ‏עוש‎ be exposed, ‏עור‎ be dark, ‏עוף‎ ‏עול, עדר, סעה‎,
‏פון, עתם‎, ‏עלל‎ ‏ענד, ענה‎ be occupied, ‏עפל, ערג, ערף‎ drip, ‏עלם‎,
‏צפר, צעה‎ disappear, ‏פסם‎ be scattered, ‏פוש‎ ‏פוש‎ spring about,
‏קוט, קוש, קיה, קשח, רגע‎ harden, ‏רגע‎ disturb, ‏רהה, רוד, רנה, רעל‎,
travel, ‏שור‎ be abundant, ‏שוק, שוע, שגל, שאה, רתם, רצד, רעף‎ reel,
‏שקק‎, be smeared, ‏שעע‎ ‏שסם‎, spoil, ‏שסה, שלו, שלה‎ behold, ‏שור‎
‏תזז, תאה‎.

85. (2) Verbs common to BH and Aram.: ‏אלף, אלם, אזל‎,
‏כתר, כפן, יהב, יאב, טלל, טאטא, חרג, חלש, חזה, חוה, גיח, אתה‎,
‏סגד, נכל, נכא, נחת, (משא =) (מרע =), משה (=) מרץ, מוק, מגר‎ (Pi'el),
‏צלח, צום‎ be wide, ‏פצה, פצח, פצה, פעל, פרע, עתר, עשת, עוק, עבט‎
‏שגה, שגא, רחם‎ love, ‏שבר‎ hope, ‏רזה, קמל, קטל‎, (‏טלל‎ =) ‏צלל‎
‏תכן, (סיב =) שיב, שחה, שוט, שוה‎ set, (‏סגי‎ =), ‏שוה‎ (=)‏.

86. (3) Verbs frequent in BH: ‏התאפק, אפס, האזין, איב, אבה‎,
‏חסה, חדל, (תלל) התל, דפק, גער, גיל, גור, בתר, בוך, בגד, אשם, אצל‎,
‏מחא, מוג, התמהמה, לוט, יקע, יצג, ינה, יהד, יגר, טחוה, חשף, חרב‎,
‏העתיר, ערב, עלו, עוז, סכר, סכל, סחב, סוג, נצב, נחה, נוט, נגש, מעד‎,
‏שעה‎ gaze, ‏שית, שגע, שאנן, רעה, רמש, רכש, רוש, קדד, פצר, פצץ‎,
‏שרה‎.

(4) Denominative Verbs: ‏נסס, נכר, נהר, מהר, לחם, גבל, אפד‎,
‏קרן, עלל, נפש‎.

87. (5) BH Verbs used in MH in cognate roots only: ‏יעף‎ =
‏סוך; נכה—נכא; רקק—ירק; ירה—ירא; קוץ—יקץ; נפח—יפח; עיף‎,
‏טען—צען; פקק—פוק; יעץ—עוץ; עפש—עבש; (סריג) סוג—שוך‎;
‏תקן—תכן; תלה—תלא; רום—רמם; רמז—רזם; נקר—קור‎.

88. (6) The following is a list, by no means exhaustive, of the equivalents used in MH for older BH verbs: יאב, חפץ, אבה‎, ;בא—אתה‎ ;חזק—אמץ‎ ;למד—אלף‎ ;שנא—אֵיב‎ ;רצה—הואיל‎ ;גער‎ ;פחד, ירא—גור, יגר‎ ;חתך—בתק‎ ;גזל—שסה, חמס, בזז‎ ;זרם‎ ;כעס—קצף, זעף, זעם‎ ;לגלג, לעג—תלל, התל‎ ;נזף—כהה‎ ;כבד—טאטא‎ ;יבש—נתש, חרב‎ ;נהג—יבל‎ ;בטח—עוז, חסה, שטף‎ ;יצג‎ ;התגייר—התיהד‎ ;נתן—יהב‎ ;התחיל—החל‎ ;שתק—החריש‎ ;נגש—מרד—מרה—מעד‎ ;הוחלק—לאט, לוט‎ ;כסה—לאט, לוט‎ ;העמיד—נצב‎ ;סגד‎ ;מסר—סַגַּר, נָבַר‎ ;נפרע—נקם‎ ;נהג—נחה‎ ;בא אצל, קרב‎ ;חכה‎ ;משכן—ערב, עבט‎ ;שוטה—סכל‎ ;גרר—סחב‎ ;השתחוה—קדד‎ ;עשה—פעל‎ ;פגע—קרה, פגש‎ ;שמח—גיל, עלם, עלז, עלן‎ ;המתן—קוה‎ ;משל, שוה‎ ;כחש—רזה‎ ;עני—דלל, ריש‎ ;הרג—קטל‎ ;התענה—צום‎ ;דין—פלל, שפט‎ ;דמה‎.

89. Of the 300 new verbs in MH, only a very small proportion are loan words from Aram. The majority are old Hebrew expressions which occur in BH either in cognate verbal roots, or in derivatives, usually substantives. A further large number of these new verbs are real denominatives which are consciously formed by MH from nouns found in BH. Of the residue which cannot be traced to BH sources, a very large proportion belong to the original stock of the old Hebrew vocabulary, which by mere accident have not been preserved in the scanty and fragmentary remains of BH literature. Some of these are found also in Aram. and in other Semitic languages, and are thus of a general Semitic character. Others are found in MH and in Aram. only, and are, probably, at least in most cases, as original in MH as in Aram. Others, again, are peculiar to MH, or may be also found in other Semitic languages, but not in Aram. The remainder (about thirty verbs) are direct borrowings from Aram., and a few more are derived from Greek.

It will, therefore, be seen that the Aram. influence on the lexical character of the MH verb is far less extensive than has been supposed. It may safely be said that the MH influence on the Aram. vocabulary was greater than that of Aram. on MH, particularly in the sphere of religion and the higher life.

We give in what follows a classified list of the new verbs in MH.[1]

(B) *MH Verbs not found in BH.*

90. (1) MH verbs, found in BH in a different form.

(*a*) In cognate roots: אנה—ינה ; ותר—יתר ; זוח—זחח ; זול—
זלל ; חשש—חוש ; טוח—טחה ; נפש—פוש ; שפף—שוף ; שתת—שתה.

(*b*) With mutation of sound: בגר—בכר ; זבל—זבח[2]; חזם—
גזם ; טמע—טבע ; מהה—מחה ; מלג—מלק ; מרד—ירד ; נגל—נבל;
נשר—נשל ; סים — שים (?); סתר — שתר ; עוג — חוג ; עכב—עקב;
עסק—עשק ; עפש—עבש ; עקם—עקל ; פכח—פקח ; פקע—בקע ; פשר—
פתר—קטע ; קצע : קמו—קמין ; קמע—קמט ; קפל—כפל ; קרד—גרד;
ריקן—ריקם ; תפח—נפח ; תשש—נתש.[3]

(*c*) By transposition of sound:[4] זקר—זרק ; חגר—חרג ; עלב—
לעב ; עמץ—עצם.

91. (2) MH verbs found in BH in derivatives: אחה, אגר,
גבל knead (BH גבלות), גבה (BH גבים, &c.), גבב, גבה, בור, בהק,
דרג, גנו (גף BH), גפף (גם BH), גמם (גדיש, גדלים), גדל twist (גבש,
הבהב, זוז, זלג, חדק, חלד, חמר heap, חפף, חרר bore, חרר be free,
חשר, יהר, ירק, כבל, כמן, כפת (?כפתור), כרך, מרא, מתן (מתנים ?),
נגב, נסר, נקד, סגל, סדר, סכה look, סרב, סרק (שרק=), עגל, עטן,
צנן, צמם, ציין dye, צבע, פרך, פרן, פרז, פחת, ערס knead, ערם mix, ערב
שפע, שחף, שחן, שגר, רתת, רטמ, רהט, קרש, קלם, קלט, קלח, צרך.

---

[1] For further details about the derivation of these verbs, the reader is referred to Kohut's *Aruch* and to Jastrow's Dictionary.

[2] Of heathen sacrifices, probably an artificial change in a contemptuous sense as mere זֶבֶל dung. Cf. Kohut, iii, p. 265, and reff. to Tosaphot on 'AZ. 18 b

[3] Cf. further in the Phonology above, §§ 43, 45 ff.

[4] Cf. above, § 61.

92. (3) Denominative Verbs.

(*a*) From BH nouns : גבן (from אשכן ,(אשך (from אפל ,אפל ,אלמן
fish חבּה ,זפת ,(זפת from) זפף, face south דרם ,דגש ,גפר ,(גבינה)
hook חלב ,חמר (from חמור) ,חסד ,חפן ,חרש (from חרשׁ), יבל (from
יבלת) ,ימן (from ימין), כבר sift, כרכב ,כרכם ,כתף ,נבל (from נבלה)
נגב face south, נפה sift, סלת ,סרם ,עבב ,עיין (from עראם ,(ערשׁ ,פגל ,פחם
צבע (from אצבע) ,צדד (from צד) ,ציין (from ציית) ,צמת ,צפן
(from צפון), ריקם (Aramaized for רעל (from רעלות) ,(ריקם from) רוקן
שמן (from שמן) ,שרבט ,שרב ,שרבט (from תלם ,תמר ,(שרבט תוך) תחל (from
תשע be nine. תרם (from תרומה) ,תרע (from תרועה), תרם (from תמר)

(*b*) From MH nouns : זבל ,דמע ,גשר גרע (from גרעין), רבב
משכן ,(אמצע) מצע (from מוממחה) מחה (from מֶבֶל), טבל (from זרד ,זרד
שתף ,(שובר) שבר (from מרתף) רתף ,רמץ ,(עיסה) עסם (from
תבל (from תבלין), תחם ,תמר ,תרמל.

(*c*) From Aram. nouns, only a few like קטם (=סמי) ,סמא ,סטר.
Perhaps also רמץ ,רוקן, and a few more.

(*d*) From the Greek, cf. below, § 96.

93. (4) Old Hebrew verbs not found in Aram.: חרס (חדס הדס),
נונה ,מסק ,מחל ,לקה ,לבלב ,כמש ,כחח ,טנן ,חפת ,חטט ,חבץ ,חבס,
רתך ,רהן ,קרטע ,קרטם ,קמע ,פשל ,פחם ,פחח ,פזל ,סתת ,ספת ,סנק
תרף ,תרז ,תרה ,תסס ,תחב ,שגם.

94. (5) Old Hebrew verbs found also in Aram: אמד (or עמד),
נקן ,נען ,נתן ,נבש ,בער ,חבר ,חזר ,דרם ,גנה ,גהץ ,בלש ,בלט ,בחל
קוּיץ (Aram. קרר (or קדד), צלף ,צלב ,פקר ,פלה ,פגן ,פגם ,סרח ,סכם
שמש ,שדל ,רתע ,רשה ,רסק ,קרצף ,קנה ,קלח ,(כּוּיץ).

95. (6) Old Hebrew verbs found also in other Semitic languages
beside Aram.: גרם ,גמר ,גנה ,גשר ,הנה ,זוּג (?), זוף ,זרז ,חוץ ,חכך,
פרכס ,פסד ,פהק ,סנן ,סגף ,נחר ,נזק ,נוף ,לתת ,כדן ,חשד ,חלט
תמם ,שתף ,שלק ,שחם ,שחל ,רמז ,רכן ,קפח ,קנב ,lop, קטם פתק ,פתק
תקל stumble.

96. (7) Verbs borrowed from Aram.: נגם, טוש, חצף, תהא, דבב, ארע, קנתר, קנט, קלף, קטם ashes, קרע, פתך, פתם, סמא, סייע, סִים (?), סמר, שמה, שהה, שבש, רשל, רמץ, (?), רוקן, קשט, (כרבש), קרקש.

(8) Verbs borrowed from Greek:[1] לסטם ληστής, ספג σπόγγος, פקם φυκόω, פרף πόρπη, קטרג κατηγορέω, קמר καμάριον, תרם θυρεός. The following are doubtful: זֵוֵג (from זוג) ζεῦγος, פקר (from אפיקורום) Ἐπίκουρος, קלם καλῶς, קנם κῆνσος, טנן τήγανον.

97. (9) A few new formations are of an onomatopoetic character: כשבש or קשקש knock, פטפט chatter, babble, קעקע cackle, קרקר cackle, שכשך shake, knock. Perhaps also טפטף to drip, כסכם to chew, לגלג to mock.

98. A large number of verbs which MH has inherited from BH., have undergone certain changes in usage and meaning. Thus, many verbs which were common in BH have become rare in MH. Most of these belong to the elevated diction of BH literature. But a considerable number are quite ordinary prosaic expressions which for some reason or other went out of ordinary use in MH. Again, a number of verbs which were rare in BH have become very common in MH. Many of these will be found to belong also to the Aram. vocabulary. Finally, many verbs have developed in MH a new significance, sometimes analogous to their usage in Aram., sometimes of a technical or legal character Often this new significance is expressed by a new verbal stem not found in BH (cf. below, §§ 108 ff.). A small group of verbs is of special interest. These have preserved in MH their primary significance, while in BH they only occur in a derived and secondary sense.

(C) *BH Verbs with a different usage in MH*

99. (1) Verbs more common in BH than in MH: אטם, (צעק =) זעק, זעם, זכך, הרם, המם, המה, הדר, הגה, בחר, בהל, ארב,

---

[1] Cf. Krauss, *Lehnwörter*, i, pp. 144–52. His etymologies, which are not always reliable, should be checked by Kohut and, especially, by Jastrow.

יָגַע, יָבֵל be foolish, יָאַל טבח, חשה, חרד, חפשׂ, חרה, חמם, חמל, חבא,

מלל, מלט, מחץ, מוש, לכד, לאה, כלם restrain, כלא יעל, יטב, יחל

speak (Aram.), מסה, מסך (= מזג), מרה, נאץ, נבט, נגר, נגשׂ, נגש,

נטש, נטר (common in Aram.), נזל, נום, נוד, נוב, נהל, נהר, נדח, נדה,

סחר, סור (common in Aram.), סוף נתש, נתח, נקם, נצר, נעם, נסע,

(common in Aram.) עזר, עזז, עזֵר, עזה, עוד repeat, ספה, סער, סלף,

עטף be faint, עיף עלץ, עצב be grieved, עצם be strong, ערץ, עתק,

פאר, פסח, פעם, פער, פרה, פשע, צדה lie in wait, צדה lay waste,

צהל צות (common in Aram.), ציץ, עוק, צחק (= שׂחק), צפה look out,

רגן, קשב, קרה, קצב, קלה be light, קוץ, קוה wait for, צרח, צמן,

שׁוט, שׁדד, שׂגב, רעשׂ, רעץ, רעד, רנן, רמס, ריב, רגע be at rest,

despise, שׂים, שׂישׂ, שׁחר be early, שׁטם, שׂכל, שׁלל, שׁעע take

delight, תעב.

100. (2) Verbs more common in MH than in BH : בדה, אנס,
זמן, זכה, זהם, דמע, דין, דחק, גרם, געל, גמר, גזר, בקר, בטל, בדק,
טמן, טול, חתר, חנף, חנך, חלף, חלם, חלט, חטף, חוש, חוב, חבב, חבל, זקק,
מלך, לחש, כשר, כפה, כנס, (יחם =) יחשׂ טרח, טרד, טפל, טען,
counsel, מרח, מתח, נאה, נאם, (נום =) נדה, נטל, נתר, סבן, סלק,
קבל, צער, צמק, (פרס =) פרשׂ, פרט, פרח fly, פרט, פטר, ספק sufficient,[1]
תקן, שׂגח,[1] שבח, רוח, (כרסם =) קרטם, קרם, קפד.

101. (3) Verbs which show a change of meaning in MH :
גדל, ברר, ברך, בקר ; אסר, אנס, אכל, אחר, אחז, אות, אבק, אבד
דקק, דמע, דמה, דלל, דלה, דלג, דלה, דחה, דוח, דדה, דבק ; גרר, גרם, גזר,
חלל, חלם, חלט, חטא, חוש, חזק, חול ; זקק, זנב, זמן, זמם, זכה, זחל ; הלך
טבע, טבל ; חתם, חתך, חשך, חשב, חרט, חקה, חצן, חנק, חנף, חלף
ישׁן, ישׁב, יקר, יצא, יפה, ילד ; טרף, טרד, טפל, טפח, טען] טול,
מחה, מול, מאן ; לקח, לוה, לבן ; בשר, כרע, כפר, כפה, כנס, כון, כבד
סבר, סבב ; נתר, נתך, נשׁך, נבל ; מרח, מצא, מנה counsel, מלך מחק
ערר, ערך, עצם, ענה, ענה, עלה, עבר, עבד ; ספר, ספק, סעד, סמך, סכך
צרף, צער, צלל, צחח ; פשט, פרע, פקד, פסל, פנה, פלל, פטר, פוג

---

[1] Cf. Sirach xxxix. 16, 33 ; xlii. 17 ; xl. 29 ; l. 9.

קרסם, קצה, קפץ, קפד, קנה, קמץ, קלם, קלל, קדש, קדם, קדח, קבל,
רקם, רקד, רצה, רעם, רכס, רחם, רווח, רגש, רגל, רבץ, ראה; קשה;
תקן, תנה; שקע, שפה, שער, שנה, שמן, שמד, שלש, שלל, שכר, שבח.

102. (4) Verbs with the primary meaning in MH and a
secondary meaning in BH.

כסף BH long, MH grow pale; מהל BH mix, MH circumcise; עין BH look with envy, MH look intently; סלד BH spring
back, MH be scalded; סמר BH bristle up with fear, MH stud with
nails; פלט BH escape, MH discharge, spit out; פצע BH bruise,
MH split; פקח BH open the eye, MH open up; פרר BH
frustrate, annul, MH break, crumble; פשק BH part, open wide,
MH split, cut; צנע BH be modest, MH hide, retire; cf. also
דלק, געל, בצע.

2. GRAMMATICAL

103. The differences between the BH verb and the MH verb
are as marked on the grammatical side as on the lexical side.
Many verbs in MH show a loss of verbal stems found in BH.
Thus, the Qal has been lost in most verbs of an intransitive
character, especially in the Babylonian dialect of MH. Of the
Puʻal only the participle has been preserved as a living form.
Formations that are rare in BH, like the Poʻel, Polʻel, and their
derivative stems, have either disappeared entirely, or survived in only
a few verbs. The common and regular stems have disappeared
in those verbs in which their occurrence was rare in BH.

Against these losses, MH can, however, show some important
gains. It has increased its quadriliteral formations, often, no doubt,
under Aram. influence, either by reduplication, Piʻlel, Pilpel, &c.,
or by augmentation, Šafʻel, Pirʻel, &c. Further, MH has extended
the use of Piʻel to ע"ו verbs, again often under Aram. influence.
Finally, MH has applied the common and regular stems to many
verbs in which these stems were lacking in BH.

104. In the field of syntax, MH has lost many constructions which imparted much beauty and distinction to BH, such as the use of the cohortative and jussive, and of the consecutive tenses; the manifold applications of the perfect and imperfect; the variety of constructions with the infinitive, &c. On the other hand, MH has developed and extended constructions which were rare or unknown in BH, e. g. the rise of a present tense in the participle; its use with the auxiliary verb הָיָה; the combination of two verbs to express continuous and progressive action (cf. below, §§ 364–5), and the periphrasis of the future with עָתִיד.

For these syntactical changes in MH the reader is referred to the Third Part of this work (§§ 306 ff.). On the Pu'al, cf. below, §§ 125–30. Here we append tables showing the changes which the verb has undergone in MH in regard to stem formation.

(A) *BH. Stems not found in MH.*

105. (1) Formations that are rare in BH.

Po'el in the following verbs: דמם, הנה, הלל, הרה, חנן, חקק, ידע, יעד, לשן, מדד, נדר, סבב, עלל.

Po'lel: בוש, חול, לין, מות, נזם, נזף, סור, צוד.

Po'lal: חול, עול, רום, רוע.

Pi'lel: צמת, נאה (נאוה).

Pe'al'al: חמר, יפה.

Tiph'el: רגל.

Hithpo'el: אנן, בלל, גלל, הלל, מדד, נאץ, נדד.

Hithpo'lel: בוש, גור, חול, מול, נום, עוד, עוף, רוע.

Hithpalpel: חול.

Hothpa'el: דשן, טמא, כבם, פקד.

106. (2) Regular stems of rare occurrence in BH in particular verbs:

Qal: אמן, ברה, דבר, דגל, חבב, חוָר, חרך, ידה, מכך, מסם, נאץ, שבע, שאר, רנן, קרם, קשב, צפה, עתק, סער, סמר, נוף.

Niph'al: נסע, נכה, נגע, מטר, לבט, זחח, דכא, דוש, דגל, גרש, ברך,
פשע, עגן, פוג, סער.

Pi'el: נגע, כתב, ידע, ידה, הרס, גרע, ברה, ברא, בעת, אסף, אחז,
רתח, קפד, קהה, עתד, נכה.

Pu'al: ידע, חקה, חטב, חבל, זנה, הרה, הרג, דעך, גשם, אסר, אסף,
רדף, עשק, נקר, כתת, יצר.

Hithpa'el: אמר, באש, גרד, דכא, חקה, מכר.

Hiph'il: כפש, כזב, חתם, חלם, חבר, גשם, גמא, אמר, אטם, אבל,
שבר, רדף, צרח, צעק, עקד, אמד, עצב, עדה, נפח, נאץ, מלט, כתת.

Hoph'al: מכך, כתת, כשל, יצר, טבע, זון, הפך, דוש, דבק, בקע, אחז,
רוה, צהב, עלה, נתק.

107. (3) Qal of the following intransitive verbs. This is usually
expressed in MH by the corresponding adjective with היה, e.g.
היה טמא, היה חולה, or in some cases by the Internal Hiph'il, האדים,
הזקין; or by the Hithpa'el, התאבל, התגאה, הזקן, הגדיל.

יבש, טמא, טוב, חמם, חלה, חזק, זקן, דקק, ארך, אור, אדם, אבל,
ערם, (עני =), ענה, עמק, עזז, עזז, עור, עגה, נקה, מרר, מעט, מלא, כבד, יפה,
שבע, רעב, רחק, רחב, קשה, קצר, קטן, צער, צמא, פרה, עשן.

(B) *MH stems not found in BH.*

108. (1) *Quadriliterals.* These forms are found also in BH
and in other Semitic languages.[1] MH has more of these forms
than BH, but, unlike Aram., it has exercised a certain restraint
in their formation.[2]

(a) By Reduplication.

1. Doubling the third radical (Pi'lel), שרטט, ערבב.
2. By repeating the whole root, only in verbs ע"ו and ע"ע.
   ע"ו: בעבע (BH אבעבועות), נמנם, נענע, נפנף, ספסף.
   ע"ע: (הרר = הרה), הרהר (הבהבי BH), הבהב, דקדק, דלדל, בצבץ,
   רפרף, רברב, צחצח, פלפל, עמעם, עלעל, משמש, מקמק, כסכס.

---

[1] Cf. Ges.-K., § 56, i, p. 510 f.; pp. 515–20.
[2] Cf. Nöldeke, *Syr. Gr.*, § 180; Dillmann, *Ethiop. Gr.*[2], p. 251.

(b) By Augmentation.

1. The Causative stem Šaph'el, cf. below, §§ 149, 150.

2. By inserting ר after the first radical: קרצף ,כרסם. Cf. also
   קרזל (מקורזל) rounded, t. Sab. xiii. 17); ר added at the
   end: קנתר (קנטר, Aram. loan-word). Further with מ at
   the end: פרסם from פרס = פרש. With ס at the end:
   פרנס ,פרכס. Cf. Jastrow, s. vv.

(c) Denominatives: שרבט ,כרכם ,כרכב ,אשכן ,אלמן. Cf. above,
§ 92.

109. (2) The Intensive stem (Pi'el, &c.) in verbs ע״ו, ע״י.

סיֵּג ,(טוש=) טָיֵּל ,טִיֵּל ,טַיֵּב ,דִּיֵּר ,גִּיֵּף ,גִּיֵּר ,בַּיֵּר ,בַּיֵּשׁ,
קוֹיֵן) קַיֵּים ,קַיֵּים ,(ציצית) צִיֵּין ,(פִּיַּח) פִּיֵּם ,(סוֹף) סִיֵּף ,(? שׂים) סִיֵּם סִיֵּר
thorn), בַּוֵּן ,קַוֵּץ (קוֹיֵן thorn), רַוֵּח.

110. (3) Application of the regular stems to verbs in which they
were lacking in BH.

Qal: ארשׁ ,בדל ,זון ,חוב ,חתך ,נקף ,סבר (= שׁבר), עגן (partic.
pass.), עדר ,עקר ,פשׁח ,צהב ,קדם ,רפף ,שׁבח.

Niph'al: אנס ,בדק ,גמר ,געל ,דמה ,דמע ,דקק ,זון ,זמם ,זקק ,חסם,
(go) נקף ,נטל ,נדר ,מתח ,מלק ,לוש ,כפה ,כנס ,כלל ,טפל ,טען
round), צבה ,פשׁח ,פרט ,פצע ,פסק ,פטר ,עקר ,סבך ,נתר ,נשׁך
שׁלה שׁכר ,שׁחק ,שׁדף ,שׁכב ,קמץ ,צלה.

Pi'el: אבק ,אהב ,אנס ,ארח ,בזה ,גמר ,גרף ,דור ,דמע ,זון ,חמץ,
מתק ,מתח ,מעך ,לוה ,לבן ,כון ,יתר ,טרף ,טול ,טבל ,חתם ,חתך,
פרר ,פהח ,פצע ,פסע ,פסל ,עשׂה ,עשׁן ,עדר ,ספק ,סבך ,סוף ,נסף,
רקם ,רכס ,רדד ,רגש ,רבע ,רבע ,קמץ ,צנע ,צמק ,צבה ,פרשׁ ,פרשׁ,
שׁתק ,שׁרט ,שׁקע ,שׁער ,שׁמד ,שׁלה ,שׁאר.

Pu'al (only participle): אהב ,אחר ,בזה ,בצר ,דלל ,דמה ,דמע ,זון,
פרט ,עשׁן ,סלק ,סבך ,סוף ,כנס ,כון ,יתר ,ישׁן ,טפל ,חלט ,זמם,
שׁקע ,שׁמד ,שׁבח ,שׁאר ,רמה ,קום.

Hithpa'el (Nithpa'el): אבק ,אהב ,אכל (עכל), ארח ,ארשׁ (ארס),
טרף ,טפל ,חסם ,חוב ,זקק ,זמן ,זמם ,דלל ,דור ,געל ,בקר ,בצר,
סבך ,נסה ,נהג ,נבל ,מתך ,מעך ,לבן ,כשׁר ,כנס ,כון ,יתר ,ישׁן ,יסף,

פרש, פקח, פצע, פסק, פסע, פלג, עשן, עקר, עצם, עטף, ספק, סלק, סוף,
רעם, רגש, קרד, קרר, קטן, קבל, צרף, צרע, צער, צמק, צוה, פתה, פרש,
שתק. שקע, שקע, שער, שמן, שמר, שלח, שדף, רפף

Hiph'il: אהב, בקר (פקר), (פקר), זול, זקף, חלם, חמם, חמץ, חמין, טען, טרף, כנס,
ספד (שבר), סבר (שבר), נשך, נקע, נצץ, נקע, נסח, נהג, נהג, נדר, נדר, ננח, לקח, לוה,
קמץ, קטן, קדח, צלל, צהב, פרש, פצע, פצע (פשע), פסע, פלג, פוג, עשה,
תנה, שלש, שכר, שחט, שבח, רכס, רוח, רגש, רגל, קרם, קרא,

Hoph'al: בדל (participle), זול, זקף, חמם, נדר, נקף (knock off), נקף,
קרר, קדש, קדם, קבל, צנע, פרש, סנר, סבך, נתר (go round),
שחר (be black), שלש, תאם.

B. The Stems.

1. The Simple Stem.

111. (1) The *Qal*. The Qal is identical, both in form and meaning, with the Qal in BH. The form *Qaṭel* is exhibited in the intransitive verbs: בָּטֵל, Ab. v. 16; כָּשֵׁר, Ḥul. ii. 10; עָמֵל, Ab. ii. 14; קָרֵב, Pᵉs. ix. 61, &c. *Qaṭol* is found only in the common verb יָכוֹל. These, however, occur only as participles.

112. The *Participle* coincides almost completely with the partic. in BH. The fem. sing. ends in ת, e. g. גּוֹזֶלֶת robbing; נוֹשֶׁרֶת dropping (of leaves), ʿAZ. iii. 8; טוֹחֶנֶת grinding, Giṭ. v. 9; תּוֹבַעַת claiming, ib. iv. 8. In verbs ל״ה, ע״ו, and frequently also in ל״א, it ends in ה: בָּאָה coming, Yᵉb. xv. 10; בּוֹשָׁה ashamed, Dam. iii. 6; רוֹצָה desirous, ib.; חוֹתָה poking, Ṭoh. vii. 9; יוֹצְאָה going forth, Šab. v. 1; but also יוֹצֵאת, Kil. iv. 6; נוֹשֵׂאת וְנוֹתֶנֶת taking and giving, i. e. trading, Šᵉbu. vii. 8.

113. The Partic. of intransitive verbs, being treated as an adjective, forms the fem. with ה: טְמֵאָה unclean, Nid. iii. 1; בְּטֵלָה ceases, Ab. ii. 2; קְרֵיבָה comes near, Pᵉs. ix. 6, &c.

The Passive Partic., which always expresses in MH a state or condition, is also treated almost like an adjective, and the fem.

sing. always ends in הָ, גְּרוּשָׁה divorced, Yᵉb. vii. 1 ; נִשׂוּאָה married,
ib. i. 2 ; שְׁרוּיָה dwelling, Ab. iii. 2.

114. In this frequent use of the older termination ת for the
fem. sing., MH has remained faithful to the BH tradition, in
which this termination is far more common than the younger
termination ה (cf. Ges.-K., § 94 d). In Aram., on the other hand,
the fem. partic. always ends in אָ֑—.

115. (2) Niph'al. The Niph'al also agrees in form and in
meaning with the Niph'al in BH.

In the Infinitive the preformative ה is usually elided after the לְ.
In most texts the short *i* of the לְ is then written *plene* with י, in
order, presumably, to differentiate it from the inf. Qal. Thus,
לְהִבָּטֵל = לִיבָּטֵל to cease, Yᵉb. vi. 6 ; לְהֵהָרֵג = לִיהָרֵג to be slain,
'Ar. i. 3 ; לֵיהָנוֹת to enjoy, Kᵉt. vii. 1 ; לִיטָהֵר to be purified,
Kel. iii. 1 ; לִיטָּמֵא to be defiled, Mᵉi. iv. 6 ; לִיכָּנֵס to enter, BB iii. 6 ;
לִיסָּקֵל to be stoned, San. vi. 6.

The full form is, however, also common, especially in weak
verbs : לְהִבָּרְאוֹת to be created ; לְהִפָּרַע to be paid, Ab. v. 1 ; לְהִוָּדַע
to be known, ib. iv. 22 ; לְהִנָּטֵל to be taken, Šᵉbi. iii. 9 ; לְהִסָּקֵל to
he stoned, BQ iv. 8 ; לְהִשָּׁעֵן to lean, So. ix. 15.

Often the texts waver, thus : לִיגָּזֵז, L. לְהִגָּזֵז to be shorn, BQ
ix. 1 ; לִיבָּלַע, L. לְהִבָּלַע to break open, Nid. viii. 3 ; לִינָּשֵׂא, L. לְהִנָּשֵׂא
to be married, Yᵉb. ii. 10 ; לִיפָּרַע [היפרע] BM iv. 2 ; לְהִקָּרֵא, L.
לִיקָּרוֹת to be called, 'Ed. v. 6 ; לִישָּׁבַע, L. לְהִשָּׁבַע to swear, BM iii. 1.

116. In one case, the frequently occurring technical expression
הִכָּרֵת (derived from Num. xv. 31, &c.), the preformative ה is
dropped even when not preceded by לְ : כָּרֵת, e.g. Pᵉs. iii. 5, &c.
Often, however, particularly when preceded by בְּ, and especially
in Palestinian texts, the full form הִכָּרֵת is found : Ḥal. i. 2 ; Pᵉs.
ix. 1 ; Kᵉri. ii. 6, &c.

117. This elision of the ה is merely an extension to the Inf.
when preceded by a preposition, of the phonetic principle followed

in the formation of the Imperfect. Cf. also the elision of the
article after a preposition, and other cases of the elision of the ה in
Ges.-K., § 23 k. It is found in the Inf. Niph. in isolated cases
also in BH (Ges.-K., § 51 l., 53 q.), and may have been quite
common in the colloquial language.

118. The fem. Partic. always ends in ת, even in verbs ל״א, ע״ו,
and ל״ה (cf. above, § 112), e.g. נִמְכֶּרֶת to be hidden, So. iii. 3 ; נִמְכֶּרֶת
to be sold, Ket. iii. 7 ; נִזּוֹנֶת, to be fed, Ket. xii. 2 ; נִקְרֵאת to be
read, Meg. i. 1 ; נֶהֱנֵית to enjoy, Ned. vii. 9.

Signification of the Niph'al.

119. (i) Reflexive : נֶחְלְקוּ they divided themselves—disagreed,
'Er. i. 2 ; נִטְמַן hiding himself, 'Ar. ix. 4 ; תִּכָּנֵס to gather oneself, to
enter, Ned. x. 4 ; נִמְנוּ to count oneself, Šab. i. 4 ; נִפְטָרִין to depart,[1]
Ab. i. 8 ; נִשָּׂאוּ to marry oneself, Ket. vii. 10.

In a few cases it is found in a tolerative sense : נִגְנַב to allow
oneself to be stolen from, t. BQ vii. 8 ; נִשְׁאַל to allow oneself
to be consulted, t. Dam. ii. 24 ; הִשָּׁמְעִי to consent,[2] San. 82 a,
Sifre, Num. xxv. 1.

120. (ii) Middle : נֶהֱנֶה to enjoy, Ab. iv. 5 ;[3] נִזְכַּר to recollect,
Ber. iii. 5 ; נִמְלַךְ to change one's mind, Dam. iii. 2 ; נִפְרַע to obtain
payment, Ab. iii. 16 ; נִשְׁאַל to consult, MQ iii. 1 ; נִשְׂכַּר to make
profit, Šebi. ix. 10 ; נִפְסַד to incur loss, Pes. 50 b ; נַעֲנֶה to answer
Šab. 33 b.

121. (iii) Passive to Qal : נֶאֱכָלִין to be eaten, Ber. i. 1 ; נִגְמַר
to be finished, Pea iv. 8 ; נִשְׁכַּב to be lain with, San. 54 b.[4]

As passive to Pi'el : נִדְמְעוּ to be mixed with tithe, Ter. v. 6

---

[1] Cf. 1 Sam. xix. 10 in Qal.

[2] To sexual intercourse, by the woman. Perhaps, however, שמע in this
sense is equivalent to the Aram. שמש = שַׁמֵּשׁ to serve, and the Niph'al
would, therefore, be passive to Pi'el שִׁימֵּשׁ, sc. הַמִּטָּה

[3] So Sirach xxx. 19, &c.

[4] Of illicit intercourse, cf. שכב את in BH. See *BDB.*, s.v., p. 1012 (3).

(cf. ib. 5). To Hiph'il : נִגְעַל to be cleansed by boiling, j. Tᵉr. xi. 5 (cf. 'AZ. v. 12).

As passive to an intransitive verb : חֵרֵשׁ רוֹמֵז וְנִרְמָז . . . קוֹפֵץ וְנִקְפָּץ A deaf mute makes signs (with his hand or head), and signs are made to him . . ., makes signs with his mouth, and signs are made to him,[1] Giṭ. v. 7.

Denominative verbs in the Simple Stem are but few. Examples are : חוֹלֵב Šab. 95 a ; לֵיחָלֵב to milk, ib. 53 b ; חָפַן to take a handful (from חפנים), MŠ. ii. 5 ; כּוֹבְרִין to sift (כברה—), Šab. xx. 3 ; סוֹפֵג to absorb (ספוג— = σπόγγος). Tᵉm. i. 1 ; נִפְסַח to be lame, j. Bᵉr. i. 5.

2. THE INTENSIVE STEM.

122. (1) *Pi'el*. The Pi'el is identical with the BH Pi'el, except that it is often spelt with י after the short ḥireq. This is merely an orthographical device to prevent its confusion with the Qal, and has no grammatical significance whatever.[2]

The fem. of the Partic. sing. ends in ת, as מְבַשֶּׁלֶת cooking, מְכַבֶּסֶת washing, Kᵉt. v. 2, except in verbs ל״א, ל״ה, in which it has ה : מְטַמְּאָה defiling, Ḥul. i. 1 ; מְדַדָּה causing to hop, Šab. xviii. 2.

Signification of the Pi'el.

123. (i) Intensive or iterative : תְּהַלֵּךְ to walk,[3] 'Er. x. 2 ; וְזִנְּתָה to commit fornication (repeatedly), San. vii. 5 ; מְחַמְּדָתָן she covets them, Mak. iii. 5 ; מְחַתְּכוֹ he cuts it up[4] ; מְעַבְּדוֹ he tans it, Šab. vii. 2 ; מְנַשֶּׁבֶת blows, Mᵉn. x. 4 ; מְחַלֵּשִׁין plucking violently, Yo. vi. 4.

---

[1] The Niph'al is used here loosely, in order to preserve the personal construction with the subject which is characteristic of MH style. With these uses of the Niph'al in MH, cf. BH, Ges.-K., § 51 c–g.

[2] Similarly the Pu'al is spelt with י after the short u, see below, §§ 126, 129, and above, § 39. So regularly in Aram. Stein's suggestion (*Das Verbum*, p. 31) that this spelling signifies a lengthening of the vowel consequent upon the dissolution of the doubling, cannot be entertained at all.

[3] Contrast Qal הוֹלֵךְ to go, Yᵉb. vii. 5.

[4] Contrast Qal חוֹתֵךְ to cut, 'Er. x. 13.

124. (ii) Causative : טִיהַרְתֶּם ye have declared to be clean,
'Ed. i. 14 ; יִפּוּהָ they beautified her, Nᵉd. ix. 10 ; מִיעֵט diminish;
רִיבָּה increase, BQ viii. 4 ; סִילֵק to put aside, 'AZ. iii. 7 ; עִיבְּרָהּ he
caused her to be pregnant, Yᵉb. vii. 5 ; לְשַׁכַּח to cause to forget,
'Er. vii. 9 ; מְשַׁתְּקִין they silence, San. v. 2 ; חֵירְשׁוֹ he caused him to
be deaf, BQ 86 a.

125. (iii) Denominative : מְחַבְּרִין to angle (— חַבָּה), BQ 81 a ;
לְכַתֵּף to carry on the shoulder, Šab. 5 b ; מְסַלֵּת (— סֹלֶת), Tᵉr. xi. 5.
Some of these have a privative force : מְדַשֵּׁן to remove ashes,
Yo. ii. 3 ; מְזָרְדִין to nip off shoots ; מְיַבְּלִין to remove wens (= יַבֶּלֶת) ;
מְסַקְּלִין remove stones ; מְפָרְקִין remove faded leaves, Šᵉbi. ii. 2, 3 ;
מְזַנְּבִין to trim, ib. iv. 6 ; לְקַוֵּץ to remove thorns, MQ 6 a ; מְתַלַּע to
remove vermin, j. Šab. vii. 2.[1]

126. (2) *Puʻal*. Of the Puʻal only the Partic. is common. Of
the other parts of the stem only the following examples have been
preserved : אוֹרַע it happened, t. Šebu. 1, 2 ; חוּיַּבְנוּ we were
made liable, Mak. 3 a ; יְחוּלַּל to be rendered common, Qid. 77 a ;
יְחוּנְּנוּ to find favour,[2] So. ix. 15 ; חוּתַּךְ (so pointed in L.) to be cut
up, Ḥul. iv. 1 ; יוּפִּי to be made fair, good,[3] Pea vi. 6 ; לוּקַּט be
gathered, ib. v. 1 ; יְנוּגְּבוּ they will be dried up,[4] Makš. v. 3 ; נוּפַּל
to be taken away,[5] Kel. iii. 2 ; תְּעוּבַּר צוּרָתוֹ let its form be made to
pass away,[6] Pᵉs. vii. 9 ; תּוֹרְמָה to be tithed, t. Maʻa. ii. 2.

---

[1] Cf. with BH, Ges.-K., § 52 f-h.

[2] In elevated style. The whole passage is a later addition to the Mishna,
not found in the *Editio Princeps*. The form may, however, be Poʻal. L. has
יוֹחֲנֵנוּ, Hophʻal.

[3] The reading is uncertain. L. has יוּפִּי ; other texts have יְפִי, יִיפָּה, יָפָה.
The form יָפָה is given in all texts in the same phrase in Kᵉt. viii. 4, where it is
also parallel to הוּרַע. Cf. also Krauss, *ZDMG.*, lxvii. 732.

[4] So in most texts. In L. the whole passage is missing.

[5] Some texts, including L., reads נִיטַּל.

[6] This is a common technical expression in connexion with sacrifices. Cf.
the active עִיבֵּר צוּרָה, Bᵉr. 40 b, and the noun עִיבּוּר צוּרָה, Pᵉs. 82 b. The
reading of the Puʻal is not, however, quite certain. T. has תֵּעָבֵר, תַּעֲבִיר,
Pᵉs. vi. 6, &c.

Further, as an imitation of BH : וַיְבֻקַּשׁ הַדָּבָר Qid. 66 a.[1] The
following are doubtful : קְדִשׁוּ to be sanctified, parallel to נִטְמְאוּ,
Men. xii. 1, but probably read Qal, קָדְשׁוּ;[2] פּוּתֵּיתִי I have been
enticed, Gen. R., § 71.

127. The finite parts of the Pu'al have been replaced by the
Hithpa'el (Nithpa'el), which latter has greatly extended its usage
as a passive, in the same way as the old passive of Qal was already
in BH replaced by its corresponding reflexive, Niph'al. The
Partic. alone has been preserved in the Pu'al as a living form, but
only in an adjectival sense to express a state or condition.[3] Thus,
the Partic. Pu'al bears the same relation to Pi'el as the passive
partic. *Qaṭul* bears to the Qal (cf. above, § 112).

128. In the formation of the fem. sing. of the Partic., the same
rule is observed as in the Pi'el. The short vowel *ŭ* is regularly
followed by ו, to prevent confusion with the Partic. Pi'el.

129. The following are examples of the Partic.: מְאוּכָּלוֹת consumed,
Tam. i. 4; מְבוּצֶּרֶת fortified (of an eruption surrounded by sound
flesh), Neg. i. 3; מְגוּלֶּה uncovered, open, Šab. xix. 1; מְזוּיָּן armed,
BQ 57 b; מְחוּיָּל made common, Dam. v. 1; מְכוּוֶּנֶת direct, Mak.
ii. 5; מְיוּפָּה beautified, j. Giṭ. ii. 1; מְנוּדֶּה excommunicated, Ned.

---

[1] An imitation of BH derived from Esther ii. 23. This *Baraita*, so different
from the ordinary oral *Baraita*, seems to be an extract from a historical chronicle.
It exhibits a number of other imitations, such as the use of the consecutive
tenses (cf. below, § 156), and poetical expressions. Cf. also above, § 16.

[2] In some texts קפלה and הבהבה, Šab. 33, 3, are also pointed as Pu'al :
קְפָּלָה, הֻבְהֲבָה. יבוקר, 'Ed. iv. 5 in L. is an error for יבקר, as in Pea
vi. 1 in L.

[3] Cf. MŠ. v. 11, where מְחוּבָּר joined to the soil, is parallel to תָּלוּשׁ
plucked from the soil, and both these participles are parallel to יָשָׁן, חָדָשׁ.
So. ib. 6 מִתְבָּעֲרִים has the force of a present participle, ' may be cleared
away ', whereas מְבוּעָר, represents a past participle, expressing a condition,
almost like an adjective, ' cleared away '. Cf. also the adjectival use of מְזוּמָּן
appointed, as contrasted with the verb נִזְדַּמְּנוּ, Ab. deRN. ii. 3.

i. 1 ; מְעוֹרֶבֶת mixed, Šab. xvi. 3 ; מְקוּיָם confirmed, BM 7 a ; מְרוּבַּעַת squared, Kil. v. 5 ; מְתוּלָּעַת wormy, BB vi. 2 ; מְתוּקָּן prepared,[1] Ab. iii. 16 ; מְתוּשָּׁעִים divided into nine, j. Šᵉbi. i. 4.

130. In a few cases the preformative מ has been dropped : חוּתָּךְ = מְחוּתָּךְ cut up, 'Uq. iii. 2 ; מוּעָטִין = מְמוּעָטִין (as in L.) few, Bᵉr. vii. 3 ; Dam. v. 5, &c. ; עוּבָּרוֹת = מְעוּבָּרוֹת pregnant women, Par. iii. 2 (L. has עברות, so Yo. x. 5). So probably תּוֹעָב = מְתוֹעָב abominable, 'Er. 68 b. Cf. above, § 62. So sometimes also in BH, Ges.-K., § 52 s.

131. The disappearance of the finite parts of the Puʻal, and their replacement by the originally reflexive Nithpaʻel, is evidently due to the decay of the inflexional power of the language. It was no longer capable of expressing the modification of the stem idea by internal change alone without the aid of external additions to the stem. The partic. with its firm preformative has been preserved, and even extended to newly acquired verbs. But the imperfect, with its continually changing preformatives, and, especially, the perfect which has no preformatives at all, were no longer able to maintain themselves. This decaying tendency was already strong in BH, in which the finite parts of the Puʻal are very scarce, as compared with other stems.[2] The same tendency was at work in the disappearance of the old passive of the Qal,[3] and its replacement by the reflexive Niphʻal.

The same phenomenon appears in all the other Semitic languages. In Assyrian the reflexive stems were gradually supplanting the passives. In Ethiopic, Modern Arabic, and Aramaic the passive forms have disappeared, and been replaced by the corresponding

---

[1] L. has Hophʻal, מוּתקן. So wherever this verb occurs in the passive, e. g. Para iii. 3, &c.

[2] The finite parts of the Puʻal are not found at all in Joshua, 1 Samuel, Micah, Jonah, Habakkuk, Chronicles, Nehemiah, and Daniel, and only once or twice in Judges, 2 Samuel, Amos, Lamentations, Canticles, and Ecclesiastes.

[3] Cf. Ges.-K., § 52 e, s. 53 u, and the reff. to Böttcher and Barth.

reflexives.[1] MH, however, did not go so far, since it has preserved remnants of the Pu'al, and in addition has retained the Hoph'al as an active and living stem in all its parts.

132. (3) *Hithpa'el—Nithpa'el.* The reflexive of the intensive stem in MH is, with a few exceptions, Nithpa'el instead of the BH Hithpa'el. These two formations are identical both in form and in meaning, except that in the perfect the one has ה as the preformative, the other נ. There can be no doubt that they are really one and the same stem. The preformative —הָ was in the course of time changed in popular speech into —נָ, on the analogy of Niph'al. In the popular mind ה became associated with the causative idea, through the influence of Hiph'il, Hoph'al, and —נָ with the reflexive idea, through the influence of Niph'al. This change extended only to the perfect. For in the imperfect there is no room for either of these preformatives, and in the infinitive and imperative Niph'al itself has —ה, hence also Hithpa'el-Nithpa'el has retained —ה (e.g. לְהִתְגַּדֵּל to magnify oneself, Ab. iv. 5; לְהִתְקַיֵּם to exist, v. 7; הִסְתַּכֵּל consider, iii. 1, &c.). In the participle the preformative —מְ has maintained itself, in spite of the Niph'al partic. נקטל, through its firmly established nominal force. Besides, it would be unreasonable to expect that an analogy-formation of this kind should be worked out to its full logical extreme.

133. The preformative —הָ survives only in a few cases: וְהִשְׁתַּחֲוָה and he bowed down, Bik. iii. **6** (probably a reminiscence of וְהִשְׁתַּחֲוִיתָ Deut. xxvi. 10); הִתְפַּלַּלְתְּ thou hast prayed, Ta'a. iii. 8 ; in the legal phrase הִתְקַבַּלְתְּ thou hast received; הִתְקַבַּלְתִּי, K^{et}. ix. 8 ; [2]

---

[1] Cf. Delitzsch, *Assyr. Gr.*, § 115; Dillmann, *Ethiop. Gr.*, § 80; Spitta, *Gram. d. Arab. Vulg. Dialect von Aeg.*, § 90 a (4); the various Aram. Grammars.

[2] Four times. L. has twice נתקבלתי. So in v. 1 L. has ניתקבלתי for edd. התקב/. Contrast also t. K^{et}. ix. 4 with xi. 1.

הִתְנַדֵּב he 'donated', Men. xii. 3 (L נתנדב); הִתְעַנִּינוּ we fasted,
'Er. 41 a; הִשְׁתַּעְבַּדְתֶּם ye were enslaved, Šab. 88 b; הִתְכַּעַרְתִּי
I made myself ugly, Gen. R., § 17 הִתְמַלְּאוּ, הִתְמַלֵּאתִי ib., § 33.[1]

The Nithpaʻel agrees with the BH Hithpaʻel both as regards its
meaning and its formation (cf. Ges.-K., § 54).

134. *Formation.* The preformative syllable is, as stated above,
נִתְ— in the perfect, in the other parts it is exactly like Hithpaʻel
in BH. The fem. sing. of the participle follows the rules given
above (§§ 112, 122).

The phonetic rules regulating the preformative are the same as
in BH. (i) When the first radical is a sibilant ז, ס, צ, שׁ, the ת
is transposed after the sibilant. In the case of the ז, the ת is
changed into ד, as in Aram. (cf. Dan. ii. 9), and of צ, into ט.
Exx.: הֻזְדַּיֵּף to be forged, Giṭ. ii. 4; מִזְדַּוְּוגִין to join themselves
together, San. v. 5; נִסְתַּחֲפָה to be swept away, Ket. i. 6; מִצְטָרְפִין
to be joined, Naz. vi. 1; מִצְטָעֵר to be grieved, San. vi. 5; נִשְׁתַּיֵּיר
to be left over, Yeb. viii. 2.

135. (ii) When the first radical is ד, ט, or ת, the preformative ת
is assimilated to the first radical. The short *i* of the preformative
syllable is then often written with י, as in Piʻel: נִדַּיְירָה to be
manured by cattle; נִטַּיְּיבָה to be improved, Šebi. iv. 2; מִיטַּהֲרִים
to be purified, Yo. viii. 9;[2] נִיטַּמֵּאת to become unclean, Ḥag. iii. 2;
הִתַּלֵּשׁ to be plucked out, Šebi. vi. 3; מִיתַּרְגֵּם to be translated,
Meg. iv. 1.

Assimilation of the ת is sometimes found also with other consonants, מְנַתְּתִין to squirt off, BQ ii. 1; so, perhaps, מְקַדְּשִׁין to
become holy, 'Or. iii. 3.

---

[1] The forms נְכַפֵּר, Deut. xxi. 8, and נִסְּרוּ, Ezek. xxiii. 48, are also usually
explained as Nithpaʻels. Cf., however, Eitan, *JQR.* (N. S.), xii, p. 25, who
holds that these two forms are survivals of a stem *Nippaʻel*, reflexive of Piʻel
corresponding to Niphʻal in the Simple Stem.

[2] But also מִתְטַמֵּא, Naz. iv. 3. Cf. especially, Kel. ii. 1.

Signification of Nithpaʿel. The Nithpaʿel bears the same relation
to the Piʿel as the Niphʿal to the Qal.

136. (i) It is primarily Reflexive : מִתְאַבֵּק to cover one self with
dust, Ab. i. 4 ; תִּתְוַדַּע to make oneself known, ib. i. 10 ; מִתְחַכֵּךְ to
rub oneself, BQ iv. 6 ; לְהִתְכַּסּוֹת to cover oneself, Nᵉd. vii. 3 ;
תִּתְלַבֵּשׁ . . . תִּתְעַטֵּף . . . תִּתְכַּסֶּה . . . ; נִסְתַּפֵּג to dry oneself, Yo. vii. 3 ;
תִּתְאַזַּר clothe, wrap, cover, gird thyself, Bᵉr. 16 b. It is sometimes
strengthened by the addition of a reflexive pronoun : הֵן מִתְעַצְּמִין
מֵאֲלֵיהֶן they shut of themselves, Šab. 151 b.

137. (ii) Internally reflexive, or in a middle sense : תִּתְיָרֵא to
fear, So. vii. 8 ; נִתְכַּוַּנְתִּי I intended, Mᵉn. xiii. 4 ; מִתְנַדְּבִין to ʿdonate',
Zᵉb. x. 8 (cf. Ezra iii. 5 ; 1 Chron. xxix. 17); תִּתְיָאֵשׁ to despair,
Ab. i. 7 ; הִסְתַּכֵּל to consider, ib. iii. 1 ; הִשְׁתַּדֵּל to strive, ib. ii. 5.
Further, the performance of an act in which the subject is interested,
which thus assumes a purely active significance : הִתְקַבֵּל to receive
(for oneself), Kᵉt. ix. 8.

138. (iii) Inchoative, to describe the entry into a new state
or condition, especially of the body or mind : נִתְאַרְמְלָה (= נִתְאַלְמְנָה,
cf. above, § 54) she became a widow, Yᵉb. xiii. 4 ; נִתְגַּיְּירוּ they
became proselytes, Kᵉt. iii. 1 ; נִתְחָרֵשׁ to become deaf-mute,
Yᵉb. xiv. 1 ; נִסְתַּמֵּא to become blind, ʿAr. 17 b ; נִתְפַּקַּח to regain
one's hearing ; נִשְׁתַּפָּה to regain one's sanity, BQ iv. 4 ; נִשְׁתַּטָּה to
become mad, Giṭ. ii. 6 ; נִשְׁתַּתֵּק to become dumb, ib. vii. 1.

139. (iv) Reciprocal : נִתְעָרְבוּ they become mixed up one with
the other, Yᵉb. xi. 5 ; נִצְטָרְפוּ they joined one another, ʿOr. ii. 11 ;
נִשְׁתַּתְּפוּ they joined each other in partnership, Dam. vi. 8. Often,
however, the reciprocal idea is strengthened by the addition of
reciprocal pronouns : נִתְעָרְבוּ זֶה בָּזֶה Pᵉs. iii. 5 ; נִתְעַצְּמוּ זֶה בָּזֶה they
quarrelled, t. BM i. 16 ; מִתְרַצִּים זֶה לָזֶה they become reconciled
to each other, Nᵉd. v. 6 ; נִתְקַבְּלוּ . . . . זֶה מִזֶּה MŠ. v. 9 they received . . .
from each other.

140. (v) Finally, the Nithpaʻel is extensively used in a passive sense, serving as a substitute for the Puʻal (§ 127); נִתְבַּשְּׁלוּ to be boiled, Nᵉd. vi. 6 ; נִזְדַּבְּלָה to be manured, ʻAZ 49 a ; מִתְחַלֵּל to be profaned, Ab. i. 11 ; יִתְמַעֵךְ to be pressed, Mᵉn. x. 4 ; נִתְנַסֶּה to be tried, Ab. v. 3 ; נִתְפַּצְעוּ to be cracked, ʻOr. iii. 8 ; נִתְפַּתְּתָה to be seduced, Kᵉt. iv. 1 ; נִתְקַוְּצָה to be cleared of thorns (privative) Šᵉbi. iv. 2 ; מִתְקַדֶּשֶׁת to be betrothed, Qid. ii. 1,[1] corresponding to the Piʻel active : בשל, זבל, חלל, מעך, נסה, פצע, פתה, קווץ (cf. MQ 6 a), קדש.

This passive use of a reflexive stem is common to all Semitic languages in their later stages, cf. above, § 131. In BH it is comparatively rare in the Hithpaʻel, cf. Mic. vi. 16 ; Prov. xxxi. 30 ; Qoh. viii. 10, and the cases cited in the Note to § 133. See Ges.-K., § 54 g.

141. (4) *Poʻel, Poʻal, and Hithpoʻel*. These stems, already rare in BH, have practically disappeared in MH (cf. above, § 105). Poʻel is found in a few ע″ע verbs, cf. below, § 191. In the strong verb it is found only in the forms מְשׁוֹעֲרִים gate-keepers, by analogy from the parallel מְשׁוֹרְרִים singers, ʻAr. 11 b,[2] and רוֹקֵן to empty, Lev. R. 24, a secondary form of רִיקֵן San. 60 b. This is a denominative of רֵיקָן, BH רֵיקָם ; cf. above, § 54. Of the Poʻal no trace is to be found in MH. The Hithpoʻel is found as Nithpoʻel in a few ע″ע verbs, cf. below, § 191, and in the form נִתְרוֹקְנָה she was made empty, Nᵉd. x. 2.

3. THE CAUSATIVE STEM.

(1) *Hiphʻil*. The Hiphʻil is identical with the Hiphʻil in BH, both in form and in meaning.

142. The preformative א, instead of ה, is found in some texts in אוֹנִיתַנִי thou hast cheated me (= הוֹנִיתַנִי, as in L, cf. Exod.

---

[1] Of a woman. The corresponding reflexive is קִדְּשָׁה אֶת עַצְמָהּ, Qid. iv. 9
[2] But the verb is in the Piʻel : שִׁיעֵר, ib.

xxii. 20, &c.), BM iv. 4, no doubt on the analogy of the cognate verbal noun אוֹנָאָה, ib. (L הוֹנָאָה). For BH cf. Ges.-K., § 53 k, p.

143. In the Infinitive the ה is elided in לָרְבּוֹת (= לְהַרְבּוֹת) to increase; לַשְׁהוֹת (= לְהַשְׁהוֹת) to cause delay, 'Er. x. 15; לָדִיחַ (= לְהָדִיחַ) to rinse, j. 'AZ. iii. 5.[1] Cf. above on Niph'al, § 119, and for BH Ges.-K., § 53 q. Elsewhere the ה is preserved: לְהַבְעִית to frighten, Yo. v. 1; לְהַחֲמִיר to be strict; לְהָקֵל to be lenient, Kil. ii. 2; לְהַכְנִים to bring in, Ket. vi. 3; לְהַצְנִיעַ to hide, Dam. iii. 3, &c.

144. The fem. sing. of the Partic. follows the rule given above, § 112: מַשְׁכַּחַת causing to forget, Ab. ii. 2; מַתְרַעַת blowing the horn (denom. of תרועה, cf. above, § 92), Ta'a. iii. 3, 4; but מְטִיבָה doing good, San. vii. 10; מְנִיקָה nursing, Ket. v. 5; מְרֵעָה doing evil, San. vii. 10.

The shortened Hiph'il (Jussive) is rare: תַּשְׁכֵּן mayest thou cause to dwell, Ber. 16 b; אַל תַּאֲמֵן do not believe, Ab. ii. 4 (L most texts have תַּאֲמִין); אַל תַּחֲזֵק טוֹבָה ib. ii. 8 (L).

145. *Signification.* (i) Usually Causative: לְהַבְטִיל to cause to cease, Suk. v. 5; מַקְרִיא to make to read, to read to, Bik. iii. 7; הִשִּׁיךְ to cause to bite, San. ix. 1; הִקְדִּיחָה to cause to burn, BQ ix. 4, &c.

146. (ii) Inchoative, or Internally Causative, describing the entry into a state or condition. This usage is even more frequent in MH than in BH (cf. Ges.-K., § 53 e). Exx.: יַבְרִיא to become healthy, Šab. xix. 5; הִבְרִיקָה to become bright (euphemistically— blind), BM vi. 2; תַּגְדִּיל to grow up, come of age, Ket. vi. 6; הֶעֱשִׁיר .... הֶעֱנִי to grow rich, poor, ib.; יַעֲנוּ they will become poor, Me'il. 17 a; מַחְכִּים to grow wise, Ab. ii. 5; יַבְחִילוּ, הִבְאִישׁוּ, יַאֲדִימוּ to become ripe, ill-smelling, red, Ma'a. 1, 2; הֶחֱמִיץ, הִרְקִיבוּ, הִזְקִינוּ

---

[1] לִשְׁטִיחַ, cited by Stein (p. 10 b) and by Albrecht (§ 101 b) is a noun, for a spread, or mat, cf. Bertinoro to Ḥul. ix. 3.

to become old, rotten, sour, BQ ix. 2 ; הִשְׁחִירוּ ,הִקְצִירוּ to become
black, short, Neg. i. 5 ; הֶאֱרִיכוּ ,הִלְבִּינוּ to become white, long, ib. 6.

Examples of Denominative verbs in Hiph'il are (תְּחִלָּה—) הִתְחִיל
to begin, Šab. 1, 2 ; (אצבע—) הַצְבִּיעַ to put up the finger, Yo.
ii. 2 ; הִנְמִיב to face south (—נגב), 'Er. 53 b ; יַצְפִּין ,יָדְרִים to face
south, north, BB 53 b, &c.

147. (2) *Hoph'al.* The Hoph'al is extremely common. It
differs in no respect from the BH Hoph'al, except that it takes
the vowel *ŭ* after the preformative, always written *plene* with וֹ:
—הוּ, —מוּ,¹ &c., even in strong verbs, instead of the usual BH *hŏ*.
This form of the vowel is found occasionally in BH in strong
verbs (Ges.-K., § 53 s), and regularly in most of the weak verbs,
viz. ע"ע, פ"נ, פ"ו, ע"ו, and ל"א. As *ŭ* is also the regular vowel of
the Pu'al it must have become in the popular mind the only
characteristic vowel of the passive stems, resulting in the total
suppression of the vowel *ŏ*.

148. Examples of Hoph'al : הוּחְזְקוּ to be made strong, confirmed,
Yeb. xii. 6 ; הוּסְבַּךְ to become intertwined, Pe. vii. 3 ; מוּסְגָּר to
be shut up, Neg. i. 7 ; מוּצְנָע to be hidden, Ter. viii. 8 ; מוּקְדָּמִים
early, Šebi. x. 5 ; הוּשְׁחָרוּ to be made black, Ḥag. 22 b ; הוּשְׁלַשׁ to
be deposited with a third party, Ket. vi. 7 ; הוּרַע to become bad,
Pe. vi. 6 ; הוּזְלוּ to become cheap ; הוּקְרוּ to become dear, BM
v. 8 ; מוּדָּר to be forbidden by vow ; מוּפְרָשׁ to be separated, Ned.
i. 1 ; מוּדְרָמוֹת facing south, Men. 85 a : תוּדַח to be rinsed, Makš.
iv. 3 ; יוּרַע to be made bad, BB x. 5 ; יוּצַן to be made cold ; יוּתַּץ
to be destroyed, 'AZ iii. 9, &c.

149. (3) *Saph'el.* This old stem is found in the verb סְרֵב ²

---

¹ This traditional pronunciation as *ŭ* is proved to be correct by the invariable spelling with וֹ. So also in BH even in strong verbs, according to the
Babylonian punctuation, cf. Kahle, *Masoreten d. Ostens*, p. 193.

² Also in Sirach iv. 25 a ; xli. 2, and, probably, also in the BH noun
סָרָבִים.

(contracted from סְרְהַב), to rebel, refuse; מְסָרְבִין Nᵉd. viii. 7; Bᵉr. 4 a, &c., and in סִרְגֵּל to draw lines; מְסַרְגְּלִין j. Mᵉg. i. 9; Sopherim i. 1.

150. (4) *Šaph'el.* The causative stem Šaph'el is found in the following verbs: שִׁחְרֵר to liberate, manumit; שִׁעְבֵּד to enslave, subject; שִׁכְלֵל to furnish, decorate; שַׁלְהֵב to be aflame; שִׁעְמֵם to be dim, dull; and שִׂרְבֵּב to be much, great.

Examples. Active: שִׁחְרְרוּ Yᵉb. xi. 5; Passive Participle: מְשׁוּחְרָר Giṭ. iv. 4; מְשׁוּחְרֶרֶת Yᵉb. vi. 5; מְשׁוּחְרָרִים MŠ. v. 14; Ništaph'el, in a passive sense; נִשְׁתַּחְרֵר BQ viii. 4; נִשְׁתַּחְרְרָה Yᵉb. ii. 8; נִשְׁתַּחְרְרוּ ib. xi. 2; תִּשְׁתַּחְרְרִי, אֶשְׁתַּחְרֵר Qid. iii. 5.

Active: מְשַׁעְבְּדִין RH iii. 8; Passive: מְשׁוּעְבָּדִים mortgaged, Keṯ. ix. 7, 8; Ništaph'el: יִשְׁתַּעְבֵּד Giṭ. iv. 4.

שִׁכְלְלָן he furnished them, San. 38 a; מְשׁוּכְלָל Sifra (Weiss) 88 c; מְשׁוּלְהָב Qoh. R. i. 5; מְשׁוּלְהָבִין Mᵉkil. (Weiss) 79; מְשׁוּעֲמֶמֶת BM 80 a; נִשְׁתַּעְמְמוּ Num. R. x. 8; שִׂרְבַּבְתָּ Bᵉr. 54 b; נִשְׁתַּרְבְּבָה she became prolonged, So. 53 a.[1]

These formations are found in all Semitic languages, including BH.[2] Nevertheless, these verbs may, perhaps, be loan-words in MH from Aram.

C. The Tenses.

The inflexion of the verb in MH follows generally the verbal inflexion in BH. The following few variations may be noted.

151. (1) The second masc. sing. of the perfect is sometimes spelt with ה at the end, especially in Palestinian texts: קַיַּמְתָּה

---

[1] In the partic. מְהַלְקְטִין to cause birds to pick up corn from the hand, we have a secondary Hiph'il of לקט with the retention of the preformative ה, formed on the model of Šaph'el, as distinguished from the regular Hiph'il— מַלְקִיטִין to cause birds to pick up corn from the ground, t. Šab. xviii. 4; cf. Šab. 155 b.

[2] Cf. Ges.-K., § 55 c. Also the nouns enumerated below, § 262.

thou hast fulfilled, Suk. ii. 9 (L); עֲבַרְתֶּה‎, נָתַתֶּה‎, but also עברת‎ Zᵉb.
viii. 11 (L); הֶקְלִתָּה‎ Sifra (Weiss) 15 b; הֶחֱמַרְתָּה‎ ib. 48 d, &c.

152. (2) The second masc. plur. of the perfect often ends in
תֶּן‎, instead of תֶּם‎, e.g. עֲשִׂיתֶן‎ Mid. ii. 2 (but עֲשִׂיתֶם‎ in Ab. ii. 3).
This is a common phonetic change, which may, however, have
been assisted by Aram. influence.[1]

153. (3) In the Imperfect the form תִּקְטֹלְנָה‎ (second and third
fem. plur.) has entirely disappeared from MH.[2] Both genders use
יִקְטְלוּ‎ and תִּקְטְלוּ‎, just as in the perfect they both use קָטְלוּ‎, and
sometimes in MH, קָטַלְתֶּן‎, e.g. הַנְּשׂוּאוֹת יִתְאָרְסוּ וְהָאֲרוּסוֹת יִנָּשְׂאוּ‎
women who had been married may become betrothed, and women
who had been betrothed may be married, Yᵉb. iv. 10; הַבָּנוֹת יִזּוֹנוּ‎ the
daughters must be fed, Kᵉt. iv. 6; xiii. 3.

So also in the Imperative the form קְטֹל‎ is used also for the fem.,
e.g. וְרִקְדוּ‎ . . . וְאָמַר לְאִמּוֹ וּלְאִשְׁתּוֹ רַחֲצִיהָ‎ he said to his mother and to
his wife: bathe her . . . and dance before her, Ab. dᵉRN. xli. 13.

In this MH has merely developed to the full a tendency already
strong in BH.[3] Modern Arabic has gone further in this respect
than MH, and has given up all the fem. plural forms, both in the
perfect and the imperfect.[4] Aram., on the other hand, has carefully
preserved the distinction of gender in all its dialects.[5]

154. (4) The imperfect and imperative Qal is spelt *plene* with וֹ,
קְטוֹל‎, יִקְטוֹל‎. The plur. is קְטְלוּ‎, יִקְטְלוּ‎, except in pause where they

---

[1] Cf. above, § 70, and *JQR.*, xx. 680 f.

[2] The few cases found are all imitations from BH. Thus: כִּלְיוֹתֶיךָ תַּעֲלֹזְנָה‎
מֵישָׁרִים‎, Bᵉr. 17 a, from Prov. xxiii. 16; תִּכְהֶינָה עֵינָיו‎, Pea viii. 9 (L; editions
have עֵינָיו כֵּהוֹת‎, from 1 Sam. iii. 2), from Gen. xxvii. 1; וְתֶחֱזֶינָה עֵינֵינוּ‎
(Singer, p. 51), from Isa. xxxiii. 17; Ps. xvii. 2.

[3] Cf. Gen. xxx. 39; Lev. xxvi. 33 b; Judges xxi. 21 a; Cant. ii. 7; iii. 5;
v. 8; vi. 9; viii. 4—ten examples of MH usage against three examples of
the older BH usage, viz. iv. 11 and iii. 11 (imperatives).

[4] Cf. Spitta-Bey, op. cit., § 90 a (1).

[5] Mandaic forms the only exception, cf. Nöldeke, *Mand. Gr.*, § 162.

are יִקְטוֹלוּ. Exx.: יַחֲלוֹקוּ they shall divide,[1] BM i. 1, 2; יִטְבּוֹלוּ they will bathe, Ṭoh. x. 3; אַל תִּכְתּוֹבוּ do not write, Giṭ. vii. 1 (L); יִמְתּוֹקוּ they will become sweet, 'Uq. iii. 4; יִפְלוֹטוּ they shall spit out, Ter. viii. 2; יִשְׁטוֹפוּ they will overflow, Miq. i. 5; יִתְרוֹמוּ they will tithe, Ter. i. 1. Cf. also the pointing in L: יֵגָּנוּ they shall be hidden, San. x. 9.

Imper.: כְּתוֹבוּ write ye! חֲתוֹמוּ seal ye! Giṭ. vi. 7; vii. 2; שְׁתוֹקוּ be ye silent! Šebi. viii. 9, 10; תֵּינוּ give ye! t. Giṭ. vi. 8.

155. (5) The lengthened forms of the imperfect and imperative (cohortative) are not found in MH. The shortened form of the imperfect (jussive) is found only occasionally; cf. for the Hiph'il above, § 144, and for ל״ה verbs below, §§ 205, 212.

156. (6) The Consecutive Tenses have practically disappeared from MH. In the few cases where they occur, they are conscious imitations of BH. Thus הִשָּׁבַע לִי וַיִּשָּׁבַע לוֹ Mekil. (Weiss), 66, from Gen. xxv. 33. Five examples occur, besides more than a dozen simple tenses, in that remarkable *Baraita* in Qid. 66 a, which must be a fragment of some historical work written in a mixed style of BH and MH (cf. above, §§ 16, 126 n.). They are וַיֹּאמֶר (three times), וַיְבַקֵּשׁ הַדָּבָר (Esther ii. 23); וַיִּבָּדְלוּ they were separated (Ezra x. 16; Neh. ix. 2); וַתּוּצֵץ הָרָעָה and the evil sprouted forth; וַיֵּהָרְגוּ and they were slain. They are found occasionally in the older, but not the oldest, parts of the liturgy: וַתִּתֵּן (Singer, op. cit., pp. 228, 230, &c.); וַתְּלַמְּדֵם (p. 39); וַתְּלַמְּדֵנוּ, וַתַּבְדֵּל (pp. 46, 227, 240, six times beside one perfect with simple *waw*); וַתִּפְקְרֵהוּ (p. 250); וַתַּשְׁמִיעֵם (p. 252); וַתְּלַמְּדֵנוּ, וַתַּכִּירֵהוּ (p. 267); וַיַּהַרְגֵנוּ, וַיַּטִּילוֹ, וַיִּירָשׁוּהָ, וַיְבַלְּעוּהָ [2] (p. 49): וַיְכַסּוּ (p. 43) is a quotation from Psalms cvi. 11.

---

[1] The occurrence of this form not in pause is due to scribal error. Thus, in Ket. viii. 6; BM. viii. 8, read יַחֲלוֹקוּ, as in L. So Ab. iii. 16. L has יַחֲלֹקוּ, but edd. יַחֲלוֹקוּ may also be right.

[2] Cf. j. Ta'a. 11. 2.

157. As is well known, numerous passages are found even in the oldest portions of the Bible, in which the simple tenses are used in place of the usual consecutive tenses. This becomes more frequent from the time of Jeremiah onward, until in Qohelet the relation between the consecutive and simple tenses is reversed, i. e. the use of the simple tense becomes regular, while that of the consecutive sense becomes exceptional. The explanation of this phenomenon as due to Aram. influence is inapplicable to the numerous cases in the earlier books of the Bible.[1] Probably this irregularity in the use of the simple for the consecutive tense arose at an early time within the Hebrew language itself, and independently of outside influence. It may even be doubted whether the consecutive construction ever attained in popular speech that dominating position which it occupies in the literary dialect. It may be plausibly assumed that the more convenient construction with the simple tenses had survived in the every-day speech side by side with the more difficult construction by means of the consecutive tenses.[2]

Similarly in Phoenician, which also possesses the consecutive tenses, the simple tenses are used very often where BH would employ the consecutive tenses. Thus: וּפָעַל . . . ושמע (Cooke, *N. Sem. Inscriptions*, No. 3, l. 8); וּפעלת אנך וַיְקַדִּשְׁתְּ (No. 29, l. 13); בן וּפָעַל (No. 33, l. 3), פָּעַל וְחִדֵּשׁ (No. 38, l. 1); and the common phrase יתן ויטנא (No. 13, l. 2, &c.), both of which verbs are perfects.

The contact with Aram. naturally strengthened the simpler construction, until eventually the consecutive construction disappeared from the living speech, and survived only in literature, largely by the force of the literary tradition, as in the later books of the Bible, in Sirach, and other literary productions of the MH period.

---

[1] Cf. Driver, *Hebrew Tenses*, § 133.
[2] Cf. also H. Bauer, *Die Tempora im Semitischen*, p. 37 f.

D. Weak Verbs.

(1) Guttural Verbs.

158. In the absence of a trustworthy system of punctuation in MH texts, it is not possible to determine whether the Guttural verbs have suffered any change in MH, as compared with BH. It may, however, be safely assumed that these verbs obey the same phonetic rules in MH as in BH. (Cf. above, §§ 36, 40.)

Examples of Guttural Verbs.

159. Guttural in the First Radical. Qal: לַחֲזוֹם to trim, Dam. ii. 2; יַעֲלֶה to go up, Bᵉr. i. 1; עֲמוֹד stand up, Yo. i. 7. Niph'al: נֶעֱגָּל to be round, j. 'AZ 41 b: נַעֲנוּ they answered, Qid. 40 b; לְהֵחָיוֹת to be revived, Ab. iv. 22. Hiph'il: הֶחֱשִׁיךְ he remained till darkness, Šab. xxiv. 1; יַעֲצִים to shut (eyes), Qid. 32 b; מַחֲכִיר to farm, BM 104 b.

160. Guttural in Second Radical. Qal: צָהֲבוּ to be bright, Mᵉn. 18 a; סוֹחֲטִין to squeeze, Šab. xxii. 1. Pi'el: אֲחַרְתִּי to delay, Pᵉs. ix. 9; עֵרָה (L points עֵירָה) to empty, 'AZ. v. 7 (L 10); מְאָרֵחַ to entertain, Bᵉr. 63 b; יְשָׁרֵשׁ to uproot, Šᵉbi. iv. 4. Pu'al: מְכֹעָר ugly, Kᵉt. 105 a. Nithpa'el: נִסְתַּחֲפָה to sweep away, Kᵉt. i. 6; יִתְאָרְסוּ to be betrothed, Yᵉb. iv. 10.

161. Guttural in Third Radical. Qal: נוֹבֵעַ bubbling up, BB x. 8; רוֹוַחַת spread wide, t. San. vii. 1; לָקוּחַ bought, MŠ. iii. 11. Niph'al: נִיטַּע to plant; נִזְרַעַת to sow, Oh. xviii. 5. Pi'el: מְפַצֵּעַ to split, Šab. 145 a; מְקוּפַּחַת cut, fragmentary, Oh. xvi. 1. Hiph'il: הַגְבֵּהַּ lift up, Yo. iv. 1; מַתְרַעַת to blow trumpet, Taʿa. iii. 3; Hoph'al: מוּצַעַת spread out, 'Ar. vi. 3.

162. The verb שאר to leave, hardens the א into י in the Pi'el and Nithpa'el: שִׁיֵּיר Pea iii. 2, 3; יְשַׁיֵּיר Kil. ii. 3; מְשַׁיֵּיר Pᵉs. i. 3; נִשְׁתַּיְירוּ Kil. vi. 6. Contrast Partic. Pu'al: מְשׁוֹאָר Pea iii. 3; Zᵉb. viii. 12.

(2) Verbs פ״א.

163. These verbs follow generally their BH models. Thus,
Qal: יֶאֱרַע to happen, Yo. i. 1; יֹאכַל Pes. x. 1; אוֹכַל Ned. i. 3;
אוֹמַר I shall eat, say, Šebi. viii. 9; תֹּאפֶה (but L תוּפה) to bake,
Pes. iii. 3; לֶאֱגוֹד to bind, Šebi. viii. 3; לֶאֱכוֹל Ber. i. 1. The
Palestinian texts, however, often have לֶאֱכָל = לוֹכַל ('Er. iii. 1, &c.)
on the analogy of the imperfect יֹאכַל, &c. So, usually, in all texts
לֶאֱמַר = לוֹמַר Šab. ii. 6; Ab. v. 1, &c., on the analogy of יֹאמַר.

Niph'al: נֶאֶנְסָה she was violated, Ket. i. 10; נֶאֱנַסְתִּי ib. 6;
נֶאֱמֶנֶת ib. 7; נֶאֱגָר, יֵאָגֵר Ma'a. i. 5; תֵּאָכֵל Be. i. 1. Pi'el: אִיהֵל
to make a tent, Me'il. 17 a; אֵירְעוּ Ta'a. iv. 6; אֵחַרְתִּי to delay,
Pes. ix. 9; יְאַבֵּד to destroy, 'AZ iv. 7. Pu'al: מְאוּחָר delayed,
Pes. 6 b. Hiph'il: הֶאֱהִיל Oh. iii. 1; מַאֲפִיל to make dark, Šab.
86 a; מַאֲחִיזִין to cause to take hold, kindle, Šab. i. 11. Some texts
(L, &c.) have מַחִיזִין, with א elided. Similarly מָאֲגִירוֹת = מוֹגִירוֹת =
מַאֲגִירוֹת t. Dam. i. 10, from אגר to store. Hoph'al: יוּאָחָר
j. Yo. iii. 4.

164. Note. The verb הפך forms the imperfect Qal on the
analogy of the פ״א verbs. Thus, אוֹפַּךְ = יֶהְפַּךְ; יֹאפַּךְ = יֹופַּךְ =
אֶהְפֹּךְ = אֹאפַּךְ Kil. ii. 3, 4; Ter. ix. 3. The ה in this verb seems
to have been weakened into א. Cf. R. Jonah, *Riqmah*, p. א.

(3) Verbs פ״י.

165. MH has preserved the distinction between the three
classes of verbs, as in BH. (i) Original פ״ו; (ii) Original פ״י;
(iii) With י assimilated to a following צ.

Qal. (i) תֵּרְדְעוּ Šebu. iv. 9; תֵּצֵא Yeb. iii. 5; צֵא Pes. iv. 2; but
also יִישַׁן Šab. 25; אִישַׁן Šebu. iii. 5. (ii) יִיבַשׁ Šebi. iii. 1; יִינַק to suck,
So. 12 b; יִירַשׁ to inherit, BB viii. 5; תִּירָשֵׁנִי ib.; יִישַׁר to be straight,
strong, Ber. 42 a. (iii) לָצוּק to pour, Šab. xvii. 5.

The Infinitive is formed on the analogy of the imperfect. Thus:
לֵידַע Ab. iv. 22; לֵילֵד Yeb. iii. 10; לֵירֵד 'Er. iv. 2; לִישַׁן BB ii. 3;

לִינַע j. Ber. ix. 5 ; לִינַק Pes. 112 a ; cf. the imperfects יֵרֵד, יֵלֵד, יֵדַע,
יִינַק, יִינַע, יִישַׁן.[1] Exceptions are : לָצֵאת Šeq. iii. 2, and לִירָאָה
Ber. 16 b (a liturgical phrase), which are formed as in BH.[2]

Niph‘al: נוֹלָד Ab. ii. 9 ; נוֹתָר Ker. iii. 4 ; נוֹצַרְתְּ Ab. ii. 8 ; לְהִוָּדַע
ib. iv. 22 [3] ; לְהִוָּדַע Šebu. 9 b ; יִוָּדַע ib. i. 4 ; יִוָּלֵד Bek. v. 3. (iii) נָצוֹק
Makš. v. 9.

166. Pi‘el, Pu‘al retain the י, as in BH : יִחֵסוּ to give a pedigree,
San. 82 b ; יִיפִּיתָה to make fair, good, j. BB viii. 1 ; מְיַיֵּסֵּר to chasten
San. 39 a ; מְיַיַּתֵּם to make orphaned, Pes. 49 a ; יִיֵּבֵּם to marry a
brother's widow, Yeb. xv. 10 ; יַיְחַרְנוּ to set apart, Ṭoh. viii. 6 ;
לְיַגְּעָהּ to weary her, So. ii. 1 ; לְיַישְּׁנָן to make old, BB 91 b ; מְיֻגָּעִין
Keṭ. 8 b ; מְיֻיֶחֶדֶת BQ i. 2 ; מִיֻיפָּה j. Giṭ. ii. 1 ; מִיֻישָּׁן Ned. ix. 8.

Nithpa‘el. (i) תִּתְוַדַּע Ab. i. 10 ; הִתְוַדֵּה (imperat.) ; לְהִתְוַדּוּת to
confess, San. vi. 2, but also מִתְיַשֶּׁבֶת Kin. iii. 6 ; נִתְיַישְּׁבָה Ber. 31 a.
So the forms נתוספו 'Er. vii. 7 ; יתוספו Pes. 87 b ; מתחספת to be
added, Šab. 152 a ; מתוקדת to be burnt, Lev. R. 7 ; נתותרו to be
left over, Pes. 159 b ; Yo. 46 a, traditionally pronounced like the
Aram. Ittaph‘al : נִתּוֹסְפוּ, מָתּוֹסֶפֶת.[4] (ii) נִתְיַחֵד נִתְיַחֵד נִתְיָארִי, מִתְיַקֶּרֶת, מִתְוֹקֶרֶת,
Giṭ. vii ; נִתְיַבְּמוּ Yeb. i. 4 ; נִתְיַפְּתָה Taʿa. 23 b ; נִתְיַפֵּית Gen. R. 59 ;
תִּתְיָאֵשׁ to despair, Ab. i. 7 ; תִּתְיַפִּי Taʿa. 23 b ; יִתְיַחֵד Qid. iv. 12 ;
מִתְיַבְּמוֹת Yeb. 3. 1 ; לְהִתְיַהֵר to be haughty, BB 10 b.

167. Hiph‘il : (i) הוֹאִיל Kil. v. 1 ; הוֹדִיַע Ab. iv. 22 ; הוֹתִירָה

---

[1] Albrecht's suggestion (§ 106 e) that these and similar infinitives (לֵאמֹר,
לֵיתֵן, &c.) are a combination of the imperf. with the preposition (= לֵירֵד,
לֵיתֵן, לֵאמֹר) is against the spirit of the language.

[2] לִירָתה Keṭ. iv. 3, cited by Albrecht (§ 111 b), is not an infin , but a verbal
noun : לִירָתָהּ = יְלִידָתָהּ ; cf. below, § 228, and above, § 62.

[3] The preformative ה may have been preserved here because of the assonance
with the preceding לְהוֹדִיַע ; cf. above, § 115.

[4] This traditional pronunciation seems to be more correct than that of the
simple Nithpa‘el : נִתוֹסְפוּ, מִתוֹסֶפֶת, מִתוֹקֶרֶת, נִתוֹתְרִי. In this latter the ו,
as a consonant, would have been written twice ; cf. above, § 57. Cf. also
the Targum : אִתּוֹקַד, Lev. x. 16 ; 2 Sam. xxiii. 7.

Ter. v. 9; אוּנְתַּנִי (cf. above, § 142); הוֹקִירוּ to become dear, BM
v. 9; הוֹתַרְתֶּם ib. vii. 2; מוֹצִיא, יוֹצִיא Ket. viii. 4; הוֹשַׁע save! Ber.
iv. 4; הוֹדוּ to agree, Pes. iv. 9; מוֹרִיקוֹת to become yellow, So. iii. 4;
לְהוֹדִיעַ Ab. iv. 22.

(ii) יֵישִׁירוּ Ber. 17 a (from Prov. iv. 25); מְטִיבָה San. vii. 10;
מֵנִיק Bek. 7 b; מֵנִיקָה Ket. v. 5; מֵינֶקֶת Ket. 60 a; לְהָנִיק Pes. 112 a;
לְהֵיטִיב ¹ Yo. iii. 4.

(iii) הִצִּית BQ 22 b; יַצִּית ² to kindle, Yo. vi. 7; מַצִּיעִין to spread,
Šab. xviii. 3; מַצִּיק Ker. 5 b.

Hoph'al: הוּקְרוּ BB. v. 8; מוּבָל to be led, Toh. vii. 5; מוּסָף to
be added, Šebu. i. 6: מוּטָב San. vii. 10; מוּעֶצֶת 'Ar. vi. 3; מוּצֶּתֶת
Num. R. 12.

168. The two verbs יתר, יער (original פ"ו), have formed in MH
secondary roots ותר, ועד. Exx. Pi'el: וִיעֵד Lam. R. ii. 13;
לְהִתְוַועֵד, נִתְווֹעֲדוּ Num. R. 14. Qal: וְיִתְרוּ j. Suk. v. 5; Cant. R.
i. 6. Pi'el: מְוַותֵּר San. xi. 5. Nithpa'el: יִתְווַתְּרוּ BQ 50 a. These
may, perhaps, be loan-words from Aram.

The verb הלך forms the imperfect Qal and the whole of the
Hiph'il from ילך, as in BH. Exx. Qal: יֵלֵךְ Ket. xiii. 7; תֵּלֵךְ
ib. vii. 4; תֵּלְכִי Ned. vii. 9; נֵלֵךְ, אֵלֵךְ 'Er. iii. 5, Inf. לֵילֵךְ ib. iv. 10;
BQ i. 1, but also לָלֶכֶת ³ Nid. iv. 2; לְכִי Ket. xii. 3; San. vii. 10,
Hiph'il: הוֹלַכְתֶּם Šebu. vii. 6; מוֹלִיךְ Ket. xii. 1; מוֹלִיכִין 'Er. vi. 7;
הוֹלֵךְ (imperat.) Git. vi. 1; יוֹלִיךְ 'AZ iii. 9; לְהוֹלִיכוּ Pea vi. 3. The
Intensive stem is formed throughout from הלך.

(4) Verbs פ"נ.

169. These verbs conform generally to the BH פ"נ verbs. The
נ is regularly assimilated to the following consonant whenever

---

¹ Some of these forms may be derived from the cognate ע"ו roots: טוב,
נוק; cf. below, § 185.

² L and other texts have יִצַּת = יצת, Qal.

³ The form להלוך in edd. is an error for לְהַלֵּךְ, Pi'el, as always in L, and
also in edd. BQ ii. 1, &c.

preceded by a preformative with a vowel, or it is dropped altogether where it would have to begin a word with a *shᵉwa* as in the imperative Qal.

(i) Qal. Imperfect: תָּגוּב, יָגוּב to dry up, 'AZ v. 3 ; יִגּוֹם to bite off, 'Uq. ii. 6 ; יִגַּע to touch, BM ii. 3 ; תִּטְלִי, תִּטּוֹל to take up, Yeb. xv. 3 ; אֶטּוֹל Pe. vi. 11 ; אֶטַּע to plant, Kil. i. 8 ; יִקּוֹב to bore, Šab. ii. 4 ; יִקְבֶנָּה ib. xxii. 3 ; יִתֵּן to give, ib. iii. 5 ; יִתְּנֶנָּה ib. ii. 4 ; יִדּוֹר to vow, Naz. viii. 1 ; אֶתֵּן Ter. x. 6 ; תִּשּׁוֹךְ Šab. xvi. 7 ; יִטְלוֹ Keṯ. x. 2. The vowel *ō* is sometimes retained on the analogy of ע״ע verbs (— יִסּוֹבּוּ, תִּסּוֹבִּי) in the second fem. sing. and in the plural : תִּדּוֹרִי Neḏ. x. 7 ; יְשׁוֹכוּ to bite in, adhere, Ḥal. ii. 4.

Imperative : דּוֹר San. iii. 5 ; טוֹל Yo. vi. 4 ; טְלִי Giṭ. 78 a ; טְלָה Ma'a. ii. 1 ; but also טוֹלִי Meʿil. vi. 1 (L טְלִי) ; תֵּן Giṭ. vi. 1 ; תְּנוּ ib. i. 6 ; תֵּינוּ in pause, t. Giṭ. vi. 8 ; שָׂא lift, Ta'a. iv. 8.

The Infinitive is formed from the Imperfect : לִידּוֹר Neḏ. iii. 1 (BH לִנְדּוֹר Num. vi. 2) ; לִיגּוֹף to strike ; לִישׁוֹךְ BQ i. 4 ; לִיטּוֹל Ab. v. 8 ; לִיזוֹר to become a Nazirite, Neḏ. 3 b ; לִיתּוֹר to loosen, j. Bik. i. 8. So לִישָּׂא to marry, Yeb. i. 4 ; לִיתֵּן Šab. i. 8, except in the standing expression לָשֵׂאת וְלָתֵת 'AZ i. 1 ; ii. 3, &c. (literally : to take and give, i.e. to buy, to deal), where the old forms have been preserved for their assonance.[5]

These infinitives may, perhaps, be older than the BH forms with the termination ת. Cf. לִתֵּן 1 Kings vi. 19, which may be a *forma mixta* of a colloquial לִתֵּן and the literary לָתֵת. So, perhaps, לתן ib. xvii. 14 (Kᵉtib), is a *forma mixta* of תֵּן (לִתֵּן) and תֵּת.

170. When the second radical is a guttural, the נ is preserved : יִנְעוֹל to put on a shoe, Para viii. 2 ; תִּנְעוֹל Yo. viii. 1 ; לִנְעוֹל Šab. xiii. 16 ; לִנְהוֹג Ab. vi. 3. So also sometimes in other cases : תִּנְזוֹר Naz. 17 a ; נְצוֹר guard, Bᵉr. 17 a (liturgical) ; לִנְטוֹעָה Kil. ii. 4 (cf. לִנְטוֹעַ Jer. i. 10).

---

[1] Cf. the writer's remarks, *JQR.*, xx, p. 686, footnote 3.

171. (ii) Niph'al. Perfect: נִיקַב ,נִיקְּבָה Ḥul. iii. 1 : נִיקְּרוּ to be bored,
j. Ter. viii. 5 ; נִשַּׂאת Ket. iv. 4 ; נִישָּׂאוּ ib. v. 2 ; נִשָּׂאתֶם t. BB viii. 9
(fem. !) Imperfect : תִּנְּשֵׂא Yeb. ii. 9 ; יִנָּקְדוּ to be spotted, Ma'a. i. 3 ;
יִנָּתְנוּ Ket. ix. 2. Infinitive: לְהִנָּטֵל Para v. 9 ; לִינָּשֵׂא Yeb. ii. 10 ; לִזּוֹק to
be injured, Pes. 8 b (cf. לִידּוֹן below, § 177). Participle : נִידָּב to be
donated ; נִידָּר Meg. i. 10 ; נִידָּרִים 'Ar. i. 1 ; נִיטַּעַת Oh. xviii. 3 ;
נִשֵּׂאת Ket. i. 1 ; נִישָּׂאוֹת t. BB xviii. 19 ; נִתַּז to squirt, Ḥul. vi. 6 ;
נִיתָּזִין [1] Makš. v. 2 ; נִיתָּנִין Zeb. viii. 9. Some show ō in the second
syllable instead of ā : נִיזּוֹקִין Pes. 8 b ; נִסּוֹק to be kindled, Kel. v. 6 ;
נִיסּוֹקֶת j. Ber. ix. 4 ; נִיצּוֹל to deliver, Šab. 32 a ; נִצּוֹלֶת ,נִצּוֹלִין Para
xi. 1 ; נִשּׁוֹל to slip off, Lev. R. 37 ; נִיתּוֹרִין j. Bik. i. 8 ; נִיתּוֹשׁ to
pluck out, Gen. R. 56.

נ is retained in verbs with second radical ע : נִנְעֲלוּ to be locked,
Pes. v. 5 ; נִנְעֶלֶת 'Ed. v. 6 ; נִנְעַר to be shaken, BB 74 b.

The Intensive Stem is regular.

172. (iii) Hiph'il : הִגִּיעַ to reach, Bik. iii. 3 ; הִדִּירוּ Ned. iii. 3 ;
הִדִּרְתָּה Ned. 23 a ; הִדַּרְתִּי Šab. 127 b ; הִזִּיק BQ i. 2 ; הִיסֵּתִי to incline,
Ber. i. 3 ; הִפִּיקוּהָ to kindle, Šab. iii. 1 ; הִכִּישָׁה to strike, BM 30 b ;
הִשִּׂיא Ket. vi. 6 ; הִתַּרְתֶּם to permit, Yeb. xv. 3 ; but also with נ
retained : הִנְהִיג to lead, Kil. viii. 2, 3 ; הִנְעִילוֹ Qid. 22 b ; הִנְגִּיב to
face south (denom. from נגב), 'Er. 53 b. Imperfect : יַגִּיחוּהוּ BQ
iv. 4 ; יַסִּיחַ to move, Šab. 82 b ; יַסִּיק Kel. v. 1 ; תַּתִּירוּ Yeb. xv. 3 ;
but also יַנְקִידוּ j. Ma'a. i. 3. Infinitive : לְהַזִּיק BQ i. 1 ; לְהַסִּיעַ to
move, Kel. v. 7 ; לְהַקִּישׁ to compare, BM ii. 5 ; לְהַשִּׂיאוֹ Qid. 29 a.

Participle : מַדִּיר ,מַדֶּרֶת So. iii. 8 ; מַטִּיל Yo. iii. 2 ; מַקִּיף to strike,
Bek. vii. 6, but also מַנְקִיף So. 22 b ; מַשִּׁיר to drop, Šab. 67 a ;
מַשֶּׁרֶת Naz. vi. 3 ; מַשִּׁילִין to cause to drop, Be. v. 1.

173. (iv) Hoph'al. Perf. : הוּזַר Qid. iii. 5 ; הוּזַּק ,הוּזְּקוּ BQ
iii. 2 ; הוּפַק Kel. v. 4 ; הוּקְּשָׁה to be compared, Ker. 3 a. Imperf. :
יוּדַּח San. x. 4 ; יוּתַּז Ḥul. 27 b ; יוּתַּךְ Me'il. ii. 3 ; יוּתַּז 'AZ iii. 2.

---

[1] L has Qal in both passages : נותן, נותזים.

Partic.: מוּגָּה corrected, Pes. 112 a; מוּדָּר Ned. iv. 1; מוּזָּה Pa. xii. 8; מוּכָּה Ket. vii. 11; מוּבַּת ib. i. 3; מוּטִּין Kel. x. 1; מוּטָּה Oh. ix. 9; מוּקֶּפֶת surrounded, Suk. i. 10; מוּקָּפוֹת Meg. i. 2.

174. The verb לקח forms the imperfect Qal on the analogy of the פ"נ verbs, as in BH: יִקַּח Yo. vi. 1; יִקְחוּ.

The Niph'al is regular, but some later texts show assimilation: נִקַּח 'Er. iii. 1 (L נלקח); נִקְחִין, נִקְחֵית Men. 42 b.

(5) Verbs ע"ו, ע"י.

175. In this class of verbs, MH follows faithfully the model of BH, but has carried certain forms to a fuller development, especially in the Intensive Stem. The ע"י forms, like דִּישׁ, דִּין, בִּין, לִין, זִיז, &c. differ very little from the ע"ו forms, and the two classes may be treated together.

176. (i) *The Simple Stem.*

Qal. MH has preserved the distinction between transitive verbs which have the vowel $\bar{a}$ in the perfect, and intransitive verbs which have $\bar{e}$ or $\bar{o}$ in the perfect.

Exx. Transitive: גְּפָם he corked them, MŠ iii. 12; זָן to feed, Ber. 58 b (Singer, p. 319); סָג to fence, Ab. deRN. i. 7; עָג to draw a circle, Ta'a. iii. 8; חָס to pity, Neg. ii. 5; with the older fem. termination ת: שָׁבַת to return, Lev. R. 23; חַבְתִּי to be guilty, BQ i. 2; חָסוּ j. Ket. iv. 14; דָּשׁ ע"י to thresh, Ber. 58 a; זָזָה to move, Ket. ii. 9; זָזוּ 'Er. iv. 1; נָרָה to harrow, 'Ar. ix. 1; שָׂמְתָ to put, Ber. 28 b; דַּנְתִּם to judge, San. vi. 6; דַּנְתִּי Sifre Num. xix. 2.

Intransitive: מֵת, מֵתָה, מֵתוּ to die, Yeb. i. 2; מַתִּי Git. vii. 3; בּוֹשָׁה to be ashamed, Qid. 81 b; בּוֹשְׁתִּי t. Oh. v. 11; בּוֹשׁוּ So. ix. 15; בָּא to come, Naz. iii. 6; בָּאָה Yeb. xv. 6; with termination ת: בָּאת Ned. ix. 5; בָּאתָה Yeb. xv. 1 (L בָּאת); בָּאנוּ, בָּאתֶם Ber. 63 a.

Imperf.: יָדוּךְ to pound, j. Be. ix. 9; יָזוּן, אָזוּן to feed, Ket. xii. 1; יָזוּעַ to sweat, Toh. ix. 1; יָחוּץ to form a partition; תָּחוּץ Zeb. 19 a; יָחוּצוּ Makš. iii. 8; תָּזוּחַ to move, be elated (with דַּעַת as subject)

Kᵉt. 67 b; תָּפוּג to grow cold, weak, Yo. iii. 5 (L and other texts
יְשׁוּפְנוּ (תְּפִיג); to rub, Kel. xiv. 5; יְשׁוּפֵם ib. xvi. 1; יָזוּנוּ Mid. iv. 5;
נָשׁוּט to go to and fro, Bᵉr. 18 a; אָדוֹן BQ ii. 10 (L אָדִין); תָּמוּת
Tᵉm. iv. 2; תְּחוּבוּ Ab. i. 11; יָבֹא Naz. iii. 6; תְּבוֹאוּ Šᵉbu. iv. 5.

Infin.: לִדוּכָה Be. 14 a; לְזוּנָה Kᵉt. xii. 3; לָזוּ ib. 1; לָחוּץ
'Er. iii. 1; לָמוּל to circumcise, Šab. xix. 4; לָסוּךְ to anoint, Dam.
iii. 1; לָשׁוּחַ to bend, Ab. iii. 21.   Imperat.: לִין 'Er. 52 a; בוֹאִי
Bᵉr. 18 b; בוֹאוּ Yo. ii. 4.

Partic.: זָנָה, זָנִין Kᵉt. xii. 1; חָב BQ i. 1; חָבִין 'Er. vii. 11; חָלוֹת
dance, L (ed. חולות), Taʻa. iv. 8; לָשׁ to knead, Šab. vii. 2; לָשׁוּת
Pᵉs. iii. 9; צָד to catch, Šab. vii. 3; צָדִין Be. iii. 1; דָּשׁ Šab. vii. 2;
דָּן, דָּנִין San. ii. 1; מֵת Yᵉb. xvi. 6; גֵּר proselyte, Yad. iv. 4; עֵר
awake, BQ ii. 5; בָּא BQ iii. 5 (ā because of א), but בּוֹר; בּוֹרָה to
be waste, BM 101 a; בּוֹשׁ Maʻa. iii. 5; בּוֹשָׁה Dam. iii. 6; בּוֹשִׁין
Kᵉt. viii. 1; חוֹצָה Miq. x. 3; נוֹחַ easy, Mᵉn. x. 3; נוֹחִין Gen. R. 11.

Passive: טוּחַ to plaster, Mid. iv. 1; טוּחוֹת Nid. 24 a; לוּשָׁה
j. So. ix. 14; מוּלִים Pᵉs. v. 3; סוּכוֹת j. Bik. i. 3; שׁוּמָה to value,
t. BQ x. 1; נִירָה t. BM ix. 29; נִירוֹת נִיר 'Er. 17 b.

177. *Niphʻal*. Perfect: The preformative נ is pointed with
ḥireq (נִי—), evidently on the analogy of the strong verb. Exx.
נִידוֹנוּ RH 12 a; נִיטּוּחַ Ab. dᵉRN. xxiv. 5; נַלּוֹשָׁה Ḥal. ii. 2;
נִיּוֹחוּ Gen. R. 13; נִיצּוֹד Šab. 106 b; נְצוֹדוּ Be. iii. 2; נִיזַּחֵם (fem.)
t. BB viii. 19.

Imperf.: יֵאוֹר to be light, j. Bᵉr. i. 1; יֵאוֹרוּ Yo. viii. 5; יֵאוֹתוּ to
enjoy, Bᵉr. viii. 6; יִדּוֹן Oh. vi. 3, 7; San. viii. 8, 9 (L ed. נִידוֹן
Partic.); יֵזוֹנוּ Kᵉt. xiii. 3; תִּלּוֹשׁ Tᵉr. v. 2, 3; יִלּוֹשׁוּ ib. 1; יִמּוֹל,
יִמּוֹלוּ Šab. xix. 5; יִצּוֹדוּ ib. i. 6; תֵּירוֹם to be lifted, Tᵉr. v. 2; יִשּׁוֹף
to rub, t. BM xi. 8.

Infin.: לִידּוֹן Giṭ. iii. 4; Ab. iv. 29; לִידּוֹחַ Miq.

Partic.: נִיאוֹתִין Šab. iii. 6; נִיאוֹתוֹת Yo. 11 a; נִידּוֹנִין, נִידּוֹן RH
i. 2; נִידּוֹנֶת RH 16 a; נִידּוֹכִין Bez. i. 7; נִיּוֹן Giṭ. xii. 6; נִיּוֹנֶת,
נִיזּוֹנוֹת Kᵉt. xii. 2; נִיסּוֹטִין to move, t. Zab. iv. 6; נֵעוֹר Ab. iii. 4:

נְעוֹרִין Ber. 61 b.   But with *ā* in the preformative : נָדוֹן BQ ii. 5 ;
Ya. iv. 3, &c. (cf. 2 Sam. xix. 10) ; נָלוֹז to twist, Kil. ix. 8 ; נָמוֹךְ
to be low, ib. iv. 7 ; נְמוֹשׁוֹת to feel (aged persons who grope their
way), Pea viii. 1.[1]

178. (ii) *The Intensive Stem.*   In the formation of this stem
MH has further developed the two methods already found in BH,
viz. (a) Hardening of the vowel into the cognate consonants
(ו or י) on the analogy of the strong verb, and (b) Reduplication.

(*a*) Hardening the vowel into a consonant.

(α) Into ו.   Pi'el : כִּוּן to make firm, direct, Ber. ii. 1 ; כִּוַּנּוּ
MQ ii. 3 ; יְכַוֵּן ib.; יְכַוְּנוּ Ber. v. 1 ; לְכַוֵּן Kil. v. 1 ; לְקַוֵּץ to
remove thorns, MQ 5 a ; מְזַוֵּג BM 90 b ; מְחַוְּבוֹת to halve (from
תּוֹךְ), j. Br. i. 1.   Pu'al : מְכֻוָּן Toh. iii. 2 ; מְכֻוֶּנֶת Kel. xxviii. 7 ;
מְכֻוָּנוֹת Makš. ii. 5 ; מְחֻוֶּבֶת j. Ber. i. 1.   Nithpa'el : נִתְכַּוֵּן BQ iv. 6 ;
נִתְכַּוַּנְתִּי ,נִתְכַּוְּנוּ ib. viii. 1 ; מִזְדַּוְּגִין to join together, San. v. 5 ;
נִתְקַוְּצָה Šᵉbi. iv. 2.[2]

179. (β) Into י.   *Pi'el.*   Perf. : בִּיֵּשׁ to shame, BQ iii. 10 ; טִיֵּל
to walk, Suk. 28 b ; כִּיֵּרוֹ to decorate ; סִיְּדוֹ to plaster, 'AZ iii. 7 ;
טִיְּבָה to improve, j. Šᵉbi. iv. 2 ; וַיִּפְתֶּם ,וַיִּפְתָּ to forge, j. So. vii. 3 ;
קִיְּמָהּ to confirm, fulfil, BQ iii. 9 ; קַיְּמוּ 'Ed. i. 3 ; חִיְּבוּ to declare
guilty, Šab. xii. 3 ; חִיַּבְתֶּם Exod. R. 32 ; תְּסַיֵּעַ to accompany,
assist, Šab. 104 a ; גַּיְּרֵנִי (imperat.) ib. 31 a ; לְחַיֵּף to destroy,
Gen. R. 100 ; לְפַיְּסוֹ to appease, Ber. 28 b ; מְבַיֵּשׁ BQ viii. 1 ;
מְחַיֵּב Šab. x. 6 ; מְחַיְּבִין Dam. i. 3 ; מְעַיֵּן to look, Ber. 55 a ; מְדַיְּרִין
to cause cattle to dwell on a field, to manure, Šᵉbi. iii. 1 ; מְדַיֶּנֶת,
מְדַיְּנִין Qoh. R. ii. 8.

Pu'al : מְגֻיָּד cut up (from גִּיד artery), Yᵉb. xvi. 3 ; מְזֻיָּף Git.
x. 6 ; מְצֻיָּן marked, t. Šᵉq. i. 5 ; מְקֻיָּים BM 7 a ; מְקֻיָּמִין Neg.

---

[1] Another reading has מָשׁוֹשׁוֹת ; cf. the comment of R. Simson, *ad loc.*

[2] The verb נוּל, So. i. 6 ; Naz. iv. 5, &c., cited by Albrecht (§ 114 b) does
not belong here.   It is a MH modification of the BH verb נבל ; cf.
above, § 58.

v. 3 ; מְצוּיָצוֹת with fringes, Šab. 25 b : מְצוּיָירוֹת painted, Kel.
xxviii. 4.

Nithpaʻel: נִדַּיֵּר to be manured, Šᵉbi. iv. 2 ; נִטַּיְּיבָה to be improved, ib.; נִתְפַּיֵּים Ber. 33 a ; נִסְתַּיְּימוּ j. Dam. i. 1 ; יִתְקַיֵּים Giṭ.
i. 3 ; נִתְפַּיַּירְתִּי Yeb. 47 a ; אֶתְפַּיֵּירִי, תִּתְפַּיֵּירִי Qid. iii. 7 ; לְהִתְוַדֵּיף Giṭ.
ii. 4 ; לְהִתְפַּיֵּיר Yeb. 47 a ; מִתְבַּיֵּישׁ BQ viii. 1 ; מִתְחַיֵּיב Ab. iii. 4 ;
מִתְקַיֶּימֶת ib. iii. 9.

180. Of this formation BH shows only one example with וֹ
(עוֹדְדֵנִי Ps. cxix. 61) and two examples with יֹ : חָיֵּב (Dan. i. 10 ;
cf. Sirach xi. 21), and קָיֵם Esther ix. 31, &c.; cf. Sirach xlii. 23,
and Ges.-K., § 72 m). The formation is generally considered to
have been borrowed by late BH from Aram. But it is found also
in other Semitic languages, e.g. Arabic. That earlier Hebrew
possessed this power of converting the vocalic middle radical into
a hard consonant, is shown by the cognate nouns תָּוֶךְ, מָוֶת, אָוֶן,
דַּיִשׁ, חַיִל, צַיִד, &c., and by uncontracted verbs like עֻוַּת, רָוַח, עוֹד,
צֻוָּה, קֻוָּה, which have hardened the middle *waw*, owing to the
presence in the root of another weak letter. It is, therefore, quite
probable that this formation for the intensive stem was developed
within Hebrew itself on the analogy of the strong verb. It may
even be assumed that the formation existed in the spoken language
long before it appeared in literature, and that MH received it from
the spoken language of BH times.[1]

181. (*b*) Reduplication. (*a*) Doubling of the second radical,
Poʻlel, and Nithpoʻlel. These forms are rarer in MH than in BH
Only the following examples are found in MH :

Poʻlel : יְעוֹרֵר to awake, MQ i. 5 ; לְכוֹנֵן Ex. R. 15 ; לְרוֹמֵם to
exalt, Pes. x. 5 (liturgical passage) ; מְכוֹנֵן to wheel round (denom.
of מְכַנִי μηχανή, Yo. iii. 10. L has, perhaps, correctly מְכוּנֵן, Polʻal) ;
Makš. iv. 1 ; מְעוֹפֶפֶת to fly, Ḥul. xii. 3 ; מְעוֹרְרִים MŠ v. 15 ; מְפוֹצֶצֶת

---

[1] Cf. Koenig, *Lehrgebäude*, i, p. 452 f.

to shatter, Lev. R. 27 ; מְקוֹנֶנֶת to lament, Ket. iv. 4 ; מְקוֹנְנוֹת MQ iii. 9 ; מְרוֹמַמְתּוֹ Ab. vi. 2 ; מְשׁוֹרְרִים singers, 'Ar. 11 b.

Nithpo'lel : נִתְמוֹטְטוּ to totter, Ber. 32 b ; יִתְעוֹרְרוּ Lev. R. vii. 9 ; הִתְנוֹפְפִי (imperat.), to wave, 'AZ 24 b ; לְהִתְבּוֹנֵן מִשְׁתּוֹקֶקֶת BQ 27 b ; to long, Yeb. 62 b ; Ab. deRN. i. 7 ; מִתְמוֹטְטִין BM 71 a (cf. Sirach xxxii. 2) ; מִתְפּוֹצֵץ Qid. 30 b.

182. (β) Doubling of the whole root. This is more frequent in MH than in BH ; cf. above, § 108.

Pilpel : וְעִזְעַתִּי, וְעִזְעוּ to shake, 'Or. i. 3 ; לְגַלֵּג to mock, Šab. 30 b ; נִעְנְעוּ to shake, Suk. iii. 9 ; נִעְנַעְתִּי Yeb. 121 a ; יְנַעְנְעוּ Šab. xx. 5 ; יְקַעְקֵעַ to tattoo, Mak. iii. 6 ; יְשַׁלְשְׁלוּ to let down by chain, Šebi. iv. 10 ; מְטַלְטֵל to move, 'Er. x. 4 ; מְטַלְטֶלֶת BB iv. 3 ; מְגַלְגֵּל Ber. 39 a ; מְנַפְנֶפֶת Oh. viii. 5 ; מְשַׁלְשְׁלִים, שִׁלְשְׁלוּ BQ 82 b.

Pulpal. Participle only : מְחוּלְחֶלֶת shaken, Kel. x. 3 ; מְשׁוּלְשֶׁלֶת ib. viii. 1 ; מְנוּעֲרוֹת (= מְנוּרְנָרוֹת), well harrowed, Men. 85 a : מְטוּשְׁטָשׁוֹת rubbed off, Meg. 18 b ; מְנוּעְנָעִין Be. 25 a.

Hithpalpel : נִזְדַּעְזְעוּ to be shaken, BQ 82 b ; נִתְנַמְנְמוּ to slumber, Pes. x. 8 ; תִּפַּמְמֵם (= תִּתְטַמְטַם), to be kneaded through, Ḥal. iii. 1 ; מִתְחַלְחְלִים לְהִתְנַמְנֵם Yo. i. 7 ; לִיטַּלְטֵל Kel. xv. 1 ; מְטַלְטְלִין Šab. iii. 6 ; Miq. iv. 3.

(iii) *The Causative Stem.*

183. Hiph'il : הֵמִיר to change, Temu. i. 1 ; הֵרִיחָה to smell, Yo. viii. 4 ; הֵקִיצְתִּי to awaken, Num. R. 10 ; הֲבַנְתָּה to understand, Šab. 31 a ; הֵנִחְתָּ to give rest, ib. 152 b ; הֵעַדְתָּ to testify, Yeb. vii. 3 (L הַעִידוֹתָה) ; הֵעַדְתִּי Yeb. 99 b ; הֵעַדְנוּ Mak. 3 a ; הֵמַכְתִּי to lower, t. Naz. iv. 7 ; הֵצַצְתִּי to gaze, Ḥul. 47 b ; הֵרִיחְתִּי Yo. 39 b ; הֵשַׁבְתָּה to reply, Sifra (Weiss), 113 a ; הֵשְׁבַתַּנִי Pes. 69 a.

For the omission of the separating vowel before the afformative in BH, cf. Ges.-K., § 72 k.

Imperf. : יָוִיז, יָזִינוּ to move, Be. iii. 5 ; יָמִירֶנּוּ Tem. i. 1 ; תְּעִידֵנִי Šebu. iii. 8 ; תְּעִידֵנִי ib. iv. 5 ; יָפִיחַ to blow, Šab. 49 a ; יְשִׁיבֶנּוּ Ber. v. 1 ; יָבִיא Naz. iv. 6. Imperat. : הָבֵא Pes. vi. 2 ; הָפֵג to cool,

Yo. i. 7 ; הַעֵידֹתִי Šᵉbu. iii. 8 ; הָרִיעוּ Taʻa. ii. 10. Infin.: לְהָמִיר
Tᵉm. i. 1 ; לַהֲמִיתוֹ San. 53 a ; לְהָסִיט Zab. iii. 3.

Partic.: מֵבִין Ḥag. ii. 1 ; מֵסִיט Zab. v. 1 ; מְטִיבָה San. vii. 10 ;
מְזִיוִין Ab. iii. 17 ; מְמִירִין Tᵉm. i. 1.

184. *Hophʻal*: הוּחֲלָה to occur, Bᵉr. 31 a ; הוּרְמָה to be lifted,
Ḥal. ii. 8 ; יוּנַּף to be waived, Mid. iii. 4 ; תּוּדַח to be rinsed, Makš.
iv. 3 ; תּוּצָץ to sprout forth, Qid. 66 a ; מוּכָן prepared, Bᵉ. i. 1 ;
מוּמָר Tᵉm. i. 1 ; מוּרָם Zᵉb. v. 6 ; מוּמָתִין San. vi. 2.[1]

185. Note 1. As in BH, so in MH some ע״י roots are found
also in פ״י forms. Thus, טוב to be good = יטב ; נוק to suck = ינק ;
קוץ to awake = יקץ. So also in ע״ע forms : דוך to crush = דכך ;
זוח to move = זחח : זול to be cheap = זלל ; חוץ to separate = חצץ ;
מוש to feel = משש.

186. Note 2. The verb נוח forms also a causative by assimilation, as in BH, in the sense ʻto lay down', e.g. הִנִּיחַ BB ix. i ;
מַנִּחָה Bᵉr. viii. 4 ; הִנַּחְנוּהוּ So. ix. 6 ; מוּנַּח BM iii. 4 ; מוּנַּחַת
Qid. 66 a.

187. Note 3. The verb נום (BH נאם) to speak, shows some
strange forms, probably of an artificial character. Thus נוּמִי he
spoke, Zᵉb. iv. 5 ; נוּמֵית, נוּמָה she spoke, Yᵉb. xvi. 7 ; נוּמֵיתִי
I spoke, ib. ; נוּמֵינוּ (L נוּמְנוּ) we spoke, Giṭ. vi. 7 ; but also נָם,
נַמְתִּי t. Naz. iv. 7 ; נָאַמְתִּי Sifre Num. xix. 2 ; נָאַם, ibid. xxviii. 2.

(6) Verbs ע״ע.

188. The tendency, already strong in BH, to make these
verbs approximate to the standard of the strong triliteral type is
carried still further in MH. Biliteral forms are the regular type

---

[1] In the curious expression אהיה אובין, ʻAZ iii. 5 (L) the form אובין seems
to be treated as a participle Qal, and should be pointed אוֹבִין. It is probably
a scribal expansion of אָבִין = אוֹבִין. הוּבִירָה, BM. ix. 3, is an Aramaism for
הבירה, from בוּר to be fallow, due to the influence of the following Aram.
form אוביר. L has the correct reading הבירה in BM. In ʻAr. ix. 1 L is
defective.

only in the causative stem and, to a smaller extent, in the Imperf.
Qal and Niph'al. In the other parts of the Qal and the Niph'al
triliteral forms predominate. In the Intensive Stem they are used
exclusively.

Aram., on the other hand, has preserved and accentuated more
strongly than any other Semitic language the natural affinity of the
ע״ע verbs with the ע״י verbs. The biliteral forms of the ע״ע
predominate in Aram.

189. (i) *The Simple Stem.*

Qal. Perfect. Triliteral: חֲצָצוּ to divide, Oh. xv. 4 ; מָדַד to
measure, 'AZ v. 7 ; פָּקַק to stop, Miq. iii. 2 ; רָקַק to spit, BQ
viii. 6 ; שָׁגַג to err, Šab. 95 a ; רָקְקָה Yeb. xii. 3 ; קָצְצָה to cut,
BQ 91 b ; חָקַקְתִּי to enact a law, Yo. 67 b ; טָנְנוּ to become moist,
Makš. iii. 4 ; עָמְמוּ to become dim, t. Šab. iii. 2 ; צָלֲלוּ to clarify,
t. Nid. iii. 11 ; חֲגַגְתֶּם to offer the Festival sacrifice, Pes. 70 b.

Biliteral: חַג Hag. i. 9 ; כַּח to cough, 'Er. 99 a ; רַב Hag. 9 a ;
רַבּוּ to be many, Šab. i. 7.

Imperfect: יִקְצְצֶנּוּ to cut, BQ 91 b ; יִשּׁוֹג Šab. 69 a ; יִשְׁלוֹל to
baste, j. MQ iii. 5. But usually biliteral: יָבוֹר to choose, Ab. ii. 1 ;
תָּבוֹר Git. v. 9 ; אָבוֹר Ma'a. ii. 6 ; יָגוֹר to cut, Pa. ii. 2 ; אָגוֹר BB 13 a ;
יָחוֹף to cleanse the head, Naz. vi. 3 ; יָמוֹד Ber. 30 b ; יָקוֹץ BQ x. 2.
So Imperat.: גּוֹד BB 13 a ; כּוֹף to bend, Ber. 60 b ; קוֹצּוּ Ab.
deRN. xxxix. 1 ; but also מָדוֹד Yo. 39 a.

Infinit.: לִגְזוֹז to shear, Ḥul. 138 a ; לִגְרוֹר to drag, Kel. v. 7 ;
לַחֲצֹץ Be. iv. 6 ; לְלוֹתְתָן to mix, t. Makš. iii. 7 ; לְמוֹלְלָן to hem,
MQ 26 a ; לִקְצֹץ Miq. x. 5 ; לְקוֹצְצוֹ (L לִקְוֹצוּ) Šebi. iv. 10.
Biliteral: לָבוֹז to spoil, Pe. iv. 1, 2 ; לָחוֹף to rub, Naz. 59 a ; לָמוֹד
MŠ v. 9 ; לָפוֹף Kel. xxviii. 2 ; לָקוֹץ 'AZ i. 8.

Participles, only triliteral: בּוֹזֵר San. iii. 1 ; זוֹמְמִין, זוֹמֶמֶת, זוֹמֵם,
to give false evidence, Mak. i. 1, 2, 3, &c. ; [1] מוֹזְרִין 'Er. v. 4 ; רוֹפֶפֶת

---

[1] From Deut. xix. 19.

to shake, t. Ḥul. ii. 12; שׁוֹתֵת to flow gently, Oh. iii. 5; גְּמוּם
to level, Ḥul. 59 a; רְעוּעָה ,רָעוּעַ to break, Kel. iii. 5; צְפוּפִין to
press, Ab. v. 5.

190. *Niph'al.* Perf.: נִגְמַם Šebi. i. 8; נִגְמְמוּ Bek. vi. 4; נִזְקַק to
bind, Naz. ix. 4; נִקְצַץ BM ix. 2; נִכְפְּפָה 'Ar. 19 a; נִבְזְזָה Bik. i. 8;
נִכְלְלוּ to complete, include, j. So. vii. 4. Biliteral: נִימוֹק to decay,
Nid. iii. 4; נִיפּוֹקִי Bik. i. 8 (L נימוקו).

Imperf.: יִקָּצֵץ 'AZ i. 8; תִּקָּצֵץ Nid. ii. 1; יִקָּצְצוּ Ned. iii. 5; but
biliteral forms are more common: יֵחַם to be hot, Be. ii. 5; יֵחַמּוּ
Šab. iii. 5; יִמַּסּוּ to melt; יֵצַנּוּ to be cold, Šab. xxii. 4; יֵצַלּוּ to
clarify, ib. xx. 2.

With ŏ, instead of ă, on the analogy of the ע״ו verbs: יִגּוֹלּוּ to
roll, Bᵉr. 7 a; יֵחוֹלּוּ to be common, Šebi. i. 8; יֵחוֹמּוּ Šab. 41 b; [1]
יִמּוֹקוּ (L יִמַּקוּ) Ta'a. iii. 8.

Infin.: לְהִבָּלֵל to mix, Mᵉn. xi. 4; לִיגֵּז BQ ix. 1; לְהִמָּדֵד Dam.
ii. 5; but also לָחֵם Kel. xiv. i.

Partic.: נִבְלָלִין Mᵉn. xii. 4; נָגֵר 'Er. x. 11; נִגְרֶרֶת ,נִגְרָרִין Be.
ii. 10; נִזְקָקִין Šab. 12 b; נִמְדָּדִין 'Ar. vii. 1; נִקְצָצוֹת Ned. iii. 5,
but also Biliteral: נָרוֹק to spit, Miq. vii. 1; נִימוֹק Bᵉr. 61 b; נִימוֹקִין
RH iii. 8.

191. (ii) *The Intensive Stem.*

(a) *Po'el, Po'al, Nithpo'el*: These forms are still more rare in
MH than in BH. The following are the only exx. found:
מְחוֹטֵט ,מִתְחוֹטֶטֶת to dig, cut, Mᵉg. 12 a; מְסוֹלֶלֶת to coddle, San.
69 b; מְסוֹלְלוֹת Yeb. 76 a; לְקוֹצֵץ Miq. x. 4; יְסוֹבְבוּ So. ix. 15;
חוֹנַנְתָּנוּ Singer, pp. 46, 280. An example of Po'al may be יְחוֹנְנוּ
So. ix. 15, but this is more probably a Pu'al: יְחוֹנְנוּ, cf. above,
§ 126; נִתְרוֹעֲעָה Kel. iii. 4; iv. 2 (L נתרעעה); מִתְרוֹסֵם to crush,
Ḥul. 77 a; מְשׁוֹתּוֹמֵם to be desolate, Qid. 66 a.

192. (b) *Pi'el*: בֵּרַר 'Er. iv. 5; גֵּרְרָה Pes. i. 2; סִיכֵּךְ to cover,

---

Suk. i. 4; מֵרֵרוּ to embitter, Pes. x. 5; קִינְּנוּ to make a nest, Ḥul. xii. 1; יְרַפֵּם ʿUq. ii. 6; יְקַצֵּץ ʾAZ i. 8; אֲקָרֵר, אֲצַנֵּן, to make cold, Pes. 118 a; לְבָרֵר San. 23 b; לְחַמֵּם j. Nᵉd. iv. 2; לְפָרֵר to crumble, Pes. 10 b; לְחַמְמָהּ, לְצַנְּנָהּ Šab. 53 a; מְנַפֵּף to caress, San. vii. 6; מְלַקֵּק to lick, San. 68 a; מְפָרֵר Pes. ii. 1; מְצַדֵּד to move to the side, Yo. 55 a; מְנָעֶרֶת t. Šab. vi. 1; מְסַנֶּנֶת to sift, Kel. ii. 5; מְסַבְּבִין ib. i. 7. Biliteral only: מְחַמִּין Yo. iii. 5 (unless this is Hiph'il: מְחַמִּין), and perhaps also מְלַקֶּקֶת = מַלֶּקֶת Pa. ix. 3 (מלקה L).

193. *Puʿal*: מְזוּמָם San. vi. 2; מְזוּפָּפִין pitched, BM 40 b; מְחוּדָּד sharpened, Qid. 30 a; מְסוּבֶּבֶת BB 25 b; מְסוּבֶּבֶת Suk. 8 b; מְצוּדָּדִים BB 99 a; מְצוּנֶּנֶת Ḥul. iii. 5; מְרוּדָּד, מְרוּדָּדִין beaten, Miq. vii. 7. Biliteral only, מְסוּבִּין reclining round the table, San. ii. 1, 3, &c.[1]

194. *Hithpaʿel-Nithpaʿel*: הִתְפַּלַּלְתָּ, הִתְפַּלֵּל Taʿa. iii. 8; נִתְאָרְרוּ to curse, t. So. xv. 2; נִצְטַנֵּן Šab. 129 a; נִתְקַלְלָה to curse, ʿEr. 18 a, b; מִתְחַכֵּךְ BQ iv. 6; מִתְחַלֵּל Ab. i. 11; מִתְחַמֵּם ib. ii. 10.

(c) Reduplicated Forms.

195. *Pilpel*: דִּקְדֵּק to be thin, exact, Bᵉr. ii. 3; הִרְהַרְתִּי to reflect, Ḥul. 37 b; בִּלְפֵּלוֹ to search, t. BB vii. 6; קִלְקְלָה to damage, corrupt, Yᵉb. x. 2; קִלְקְלוֹ Bᵉr. ix. 5; יְחַרְחַר to bore, ʿUq. iii. 11; תְּבַשְׁבֵּשׁ to shake, Ḥul. ii. 6; יְצַחְצְחָן to polish BM 84 a; יְקַלְקְלוּ Ḥul. i. 1; לְחַטְחֵט j. ʿOr. iii. 2; לְכַסְכֵּס to chew, Nid. ix. 7; לְמַשְׁמֵשׁ to feel, BM 21 b; מְהַרְהֵר Bᵉr. iii. 4; מְכַלְכֵּל to maintain, Naz. i. 1; מְסַלְסֵל to wave the hair, ib.; מְסַכְסֶכֶת to intertwine, t. BQ vi. 22; מְקַלְקֶלֶת Nᵉd. xi. 11; מְמַשְׁמְשִׁין BQ ii. 4.

Pulpal: מְגוּלְגָּלוֹת Pes. 7 a; מְגוּלְגָּלִין ʿAZ ii. 7; מְדוּלְדָּל to hang down, Kᵉr. iii. 8; מְדוּלְדָּלִין Ḥul. ix. 7; מְצוּחְצָחוֹת Lev. R. 1.

Nithpalpel: נִתְגַּלְגֵּל Šab. xi. 3; נִתְגַּלְגְּלָה Šᵉbu. vii. 8; נִיַדַּלְדְּלוּ to be impoverished, So. ix. 15; יִתְמַקְמֵק Taʿa. 25 b; יִתְקַלְקְלוּ Mᵉn. xi. 1; מִתְקַלְקֵל Dam. iii. 6; מִתְחַרְפֶּרֶת t. Makš. iii. 8.

(iii) *The Causative Stem.* Biliteral; triliteral forms are very rare.

---

[1] The sing. is always מֵסֵב, in Hiph'il; cf. below, § 196.

196. *Hiph'il*: הֵפֵר Neᵈ. x. 1; הֵקֵל to make light, be lenient,
MŠ iii. 2; הֶחֵלּוּ ¹ to begin, Tam. ii. 2, 3; vi. i; הֵסַבּוּ Berᵉ. vi. 6;
הֲזֵימוּם to convict of false evidence, San. xii. 5; הֲרֵעוֹתִי Qid. iv. 14.
Without separating vowel (cf. BH הֵתֵלתָּ Jud. xvi. 10; Ges.-K.,
§ 67 dd, and above, § 183): הֵמַסְתְּ Deut. R. 2; הֶעֵזְתָּ to strengthen,
Berᵉ. 62 b; הֶעֵזְתִּי BB 131 a; הֵיקֵלְתָּ Yᵉb. 88 a. Triliteral: הֻקִקְתּוּנִי
Suk. 28 a.

Imperf.: יָחֵם Be. ii. 5; יָסֵב Pᵉs. x. i; יָפֵר Neᵈ. x. 5; יָצֵן j. Hor.
ii. 5; יָקֵל Berᵉ. ix. 5; נָקֵל MŠ iii. 2; תָּנֵץ to shine, Mᵉg. ii. 4; יָנֵצוּ
Šebi. iv. 2; יָזֵימוּ Mak. i. 7; יָרֵיצוּ to crush, t. Oh. xviii. end.

Inf.: לָחֵם Šab. 40 a; לָהֵטְן to moisten, Makš. iii. 5; לָהֵפֵר Neᵈ.
x. 3; לָהֵקֵל 'Er. iv. 9; לָהֵקֵר Makš. iv. 2.

Imperat.: הָחֵל j. Berᵉ. v. 2; Singer, p. 46.

Part.: מֵדֵל to thin grapes, Pe. iii. 3; מֵיחֵל, מְחִלִּין to defile, Berᵉ.
32 a; Dam. vii. 4; מֵחֵם t. Šab. iii. 7; מְחַתִּין ² Yo. iii. 5; מֵטֵן (so
correctly L for edd. מטטן), מְטִנִּין Makš. iii. 5; מֵצֵן j. Hor. ii. 5;
מֵיצַר RH ii. 9; מֵיקֵל, מְקִילִין Šab. 129 a; מֵסֵב to recline, San.
ii. 1, 3; מֵסֵךְ Šab. vii. 2; מֵפֵר, מְפִירִין Neᵈ. x. 1, 2; מְרִיעָה to do
evil, San. vii. 10; מְמֵקְתּוּ to cause decay, Kᵉt. vii. 11; מֵצֵמֵת to
restrain (צמם), Cant. R. iv. 1; מֵתֵשֶׁת to weaken (תשש) San. 26 a.

197. *Hoph'al*: הוּפְלוּ BB v. 8; הוּנְמוּ ³ San. x. 8; הוּנְמְנוּ Mak. 3 a
(without the separating vowel); הוּחַמָּה BM vi. 3; הוּחַמּוּ Šab. iii. 4;
הוּמַק San. 92 b; הוּסַבָּה BB 112 a; הוּרַע Pea vi. 6. Triliteral:
הוּנְלְלוּ Ta'a. 21 b; הוּזְקַק BB 170 a; הוּזְקְקוּ Mᵉn. 45 b; יוּצַן 'AZ
iii. 9; יוּרַע BB x. 6.

מוּדָק j. So. ii. 2; מוּזָרוֹת smashed, San. 82 b; מוּפָר, מוּפָרִין Neᵈ.
viii. 7. Triliteral: מוּבְלֶלֶת j. Šᵉq. vi. 1 end; מוּבְכָלּ Yo. 54 b.

---

¹ Elsewhere always the denominative of תִּחְלָה = הִתְחִיל; cf. § 92. So ib.
vi. 3.

² The traditional pronunciation is מְחַמִּין = מְחַמְמִין, plur. of מְחַמֵּם; cf.
§ 192; j. Šab. ix. 3.

³ This is the traditional pronunciation, and not הוּנְלוּ, הוּנְמוּ. Cf. BH
הֻמְכוּ, Job xxiv. 24; Ges.-K., § 67 v.

(7) Verbs ל״א.

198. The inflection of these verbs follows on BH lines.
The interchange of forms between these verbs and verbs ל״ה,
already frequent in BH (Ges.-K., § 75 m, n, ff.), becomes more
frequent in MH. Sometimes we find forms combining both ל״א
and ל״ה types. Nevertheless, the distinction between these two
classes has been clearly preserved in MH. Many of the ל״ה
forms in ל״א verbs may be ascribed to the negligence and the
Aramaizing tendencies of the scribes, as is proved by comparing
different texts. MH also shows more frequently than BH the
older termination ת for the third fem. sing. in Qal, Niph'al, and
Nithpa'el (cf. Ges.-K., § 74 g).

199. *Qal.* Perfect: יָצָא Yo. v. 3; מָצָא BM ii. 1. The fem.
wavers between יָצָאת, יָצְאָה (so usually in L and other Palestinian
texts), יָצְאָה and יָצְתָה; cf. Šab. vi. 1, 3; xi. 6; Pes. v. 7; Yeb.
xvi. 1; Toh. iii. 1. So קָרְאָה and קְרָאתָה Yeb. xii. 3, in various
texts. חָטָאתִי Yo. iii. 8, but also קָרִיתִי ib. i. 6; מָצְאוּ Yeb. xvi. 6;
מְצָאָנוּ ib. xvi. 7, but also מָצִינוּ Ber. vii. 3; Kil. iii. 7; קָרִינוּ Ber. i. 1,
especially in later texts. Imperf., as in BH.

Infin.: לִקְרוֹת Ber. i. 1, but also לִקְרֹאות MŠ v. 9 (L), as Judges
viii. 1.

Imperat.: קְרָא Yo. i. 6; שְׂנָא Ab. i. 10.

Partic.: קוֹרֵא Yo. i. 6; קוֹרִין ib.; Ber. i. 1 (cf. Psalm xcix. 6);-
יוֹצֵא Šab. v. 2; יוֹצְאָה ib. v. 4; but also יוֹצֵאת Kil. iv. 6; נוֹשֵׂאת
Šebu. vii. 8; יוֹצָאוֹת, יוֹצְאִין Šab. v. 4; נוֹשְׂאִין MQ i. 7; נָשׂוּי married,
Yeb. iii. 7 (L has the mixed form נָשׂאוּי, cf. Psalm xxxii. 1); קָרוּי
Ter. iii. 7; סְמוּיָה blind, hidden, Qid. 24 b.

200. *Niph'al:* נִטְמָא Pes. i. 6; נִטְמֵאת Ter. viii. 2; So. vi. 2;
נִשֵּׂאת to be married, Yeb. vii. 2 (also spelt נִיסֵּת ib. vii. 3, 6, and
often in L and the Talmud); נִסְמֵית to be blind, Zeb. vii. 5; נִטְמֵאתָ
Ter. viii. 2; נִטְמֵאנוּ Pes. 78 b; נִטְמֵינוּ.

The imperf. as in BH.

Infin.: לִינָשָׂא Yeb. ii. 10; לְהִיקָּרֵא 'Ed. v. 6 (L לִיקָּרוֹת); and the mixed form לְהִבָּרָאוֹת Ab. iv. 1.

Partic.: נִשָּׂאת, or נִיסָּת Ket. i. 1; נִקְרֵאת Meg. i. 1; נִקְרָאִין, also נִקְרִין Git. ix. 5.

201. *Pi'el*: מִילָא, אֲמַלָּא Pa. vii. 4; יְטַמְּאֶנָּה, אֲטַמְּאָה Ter. viii. 11; נְטַמְּאָה, יְטַמְּאוּ ib. 12; יְמַּאֶנָּה Šab. ii. 4; סִימֵּא BQ viii. 1; מַלֵּא (imperat.) Be. iii. 8; מְמַלֵּא Pa. vii. 5; מְמַלְּאִין ib. 11 (L מְמַלִּין and so often, 'Er. viii. 7, &c.); מְקְרֵא to read to, Suk. iii. 10; מְקְרִין ib.; Bik. iii. 6 (L also מְקָרְאִים, beside מְקְרִין); מְקַפֵּא to congeal, Ma'a. i. 7; מְחַבְּאִין = מְחַבִּין to hide, Šab. 25 b.

The Infin. has mixed forms: לְמַלֹּאות Ket. i. 10; לְרַפֹּאותוֹ to heal, BQ viii. 1. So in BH, cf. Ges.-K., § 74 h.

Pu'al: מְדוּבְּאָן to crush, Ket. 8 b; מְקוֹרְאִין Num. R. 13.

202. *Nithpa'el*: נִסְתַּמֵּא 'Ar. 17 b; נִתְמַלֵּאת Pes. v. 5; לִיטַמֵּא Yo. 38 b; מִיטַמֵּא 'Uq. i. 1; מִיטַמְּאָה Naz. iv. 3; מִיטַמְּאִין (also מִתְטַמְּאִין) Kel. ii. 1; מִתְחַטֵּא Ta'a. iii. 8; מִתְרַפְּאִין, also מִתְרַבִּין 'AZ ii. 2.

203. *Hiph'il*: הִשִּׂיאוֹ to move, 'AZ ii. 5; יַבְרִיא to become healthy, Šab. xix. 5; יַקְפִּיאֶנָּה to ladle off, Ter. iv. 11; מַמְצִיא Hag. 5 a, but מַמְרִין to fatten, (BH מריא) Šab. xxiv. 3.

Hoph'al: מוּפְלָא distinguished, Hor. i. 4.

(8) VERBS ל״ה.

204. These verbs also conform to the BH rules. As in BH (Ges.-K., § 75 rr), ל״ה verbs sometimes assume ל״א forms. This happens usually in the third sing. and plur. of the perf. Qal when they have pronominal suffixes attached to them, and further, in the third fem. sing. perf. Niph'al, and in the fem. sing. of the Partic. Niph'al. The older termination ת— for the third fem. sing. of the perf. Qal is regularly found in Palestinian, and sometimes also in other texts. Cf. the ל״א verbs above, § 199, and Ges.-K., § 75 m.

205. *Qal.* Perfect : זָכָה to acquire, BM i. 3 ; שָׁהָה to tarry, Šᵉbu. ii. 3 ; גָּבְתָה (L נבת) to collect, Kᵉt. iv. 1 ; זָבְתָה (L זבת) BM i. 4 ; כָּבְתָה to extinguish, Šab. 21 a, but כָּבַת j. Yo. ii. 3 ; כָּהֲתָה to dim, Qid. 24 b ; עָלְתָה (L עלת) (L פשת פָּשְׁתָה) to go up, Zᵉb. ix. 1 ; to increase, Nᵉg. iv. 9 ; שָׁפְתָה (L שפת) to be quiet, Nid. iv. 4 ; שָׁתָת to drink, Pa. ix. 5 ; שָׁרָה to be loose, Qoh. R. vii. 2 ; צָבָת to swell, j. BQ vii. 1.

The original third radical י reappears in the third sing. and plur. of the perfect with suffixes : טְלָיֵיהּ to patch, Kel. xxiv. 17 ; פְּדָיוֹן to redeem, Pea iv. 8. Often, however, this י is changed into א, especially in Babylonian texts : עֲשָׂאָהּ Suk. i. 1 ; עֲשָׂאַךְ Tᵉr. viii. 1 ; כְּוָואוּ to burn, BQ viii. 1 ; אֲפָאָהּ (L אפייה) to bake, MŠ ii. 3 ; cf. below, § 216, and above, §§ 56, 58.

זָכִיתִי Ber. i. 5 ; לְוִיתְ to borrow, BB 6 a ; בְּדוּ to invent, Nᵉd. 10 a ; נָשִׁינוּ to forget, ib. 50 b ; צָלוּ to roast, Pᵉs. v. 9.

Imperf. : יִלְקֶה to be smitten, BM iii. 12 ; יִרְעֶה to feed, Yo. vi. 1. Jussive : אַל תַּעַשׂ do not make, Ab. i. 8 ; ii. 12.

Infin. : לַחְתּוֹת to take fire, Šab. viii. 7 (BH) ; לִרְדּוֹת to chastise, Yo. 40 b.

Imperat. : צְלֵה Pᵉs. vii. 2 ; שְׁנֵה to repeat, Nid. 5 b ; לְוֵי to borrow, Be. 15 b.

Partic. Active : הוֹגֶה to utter, San. x (xi.) 1 ; זוֹכֶה 'Ed. ii. 9 ; חוֹתָה Yo. iv. 4 ; טוֹוֶה to spin, Kᵉt. vii. 6 ; דּוֹחִין to push off, Oh. vii. 6 ; חוֹפִין to cover, Ḥul. iii. 7 ; פּוֹדִין to redeem, Giṭ. iv. 6 ; שׁוֹרִין to soak, Šab. i. 5.

206. A few participles are found in an adjectival form with *ā* in the first syllable : זָכֶה 'Ed. ii. 10 (L ; elsewhere always זוֹכֶה), זָכִין in the dictum : — זָכִין לְאָדָם שֶׁלֹּא בְּפָנָיו וְאֵין חָבִין לְאָדָם אֶלָּא בְּפָנָיו one can confer an advantage upon a person in his absence, but one cannot confer a disadvantage upon a person, except in his presence, 'Er. vii. 11; Gi̇ṭ. i. 6. The form זָכִין may perhaps be due to assonance with חָבִין. So זָכִין Yo. ii. 3; זָכוֹת Gi̇ṭ. vi. 2, in L, for זוֹכִין, זוֹכוֹת in other texts. Further, כָּבָה, fem. כָּבָה to be extinguished, Šab. 151 b; כָּלָה to come to an end, Tᵉr. vi. 7; כָּלִין San. 17 a; פָּרָה וְרָבָה fruitful and multiplying (a standing expression, derived from Gen. i. 28); פָּרִין וְרָבִין Šab. 107 b; Ab. dᵉRN. xxxvii. 2, 3.

Partic. Passive: טָוּוי Kil. ix. 8; צָפוּי to see, Ab. iii. 15; רָאוּי fit, Nid. vi. 4; כְּרוּיָה to dig, Kel. iii. 5; שְׁבוּיִים to capture, Šᵉq. ii. 5; שְׁרוּיָה to dwell, Ab. iii. 2.

207. *Niph'al*. The third fem. sing. of the perfect is identical in form with the fem. sing. of the Participle. They usually both end in יִת ָ, or ת ָ in L, as in the ל״א verbs (§ 200).

Perfect: נֶהֱנִית to enjoy, BQ ii. 2; נִפְדֵּית Kᵉt. iii. 2; נִשְׁבֵּית ib. ii. 5; נַעֲשֵׂית 'Er. v. 6; Šab. xi. 6 (L נעשתה); נִמְנֵית, נִמְנִינוּ to count, Pᵉs. ix. 10; נִפְנֵיתִי to have leisure, Ab. dᵉRN. xxv. 3; נִשְׁבֵּיתִי Kᵉt. ii. 5; נַעֲנֵתִי to be humble, Bᵉr. 28 a; נַעֲנָה Zᵉb. 57 a; נַעֲנוּ to answer, Qid. 40 b; נִימְחוּ to wipe out, dissolve, Ṭoh. iii. 1; נִשְׁרוּ to soak, Šab. xxii. 4.

Imperf.: יִדָּחֶה Mᵉg. 5 b; תִּפָּנֶה, אֶפָּנֶה Ab. ii. 4; יִפָּדוּ Tᵉr. v. 1; תִּצָּלֶה Šab. iii. 3; written *plene* יִצּוֹלוּ ib. i. 10; so יֵשּׁוֹרוּ ib. i. 5.

Partic.: נִדְחֶה Mᵉg. 5 b; נִפְדֶּה MŠ iii. 10; נִתְלֵית, נִתְלָה (L נִתְלַת), נִתְלִין to hang, San. vi. 4; נִכְסִין, נִכְסֶה to cover, ib. ii. 1; נִבְנֵית to build, ib. x. 6; נַעֲשֵׂית Pa. iii. 7; נִקְנֵית to acquire, Qid. i. 1; נִכְווֹת Kᵉt. 5 b.

Infin.: לִנָּבוֹת BM 59 a; לִיהָנוֹת Kᵉt. vii. 1; לֵיעָשׂוֹת 'Ed. v. 6; לִיפָּנוֹת to ease oneself, Šab. 82 a.

The Intensive Stem is regular, as in BH.

208. *Pi'el*: וִיכָּה BB viii. 6; וְזִנְּתָה to commit fornication, San. vii. 2; לִיבָּה to kindle a flame; לִיבְּתָה BQ vi. 4; עֵרָה to pour out, Yo. v. 4; דִּימּוּ to imagine, ib. iii. 2; פִּתֵּיתִי to seduce, Kᵉt. iii. 9.

יְרַצֶּה to make acceptable, Yo. viii. 9; יָחַפֵּהוּ to cover, Šᵉbi. iv. 5,

נַפֵּה (imperat.) to sift, Men. 85 a; לְיַפּוֹת to make fair, good, BB vii. 2; לְעָרוֹת MŠ iii. 10; מְדַדֶּה, מְדַדִּין to cause to hop, Šab. xviii. 2; מְכַסֶּה Ket. vi. 5; מְעָרֶה MŠ iii. 13; מְקָרֶה to cover a ceiling, Suk. i. 8.

209. *Pu'al*: יֻפִּי to be made good, Pea vi. 6 (cf. above, § 126).

Partic.: מְהוּגָּא, L מְהוּגָהָ worn out (מחה = מהה), cf. L נימהו = נימחו Toh. iii. 1) Kel. xxiv. 17; מְנוּדֶּה excommunicated, MQ iii. 1; מְנוּפֶּה, מְנוּפָּה sifted, Men. vi. 7; מְעוּבֶּה thickened, Suk. ii. 2; מְעוּשֶּׂה forced, Git. ix. 8; מְרוּבֶּה, מְרוּבִּים, מְרוּבּוֹת many, Ḥag. i. 5.

210. *Nithpaʻel*: נִוְדְּבֶּה San. 30 a; נִתְנַסּוּ, נִתְנַסֶּה to be tried, Ab. v. 3; נִתְגַּלְּתָה to uncover, Suk. iv. 10; נִתְלַבְּתָה Šab. 37 a; נִתְפַּתְּתָה Ket. iv. 1; but also נִשְׁתַּטֵּית she is become insane, Yeb. xiv. 1; נִצְטַוֵּוִינוּ, נִצְטַוּוּ to command, Qid. 38 a, b; נִשְׁתַּהוּ to be delayed, RH iv. 4; הִתְעַנִּינוּ to afflict, 'Er. 41 a; יִתְנָאֶה to become beautiful, RH 26 a; יִתְעַלָּה to be elevated, Šab. 33 b; תִּתְיַיפִּי Taʻa. 23 b; יִתְקַשּׁוּ to be hardened, t. Nid. vi. 4; לְהִתְכַּפּוֹת Ber. iii. 4; מִתְכַּפָּה Ket. v. 8; מִתְכַּבְּפִין Taʻa. i. 1; מִתְעַנֶּה ib. iii. 3, 4.

The Causative Stem is exactly as in BH.

211. *Hiphʻil*: הִלְוָה to lend, BM v. 1; הִתְנָה to stipulate, Ket. ix. 1; הִתְרוּ to warn, Mak. i. 12; הִרְצֵתִי to discourse, t. Nid. vi. 6; תַּרְשֵׁנִי to permit, Ḥag. 14 b.

Imperat.: הַעֲלֵם, הַעַל MŠ iii. 1; הַשְׁנִינִי teach me, Lam. R. i. 6.

Infin.: לְהַקְווֹת to collect water, t. Šeq. i. 2; with elision of the ה (cf. above, § 143); לַמְחוֹת to object, BM x. 6 = לְהַמְחוֹת; לַשְׁהוֹת = לְהַשְׁהוֹת 'Er. x. 5.

Partic.: מַמְחֶה to wipe, cleanse, BB v. 10; מַמְחָה, מַמְחִין j. Pes. viii. 5; מַשְׁקִין to give to drink, 'Ed. v. 6; מַשְׁחִין Nid. 31 a; מַתְעֶה to lead astray, San. 55 a.

Note.—The denominative Hiphʻil of עני poor, preserves the י in the sing.: הֶעֱנִי 'Ar. iv. 2; יַעֲנִי Šeq. iii. 2; Ned. ix. 4, but plur.: הֶעֱנוּ Ber. 33 a; יַעֲנוּ Meʻil. 17 a.

Hophʻal: הוּמְנָה t. Pes. vii. 2; הוּקְשָׁה Num. R. 16; הוּרְצָה Yo.

7 a; הוּרְאוּ j. MQ iii. 5; הוּשְׁווּ to be like, Šab. 15 a; הוּרְשֵׁיתָ Ḥag. 13 a (from Sirach).

Partic.: מוּמְחֶה expert, Bᵉk. iv. 4; מוּפְנֶה free, Yᵉb. iii. 5; מוּטְעִין in error, RH 25 a; מוּטֶּה bent, Kel. iv. 3; מוּטִּין ib. x. 1; מוּטָּה Oh. ix. 11; מוּטּוֹת ib. xv. 3.

212. Note.—The verb היה has in the imperf. Qal the following shortened forms: יְהֵא Yo. i. 3; אֱהֵא, תְּהֵא Naz. iii. 6.[1] יְהוּ Kil. iv. 5 (L often יהוא, cf. Qoh. xi. 3). The Imperat. is formed from הוה: הֱוֵי Ab. i. 4 (cf. BH Gen. xxvii. 29; Isa. xvi. 4); plur.: הֱווּ ib. ii. 3. The partic. is always הוֹוֶה Šab. vi. 6, 10; ʻEr. i. 10, as already in BH: Qoh. ii. 22; Neh. vi. 6. Examples of the Piʻel, causing to be, are found in the partic. only: מְהַוֶּה Kᵉt. 40 b, but also מְהַיֶּה Qid. 58 a and parallels.

The rest of the verb is regular, and even for the forms given above, the regular forms are also found.

Note also the jussive forms תְּהִי, יְהִי Ab. iii. 10, &c.

(9) Verbs with Pronominal Suffixes.

213. The object of a verb can be expressed in MH, as in BH, by a suffix. The phonetic rules governing the modification of the verb when it assumes a pronominal suffix, are the same in MH as in BH. The following points may be noted:

The third sing. imperf. usually inserts the so-called *nun energicum* before the suffix of the third sing. masc. and fem. (cf. Ges.-K., § 58 i).

In ל״ה verbs the original י reappears before the suffix in the third sing. and plur. of the perfect Qal, or is softened into א (cf. § 205).

These suffixes are used in MH somewhat less frequently than in BH, their place being taken by את. The most common suffixes

---

[1] These forms also occur sometimes in Aram.; cf. Dalman, § 73 (p. 354); Nöldeke, *Syr. Gr.*, § 183 (8), but they are more common in MH.

are those of the third person sing. and plur. The suffixes of the
first person are also fairly common, especially in the sing. The
suffix of the second person sing. is much rarer, and that of the
second person plur. is exceedingly rare, just as in BH.

Examples of Verbs with Suffixes.

(1) Suffix of the First person.

214. Sing.: מְצָאַנִי to find, Yᵉb. xvi. 7 ; נְשָׁכַנִי to bite, ib. 6 ;
עֲקַצְתַנִי to sting, Ab. dᵉRN. i. 7 ; נְשָׂאתַנִי to marry, Kᵉt. ii. 1 ;
קִדְּשַׁתַּנִי to betroth, Qid. iii. 3 ; דַּנְתּוּנִי to judge ; חֲשַׁדְתּוּנִי to suspect,
Šab. 117 b ; תְּשַׁמְּשֵׁנִי to serve, Giṭ. vii. 7 ; תִּירָשֵׁנִי, יִירָשֵׁנִי BB viii. 6 ;
תּוֹצִיאֵנִי to bring forth, Bᵉr. 60 a ; גַּיְּרַנִי to make a proselyte,
Šab. 31 a.

Plur.: גְּאָלָנוּ to redeem ; הִגִּיעָנוּ, יַגִּיעֵנוּ to cause to reach, Pᵉs.
x. 5 ; לְפַדְּתָנוּ to teach, Bᵉr. ii. 8 ; יְלַמְּדֵנוּ Pᵉs. 48 b ; תַּעֲמִידֵנִי to
place ; תַּצִּילֵנִי to deliver, Bᵉr. 17 a ; רַחֲקֵנוּ to remove ; דִּשְּׁנֶנּוּ to
fatten, ib. 29 a.

(2) Suffix of the Second person.

215. Sing.: מְכָרָךְ to sell ; נְתָנָךְ to give, Tᵉr. viii. 1 ; הִגִּיעָתָךְ 'Ar.
viii. 1. ל״ה verbs: עֲשָׂאָךְ to make, Tᵉr. viii. 1 ; הֲנָאָךְ to give
pleasure, ʿAZ 16 b ; נְשָׂאתִיךְ Kᵉt. ii. 1 ; גֵּרְשֵׁךְ to divorce, Tᵉr. viii. 1 ;
קִדַּשְׁתִּיךְ Qid. iii. 1 ; יְבָרְכוּךְ to bless, Mᵉg. iv. 10 ; יְקָרְבוּךְ to bring
near; יְרַחֲקוּךְ ʿEd. v. 9 ; אַרְאָךְ to show, Qid. iii. 2 ; נַעֲשָׂךְ ʿEd. v. 6.

Plur.: The following are the only exx. found : לְהָקִימְכֶם to raise ;
לְהַחֲיוֹתְכֶם to revive, Bᵉr. 58 b ; cf. Singer, p. 319. (Contrast with
four times אֶתְכֶם in the following finite verbs.)

(3) Suffix of the Third Person.

216. Sing. Masc. Perfect: שְׁכָחוֹ to forget, Pea vii. 7 ; סִיְּידוֹ to
plaster ; כִּיְּירוֹ to decorate, ʿAZ iii. 7 ; הֲשִׂיאוֹ to move, ib. ii. 8 ; הִכָּהוּ
to strike, Pea iv. 8 ; הֶרְאָהוּ Kil. vi. 4 ; כְּוָאוֹ to burn, BQ viii. 1 ; צְלָאוֹ
to roast, Pᵉs. v. 9 ; סִיעֲרַתּוּ to carry off by storm, Kil. v. 7 ; גְּנָבַתּוּ

to steal; הַכַּחוּ Ned. iii. 2 ; טָוָאתוּ to spin, Zeb. 79 b ; נְתַתּוֹ ,נְחַתִּיו Šebu. vii. 7 ; הֲבֵאתִיו to bring, MŠ v. 12 ; שְׁכָחוּהָ Pea vii. 7 ; רָאוּהוּ to see, RH iii. 1 ; הוֹלִיכוּהוּ to lead ; הֶחֱזִירוּהוּ to return; נְתָנוּהוּ 'Er. iv. 1 ; פְּטָרְנוּהוּ to dismiss ; רְאִינוּהוּ ,הַנַּחְנוּהוּ to leave, So. ix. 6.

Imperfect : יְשִׁיבֶנּוּ to answer, Ber. v. 1 ; יְכַסֶּנּוּ to cover, Šab. iv. 2 ; יַנִּיחֶנּוּ Pes. i. 3 ; יַסְפִּידֶנּוּ to lament, MQ i. 5 ; אֲלַקְּטֶנּוּ to gather, Kil. v. 6, but also תִּתְנֶהוּ ,תְּנֵהוּ Šebu. vi. 2 ; יַחְפֶּהוּ to cover, Šebi. iv. 5 (L יְחַפֶּה).

Infin. : לְפַיְּיסוֹ to appease, Ber. 28 b ; לְיוֹרְשׁוֹ BB viii. 5 ; לִיתְנוֹ Šebu. vi. 1.

Partic. : מְלַבְּנוּ to whiten, wash ; מְנַפְּצוֹ to beat ; צוֹבְעוֹ to dye ; שׁוֹחֲטוֹ to slay ; מַפְשִׁיטוֹ to skin, Šab. vii. 2, 3 ; מַטֵּהוּ to bend, Be. i. 4 ; חוֹצֵהוּ to divide, Men. iv. 7 ; עוֹקַרְתּוֹ to uproot ; הוֹפַכְתּוֹ to over-throw, Ab. iii. 17 ; מַאֲכִילָתּוֹ to give to eat ; מְשַׁמַּשְׁתּוֹ Ket. vii. 6 ; מְנִיקַתּוֹ to suckle, Gi. vii. 6.

Sing. Fem. Perfect : דָּרְשָׁה to expound, Ber. i. 8 ; קָרְאָה to read, Meg. ii. 1, 2 ; אֵירְשָׁה to betroth ; גֵּירְשָׁה Ket. iv. 3 ; אָפְאָה to bake, MŠ ii. 3 (L אֲפָיָה); עֲשָׂאָה Suk. i. 1, 2 ; שְׁפָיָה to rub, 'AZ iii. 10 ; טְלָיָה to patch, Kel. xxiv. 7 ; פְּדָאַתָּה (L פדיתה) to redeem, Ḥal. iii. 3 ; הִקְדִּישַׁתָּה to sanctify, ib.; הִבַּתָּה Kel. vii. 11 ; עֲקַצָתָה to sting, Ab. deRN. i. 7 ; פְּדִיתִיהָ ,גֵּרַשְׁתִּיהָ ,קִדַּשְׁתִּיהָ Qid. iii. 8 ; הֶאֱדִימוּהָ to be red ; הִלְבִּינוּהָ Oh. xvii. 4 ; מִלֵּאנוּהָ to fill ; נְקַבְנוּהָ to bore ; הַנַּחְנוּהָ Šab. 29 b.

Imperf. : יִתְּנֶהָ Šab. ii. 4 ; יַפְקִיעֶנָּה to break, ib. iii. 3 ; יַסְפִּיאֶנָּה to congeal, Ter. iv. 11 ; וְיַלְבָּה ,יְכַסֶּנָּה ,יַנִּיחֶנָּה ib. viii. 8.

Infin. : לְנָטְעָה to plant, Kil. ii. 4 ; לְדוּכָה to pound, Be. 14 a ; לְנָאוֹתָה to beautify, Suk. 10 a.

Partic. : מַנִּיחֶנָּה Ber. viii. 3 ; מַשִּׂיאָה Be. iii. 7 ; מַשְׁבִּיעָה Ket. ix. 4 ; כּוֹפָה to force, ib. v. 5 ; מְטַהַרְתָּה Ḥul. iv. 4.

Plur. : רִיסְּקָן to crush, Šab. xxii. 1 ; שִׁיְּנָן to change, Pes. v. 6 ; וְזַעֲזְעָן to move, Šebi. iii. 7 ; פְּדָאָן Pea iv. 8 (L פדיין); נְתָנָתַם Kin. iii. 6 ; הוֹלַכְתָּם ,הִשְׁלַכְתָּם to throw ; נְתַתִּים Šebu. vii. 6 ; הֱזִיזוּם to

3096   H

convict of false evidence, Mak. i. 5 ; יִזְרְעָם to sow, Kil. ii. 10 ; יְזִיזֵם to move, Be. iii. 5 ; יְשׁוּפֵם Kel. xvi. 1 ; יִטְּלֵם to take, Dam. iv. 4 ; הַעֲלוּם to bring up, Suk. ii. 5 ; לְלָוִתְהָן to mix, t. Makš. iii. 2 ; Pes. 36 a ; לְמְוִּלְלָן to hem, MQ 26 a.

זוֹרְעָם Kil. ii. 9 ; מְהַנָּן to benefit ; מַפְסִידָן to cause loss, Yad. iv. 3 ; מְבַשְּׂרְתָּן to bring good tidings, So. ix. 6 ; מְסַעֲיַעְתָּן to assist, Ab. ii. 2.

III. THE NOUN

1. General Survey.

217. As in the other parts of speech, so also in the treatment of the noun MH has followed faithfully the traditions of BH. This is true of the formation of the noun and also of its inflexion. With regard to the formation of the noun, MH has retained the original forms of those BH nouns which it still uses. Further, all its new nouns are formed on the basis of the old BH ground-forms.

Noteworthy features in the MH noun formation are : (a) the wide development of the verbal nouns to replace the old BH infinitive construct, viz. the forms קְטִילָה for the Simple Stem (§ 228); קִטּוּל and קַטָּלָה for the Intensive Stem (§§ 237, 241); הַקְטֵל and הַקְטָלָה for the Causative Stem (§§ 251–2) ; (b) the more frequent use of Reduplication (§§ 244–8) ; (c) of the nomen agentis (קָטוֹל (§ 235) ; (d) of the use of the suffixes ָן‎, וֹ‎—, and ־נִי (§§ 267–8, 270) ; (e) and the various forms of the Diminutive (§ 276). But all these forms are based on BH ground-forms, and have parallels in the BH vocabulary.

218. As regards the lexical character of the MH noun, the results of our review of the MH verb (§§ 83 ff.) apply also to the MH noun, except that the noun has borrowed more freely than the verb from Aram., from Greek, and, to a less degree, from Latin. The nouns which are most common in MH are also found in BH. A number of BH nouns have disappeared in MH, especially nouns of a poetical character or of rare occurrence in BH, though common in Aram. (e.g. בְּעִיר, גֶּרֶם, &c.). The new MH nouns are usually formed from BH roots, or from old Hebrew roots not found in BH. Many of these MH nouns occur also in Aram., just as many old BH nouns occur in Aram. But the majority of such nouns are native in MH.

219. Even Aram. loan-words usually receive a Hebraic form, like רֶמֶץ, זָוִי, &c. This has also happened in the case of a number of Gk. and Latin nouns, e.g. אִצְטְלִית στολή, Yo. vii. 1 ; קִילּוֹרִית κολλύριον, Šab. viii. 1 ; מַרְגָּלִית μαργαρίτης, Ab. vi. 9 ; בַּלָּן βαλανεύς, Šᵉbi. viii. 5 ; קָרוֹן carrus, ʿAZ v. 4 ; אַכְסַנְיָא ξένος, Dam. iii. 1, &c.[1]

MH also follows BH in the other grammatical changes of the noun, viz. in the formation of the feminine (§§ 277 ff.) ; the plural (§§ 281 ff.) ; the dual (more frequent in MH than in BH, § 293) ; the construct state (§ 380), and the use of the noun with pronominal suffixes.

For the forms of nouns derived from Greek and Latin cf. Albrecht, § 82.

2. Formation of Nouns.

(1) *Nouns derived from the Simple Stem.*

(i) Ground-form *Qaṭl, Qiṭl, Quṭl.*

220. (*a*) *Qaṭl.* Strong Verb. Concrete : דֶּקֶל date-tree, Pea iv. 1 ; זֶבֶל manure, BM v. 7 ; דֶּקֶר mattock, j. Be. i. 2 ; כֶּבֶשׁ preserves, Tᵉr. ii. 6 ; לֶבֶד felt, Kil. ix. 8 ; סֶדֶק slit, Pᵉs. iii. 2 ; קֶרֶץ partition, Kel. viii. 6 ; רֶמֶץ hot ashes, Nᵉg. ix. 1. With guttural in second or third radical : בַּעַץ tin, Kel. xxx. 3 ; נַחַר jetty, Oh. viii. 2 ; שַׁחַת fodder, Pea ii. 1 ; נֶקַע cleft, Kil. v. 4 ; קֶלַח stalk, Pea iii. 3 ; שֶׁבַח improvement, MŠ ii. 1.

[1] Cf. Krauss, i, §§ 326 ff. ; Albrecht, § 82 g–h.

Abstract: חֶנֶק strangulation, San. vii. 1 ; פֶּרֶךְ cracking, 'Or. vii. 7 ; וַעַד assembly, Ab. i. 4 ; צַעַר pain, BQ viii. 1 ; קֶבַע permanence, Yo. vi. 3 ; שֶׁבַח praise, ib. iii. 9, 10.

ע׳׳ע, ע׳׳ו : גַּיִס troop, Pes. iii. 7 ; סַיִף sword, Šab. vi. 4 ; נוֹי beauty, 'AZ iii. 4.

ע׳׳ע : חַף pivot of door, Šab. viii. 6 ; סַם spice, Giṭ. ii. 3 ; גַּס gross, Ab. iv. 7.

ל׳׳ה : גְּמִי reed-grass, Šab. viii. 2 ; טְנִי basket, Kel. xii. 3 ; לְחִי cheek, board, 'Er. i. 2.

Fem.: חַרְבָּה knife, Šebi. viii. 7 ; צֵחָנָה offensive matter, Ter. x. 1 ; גַּפָּה stone fence, Pea iv. 2 ; אַשְׁפָּה dung-hill, BM ii. 3 ; שַׁעֲוָה wax, Šab. ii. 1 ; שַׁקְיָא irrigation, Ter. x. 11 (L has the masc. form : שַׁקְי).

221. (b) *Qiṭl.* אֵבֶר limb, Šab. viii. 1 ; חֵלֶשׁ lot, ib. xxiii. 2 ; סֵדֶר order, Yo. i. 3 ; סֵבֶר countenance, Ab. i. 15 ; עֵסֶק business, ib. iv. 10 ; עֵקֶל bale for pressing, Ma'a. i. 7 ; דִּיר shed, 'Er. iv. 1 ; צִיר hinge, ib. xi. 2 ; פִּיַּח ¹ phlegm ; נִיַע mucus BQ 3 b ; זִיק spark, BQ vi. 6 ; ל׳׳ה : רְעִי excrements, Kel. xvii. 2.

Fem.: אִכְפַּת pressure, BM iii. 7 (with older fem. termination אִכְפָּה = ת—֜ j. So. v. 2 ; Sirach xlvi. 5, 16); צִנְעָה privacy, Pes. i. 3 ; שִׁכְחָה forgetfulness, Pea iv. 6. ל׳׳ה : גְּנוּת disgrace, Pes. x. 4 ; רְשׁוּת permission, ib. iii. 7.

222. (c) *Quṭl.* The vowel *u* is represented by וֹ. בּוֹרֶךְ knee, Kel. xxii. 2 ; דּוֹפֶן side, Ker. i. 5 ; חוֹמֶשׁ fifth part, Yo. vii. 1 ; סוֹרֶג lattice work, Mid. ii. 3 ; עוֹקֶץ point, Tam. iii. 1 ; רוֹמֶב broth, Pes. vii. 2 ; אוֹנֶס force, Kil. vii. 2 ; גּוֹדֶל full age ; קוֹטֶן minority, Ket. ii. 11 ; כּוֹשֶׁר fitness, Yeb. viii. 4 ; צוֹרֶךְ need, Ab. ii. 3 ; מוֹהַל (or מוֹחַל) secretion, Ṭoh. ix. 2 ; פּוֹתַח opening, Kel. xi. 3 ; רוֹבַע quarter, Oh. ii. 1 ; דּוֹחַק need, Ab. ii. 3 ; כּוֹרַח force, ib. iv. 22.

ע׳׳ו : דּוּר rim, Kel. xvi. 3 ; כּוּךְ sepulchre, MQ i. 6 ; כּוּי a kind of

---

¹ From כחח, by assonance with ניע, with which it is always combined.

antelope, Bik. ii. 8; בּוּר uncultivated, Ab. ii. 5; נוֹחַ pleasing,
ib. 10; ע"ע : רוֹק spittle, Yeb. xii. 6; זוֹל cheapness, MŠ iv. 1; קוֹל
lightness, Ḥal. iv. 7; ל"ה : קוֹשִׁי hardness, Nid. iv. 6; שׁוֹפִי ease, ib.;
יוֹפִי [1] beauty, Suk. iv. 5.

Fem.: זוֹחֲמָה filth, Ter. x. 1; חוּלְדָּה mole, Kel. xv. 6; עָרְלָה
forbidden fruit of a tree under four years old (cf. Lev. xix. 23),
'Or. i. 1.

ע"ו : חוֹבָה duty, San. iv. 1; עוּקָה cavity, Ma'a. i. 7.

ע"ע : גוּמָה, hole, Ḥul. ii. 9; קוּפָּה basket, Kel. viii. 2.

ל"ה : חוּלְיָה limb, looseness, Kel. v. 10.

223. To this ground-form belong also nouns in which the
characteristic vowel has been moved forward to the second radical:
Qaṭl, דְּבַשׁ honey, Ter. xi. 3; גְּמַר completion, Šab. xxii. 2; צְבַת
tongs, Ab. v. 6; ל"ה : הֲבַאי (L הווי) vanity, Ned. iii. 1; חֲשָׁאי
modesty, privacy, Šeq. v. 6; כְּדָאי worthy, Nid. 9 b; פְּנַאי leisure,
'AZ v. 6; תְּנַאי condition, Qid. iii. 4.

Qiṭl: בְּאֵר well, 'Er. x. 14; זְאֵב wolf, BQ i. 4. Fem.: כְּרֵישָׁה
leek, Šab. viii. 5.[2] Cf. Ges.-K., § 84 A e.

Some texts point in this fashion many nouns which properly
belong to the regular *Qaṭl* type, like קֶבַע, פְּלַג half, Ber. iv. 1, &c.
The extension of this form by the scribes is no doubt due to the
influence of Aram., in which this is the regular form for the *Qaṭl*
(cf. Nöldeke, *Syr. Gr.*, §§ 93–4). So, sometimes, in BH: גְּבַר
beside גֶּבֶר; חֲדַר and חֶדֶר, &c. Cf. Stade, § 191 c.

(ii) Ground-form *Qaṭal, Qaṭil, Qaṭul.*

224. (a) *Qaṭal*: אָבָק dust, Šab. iii. 3; בָּקָר kine, San. iii. 2; זָרָז
girdle, Kel. xxiii. 2; כְּרָךְ city, Ber. ix. 4; נָגָר bolt, Zab. iv. 3; רְקָב
rottenness, Naz. vii. 2.

---

[1] This full form is the only one found in MH, even when not in pause.

[2] כְּרֵישָׁה belly, cited by Albrecht, § 41, does not belong here. It is כְּרֵיסָה,
from כֶּרֶשׂ = כֶּרֶס; cf. כְּרֵיסוֹ his belly, Šab. 151 b.

ע"ע: חָלָל defiled priest, Qid. iv. 6 (from Lev. xx. 7); מָלַל hem,
Kel. xxviii. 7; פְּקָק stopper, Šab. xvii. 7.

ל"ה: טָלֶה lamb, Tam. iii. 3; יָפֶה worth, BQ viii. 1; נָאֶה beautiful,
Ab. iii. 7; שָׁוֶה worth, BQ iv. 1; עָנָיו humble, Bᵉr. 6 b.

Fem.: הֲלָכָה rule, Šab. i. 4; חֲזָקָה possession, usucaption, BB
iii. 1; חֲזָרָה return, Yᵉb. xiii. 6; סְבָכָה net work, hairdress, Nᵉg.
xi. 11; עֲדָשָׁה lentil, Šab. x. 5; צְוָחָה cry, Bᵉr. ix. 3; חֲטֶרֶת hump,
Hul. ix. 2; מְלֵחָה saltiness, Oh. iii. 7; צַלֶּקֶת scar, Nᵉg. ix. 2;[1]
ע"ו: נָפָה sieve, Šab. viii. 2; זְוָעָה earthquake, Bᵉr. ix. 2.

ע"ע: גְּבָבָה rakings, Šab. iii. 1; חֲרָרָה cake, ib. i. 10; סְכָכָה
covering, overhanging boughs, Naz. vii. 3; קְטָטָה strife, Yᵉb. xv. 1;
שְׂרָרָה dominion, Mak. ii. 8.

ל"ה: הֲנָאָה enjoyment, benefit, ʿAZ ii. 3; לְוָיָה escort, So. ix. 6;
רְאָיָה proof, Šab. viii. 7.

225. (*b*) *Qaṭil*: גָּדֵר stone fence, Pea ii. 3; חָבֵר associate, Dam.
ii. 3; כָּרֵס belly, j. San. iii. 9; כָּתֵף shoulder, Šᵉbi. iii. 9; סָפֵק
doubt, Yo. viii. 6; בָּטֵל nought, Kᵉt. ix. 1; טָפֵל subordinate, Bᵉr.
vi. 7; כָּשֵׁר proper, legal, Šab. vii. 3.

Fem.: אֲבֵדָה lost property, BM ii. 7; גְּוֵלָה robbed property,
Yᵉb. xv. 7; בְּרֵיכָה pond; פְּסֵיקָה pool, MQ 4 a; עֲרֵבָה kneading
trough, Pes. iii. 2; קְדֵרָה pot, ʿOr. ii. 15; דְּלֵקָה conflagration, Šab.
xvi. 1; חֲשֵׁכָה darkness, ib. i. 3; עֲבֵרָה transgression, Yo. viii. 8.

226. (*c*) *Qaṭul*. The vowel *ŭ* = *ŏ* is represented by ו, ֹ.

רְמוֹב birdtrap, Kel. xxiii. 5; חָשׁוֹךְ dark, Bᵉk. vii. 8; יָרוֹק yellow,
ʿEd. v. 6; מָתוֹק sweet, ʿEr. 18 b; עָגוֹל round, Nid. viii. 4; עָמוֹק
deep, t. Nᵉg. i. 5.

(iii) Ground-form *Qaṭāl*, *Qaṭil*, *Qaṭul*.

227. (*a*) *Qaṭāl*, with *ā* obscured into *ŏ*. Concretes are rare:
מָרוֹר bitter herbs, Pᵉs. ii. 6. Usually abstract nouns and adjectives

---

[1] רְכָבָה, Šᵉbi. ii. 6, cited by Albrecht, § 42, is an error. The text has
הַרְכָּבָה grafting, a verbal noun; cf. below, § 252.

derived from BH, e.g. כָּבוֹד honour, Ab. ii. 10; שָׁלוֹם peace, ib.
i. 12; גָּדוֹל great, ib. vi. 5; קָדוֹשׁ holy, ib. v. 4; טָהוֹר pure,
Kel. xii. 2.

228. (*b*) *Qaṭíl*: אָרִיחַ lath, 'Er. i. 3; אָרִיג web, Šab. xiii. 1;
בָּזִיךְ dish, Yo. ii. 5; חָרִיץ trench, Kil. v. 3; יָרִיד a fair, 'AZ 13 a;
אָסִיף gathering; זָמִיר pruning; חָרִישׁ ploughing, Sifra 105 b, c, d;
מָסִיק olive gathering, Ḥal. iii. 9; זָהִיר careful, Ab. i. 9; חָבִיב
beloved, ib. ii. 10; צָרִיךְ necessary, Šab. ii. 7; רָגִיל accustomed,
Yo. i. 3; בָּקִי לְ"ה: experienced, San. vii. 2; נָקִי clean, t. Ṭoh.
iii. 8.

The Fem. form *Qeṭílā* is exceedingly common in MH as a
nomen actionis for the *Qal*, taking the place of the old BH construct
infinitive. The form is also found in BH with the same significance, both in early and in late texts. Thus, שְׁרִיקוֹת Jud. v. 16;
אֲכִילָה 1 Kings xix. 8; שְׁגִיאוֹת Psa. xix. 13; שְׁחִיטָה 2 Chron.
xxx. 7; יְגִיעָה Qoh. xii. 12; perhaps also פְּצִירָה filing, 1 Sam.
xiii. 21. In ע"וּ: קִימָה Lam. iii. 63, and in a derived concrete
sense: מְלִילָה Deut. xxiii. 26; בִּיאָה entry, Ezek. viii. 5. It is also
found in Sirach: גְּוִיעָה xxxviii. 16; שְׁעִיָּה ib. 25; שְׁקִידָה ib. 26.
The form is used in Ethiopic in exactly the same way as in MH,
cf. Dillmann, *Eth. Gr.*, § 124; Barth, *Nominalbildung*, p. 137.
In Aram., however, it occurs only occasionally in Jewish dialects,[1]
in which it is most probably borrowed from MH. The fact that
in earlier BH it occurs only in the Song of Deborah and in the
story of Elijah may, perhaps, tend to show that it was originally
a Northern dialectal form, which was received into the literary
language only after it had established itself in the spoken language.
From the latter it may have descended into MH.

Concrete nouns in this form are comparatively few in MH, as
compared with the extremely numerous examples of abstract
nouns of a verbal nature. This seems to show that the concrete

---

[1] Cf. Dalman, p. 158, 5 and foot-note.

significance is only secondary, and that it was derived from the original abstract meaning; cf. בִּיאָה, in BH, cited above.

Exx. of concrete nouns: חֲתִיכָה piece, Ḥul. vii. 5; כְּרִיכָה bundle, BM ii. 1; מְלִילָה parched ear of corn, Maʻa. iv. 5; מְשִׁיחָה cord, Kil. ix. 9; סְרִידָה bag, Kel. viii. 3; עֲנִיבָה loop, Pes. 11 a; פְּתִילָה wick, Šab. ii. 1; קִיחָה = לְקִיחָה handle, Kel. xvi. 4.

ע״ע: חֲגִיגָה festival sacrifice, Ḥag. i. 2; חֲצִיצָה intervening object, BQ 82 a; כְּפִיפָה basket, So. ii. 1. נִבְיָה : ל״ה leaf, ʻAZ iii. 8; רְטִיָּה plaster, ʻEr. x. 13.

Abstracts (*nomina actionis*) can be formed at will from every verb. Exx.: אֲכִילָה eating, MŠ i. 7; בְּדִיקָה searching, Pes. i. 1; גְּמִיאָה quaffing, Šab. viii. 1; דְּרִיסָה treading, Šebi. v. 2; דְּרִישָׁה inquiry; חֲקִירָה investigation, San. iv. 1, 5; סְמִיכָה laying on of hands; קְמִיצָה taking of a handful; מְלִיקָה pinching bird's head, Qid. i. 8; רְחִיצָה washing, Yo. iii. 1; שְׁחִיטָה slaying, ib. i. 7; קְרִיאָה reading, Ber. i. 1; קִיחָה (= לְקִיחָה) taking, Sifra 45 c; Qid. 2 a; יְצִיאָה going out, Šab. i. 1; יְלִידָה = לִידָה birth, Ket. iv. 3.

ע״ו: בִּיאָה coming, Pes. ix. 4; טִיחָה daubing, Neg. xii. 6; לִישָׁה kneading, Men. v. 2; מִיתָה death, Yo. viii. 8; סִיכָה anointing, Šab. ix. 4 (L יסיכה: so elsewhere, e.g. Yo. viii. 1).

ע״ע: בְּלִילָה mingling, Men. vi. 3; חֲפִיפָה cleansing the head, MŠ ii. 3; פְּתִיתָה crumbling, Men. vi. 4; רְקִיקָה spitting, Ber. ix. 5.

ל״ה: אֲפִיָּה baking, Men. v. 2; דְּחִיָּה pushing, Yo. vi. 6; כְּרִיָּה digging, BQ v. 6; עֲלִיָּה going up, Šeq. viii. 2; צְלִיָּה roasting, Pes. vi. 1; רְבִיָּה increasing; פְּרִיָּה fruitfulness, Yeb. vi. 7; שְׁתִיָּה drinking, Yo. viii. 1.

A number of nouns add the abstract suffix וּת— (cf. below, § 272) to strengthen the abstract significance, e.g. אֲרִיסוּת tenancy, Pea v. 5; גְּמִילוּת doing, ib. i. 1; פְּרִישׁוּת separation, Ab. iii. 13; שְׁתִיקוּת silence, Giṭ. iv. 8, &c.

229. (c) *Qaṭûl.* To this form belong the Passive Participles *Qal*, and verbal adjectives like חָמוּר weighty, strict, Kel. i. 4;

עָרוּם subtle, So. iii. 41; פָּחוּת[1] less, Yo. ii. 5. Further, nouns: בָּחוּר young man, Ta'a. iv. 8; חָלוּק smooth, shirt, Šab. x. 3; חָרוּב carob tree, Šebi. vii. 5; חָתוּל cat, BQ 18 b.

Fem.: בְּתוּלָה virgin, Ket. i. 1; חֲבוּרָה company, Ber. vii. 51; חֲלוּדָה rust, Kel. xiii. 5; סְעוּדָה meal, Ber. vi. 6; שְׁמוּעָה report, Ber. ix. 2.

To this class may, perhaps, be reckoned also fem. nouns with sharpening of the third radical: כְּהוּנָּה priesthood, Ab. vi. 5; כְּתוּבָּה writ, marriage settlement, Qid. ii. 5; קְדוּשָּׁה holiness, RH iv. 5 cf. Barth, op. cit., § 95.

(iv) Ground-form *Qᵉṭâl, Qᵉṭîl, Qᵉṭûl*.

230. (*a*) *Qᵉṭâl*. אֱלָל offal, Ḥul. ix. 1; חֶטֶם nose ring, Šab. v. 1; כְּתָב writing, Ket. ii. 3; סְיָג hedge, Ab. i. 2; סְיָח young ass, BB v. 3; פְּרָס reward, Ab. i. 4; שְׂרָף resin, 'Or. i. 7; שְׁיָר, שְׁאָר remainder, So. vii. 7; סְתָם undefined, 'AZ i. 5; פְּגָם blemish, Mᵉil. v. 1; שְׁטָר document, Šebi. x. 1. עֲ"ע: כְּלָל general rule, Ber. vi. 2.

With *â* obscured into *ô*: בְּכוֹר first-born, Zᵉb. v. 8; חֲמוֹר ass, Bᵉk. i. 2; חָסוֹם muzzle, Kel. xvi. 7; טְחוֹל milt, Ḥul. iii. 2. עֲ"ע: צְרוֹר knot, Kel. xxvi. 4; צְנוֹן radish, Kil. i. 5.

Fem.: יְרוֹקָה sea-weed, Šab. ii. 1; עֲבוֹדָה service, Kil. vi. 1; שְׂעוֹרָה barley corn, 'Ed. vi. 3. Segolate forms[2]: כְּתוֹבֶת tattooing, Mak. iii. 6; נְחֹשֶׁת copper, Kel. viii. 3; נְסֹרֶת chips, Šab. iv. 1; שְׁחוֹלֶת metal shavings, Kel. xi. 3.

231. (*b*) *Qᵉṭîl*. בְּרִיד spade, Kel. xxix. 7; גְּזִיר log, Yo. ii. 5; גְּרִיד dry season, BM v. 10; גְּרִים pounded grain, Kel. xvii. 12; חֲזִיר swine, Ḥul. ix. 2; טְפִיחַ pitcher, Šab. xvii. 6; מְלִיחַ pickled food, Nᵉd. ii. 4; סְנִיף attachment, Mᵉn. xi. 6; פְּקִיעַ wick, Šeq. v. 1;

---

[1] Some texts point פַּחוּת; cf. Krauss, *MGWJ.*, li, p. 57.

[2] Cf. Stade, § 208 c; Ges.-K., § 84 A n.

קְמִיעַ amulet, Kel. xxiii. 1; שְׁבִיל path, Pea ii. 1; שְׁלִיל embryo, Ḥul. vii. 1; פְּנִים[1] interior, Šab. i. 1.

232. (c) *Qeṭāl*: גְּבוּל border, Šeq. vii. 3; כְּבוּל hair net, Šab. vi. 1; צְלוּב gallows, Šab. vi. 10; תְּחוּב shoot, t. Šebi. i. 9; תְּחוּם boundary, 'Er. iii. 4; מְלוּג usufruct, Yeb. vii. 1; פְּטוּר discharge, Giṭ. ix. 3; פְּסוּל disqualification, Yo. i. 1; שְׁבוּת resting, Pes. vi. 2.

(v) Ground-form *Qáṭāl, Qáṭīl, Qáṭūl.*

233. (a) *Qáṭāl*, the *á* obscured to *ŏ*: חוֹטֶם nose, Bek. vi. 4; חוֹתָל wrapper, Kel. xvi. 11; חוֹתָם seal, Šab. viii. 5; שׁוֹבָךְ dovecot, ib. xxiv. 3; שׁוֹפָר trumpet, RH iii. 3.

234. (b) *Qáṭīl*. To this form belongs the Active Participle *Qal* of transitive verbs. Also a number of nouns of participial origin, e.g. סוֹחֵר merchant, Šeq. vii. 2; פּוֹשֵׁר lukewarm water, Šab. xx. 3; צוֹנֵן cold water, ib. iii. 4; קוֹחֵז (= קוֹצֵץ) clods, MŠ v. 1.

Fem.: חוֹצֶלֶת mat, 'Ed. iii. 4; יוֹתֶרֶת lobe; כּוֹתֶבֶת date, Yo. viii. 2.

235. (c) *Qáṭūl*. To this class belong the following *nomina agentis* with *ū* modified to *ŏ*: טָחוֹן miller, Dam. iii. 5; BQ 99 b; BB 93 b; לָעוֹז (so L), לָעוֹזוֹת speaker of foreign tongue, Meg. ii. 1; סָרוֹק woolcomber, Kel. xxvi. 5; סָרוֹקוֹת ib. xii. 2: the following occur in the plural only: דָּרוֹכוֹת wine pressers, Ter. iii. 4; חָכוֹרוֹת tenants, Bik. i. 2; גְּרוֹסוֹת grist makers, Men. x. 4; דְּשׁוֹשׁוֹת groat makers (דִּישׁ = דְּשׁשׁ) MQ ii. 5; מָסוֹרוֹת informers, 'AZ 26 b; מְשׁוֹחוֹת measurers, surveyors, 'Er. iv. 11; לְקוֹטוֹת gatherers, BM 72 b; t. BM vi. 1; מְשׁוֹשׁוֹת j. Pea viii. 1 (cf. § 177, note); לְקוֹחוֹת purchasers, Ket. viii. 1: the sing., however, is always לוֹקֵחַ. This form may, perhaps, be due to a deliberate change of spelling by the scribes, who mistook the form לָקוֹחַ for the participle passive לָקוּחַ. To the ignorance of the scribes are also due the forms טוֹחֵן, סוֹרֵק, and לוֹעֵז, in some texts.

The form *Qáṭūl* is also found in the following names of instru-

---

[1] This is the traditional pronunciation; cf. BH. 1 Kings vi. 29.

ments : דְּקוֹר a borer, Kel. xiv. 3 ; מָחוֹק an instrument for levelling a measure of grain, ib. xvii. 6 ; שָׂחוֹר a razor, ib. xiii. 1 ; סְמוֹכוֹת supporters, artificial legs, Šab. vi. 8 ; רָחוֹשׁ reptile-shaped ornament, t. ʻAZ v. 2. Perhaps also אָרוֹם timbrel, Kel. xv. 6 (L, but So. ix. 14 : אירום, also in L).

The form is very common in Aram. (قَطُّولَا), but it also occurs in BH nearly as often as in MH, viz. יָקוֹשׁ, חָמוֹץ, בָּחוֹן, אָמוֹן, רָזוֹן, עָשׁוֹק ; perhaps also צָרוֹף a refiner, Jer. vi. 29 ; the fem. בְּגוֹדָה, perhaps also שְׂדוֹרָה (Psa. cxxxvii. 9, for שְׂדוּרָה), and as *nomen instrumenti* : תָּקוֹעַ (Ezek. vii. 4).

236. (vi) Ground-form *Qâṭâl* : גּוּדָל thumb, Nid. viii. 1 ; with prosthetic א : אֶגוּדָל Yo. ii. 1 ; כּוּפָּח small oven, Šab. iii. 2 ; שׁוּעָל fox, Šab. vi. 10.

(2) *Nouns derived from the Intensive Stem.*

(i) Ground-form *Qăṭṭal, Qăṭṭil, Qăṭṭul.*

237. (*a*) *Qaṭṭâl, Qaṭṭâl* : chiefly *nomina opificum*, describing the occupation or profession of the substantive : אַנָּס robber, Kil. vii. 6 ; בְּהָם cattle-driver, j. Pᵉs. i. 1 ; בַּקָּר cowherd, j. Be. v. 3 ; נַמָּל camel-driver, Qid. iv. 13 ; חַמָּר ass-driver ; סַפָּן sailor ; סַפָּר barber, ib. ; גַּנָּב thief, BM iii. 1 ; כַּתָּף porter, Kel. xii. 2 ; נַגָּר carpenter, t. BQ vi. 25 ; פַּטָּם poulterer, ʻEr. x. 9 ; צַמָּר wool dealer, ib. ; קַדָּר potter, BQ iii. 4.

With ר in the second radical : הָרָג murderer ; חָרָם confiscator, Nᵉd, iii. 4 ; גָּרֵד weaver, Kil. ix. 10.

ע″ו, ז″ע : רַוָּק bachelor, Qid. iv. 13 ; בַּיָּר well sinker, Šᵉbi. viii. 5 ; דַּיָּן judge, Pea viii. 9 ; חַיָּיט tailor, Šab. i. 3 ; טַיָּל man of leisure, Kᵉt. v. 7.

ל″ה, with ◌ַ in the second radical for ◌ָ, in Aram. fashion : בַּנַּאי builder, Kel. xiv. 3 ; גַּבַּאי collector, Dam. iii. 1. Adjectives : דְּמַּאי suspect, Dam. i. 1 ; וַדַּאי certain, ib. iv. 4 ; זַכַּאי innocent,

Ab. i. 8 ; חַשָּׁאי silent, modest, Šᵉq. v. 6 ; לַוּי accompanying, Nᵉg. xiv. 6 ; רַשָּׁאי permitted, Šab. xxiii. 3.

Fem. Concrete : יַבָּשָׁה dry land, Giṭ. 56 b ; עֲבָבָה rim, 'AZ v. 1 ; and with ת at the end : בַּלֶּשֶׁת¹ reconnoitring troop, t. Be. ii. 6 ; גַּמֶּלֶת caravan of camels ; חֲמֶרֶת caravan of asses, San. x. 5 ; יַבֶּלֶת wart, 'Er. x. 3 ; כַּבֶּשֶׁת pressed vegetables, t. Šᵉbi. iv. 16 ; כַּוֶּרֶת beehive, Šᵉbi. viii. 10 ; קָרַחַת bald, empty space, Kil. iv. 1.

Abstracts, including *nomina actionis*, chiefly with ה‑ָ : בַּטָּלָה idleness, Ab. iii. 4 ; הַוָיָה being, Mᵉkil. (Weiss), 85 ; Qid. 5 a ; יַבָּבָה cry, RH iv. 9 ; כַּוָנָה intention, 'Er. iv. 4 ; כַּפָּרָה atonement, Nᵉg. ii. 1 ; סַכָּנָה danger, Bᵉr. iv. 4 ; עֲבָבָה or עַקָּבָה detention, 'AZ v. 7 ; קַבָּלָה reception, Zᵉb. i. 6. Cf. BH בַּקָּרָה, בַּקָּשָׁה, נְאָצָה, &c. ; see Ges.-K., § 84, в e.

The form is comparatively rare in MH, as in BH, and cannot like the other verbal nouns *Qiṭṭûl* (§ 241) and *Qᵉṭîlā* (§ 228) be formed at will.

238. (*b*) *Qaṭṭil, Qaṭṭíl*: the infinitive of Piʻel : יַקִּיר notable, Yo. vi. 4 ; כַּשִּׁיל axe, BQ x. 10 ; סַכִּין knife, ib. iv. 9 ; פַּצִּים board, Šab. viii. 5 ; צַדִּיק righteous, Ab. i. 2.

239. (*c*) *Qaṭṭûl, Qaṭṭúl*: חַדּוּד point, Kel. ii. 9 ; חַנּוּן gracious, Šab. 133 b ; טַבּוּר navel, Šab. xviii. 3 ; כַּדּוּר ball, Kel. x. 4 ; עַמּוּד pillar, Bᵉr. i. 2 ; שַׁפּוּד spit, 'AZ v. 12.

Fem. : חַבּוּרָה wound, BQ viii. 1 ; בַּצּוֹרֶת drought, Ab. v. 8 ; מַסּוֹרֶת tradition, ib. iii. 13.

(ii) Ground-form *Qiṭṭal, Qiṭṭil, Qiṭṭul, Qiṭṭól*.

240. (*a*) *Qiṭṭāl, Qiṭṭál*: אִכָּר husbandman, 'Arak. vi. 3 ; עִיקָּר root, principal, Bᵉr. vi. 7.

(*b*) *Qiṭṭil, Qiṭṭíl*: דִּיבֵּר speech, Mᵉkil. 5 ; fem. : דִּבְּרוֹת BQ 54 b ; כִּסֵּא chair, Tam. i. 1 ; רִבִּית usury RH i. 8 ; עִדִּית choice land, Giṭ. v. 1. The form is further used, as in BH, to express a

¹ Some texts have בולשת, a participial form, § 234.

physical defect: אִלֵּם dumb, Ter. i. 6; גִּבֵּן hunchback, Bek. vii. 2; גִּדֵּם with hands cut off; חִגֵּר lame; חֵרֵשׁ deaf, San. viii. 4; עִקֵּל with crooked feet; צִמֵּם with large ears; צִמֵּעַ with small ears, Bek. vii. 4, 6; קִפֵּחַ lanky, ib.;[1] קִטֵּעַ crippled, Šab. vi. 8; and by analogy: פִּקֵּחַ hearing, Yeb. xiv. 1.

241. (c) *Qiṭṭûl.* This form is widely used as a verbal noun for Pi'el, and can be formed at will from any verb. It has primarily an abstract significance, but is also found in concretes in a derived sense.

Exx.: אִיסּוּר prohibition, 'AZ ii. 3; בִּיטּוּל idling, interruption, Šab. xvi. 1; גִּדּוּל growth, Ber. vi. 3; דִּיבּוּק joining together, Ab. vi. 5; הִילּוּךְ walking, Yo. ii. 3; חִיבּוּר joining, Kil. ix. 10; יִבּוּם levirate marriage, Yeb. i. 1; כִּבּוּד honouring, Pea i. 1; לִימּוּד learning, Ab. vi. 5; נִסּוּךְ libation, Suk. iv. 9; סִידּוּק cleaving, Pes. iii. 5; זֵירוּד trimming, Šebi. ii. 3; עֵירוּף confusion, Ber. v. 4; פֵּירוּשׁ explanation, 'AZ i. 5; צִיהוּב gilding, Ḥul. i. 5.

עִוּוּת perverting Ab. v. 8; קִיּוּם confirming, Giṭ. ii. 5; שִׁיּוּר (cf. above, § 162) remainder, Ker. ii. 5; תִּיחוּחַ crushing, Oh. xviii. 9.

בִּיטּוּי vain talk, Šebu. iii. 9; וִידּוּי confession, San. ii. 6; מִלּוּי filling, Dam. vi. 5; עִינּוּי afflicting, Ab. v. 8; רִפּוּי healing, BQ viii. 1.

Concrete: גִּידּוּלִים products, Ber. 40 b; חִילּוּף exchange, relay, Ber. iii. 1; טִינּוּף filth, Bek. iii. 1; יִשּׁוּב civilized world, Qid. i. 10; לְמוּדִים boards, MQ ii. 2; חִיסּוּם steel edge, Kel. xiii. 4; עִגּוּל round cake, BM ii. 1; עֵירוּב *'erub,* 'Er. iii. 2; צִבּוּר heap, BM ii. 2; שִׁיעוּר measure, Pea i. 1.

פֵּירוּר crumb, Šab. xxiv. 3; חִיפּוּי wrapping, Kel. xvi. 8; כִּסּוּי cover, Šab. xvii. 8; קִיפּוּי froth, Ter. iv. 11.

Fem.: בְּכּוּרָה early fig, Ter. iv. 6.

The form is found in a number of technical terms in the plural

---

[1] So יִיתֵּר one with superfluous fingers or toes, ib., in L, for יָתֵר in edd.

only : אֵירוּסִין betrothal, Yᵉb. vi. 4 ; נִשּׂוּאִין matrimony Kᵉt. i. 4 ; קִידּוּשִׁין betrothal ; גֵּירוּשִׁין divorce, Yᵉb. iii. 8 ; בֵּירוּרִין arbitration ; מֵיאוּנִין annulment of minority marriage, BM i. 8 ; זֵירוּזִין urgings (of vows), Nᵉd. iii. 1 ; also יִסּוּרִין suffering, Bᵉr. 5 a.

The form is found in BH both as abstract and concrete, in the sing. and in the plural : גְּדוּפִים, לִמּוּד, שִׁקּוּץ, צִפּוּי, שַׁלּוּם, חִבּוּק, מִלֻּאִים, &c. Cf. Ges.-K., § 84 B i ; Stade, § 228. So in Sirach : חִמּוּד xiv. 14 ; יִסּוּר xl. 29 ; לִמּוּד xli. 28 ; נִסּוּי xxxii. 1 ; xliv. 20.

242. (*d*) *Qiṭṭōl, Qiṭṭôl* : גִּבּוֹר mighty, Ab. iv. i ; גִּיחוֹר crimson red, Bᵉk. vii. 6 ; יִלּוֹד born, Ab. iv. 21 ; נִיפּוֹל young birds fallen out of their nest, BB ii. 6 ; נִיצּוֹץ spark, t. Yo. ii. 3 ; צִנּוֹר pipe, Miq. iv. 1 ; קִיפּוֹף long-tailed ape, Bᵉk. 8 a ; שִׁכּוֹר drunkard, Bᵉk. vii. 6.

Fem. : בְּקּוֹרֶת inquiry, Kᵉt. xi. 5 ; טִינּוּפֶת filth, BB vi. 2 ; קִיבּוֹרֶת contract labour, t. MQ ii. 5 ; קִיבּוֹרֶת biceps, Mᵉn. 37 a, b ; שִׁיבּוֹלֶת ear of corn, Pea v. 2.

243. (iii) Ground-form *Quṭṭal* : שׁוּתָּף partner, Pᵉs. viii. 1 (cf. Sirach xl. 24) ; אוּמָּן artisan, 'AV v. 7 ; עוּבָּר embryo, Ḥul. iv. 1.

(3) *Nouns formed by Reduplication.*

244. (i) Reduplication of the Third radical. These have the vowel *a* in the second syllable, and are mostly of a diminutive significance.

Exx. : גַּבְלוּל lump of dough, j. Ḥal. iii. 1 ; דַּבְלוּל excrescence, t. Kel. BM vii. 11 ; קַמְצוּץ compressed, bent up, j. So. ix. 1 ; סְמַרְטוּט (Saph'el of מרט to pluck, cf. above, § 149), lappet, Šab. xi. 2, and perhaps also זַאטוּט or זַעטוּט (= זַטוּט from זוּט) young man, Mᵉg. 9 a.[1]

---

[1] Kohut, iii. 283 f., holds that זַעטוּטֵי is an error for נַאטוּטֵי = νεώτατοι. The noun is also found in the Arabic dialect of Iraq, cf. Brockelmann, *Grundriss*, i, § 172 a.

The other examples are all fem. :

עֲרֻבּוּבְיָה mixture, confusion, Kil. v. 1 ; קַרְוְיָה (from קרה) hollow
pumpkin, Pa. v. 3.   With the termination ־ִית : אַדְמוּמִית redness,
Ḥul. 87 b ; לַבְנוּנִית whiteness, Nᵉg. iv. 4 ; שְׁחַרוּרִית blackness,
ugliness, Taʿa. 23 b ; מַשְׁפּוּבִית leading ram, BQ 52 b ; רַקְבּוּבִית
rottenness, Yo. 38 b ; שַׁמְנוּנִית oily substance, Be. 28 a.

Diminutives : גַּבְשׁוּשִׁית a hillock, heap, Šab. 23 b ; גּוּמָּמִית little
hole, t. Miq. iii. 4 ; גַּנּוּנִית little garden, BB 68 a, b ; דְּגוּנִית a light
fisher-boat (contracted to דּוּגִית), BB 78 b ; זַרְבּוּבִית little pipe,
Lev. R. 5 ; Num. R. 10 ; עֲפְרוּרִית little dust, BB 93 b ; שְׁלוּלִית
pool, Oh. xvi. 5 ; תְּלוּלִית hillock, ib. 7.

Cf. BH נְעֵצוּץ, נְאֲפוּפִים, שַׁעֲרוּרִיָה, &c., Stade, § 231.

A BH parallel to the diminutive significance of reduplicated
form is to be found in שְׁחַרְחֹרֶת Cant. i. 6, which can only mean
blackish, dark.   Perhaps also יְרַקְרַק, אֲדַמְדָּם [1] Lev. xiii. 42, 43 ;
אֲסַפְסוּף rabble, Num. xi. 4, and פִּרְחָח low brood, Job xxx. 12
(cf. פִּרְחֵי כְהוּנָה young priests, Yo. i. 7 ; Tam. i. 1), are to be
regarded as diminutives, the last two nouns with a contemptuous
significance.

245. (ii) Reduplication of Second and Third radicals.

אֲדַמְדָּם red ; יְרַקְרַק yellow, Nᵉg. iii. 8 ; חֲוַרְוָר spotted, white,
Bᵉk. vi. 3 ; סְגַלְגְּלָה round, Šab. 31 a ; שְׁרַפְרָף camp stool, Kel.
xxiii. 2 ; שְׁרַקְרַק gier eagle, Ḥul. 63 a.

With ō in the second syllable, cf. BH שְׁחַרְחֹרֶת, פְּתַלְתֹּל, &c.
(Ges.-K., § 84 B n) ; חֲלַגְלוֹג purslane, Šᵉbi. ix. 1 ; חַלְחֹלוֹחַ a species
of peas, t. Pea i. 7 ; יְרַקְרֹקֶת yellowish, Mᵉg. 13 a ; צְמַרְמוֹרוֹת
feverish flushes, Nid. ix. 8.

Diminutives : בְּצַלְצִיל dwarf onion, Kil. i. 3 ; פְּרוֹטְרוֹט units,
details, t. MŠ ii. 11.   So the caritative form : יְפֵיפִין very beautiful,

[1] Cf. Ibn Ezra, ad loc., and on Cant., l. c.   In Nᵉg. xi. 4 ; Sifra, xiii. 49,
however, these terms are explained as intensives.   Cf. also Brockelmann,
ib., i, § 172.

Nᵉd. 20 b; יְפֵיפִיָּה Pᵉs. 6 b; יְפֵיפִיוֹת Mᵉg. 15 a; Taʻa. 31 a, cf.
Jerem. xlvi. 20.   For the diminutive character of the vowel
ê = ai, cf. § 273.

If the third radical is ל or ר it is sometimes omitted: מְטוּטֶלֶת
(= מְטַלְטֶלֶת) plummet, Kel. xii. 8; Šab. v. 3; שְׁפוֹפֶרֶת (= שְׁפַרְפֶרֶת),
tube, ib. ii. 4.   So עֲנַקוֹקְלוֹת for עֲנַקַלְקְלוֹת (from ענק = עָנָק), un-
developed grapes, ʻOr. i. 8.

246. (iii) Reduplication of the whole Stem,[1] in ע״ו and ע״ע roots.

(a) Ground-form *Qaṭqaṭ, Qaṭqiṭ, Qaṭquṭ*: גַּלְגַּל wheel, Mid.
v. 4; גַּרְגַּר berry, Šᵉbi. iii. 7; כַּבְכָּב lid, Kel. ii. 3; קַנְקָן cylindrical
vessel, Ab. iv. 20.

Fem.: קַלְקָלָה disgrace, Ab. iv. 18; קַרְקָרָה bottom of vessel,
Kel. ii. 2; צַפְצָפָה a species of willow, Suk. iii. 3; כַּלְכָּלָה basket,
Pea vii. 3; גַּרְגֶּרֶת windpipe, Ḥul iii. 1; פַּרְפֶרֶת hash, Bᵉr. vi. 5;
שַׁבְשֶׁבֶת paste, Šab. viii. 4; שַׁלְשֶׁלֶת chain, BQ vii. 7.

Qaṭqiṭ. The Infinitives of Pilpel: קַלְקֵל, טַלְטֵל, &c., cf. §§ 182, 195.

Qaṭquṭ: דַּרְדּוּר, cask on wheels, Kel. xv. 1; חַסְחוּס cartilage,
Bᵉk. vi. 1; חַרְחוּר coulter, Kel. xiii. 3; פַּטְפּוּט peg, Šab. viii. 4.

Fem.: נְוֹגֶנֶת parasol, Kel. xvi. 7 (L); גְּרוֹגֶרֶת dry fig, Šab. vii. 4;
קְנוֹקְנוֹת (from קנה) branch sinews, Ḥul. 92 a, b.

247. (b) Ground-form *Qiṭqaṭ, Qiṭqiṭ, Qiṭquṭ.*

Qiṭqaṭ: כִּכָּר (= כִּרְכָּר) loaf, Pea viii. 7; פִּשְׁפָּשׁ wicket, Mid. i. 7;
לִשְׁלֶשֶׁת secretion, Šab. xxi. 2.

Qiṭqiṭ: פִּלְפֵּל pepper (diminutive of פּוֹל) TY i. 5; פִּשְׁפֵּשׁ bug,
Tᵉr. viii. 2.

Qiṭquṭ: This form is very common as a verbal noun of Pilpel,
corresponding to *Qiṭṭul* for the Intensive Stem (§ 241), and also in
a secondary sense as a concrete: כַּלְבּוּל growth of hair, Šab. viii. 4;
לִפְלוּף glutinous substance, Miq. ix. 4; מַלְמוּל crumbs, ib. ix. 2;
קִלְקוּל disorder, MQ 12; בַּעְבּוּעַ swelling, Miq. x. 4; דְּקְדּוּק subtle

---

[1] Here may also be mentioned the form לֵילֵי, construct of לַיְלָה night,
Suk. 48 a, and often, for BH לֵיל; cf. BDB s.v. and reff.

thinking, Ab. vi. 5 ; הִרְהוּר meditating, Naz. ix. 4 ; טִלְטוּל moving,
Šab. 43 b; לְכְלוּךְ moistening, Miq. ix. 4 ; נִדְנוּד shaking, t. Yᵉb.
iv. 8.

248. (*c*) Ground-form *Quṭquṭ* : טוּמטוּם of unknown sex, Ḥag.
i. 1 ; קָדְקֹד skull, Nᵉg. x. 10 ; גֻּלְגֹּלֶת skull, Ab. ii. 6.

(4) *Nouns formed by means of Prefixes.*

249. (i) With Prefix א: אַבּוּב flute, Kel. ii. 3 ; אֲגוּדָל thumb,
Yo. ii. 1 ; אֲגָף door-step, Nᵉd. vii. 5 ; אַרְכּוּבָה knee, Kil. vii. 1 ;
אֲשָׁבּוֹרֶן pond, Oh. iii. 3 ; אַשְׁפּוֹת ¹ dung-hill, Kel. xxvii. 11 ; אֶגְרוֹף
fist, ib. xvii. 12 ; אֶמְצַע middle, Šab. ix. 2 ; אֶפְרוֹחַ chicken, Ḥul.
xii. 3 ; אָפוּן bean, Pea iii. 3 ; also אָפוּל t. Tᵉr. x. 15 ; אַסְקוּפָה
threshold, Šab. x. 2.

In the following verbal nouns the א is a phonetic modification
of ה (cf. the next section and above, § 43) ; אַבְעָיָה search, Pea iv. 5 ;
אַגָּדָה Agadah, Nᵉd. iv. 3 ; אַזְהָרָה warning, Pᵉs. iii. 1 ; אוֹנָאָה
wrong, BM iv. 3.

250. (ii) Prefix ה. These are all verbal nouns with an abstract
significance formed from the Hiph'il. They fall into two classes :
(*a*) masculines in the form *Haqṭel*, confined chiefly to strong verbs,
and (*b*) feminines in the form *Haqṭala*, for all classes of verbs.
Some of the *Haqṭel* forms have assumed a secondary concrete
significance.

251. (*a*) *Haqṭel.* This is practically the old Infinitive Hiph'il

---

¹ From שׁפת, as is shown by the plur. אַשְׁפַּתּוֹת, Šᵉbi. i. 1–3 ; So. 42 b, &c.
The form אַשְׁפּוֹת is for אַשְׁפָּת with *ā* obscured to *ô*. אַשְׁפָּת, which seems to
have survived in popular speech, was reduced to אַשְׁפָּה by the elision of the
final ת, on the analogy of the fem. termination. So Kᵉt. vii. 5 ; BM. v. 7 ;
BB. v. 3 ; Mᵉʿil. iii. 6. L and other texts have, however, אַשְׁפּוֹת. In
BM. ii. 3 also L reads אַשְׁפָּה. So often in the Talmud : Šab. 15 a (contrast
with 'Ed. i. 3) ; Pᵉs. 8 b, &c. The Palestinian Talmud has often אִישְׁפָּה :
j. Sab. ii. 3 ; j. Kᵉt. i. 10. Cf. also *JQR.*, xx, p. 715.

fossilized into a noun. The traditional, and no doubt correct,
pronunciation of the prefix with *e* for *a*, seems to have arisen
through assimilation to the *ē* in the second syllable.[1]

Exx.: הֶבְעֵר burning, BQ i. 1 ; הֶבְקֵר or הֶפְקֵר (cf. above, § 49),
ownerless property, Pea vi. 1 ; הֶפְסֵד loss, Ab. v. 4 ; הֶפְשֵׁט flaying,
Yo. ii. 7 ; הֶקְדֵּשׁ consecrated property, Tᵉr. i. 5 ; הֶרְגֵּל habit,
Šab. i. 5 ; הֶסְגֵּר shutting up, Mᵉg. i. 7.

פ״נ : הֶיכֵּר recognition, 'Er. 11 b ; הֶיסֵט shaking, Ṭoh. xi. 1 ;
הֵיקֵּף circumference, Kel. xvii. 8 ; הֶיקֵּשׁ comparison, Zᵉb. 50 a ; הֶנֵף
waving, Suk. iii. 12.

When followed by a genitive, the prefix preserves, if tradition
can be trusted, the old BH vowel. Thus : הַבְשֵׁר כָּל נִזְקוֹ rendering
fit (= responsibility for) all its damage, BQ i. 1 ; הֶעֱלֵם שֶׁרֶץ
unconsciousness of the reptile, Šᵉbu. iii. 4 ; הֶעֲרֵב שֶׁמֶשׁ setting of
the sun, Ḥal. i. 9 ; הַשֵּׂג יָד reaching of the hand, 'Ar. iv. 1 (cf. Lev.
xxvii. 8) ; הָשֵׁב אֲבֵדָה restoring lost property, BM vii. 4 ; הָנֵץ הַחַמָּה
the rising of the sun, Bᵉr. i. 2.

This substantival use of the Infin. Hiph'il is found also in BH,
e. g. הַפְצַר 1 Sam. xv. 23 ; הַשְׁמֵד Isa. xiv. 23 ; הַמְשֵׁל Job xxv. 2 ;
הוֹכֵחַ ib. vi. 25 ; cf. Stade, § 245.

252. (*b*) *Haqṭala* : הַבְדָּלָה separation, Ḥul. i. 7 ; הַבְעָרָה kindling,
Šab. ii. 6 ; הַגְבָּהָה lifting, Qid. i. 4 ; הַטְמָנָה hiding, Šab. 39 a ;
הַכְנָסָה bringing in, ib. 2 a ; הַפְסָקָה interruption, Ta'a. 4 b ; הַקְטָרָה
burning incense, Qid. i. 8 ; הַרְכָּבָה grafting, Šᵉbi. ii. 6 ; הַרְקָרָה
sifting, Pᵉs. 11 a.

ל״ה : הַשְׁקָיָה giving to drink, Mᵉg. ii. 7 ; הַזָּיָה or הַזָּאָה sprinkling,
Qid. i. 8.

פ״נ : הַגָּשָׁה bringing near, ib.

ע״ו : הֲבָאָה bringing, Pea i. 1 ; הֲדָחָה rinsing, Šab. xxii. 2 ; הֲטָבָה

---

[1] For a similar change in BH, cf. Ges.-K., § 27 p ; Stade, § 81 ; also
Sznejder, p. 231.

doing good, Šᵉbu. iii. 5; הַנָּחָה laying down, Kᵉl. viii. 8; הָרָעָה doing ill, Šᵉbu. iii. 5.

פ"י: הוֹרָאָה confessing, ib. vi. 1; הוֹצָאָה bringing out, Šab. 2 b; הוֹרָדָה bringing down, Mid. iv. 1.

For the change of ה to א cf. above, § 249.

This form which is identical with the Aram. infin. Aph'el (Haph'el) is probably older than the ordinary infin. with ē (= î) in the second syllable.[1] In BH it is found already in Isaiah: הַכָּרָה iii. 9; הַנָּפָה xxx. 28. Further, with א in אַזְכָּרָה Lev. ii. 2, &c.; besides הַנָּחָה Esther ii. 18; הַצָּלָה ib. iv. 14. In Sirach: הַשָּׁנָה xxxv. 10; הוֹרָאָה li. 17; הַגָּנֵעַ xvi. 25; xxxii. 3; cf. Micah vi. 8.

253. (c) With the prefix הְ is found the reflexive verbal noun הִשְׁתַּחֲוָאָה bowing down, Šᵉbu. ii. 3; הִשְׁתַּחֲוָיוֹת Šeq. vi. 1; Tam. vii. 3, formed on the analogy of בְּהִשְׁתַּחֲוָיתִי 2 Kings v. 18. Cf. Stade, § 254.

254. (iii) Prefix י. In a few nouns, consisting, chiefly, of names of animals and plants; cf. BH יַחְמוּר, יוֹנָה, &c. Stade, § 259, Barth, p. 226 f.

Exx.: יַבְחוּשׁ a kind of gnat, Nid. iii. 2; יַתּוּשׁ gnat, t. Šab. xii. 4; יַרְבּוּז strawberry-blight, Šᵉbi. ix. 1; יְחוֹר branch, Kil. i. 8; further, יָצוּל handle of a plough, Kel. xxi. 2; יַתּוּכִין tongs, ib. xii. 3.

255. (iv) Prefix מ. As in BH, מ is extensively used for the formation of nouns of the following classes: (1) subjective nouns, including the Participles of the derived active stems of Verbs; also a number of *nomina actionis*, e.g. מִמְכָּר, מִדְרָשׁ, מַטָּע; (2) objective nouns, including the Participles of the derived passive stems of Verbs; also a number of concrete nouns, representing the result of an action, e.g. מוֹתָר, מַעֲשֶׂה, מַאֲפֶה; (3) names of instruments and tools, e.g. מָדוֹךְ, מַכְבֵּשׁ, מַנְעָל; (4) nouns of a local significance, e.g. מְרָחָץ, מַחְצָב, מָבוֹי.

---

[1] Cf. Barth, *Nominalbildung*, pp. 73, 90.

256. (*a*) Ground-form *Maqṭal, Maqṭil, Maqṭul*.

Maqṭal: מַאֲכָל food, Šab. 10 a; מַחְצֵב quarry, Šᵉbi. iii. 5; מַנְעָל shoe, Šab. viii. 2; מַעְצָד adze, BQ x. 10. With *ă* changed to *ĕ*: מֶרְחָץ bath, Šab. i. 2; cf. Stade, § 270; also Ges.-K., § 85 h.

פ״נ: מַגָּע touch, Ḥul. iv. 4; מַדֵּף instrument for driving away, Kel. xvi. 7; מַסָּר saw, Šab. xvii. 4; מַשָּׂא or מַשּׂוֹי burden, Šᵉbi. iii. 6; מַתָּן gift, Ab. ii. 1.

פ״י: מוֹתָר remnant, Kil. v. 4; מֵיחָם heating-pan, Šab. iii. 3 (from חמם = יחם); מֵיטָב best, BQ i. 1.

ע״ו: מָאוֹר light-hole, Šab. xxiv. 5; מָבוֹי (= מָבוֹא) entrance, 'Er. i. 1; מָדוֹךְ pestle, Be. i. 7; מָזוֹן food, 'Er. iii. 1; מָחוֹל circle, Kil. iv. 2; מָקוֹף the eye of a coulter, Kel. xiii. 3.

ע״ע: מַמָּשׁ palpable, real, San. v. 4; מַגָּפַיִם greaves, Kel. xi. 8.

ל״ה: מַאֲפֶה baked, 'Er. vii. 10; מַקְלֶה roasting-place, Ta'a. iii. 1; מַקְפֶּה mess of grist, Šab. xvii. 5.

Fem.: מַחֲשָׁבָה thought, Bᵉr. 61 a; מַטְהֶרֶת gutter, Miq. vi. 11; מַקְלָעָה braid, Yo. vi. 7; מַרְדַּעַת pack-saddle, Šab. v. 2; מַרְפֶּסֶת veranda, Ma'a. iii. 6.

מַכָּה wound, So. iii. 4; מַתָּנָה gift, Zᵉb. v. 1.

מְגוּפָה stopper, Šab. xxii. 3; מְדוּכָה mortar, Kel. xxiii. 2; מְצוּדָה net, ib. xxi. 3; מְדִינָה district, RH iv. 3; מְחִיצָה partition, Kil. iv. 4; מְעִיסָה flour paste, Ḥal. i. 6.

Maqṭil: מַטְבֵּעַ coin, Šab. vi. 7; מַכְבֵּשׁ press, ib. xx. 5; מַלְבֵּן frame, Nᵉg. xiii. 3; מַלְקֵט (or מַלְקֵחַ L) pincher, Mak. iii. 5; מַסְמֵר nail, Kel. xii. 5; מַסְרֵק comb, ib. xiii. 8; מַעְבֵּר pitchfork (or מַעְדֵּר ib. 7; מַעְטֵן vat, BM v. 7; מַפְתֵּחַ key, Kel. xiv. 8; מַרְפֵּק elbow, 'Ar. v. 1; מַרְצֵעַ awl, Qid. 21 b; מַרְתֵּף store-room, Pᵉs. i. 1; מַשְׁבֵּר travailing chair, Kel. xxiii. 4; מַתְבֵּן store of straw, 'Er. vii. 5.

Fem.: מַגְרֵפָה shovel, Tam. ii. 1; מַזְחֵלָה gutter, BB iii. 6; מְאִירָה wicker-basket, Šᵉbi. iii. 2; מְאֵירָה curse, Suk. iii. 10; מַגֵּפָה wound, Makš. vi. 8.

Maqṭul, only fem. nouns. The *ū* is changed to *ō* and usually

spelt with ‎ו‎: ‎מַאֲבוֹלֶת‎ louse, Šab. 12 a; ‎מַחֲרוֹזֶת‎ string, BM ii. 1;
‎מַחֲלוֹקֶת‎ controversy, Ab. v. 20; ‎מַסְפּוֹרֶת‎ scissors, Šab. 48 b; ‎מַפּוֹלֶת‎
fall, Pes. ii. 3.

257. (*b*) Ground-form *Miqṭal, Miqṭil, Miqṭul*.

Miqṭal: ‎מִדְבָּר‎ wilderness, Ber. ix. 2; ‎מִדְרָס‎ treading, Kel.
xxiv. 1; ‎מִזְרָן‎ mattress, ib. xix. 3; ‎מִמְכָּר‎ selling, Meg. iii. 2; ‎מִנְהָג‎
custom, BM vii. 1; ‎מִשְׁתֶּה‎ feast, Ber. i. 1; ‎מִקָּח‎ taking, Ab. iv. 22.

Fem.: ‎מִדְלָעוֹת‎, ‎מִקְשָׁאוֹת‎ fields of pumpkins, of cucumbers, Šebi.
ii. 1; ‎מִזְוָדָה‎ travelling-bag, Kel. xx. 1; ‎מִכְוָה‎ burn, Neg. ix. 1;
‎מִלְוֶה‎ loan, ʿAZ iv. 10; ‎מִקְלָה‎ burning, Taʿa. ii. 1; ‎מִשְׁנָה‎ repetition,
study, Ab. iii. 7; ‎מִחִלָּה‎ cavity, t. Yeb. xiv. 6; ‎מְסִבָּה‎ winding
staircase, Tam. i. 1; ‎מְעִיסָה‎ flour paste, Ḥal. i. 6.

Miqṭil: ‎מִזְבֵּחַ‎ altar, Zeb. v. 1.

Miqṭul, only fem.: ‎מִכְמוֹרֶת‎ net, Kel. xxiii. 5; ‎מִשְׁקוֹלֶת‎ plummet,
ib. xxix. 3.

258. (*c*) Ground-form *Muqṭal*: Participle Hophʿal; further,
‎מוּנְמָר‎ perfume, Ber. vi. 6; ‎מוּקְצֶה‎ store of fruit, Maʿa. i. 5; ‎מוּרְסָה‎
blister, ʿEd. ii. 5.

259. (*d*) Ground-form *Maqṭál-Maqṭôl, Maqṭîl, Maqṭûl*.

Maqṭál. The long *á* is obscured to *ô*: ‎מַכְחוֹל‎ eye-painter,
Kel. xiii. 8; ‎מַלְקוֹט‎ bag, ib. xvi. 7.

Maqṭíl: Participle of Hiphʿil; further, fem. nouns: ‎מַעֲזִיבָה‎
plaster of ceiling, BM x. 1; ‎מַטְלִית‎ patch, lining, Šab. xxiv. 5;
‎מַרְאִית‎ sight, appearance, ib. xix. 6.

Maqṭûl: ‎מַפּוּחַ‎ bellows, t. Be. iii. 15.

260. (*e*) Ground-form *Maqaṭṭel*: Participle Piʿel; further some
fem. nouns of a participial origin: ‎מְסַנֶּנֶת‎ sieve, Kel. xiv. 8; ‎מְשַׁמֶּרֶת‎
strainer, Ab. v. 15.

261. (v) Prefix ‎נ‎: Participle Niphʿal; further the following
nouns: ‎נִבְרֶכֶת‎ pool, MQ i. 6; ‎נִבְרֶשֶׁת‎ lamp, Yo. iii. 10; ‎נִדְבָּךְ‎ stone
wall, Ber. ii. 4; ‎נַחְשׁוֹל‎ storm, Yo. 38 a; ‎נַחְתּוֹם‎ baker, Dam. ii. 4;

נְצְפָּה caper berry, ib. i. 1 ; נְמוֹשׁוֹת aged (groping), Pea viii. 1 ; cf. § 177, נִיצוֹק uninterrupted flow, Ṭoh. viii. 9.

262. (vi) Prefix ס, שׁ : Verbal nouns formed from Saph'el and Šaph'el : סְרְגּוּל drawing lines, Gen. R 25 ; שִׁחְרוּר manumission, Git. i. 4 ; שִׁעְבּוּד subjection, Bᵉr. 9 b ; שִׁעְמוּם idiocy, Kᵉt. v. 5 ; further, סְגַלְגַּל round, Šab. 31 a ; סְמַרְטוּט lappet, Šab. xix. 2 ; סָרָק empty (of a tree that bears no fruit), Kil. vi. 5.

263. (vii) Prefix תּ, chiefly in abstracts.

(*a*) Ground-form *Taqṭal*, *Taqṭil*.

Taqṭal, mostly BH nouns : תַּאֲוָה desire, Ab. iv. 21 ; תּוֹדָה thank-offering, Zᵉb. v. 6 ; תּוֹרָה law, Ab. i. 1 ; תַּרְבָּץ court, front, Ḥul. 43 b ; תַּרְוָוד spoon, Kel. xvii. 12.

Taqṭil, only fem. : תּוֹסֶפֶת addition, Bik. iii. 10 ; תְּחִיָּה resurrection, San. x. 1 ; תְּפִלָּה prayer, Bᵉr. iv. 1.

264. (*b*) Ground-form *Tiqṭal*, *Tiqṭul*.

Tiqṭal : תִּגְלַחַת shaving, ʻAZ i. 3 ; תִּקְרָה rafter, BM x. 2.

Tiqṭul, only fem. : תִּכְבּוֹסֶת washing, MQ 15 a ; תִּסְפּוֹרֶת hair cutting, Šab. 9 b ; תַּרְעוֹמֶת complaint, BM vi. 1 ; תִּקְרוֹבֶת gift, t. BB iv. 14 ; תִּשְׁחוֹרֶת youth, AB iii. 2.

265. (*c*) Ground-form *Taqṭil*, *Taqṭul*.

Taqṭil : תַּבְשִׁיל cooked food, Šab. iii. 1 ; תַּכְרִיךְ bundle, BM i. 8 ; תַּכְשִׁיט ornament, MQ 9 b ; תַּלְמִיד disciple, Ab. iv. 12 ; תַּמְצִית juice, Zᵉb. viii. 7 ; תַּעֲנִית fast, Taʻa. i. 4 ; תַּשְׁמִישׁ use, service, Yo. viii. 1.

Taqṭul : תַּחֲרוּת strife, Bᵉr. 17 a ; תַּלְמוּד study, Pea i. 1 ; תַּמְחוּי dish, ib. viii. 7 ; תַּנְחוּמִין consolation, Bᵉr. ii. 7 ; תַּרְבּוּת rearing, Nid. x. 8 ; תַּשְׁלוּם payment, BQ i. 1 ; תַּפּוּחַ apple tree, Kil. i. 4 ; תְּבוּסָה weltering, Oh. ii. 2 ; תְּמוּרָה exchange, Tᵉm. i. 1 ; תְּנוּפָה waving, Qid. i. 8 ; תְּרוּעָה blowing, RH iv. 9 ; תְּשׁוּבָה repentance, Ab. iv. 11 ; תַּעֲרוּבוֹת exchange, Yᵉb. xi. 3.

(5) *Nouns formed by means of Suffixes.*

266. (i) Suffix לֹ¹: אֶשְׁכּוֹל cluster, Mid. iii. 8; גִּבְעוֹל calyx, Pa. xii. 2; קַרְסוֹל ankle, Oh. i. 8; רִבְצָל small bag, Kel. xx. 1.

267. (ii) Suffix ‏ָן‎, ‏וֹן‎. This suffix is used to form abstract nouns and abjectives. Nouns of a concrete sense with this suffix are mostly of an originally adjectival character (cf. Stade, § 292; Barth, p. 316 f.).

(*a*) Suffix ‏ָן‎.

Ground-form *Qaṭlan*: אַרְבָּן prolonger; קַצְרָן shortener, Ber. 34 a; בַּיְשָׁן shamefaced, Ab. ii. 5; גַּמְלָן (also גַּמְלוֹן) camel-like, large, Kil. iii. 2; וַתְרָן indulgent, BQ 50 a; קַרְחָן bald, Bek. 43 b; מַקְּבָן mallet-shaped, Bek. vii. 1; סַרְבָּן stubborn (L סוּרְבָּן) Ber. v. 2; עַקְרַבָּן scorpion-like, 'Er. ii. 6; קַפְּדָן quick-tempered, Ab. ii. 5; גַּזְלָן robber, 'Or. i. 2; דַּרְשָׁן lecturer, So. ix. 15; רַצְחָן murderer, ib. 9; חַזָּן overseer, Šab. i. 3; סַדָּן block, Kil. i. 8; קַבְּלָן contractor, Šebi. iii. 9 (L קוּבְּלָן); רַצְעָן saddler, Pea iv. 6.

Qiṭlan: לִפְתָּן turnip-shaped, Bek. vii. 1; צִיקָן avaricious, Pes. vii. 8; רִיקָן empty, Yo. v. 4 (L רֵיקָם, so Ta'a. ii. 2); עִנְיָן subject, t. Meg. iv. 3; פִּשְׁתָּן flax, Šab. iv. 11; תִּלְתָּן fenugreek, Kil. ii. 5.

Quṭlan: מוּרְסָן bran, Ḥal. ii. 6; קָרְבָּן sacrifice, Ned. i. 4; some *Qaṭlan* forms are in certain texts given as *Quṭlan*, e. g. סוּרְבָּן, קוּבְּלָן, in L, cf. above.

Cf. also the adverbial ending ‏ָן‎ (= ‏ָם‎) in כָּאן, מַעְלָן, לְהַלָּן, מַטָּן, § 295.

268. (*b*) Suffix ‏וֹן‎.

Adjectives: אַחֲרוֹן last, BQ iv. 1; חִיצוֹן external, Zeb. v. 1; עֶלְיוֹנָה uppermost, BM iv. 2; תַּחְתּוֹן lower, San. viii. 1; תִּיכוֹן middle, Ber. 3 b; פִּילוֹן wedge-shaped, Bek. vii. 1; קֵיצוֹן of summer, Šebi.

---

¹ These are probably diminutive forms, cf. Prätorius, *ZDMG.*, lvii, p. 530 ff. Brockelmann, ib., p. 402.

v. 4 ; also adjectival nouns : אֶבְיוֹן needy, BM 111 b ; אַלְמוֹן widower, Ket. 7 a ; אֵילוֹנִית barren woman, Yeb. i. 1.

Abstract : חֶסְרוֹן loss, t. Ta'a. i. 2 ; חֶשְׁבּוֹן reckoning, BB 9 b ; סִירְחוֹן stench, Pes. 35 a ; פִּדְיוֹן ransom, Bek. i. 6 ; כִּבְשׁוֹן secret, Ḥag. 13 a.

With sharpening of the second radical : גֵּרְעוֹן diminution, 'Ar. ix. 7 ; הֶשְׁבּוֹן restoration (from השב), BM 58 b ; זִכָּרוֹן remembrance, RH iv. 6 ; חִיסָּכוֹן saving, Men. 86 b ; נִסָּיוֹן trial, Ab. v. 3 ; נִצָּחוֹן victory, So. viii. 1 ; עִשָּׂרוֹן one-tenth, Men. xiii. 1 ; פִּקָּדוֹן deposit, Šebu. v. 1 ; פִּרָקוֹן redemption, Ket. iv. 4 ; פִּשָּׂיוֹן spreading, Neg. i. 3 ; רִאָּיוֹן appearance, Pea i. 1.

Concretes with this ending are found only in a few denominatives with a diminutive significance : זֵרְעוֹנִים seeds, Kil. iii. 2 (only plur., cf. Dan. i. 16) ; צְמָחוֹנִים green buds, MŠ ii. 3 (only plur.) ; חֲבִיּוֹנוֹת little jars (from חָבִית), Kel. ii. 2 ; כִּידוֹן, נִיקוֹן little javelin, ib. xi. 8 ; קָנוֹן little reed-basket, Be. i. 8.

Cf. BH אִישׁוֹן, שַׁהֲרוֹנִים (Stade, § 296 c ; Ges.-K., § 86 g ; Barth, p. 348 f.). The form is as scarce in MH as in BH. In Aram., on the other hand, it is extremely common, and can be formed at will from any noun, cf. Nöldeke, *Syr. Gr.*, § 131.

269. (iii) Suffix י ְ , usually spelt אִי–, or יִ– (in Palestinian texts), to distinguish it from the vowel letter יִ–. It is only found in a few nouns : אַחֲרִי responsible, Dam. iii. 5 (cf. Prov. xxviii. 23) ; בַּרְקַאי (or בּוּרְקַי) morning star, Yo. iii. 1 ; גּוֹבַאי a kind of locust, Ber. vi. 3 ; and לִפְנַי within, Zeb. 52 a (cf. 1 Kings vi. 17 ; Stade, § 301 ; Ges.-K., § 86 i).

270. (iv) Suffix יִ–. To this formation belong denominative adjectives describing origin.

Of names of peoples : אֱדוֹמִי Edomite, Pes. iii. 1 ; אִיטַלְקִי Italian, Šebi. i. 3 ; אֲרַמִּי Aramaean, Pes. x. 4 ; יִשְׂרְאֵלִי Israelite, Qid. iv. 1 (but more often without suffix ; יִשְׂרָאֵל 'AZ iv. 9, 12). Of names of places : גְּלִילִי Galilean, Pes. vii. 1 ; דְּרוֹמִי southern, Šeq. vi. 3 ;

יְרוּשַׁלְמִית Jérusalemite; מִדְבָּרִית belonging to the wilderness, Men.
vii. 1 ; בֵּישָׁנִי of Beth Shean; and with נ inserted: חֵיפָנִי of Haifa,
Meg. 24 b; so טְבַרְנִית Tiberian, j. Šeq. iii. 2 ; [1] כּוּפְרִי rural, wild,
Kil. i. 6.

Of numbers, Ordinals: שְׁלִישִׁי, רְבִיעִי Yo. ii. r. 4 ; שְׁלָשִׁית ; רְבָעִי
three, four years old, Pa. i. 1 (cf. below, § 398).

Of other nouns : אֱלוּלִיִּים born in the month of Elul, Bek. ix. 5 ;
אֶמְצָעִית middle, Kil. v. 2 ; אֶצְבָּעִי smallest, dwarf, Bek. 48 b ; בֵּיתִיוֹת
domestic, Be. v. 7 ; יְחִידִי alone, Ab. iii. 4 ; עוֹלָמִית ever, Yeb. iii. 9 ;
פְּנִימִי inner, Tam. i. 4 ; צוֹאִי filthy, Ḥul. xi. 2 ; פִּשְׁתָּנִי flax dealer,
j. Yeb. xiii. 1 ; שֻׁלְחָנִי money changer, BM ii. 4.

Sometimes the suffix ִי‑ is combined with נ‑, וֹן‑ : חֶנְוָנִי shop-
keeper, Ned. iv. 7 ; טוּבְעָנִי flooded ; יוּבְשָׁנִי rainless, dry, Ta'a. 10 a ;
קַרְתָּנִי villager, Dam. vi. 4 ; רְחִיטָנִי clipper, Mak. iii. 5 ; רֵיחָנִי
aromatic, Nid. 52 a ; בֵּינוֹנִי middle, Ter. iv. 3 ; עִירוֹנִי urban,
'Ed. ii. 5 ; פְּלוֹנִי So-and-So, Giṭ. vi. 3 ; גַּרְגְּרָנִיוֹת a species of berry,
Ber. 57 b.

271. (v) Suffix ‑ִית, Fem. and chiefly denominative : גִּגִּית tub,
Šab. xxiv. 5 ; זְבּוּרִית poorest soil, Giṭ. v. 1 ; זַרְעִית family, San. iv. 5 ;
חָבִית cask, Šab. xvi. 3 ; חַרְסִית pottery, MŠ v. 1 ; טַלִּית shawl, Me'il.
vi. 4 ; יַבְלִית pulp, Kel. iii. 6 ; כַּפְנִית date berry, 'Or. i. 9 ; עִדִּית best
soil, Šebi. v. 4 ; עַרְבִית evening, Ber. i. 1 ; שַׁחֲרִית morning, ib. 2 ;
שַׁחֲצִית insolence, j. Šeq. iv. 4.

With Diminutive force : גְּדוּדִית a little band,[2] Sifra 110 c ;
ruined partition wall, 'Er. v. 1 ; כַּדִּידִית little pitcher, t. Men.
ix. 10 ; קַטְנִית pulse, Pea i. 4. Perhaps also : דּוּגִית a light fisher-
boat, BB 78 b ; סְנוּנִית a swallow, Šab. 77 b ; עֲסָסִית pounded wheat
or peas, t. Be. i. 23.

---

[1] Cf. BH. שָׁלָנִי from שָׁלָה, &c. Ges.-K., § 85 v.

[2] So Raši to Lev. xxvi. 31. But Rabad to the Sifra, l. c., explains our word
as 'foundation', and this is adopted by Levy, s. v.

Cf. also the reduplicated forms with this suffix enumerated above, § 244.[1]

272. (vi) Suffix וּת‎—, chiefly used in forming abstracts from concrete nouns: אוּמָּנוּת‎ handicraft, Qid. iv. 14; אֲנִינוּת‎ grief, MŠ v. 12; אֲרִיסוּת‎ tenancy; חֲכִירוּת‎ tenure, Bik. i. 11; גְּנוּת‎ disgrace, Pes. x. 4; זְכוּת‎ merit, So. iii. 4; חֵרוּת‎ freedom, Pes. x. 5; טָעוּת‎ error, Nᵉd. ix. 10; יַלְדוּת‎ childishness, So. i. 4; מַלְכוּת‎ kingdom, Ab. iii. 5; מְשִׁיחוּת‎ office of anointed priest, Ho. iii. 1; נְקִיּוּת‎ cleanliness, So. ix. 15; עֲנִיּוּת‎ poverty; עֲשִׁירוּת‎ riches, Qid. iv. 14; קַלּוּת‎ lightness, Ab. iii. 13; רְשׁוּת‎ permission, ib. 15; רָשׁוּת‎ authority, ib. i. 10; שָׁהוּת‎ while, RH 30 b; תַּרְפּוּת‎ obscenity, 'AZ. ii. 3.

Also in *nomina actionis*: גְּמִילוּת‎ doing, Ab. i. 2; פְּרִישׁוּת‎ separation, abstinence, So. ix. 15; שְׁפִיכוּת‎ shedding, 'AZ. ii. 1; cf. above, § 228.

This suffix is sometimes combined with another suffix: אַחֲרָיוּת‎ responsibility, BM ii. 7; פּוּרְעָנוּת‎, punishment, Ab. ii. 7; רַבָּנוּת‎ authority, ib. 10; קַבְּלָנוּת‎ contract, BM x. 4 (cf. also Dalman, p. 182).

(6) *Formation by Sound-insertion.*

273. (i) Insertion of a Vowel Sound to form Diminutives. The original Ground-form was *Quṭail* (cf. Barth, *Nominalbildung*, pp. 312 ff.; Brockelmann, *Grundriss*, i. § 137), but in MH the diphthong *ai* was contracted to *ê* and *î*. The first vowel *u* was also contracted in most cases to Shᵉwa. We thus get the forms *Quṭél*, *Qᵉṭél*, and *Qᵉṭíl*.

Quṭél. The only examples are the feminines בּוּדֵידָה‎[2] a little oil press, Šebi. viii. 6 and שׁוּמֵירָה‎[3] a watchman's hut, 'Er. ii. 5.

---

[1] Several BH nouns ending in ‎ית‎— may also, perhaps, be regarded as diminutive forms, e.g. צְלֹחִית‎, 2 Kings ii. 20, as compared with צַלַּחַת‎ (ib. xxi. 13, and, especially, 2 Chron. xxxv. 13), מְנַקִּית‎, Exod. xxv. 29, שְׁאֵרִית‎.

[2] This is the reading of the best texts, including L. Other texts have בְּדִידָה‎, like the Qᵉṭíl forms below.

So N., M., and editions. In BB iv. 8 editions have שׁוּמֵירָה‎, but N.

Qᵉṭél: חֲרִיר ¹ eyelet of a needle, Kel. xiii. 3 ; סְלִיל shuttle, Nᵉg. xi. 9. Cf. BH וְעִיר. Perhaps also פְּלֵיטָה שְׁאֵרִית, and אֱלִיל, a contemptuous diminutive of אֵל, or אַל naught.² Also Aram. וְלִילָא, וְלִיל, Targum Prov. xiv. 6 ; xii. 9 ; xxvii. 7.

Qᵉṭíl, all feminine : חֲפִיסָה a small bag, BM. i. 8 (cf. t. ib. i. 14) ; כְּנִימָה vermin, Makš. vi. 1 ; כְּפִיפָה or קְפִיפָה (L)³ basket, Tᵉr. ix. 3 ; עֲרִיסָה cradle, Kel. xvi. 1 (contrast with BH עֶרֶשׂ. A full-sized bed is always מִטָּה in MH) ; סְלִילָה a little basket, 'AZ ii. 7 (L and N. Other texts have סְלוּלָה). So in proper names : עֲקִיבָה—(עֲקִיבָא) עֲקִיבָה ; חֲנִנְיָה ; חֲנִינָה (or חֲנִינָא) from חֲנִינָה.

That the formation is original in MH, and not borrowed from Aram. (Barth, loc. cit.), is shown by its comparative frequency in MH as compared with its scarcity in Aram.

274. (ii) Insertion of a Consonantal Sound.

ר : גֵּרְדּוֹם stump, t. Pa. xii. 2 ; חַרְגּוֹל a kind of locust, Šab. vi. 10 ; חַרְטוֹם beak, Ṭoh. i. 2 ; קַרְטוֹב a small measure, Miq. iii. 2 ; קַרְפֵּף enclosure, 'Er. ii. 3.

נ : תַּרְנְגוֹל cock, fem. תַּרְנְגֹלֶת Pᵉs. iv. 7 (from רגל, רגן, if not a foreign word).

(7) *Formation of Nouns from Biblical Expressions.*

275. Certain Biblical expressions have given rise to new nouns of a technical nature. Thus, בְּרֵאשִׁית creation (Gen. i. 1) ; Bᵉr.

שׁוּמֵרָה ; t. ib. iii. 4, שׁוּמֵירָה. In Kil. v. 3, M. and edd. have שׁוֹמִירָה, N. שׁוֹמרה. L has in all these passages שׁומרה. Cf. Maimonides and other commentaries, *ad loc.*

¹ מַחַט שֶׁנִּיטַל חֲרִירָה a needle, the eyelet of which has been removed שֶׁל סַקָּיִין שֶׁנִּיטַל חֲרִירָה a needle of sack-makers, the eyelet of which, &c. Cf. Syr. ܚܪܘܪܐ.

² Cf. Sirach xi. 3 : אֱלִיל בָּעוֹף דְּבוֹרָה.

³ From כפף. L and other texts have more correctly קְפִיפָה, diminutive of קוּפָּה. So elsewhere, e.g. So. ii. 1 ; Kel. xxvi. 1. Cf. Wright, *Comp. Gr.*, p. 167 ; Kohut, iv. 298.

ix. 2 ; אַפִּין וְרַקִּין, the particles אַף and בַק RH 17b ; אְתִין the
particle אֶת אֶת BQ 41 b ; לָאַוִין prohibitionists (לֹא = לָאו) Yeb. 10b ;
עוֹדִין (L, edd. עוֹדַיִין) extras, plur. of עוֹד Men. vii. 2 ; Ter. iv. 7 ;
אוֹיִים plur. of אוֹ or א Šebu. 33 b ; 'עֲשֵׂה' (מִצְוַת) command of
affirmation ; 'לֹא תַעֲשֶׂה' (מִצְוַת) command of prohibition, Qid. i. 7 ;
'שֶׁהוּא בְלֹא יָבֹא' who is included in the command : ' He shall not
enter ' (Deut. xxiii. 3) ; Yeb. iv. 13 ; 'מִשּׁוּם לֹא תִתֵּן' because of the
command ' Thou shalt not give ' (Lev. xxv. 37), BM v. 11 ;
'אוֹתוֹ וְאֶת בְּנוֹ נוֹהֵג' the command ' It and its young ' (Lev. xxii. 28)
is in force, &c., Ḥul. v. 1.

(8) Diminutives.[1]

276. We may summarize here the various methods employed by
MH to express the diminutive. Most of these forms have already
been given above.

(i) Reduplication.

    (a) Ground-form Qaṭlul, especially with the termination
      ִית, § 244.

    (b) Ground-form Qṭalṭul, § 245.

(ii) By means of Suffixes.

    (a) Suffix וֹן, § 268.

    (b) Suffix ִית, § 271.

(iii) Insertion of Vowel-Sound (Quṭail).

    (a) Ground-form Quṭel, § 273.

    (b) Ground-form Qeṭel, § 273.

    (c) Ground-form Qeṭil, § 273.

(iv) By periphrasis with בֶּן : בְּנֵי בְּצָלִים young onions, t. 'Uq.
ii. 8 ; בֶּן גָּמָל young camel, Ḥul. 59 a ; בֶּן חָרִיץ small ditch,
BB vii. 4 ; בֶּן נֵץ young hawk, Mekil. (Weiss) 40 ; בֶּן פַּטִּישׁ small
hammer, Kel. xxix. 7. Perhaps also בַּת קוֹל the Bath Qol, Yeb.
xvi. 6. Cf. BH בְּנֵי יוֹנָה ; בֶּן בָּקָר, &c.

[1] For a full treatment of diminutive forms in BH and MH cf. M. H. Segal,
מדעי היהדות in הַצְּעִירוּת בְּעִבְרִית, vol. i (Jerusalem, 1926), pp. 139-54.

3. Formation of the Feminine.

277. In the formation of the Feminine, MH follows faithfully the rules of BH, except that it uses more frequently the older and more expressive termination תָ‍‍ַ. But the termination הָ‍ַ is still the more common of the two.

(i) הָ‍ַ is found in nouns like יְבָמָה a brother's childless widow, Yeb. ii. 3; חֲלָלָה illegitimate issue of a priest, Qid. iv. 6; לְוִיָּה a Levite woman, Qid. iii. 5; נְתִינָה female descendant of the Gibeonites, Yeb. ii. 4; גְּדִיָּה she-kid, Men. xiii. 7; חֲמוֹרָה she-ass, t. Kil. v. 4; רְחֵלָה ewe, Ḥul. xi. 2.

Further, concrete nouns : גּוּפָה hole, Ḥul. ii. 9; מְגוּפָה stopper, Šab. xxii. 3; מְחִיצָה party-wall, Kil. iv. 4. Abstracts : חֲזָקָה usucaption; קְטָטָה strife; שְׂרָרָה dominion (§ 224); חוֹבָה duty, Naz. ii. 8'; קוֹרָה cooling, Ab. iv. 17.

Verbal nouns : שְׁתִיָּה, זְרִיעָה, אֲכִילָה (§ 228); סַכָּנָה, בַּטָּלָה (§ 237); הוֹצָאָה, הֲבָאָה, הַבְדָּלָה (§ 252).

Usually in Adjectives : טְהוֹרָה pure, Ket. ii. 5; צְרִיכָה necessary, Yeb. v. 2; עֲנִיָּה poor; עֲשִׁירָה rich, Qid. iii. 5; גַּסָּה stout, big; דַּקָּה thin, small, ib. i. 4.

Participles : Exclusively in Participle active Qal of Intransitive verbs of the form *Qaṭel*, and Participle passive Qal (§ 113). Predominantly in Partic. of ע"ו (except the Intensive Stem and Hophʻal (§§ 178 ff.); ל"ה verbs, and often in ל"א (§ 112).

On the Aramaizing spelling of א‍ַ for הָ‍ַ cf. above, § 38 footnote.

278. (ii) תָ‍ַ, תֶ‍ַ (after a guttural) : גִּיּוֹרֶת woman proselyte, Yeb. vi. 5; כֹּהֶנֶת female descendant of the priests, ib. xvi. 7; מַמְזֶרֶת bastardess, ib. ii. 4; חֵרֶשֶׁת mute; פִּיקַחַת with full senses, ib. xiii. 8; אִלֶּמֶת dumb; גִּדֶּמֶת without arm, Ḥul. 79 a; קֵרַחַת bald, BB 132 a; גַּרְגֶּרֶת windpipe, Ḥul. iii. 1; עוֹלֶלֶת small bunch, Pea vii. 4; פַּרְפֶּרֶת dessert, Ab. iii. 18.

Participles: cf. §§ 111, 118, 122, 144.

279. (iii) Termination יִת_, in nouns and adjectives: חָבִית,
עֲדִית, שַׁחֲרִית (§ 271); אֲרָמִית Pes. 112 b; צוֹרִית, מַדְבָּרִית Tyrian,
Ma'a. iii. 5; אֲמָצָעִית, עוֹלָמִית, פּוּנְדָּקִית inn-keeper, Yeb. xvi. 7;
חַבְלָנִית destructive, Mak. i. 10; חֶנְוָנִית shop-keeper, Ket. ix. 4;
יוֹצָאנִית gadding about, Gen. R. 45; בֵּינוֹנִית Kel. xvii. 9 (§ 270).

280. (iv) Termination וּת_, only in abstracts: מַלְקוּת scourging,
Mak. i. 3; עַבְדּוּת slavery, Pes. 116 b; זְכוּת, גְּנוּת (§ 272).

4. The Formation of the Plural.

(1) *Masculine Nouns.*

281. The plur. termination of masc. nouns is in MH almost as
often יִן_ as יִם_. The termination יִן_ is not an Aramaism.
-*in* is probably the more original of the two terminations, since -*n* is
common to nearly all Semitic languages. It is the only one found
on the Meša' stone, though Phoenician uses only -*im*. In BH the
form -*in* is found frequently,[1] and as early as the Song of Deborah
(מִדִּין Judges v. 10). It must have been more common still in the
spoken language. Its frequent occurrence in MH can, therefore,
be explained as a purely Hebraic phenomenon. However, in very
many cases it is due to the Aramaizing proclivities of the copyists,
as is proved by comparing different texts.

282. The following peculiarities may be noted about the plur.
of masc. nouns in MH.

Nouns of the Ground-form קוֹטֶל (*Quṭl*) retain in many texts,
especially those of Babylonian origin, the vowel letter ו also in the
plur. Thus, אוֹנֶס compulsion, אוֹנָסִים Ned. iii. 1; חוֹמֶשׁ one-fifth,
חוֹמָשִׁים Ter. vi. 4; יוֹחֵס pedigree, יוֹחָסִין Qid. iv. 1. This may be
merely an orthographic peculiarity, and the first letter should
be pronounced with a short vowel *ŏ* (ָ), as usually in L. But it

---

[1] Cf. Stade, § 323 a, where twenty-five examples are enumerated.

is also possible that the traditional pronunciation of the first vowel as long (ō- יֹ) is correct. The full spelling with יֹ would, therefore, represent a dialectal variation. Cf. in BH אוֹרְחוֹתֶיךָ, אֹהָלִים, &c.; Ges.-K., § 93 r.[1]

The plur. of נֶזֶק damage, is נְזִיקִין BQ i. 1, as if from נָזִיק; cf. BH פְּסִילִים—פֶּסֶל.

The plur. of שׁוֹר is שְׁוָרִים, construct, שְׁוָרֵי Men. xiii. 9; of שׁוּק market, שְׁוָקִים Šab. 33 b; לְוָחִים, לוּחַ BM 117 a, לוּחֵי Šab. xiv. 4. Cf. Ges.-K., § 93 w.

Some nouns from ע״ע roots, show the reduplicated form in the plur., on the analogy of the tri-radicals: צַד side, צְדָדִים Šab. xx. 4, צְדָדֵי BQ ii. 2 (so L correctly for צִדֵּי in editions); טַל dew, טְלָלִים[2] Ḥag. 12 b; שֵׁן cliff, שְׁנָנִים Oh. viii. 2. סַם also inserts נ before the termination, סַמְמָנִים[3] spices, Ker. 6 a.

גַּרְדִּי weaver, Dam. i. 4, has the plur. גַּרְדִּיִּים 'Ed. i. 3, on the analogy of עֲנִיִּים.

Nouns with suffix יִ— (אִי—, cf. §§ 38, 237) reproduce the vowel letter א in the plur.: זַכַּאי innocent, זַכָּאִים Ab. i. 8; רַשַּׁאי permitted, רַשָּׁאִים ib. iv. 8. So בָּקִי expert, San. vii. 2, בְּקִיאִין Yo. viii. 5. L and other Pal. texts often have יִין—, וַדַּיִן, &c. So וַדַּיִן, בְּקִיִּין Ker. vi. 4.

Similarly, the ל״ה noun חֲצִי half, BQ iv. 9 = plur. constr. חֲצָאֵי 'Ed. iii. 1, חֲצָאִין Qid. 20 b, but also חֲצָיִין Ker. 5 a; Sifra 108 b; חֲצָיֵי Oh. viii. 6 (L. חֲצָאֵי). Cf. BH Ges.-K., § 93 x.

The plur. of שֶׂה lamb is שֶׂיִין Bek. 11 a; cf. BH שֵׂיוֹ Deut. xxii. 1. Forms ending in a vowel insert י (or א in Babylonian texts) between the final vowel and the plur. termination: מַשֵּׂהוּ (= מַה

---

[1] So also with pronominal suffix; cf. above, § 39 and foot-note.

[2] Cf. BH הֲרָרִים, so Ḥag. i. 8; Ges.-K., § 93 aa. Contrast Aram. טַלִּין j. Targ. Gen. xxvii. 28, &c.

[3] Other forms are: סַמָּנִים BQ 101 a; סַמָּנִיּוֹת Šab. xii. 3, editions, or סַמְּיוֹנוֹת L and N.

+שֶׁהוּא) something, מַשֶּׁהוּיִין 'Ev. 87 a; או or, אוּיֵי אוּיִים‎, j. Šebu.
iv. 5; אוּאִין Šebu. 33 b (cf. § 275).

שְׁאָר remainder, has plur. constr. שְׁיָרֵי Ab. i. 2. The plur. is
שִׁירִים (L) spelt in editions שְׁיָרַיִם‎, as dual and so pronounced
traditionally: שְׁיָרַיִם‎. Cf. also the verbal form, § 162, and below,
§ 293.

A few nouns of the form *Qaṭíl* take in the plur. the form *Qaṭúl*:
מָלִיחַ salty food, מְלוּחִין‎; צְלִי roasted food, צְלוּיִין Ned. vi. 3; שָׁלִיחַ
messenger, Giṭ. iv. 1, שְׁלוּחִין RH i. 3, שְׁלוּחֵי Yo. i. 5. So with
suffixes: שְׁלוּחוֹ‎, שְׁלוּחָהּ Qid. ii. 1; שְׁלוּחֵנוּ Yo. i. 5. L. has also
שְׁלוּחַ for constr. sing., Giṭ. iii. 6, but absolute: שָׁלִיחַ‎.

(2) *Feminine Nouns.*

283. (i) Feminine nouns ending in the sing. in הָ‎, or תָ‎,
תְ‎, form the plur. in וֹת‎, e.g. שׁוּרָה vow, שׁוּרוֹת Pea vi. 3;
תִּינוֹקֶת little girl, תִּינוֹקוֹת Yo. viii. 4.

Some segolate nouns ending in ת retain the ת in the plur.: דְּלָת
door, דְּלָתוֹת Tam. iv. 1; חֵמֶת leather bottle, חֲמָתוֹת Kel. xxvi. 4;
לֶפֶת turnip, לְפָתוֹת San. 19 b; כֶּסֶת bolster, כְּסָתוֹת Kil. ix. 2;
סוֹלֶת fine flour, סְלָתוֹת Šeq. iv. 3; שׁוֹקֶת trough, שְׁקָתוֹת Pa. v. 8.
Cf. for BH Ges.-K., 95 f.

The plur. of אַשְׁפָּה‎, אַשְׁפָּת dunghill, is אַשְׁפַּתּוֹת Šebi. i. 1, cf. above,
§ 249 note.

The plur. of עֶרְוָה incest, is עֶרְיוֹת Yeb. i. 2, as if from עֶרְיָה‎. This
last form is actually found in L., Hag. i. 10, and in K.,[1] 'Ed. i. 12.
Cf. also Bek. vi. 5—genitals of animal; further, Habak. iii. 9.

284. (ii) Nouns ending in ית‎ form the plur. in יוֹת‎:[2] בֵּינוֹנִית

---

[1] Cf. Krauss, *MGWJ.*, li, p. 325, note 1.

[2] The י in these forms, and also in the plur. of the nouns in the next
section, serves to remove the *hiatus* between the final vowel of the sing. (י‎
without the fem. termination ת‎) and the vowel at the beginning of the plur.
termination וֹת‎; cf. מַשֶּׁהוּיִין § 282, and the plur. of the nouns in § 286.

middle, בֵּינוֹנִיּוֹת Kel. xvii. 10; חָבִית jar, חֲבִיּוֹת Nᵉd. viii. 7; טַלִּית cloak, טַלִּיּוֹת Zab. iv. 5 (but also טַלִּיתוֹת in later texts, e. g. Num. R. 18); רְבִיעִית quart, רְבִיעִיּוֹת Pᵉs. 112 a; תַּעֲנִית fast, תַּעֲנִיּוֹת Ta‘a. ii. 1; דִּרְשָׁנִיּוֹת, חַכְמָנִיּוֹת, צַדְקָנִיּוֹת BB 119 b.

The plur. of בְּרִית covenant, is בְּרִיתוֹת Nᵉd. iii. 2 (בְּרִיּוֹת is plur. of בְּרִיָּה = בְּרִיאָה creature, San. iv. 5); so טַלִּיתוֹת above. Cf. חֲנִיתוֹת Ges.-K., § 87 k.

285. (iii) Nouns ending in the sing. in ‏ות‎— form the plur. in ‏ויּוֹת‎—: חָנוּת shop, חֲנֻיּוֹת ‘AZ i. 4; רְשׁוּת premises, רְשֻׁיּוֹת t. Šab. i. 1; Hag. 15 a.

Some nouns in ‏ות‎— take the termination ‏יּוֹת‎—; אוּמָּנוּת handicraft, אוּמָּנִיּוֹת Bik. iii. 3; זְכוּת merit, זְכִיּוֹת Yo. 86 b. So אוֹת letter of the alphabet, אוֹתִיּוֹת Šab. viii. 3 (אוֹתוֹת is plur. of אוֹת sign, Kil. ix. 10).

So also a few other nouns: בְּקַעַת log of wood, בְּקָעִיּוֹת Ḥul. 37 b; Sifre 99 d; פְּקַעַת skein, פְּקָעִיּוֹת Kel. xvii. 2; כְּנֶסֶת (בֵּית) Synagogue, כְּנֵסִיּוֹת (כְּתֵי) ¹ Ab. iii. 10; פָּרָשָׁה section; פָּרָשִׁיּוֹת sections of Scripture (פָּרָשׁוֹת) sections of the spine, Ḥul. 45 b).

(3) *Foreign Nouns.*

286. The plur. of nouns borrowed from Gk. and Lat. is formed, like that of native nouns, by attaching the plur. termination ‏ים‎—, ‏ות‎—, to the sing. in its MH form,² thus: טְפוּס (דְּפוּס = τύπος), טְפוּסִים (דְּפוּסִים) Da. v. 3, 4; סִימוֹן (= σιτώνης) סִימוֹנוֹת ib. ii. 4; אֶפִּיקוֹרוֹס (= Epicurus), אֶפִּיקוֹרְסִים, אֶפִּיקוֹרוֹסִים Ber. ix. 5; אִסָּר (assarius), אִסָּרוֹת Pea viii. 1; הֶדְיוֹט (= ἰδιώτης), הֶדְיוֹטוֹת San. x. 2.

---

¹ This gave rise to the sing. כְּנֵסִיָּה, Ab. iv. 11. L has כְּנֵסָה.

² Cf. Krauss, *Lehnwörter*, i, §§ 315–25; Albrecht, § 84 k, l. לִיסְטִים, Pea ii. 7, plur. of לִסְטִים (= λῃστής: לִסְטִים אֶחָד, Yᵉb. 25 b) forms an exception, cf. Kohut, v, p 46 a. Usually the sing. is also written לסטים. Further: אֶסְקְרִיטִים = ἐσχαρίτης, Ḥal. i. 4.

K

In the case of fem. nouns ending in the sing. in the vowel *ā*
(= אָ‑ָ, הָ‑ָ), א, or usually in Palest. texts, י, is inserted between
the final vowel of the sing. *ā*, and the vowel *ó* (= וֹת‑) of the plur.
termination, in order to obviate the meeting of two vowels. Thus:
טַבְלָה (טַבְלָא = tabula), טַבְלָאוֹת Pes. 57 a; דְּיֵיטָה, דְּיוֹטָא (= δίαιτα),
דְּיֵיטָיוֹת, דְּיוֹטָאוֹת (L), 'Er. viii. 11; גּוּזְטְרָא (= ἐξώστρα), גּוּזְטְרָאוֹת
ib. 9 (L כצוצרה, כצוצריות, cf. §§ 44, 51); גִּימַטְרְיָא (= γεωμετρία)
גִּימַטְרְיָאוֹת Ab. iii. 18. Some foreign nouns have become fully
naturalized in the language, and form their plur. regularly, e.g.
דּוּגְמָא (= δεῖγμα), דּוּגְמוֹת BQ 119 b.

This form of the fem. plur. termination for foreign nouns,
אוֹת‑ָ, יוֹת‑ָ, is also used for Gk. nouns ending in the sing. in
י‑ָ (= η): דְּיֵיתִיקִי (= διαθήκη). דְּיֵיתִיקָאוֹת אַפּוֹתִיקִי (= ὑποθήκη),
אַפּוֹתִיקָאוֹת BM 19 a; so: קַטַבְלָאוֹת, plur. of καταβολή, Šeq. iii. 4.
Further, גְּלוּסְקִין (= κόλλιξ), Da. vi. 12; also: גְּלוּסְקָא Pes. 6 b,
plur.: גְּלוּסְקָאוֹת Ket. 111 b; סַנְהֶדְרִין (= συνέδριον; also : סַנְהֶדְרִי),
plur. : סַנְהֶדְרְיָאוֹת San. i. 5 (L. סנהדראות; so Cant. R. iii. 7).

287. This plur. termination, אוֹת‑ָ, יוֹת‑ָ became very common
through the influx of Gk. and Lat. nouns into the language,
especially in later MH. As a result this termination is also found
sometimes in native nouns, thus: מִקְוֶה a ritual bath, מִקְוָאוֹת
Šeq. i. 1 (but L has מִקְווֹת; so Miq. i. 1, &c.); מֶרְחָץ a bathing
establishment, מֶרְחֲצָאוֹת (מֶרְחֲצִיוֹת) Ta'a. i. 6; מִשְׁתֶּה a feast, מִשְׁתָּאוֹת
Nid. 16 b; פַּרְפֶּרֶת dessert, פַּרְפְּרָאוֹת (beside נימטריאות!) Ab. iii. 18,
but also: פַּרְפְּרוֹתָיו Šab. 148 b; שַׁלְשֶׁלֶת chain, שַׁלְשְׁלָאוֹת 'Er. 58 a;
also the Aram. noun בֵּירָאוֹת (בירית) cisterns, 'Er. ii. 1.

The plur. of אֵם mother, is אִמָּהוֹת Qid. iv. 4; Pea iii. 4 (cf.
BH אֲמָהוֹת maids; also Dalman, p. 199), but also: אִמּוֹת אִימוֹתֵיהֶם
t. BB vii. 9. Of אָחוֹת sister, אֲחָיוֹת Yeb. ii. 6, as in BH.

288. As in BH, numerous masc. nouns form the plur. by וֹת‑,
e.g. חוֹתָם seal, חוֹתָמוֹת Šeq. v. 1; חֵן favour, חִנּוֹת So. 47 a; כְּלָל

general rule, כְּלָלוֹת 'Er. 25 a ; מִדְבָּר wilderness, מִדְבָּרוֹת Ḥul. ii. 8 ; מִקְרָא verse, מִקְרָאוֹת Ber. 32 a ; נְיָיר paper, נְיָירוֹת Pa. x. 6 ; תִּינוֹק male infant ; (שְׁנֵי) תִּינוֹקוֹת Šab. xix. 4 ; especially nouns with the suffix ‍‍ָ‍ן‍, ‍‍ו‍ן‍ָ : אִילָן tree, אִילָנוֹת Šebi. i. 2 ; זָדוֹן act of presumption, זְדוֹנוֹת BM 33 b ; סִילוֹן pipe, סִילוֹנוֹת Kel. ii. 3 ; עִנְיָן subject, עִנְיָינוֹת Šab. 61 b ; צְנוֹן horse-radish, צְנוֹנוֹת Šab. ii. 2 ; קָרְבָּן sacrifice, קָרְבָּנוֹת Zeb. xiv. 10. Further, *nomina agentis* of the form *Qaṭól* (§ 235) : לָקוֹחוֹת, דָּרוֹכוֹת, &c.

So also a number of nouns from ע״י roots ; גַּיִס troop, גְּיָסוֹת Yeb. xvi. 7 ; חַיִל army, חֲיָילוֹת Sifra 89 d, but also חֲיָילִים Mekil. 63 ; עִיר city, עֲיָירוֹת Meg. i. 1, but also עָרִים 'Er. v. 1 ; פַּיִס lot, פְּיָסוֹת Yo. ii. 3. Similarly, מַיִם water, מֵימוֹת j. So. ii. 2 ; יַיִן wine, יֵינוֹת Šeq. iv. 4.

ל״ה nouns : קָלְיָא parched corn ; קִלְיוֹת BM iv. 12 ; בְּלִי (or, perhaps, בְּלָי) בְּלָאוֹת, (L בליות ; cf. בְּלוֹיֵי and בְּלוֹיָ Jer. xxxviii. 11, 12) ; but the construct is בְּלָאֵי Suk. v. 3, בְּלוֹיֵי Kel. xxvii. 5.

The same difference between the plur. absolute and construct is found also in other nouns ; thus : שְׁטָר document, שְׁטָרוֹת BM ii. 5 ; וָלָד child, וְלָדוֹת, וַלְדֵי, in the phrase וַלְדֵי וְלָדוֹת Bek. ii. 4 ; פְּרִי fruit, פֵּירוֹת, פֵּירֵי, in the phrase פֵּירֵי פֵירוֹת Ket. ix. 1 ; אִילָנוֹת trees, Šebi. i. 2 ; אִילָנֵי So. viii. 2, 3 ; בַּת group, כְּתוֹת Pes. v. 5 ; כְּתֵּי Naz. iii. 7.

Verbal nouns of the Ground-form *Haqṭel* (§ 251), being really fossilized infinitives, have no plur. of their own. They use the plur. of the corresponding verbal noun *Haqṭala*, e.g. הֶעְלֵם concealed act, plur. הֶעֲלֵמוֹת Šab. xii. 4, 6 ; הֶקְדֵּשׁ sanctified property, Ter. i. 5 ; הַקְדֵּשׁוֹת San. i. 3, &c. So the infinitival noun כָּרֵת (§ 116) is in the plur. כָּרֵיתוֹת, from the verbal noun כְּרִיתָה (§ 228), Ker. i. 1.

289. Conversely, many fem. nouns take the masc. termination in the plur. Thus, חִטָּה wheat, חִטִּים ; שְׂעוֹרָה barley, שְׂעוֹרִים ; כּוּסֶּמֶת spelt, כּוּסְּמִין Šebu. iii. 3 ; דְּלַעַת pumpkin, דְּלוּעִין Kil. iii. 7 ;

כְּרֵישָׁה leek, Makš. i. 5, כְּרֵישִׁין Kil. i. 2 ; קִישׁוּת cucumber, קִישׁוּאִין Kil. xx. 4, 6 ; פַּגָּה fig, t. Šebi. i. 1, פַּגִּים Šebi. iv. 7 ; further, אַרְנֶבֶת hare, אַרְנָבִים Šab. 27 a ; יוֹנָה pigeon, יוֹנִים San. iii. 3 ; נְמָלָה ant, נְמָלִים Pea iv. 1 ; בֵּיצָה egg, בֵּיצִים Ḥul. xii. 3. Further, גְּדִילָה, גְּדִילִים (Deut. xxii. 12), Sifre Num. xv. 38 ; נִימָה chord, נִימִים Šeq. viii. 5. Cf. Ges.-K., § 87 q.

290. Some nouns show both plurals : פְּרִידָה pair of pigeons, פְּרִידִים Kin. iii. 6 in L ; Sifra 8 d ; פְּרִידוֹת Kin. ib. (in editions) ; BQ 38 b ; רְחֵלִים and רְחֵלוֹת ewes, Ḥul. xi. 1, 2 (in L ; cf. Ḥul. 137 b (above, § 3)) ; מַסְמְרוֹת BB 7 b, and מַסְמְרִים Gen. R. 68, nails, מְשָׁלִים So. 9 a, and מְשָׁלוֹת Ab. deRN. i. 4 ; San. 38 b, parables.[1]

Sometimes there is a variation in meaning between the two plurals : יָמִים days, Yo. i. 1, and יָמוֹת collective : season (only in constr.). Ber. i. 5 ; Šeq. viii. 1 ; Ṭoh. vi. 7 ; שָׁנִים years, Ab. v. 21, and שָׁנוֹת collective : age, only with suffix, Ber. 58 b ; עֲצָמִים single bones, and עֲצָמוֹת collective, 'Ed. i. 7 ; קְבָרִים graves, Ta'a. 25 b, and קְבָרוֹת collective, burial-place, Naz. ix. 3.[2] With a derived significance in the secondary plur. : עֲדָשִׁים lentils, Kil. xi. 8, and עֲדָשׁוֹת lentil measures, Neg. vi. 1 ; שְׂפָתַיִם lips, Ket. 61 b (also שְׂפָתוֹת San. 90 b, with suffix only), and שְׂפָיוֹת rims, Kel. iv. 4 ; רַבִּים many, 'AZ i. 7, and רַבּוֹת teachers (only with suffix), 'Er. v. 3 ; תְּמָרִים date palms, Bik. i. 5, and תְּמָרוֹת young branches of other trees, Ma'a. iv. 6, &c. ; שִׁנַּיִם teeth and שְׁנָנִים teeth of rock, cliffs, Oh. viii. 2 ; תְּפִלָּה, תְּפִלּוֹת prayer, Ber. iii. 1, and תְּפִלָּה, תְּפִלִּין phylacteries, Men. iv, 1 ; iii. 7 ; אֱלוֹהוֹת gods ; אֱלֹהִים God ; 'AZ iv. 7 ; יָדַיִם hands ; יָדוֹת handles, Yo. iii. 2.

291. In the lists given above, the reader will have observed several nouns with plur. in MH which in BH are only found in the sing., e.g. בְּרִית, יַיִן, סֹלֶת, &c. To these may be added many

---

[1] But prob. read ממשלות ; cf. Lewin, אגרת ר׳ שרירא, p. iii (נספחים).

[2] For the original collective sense of the fem. termination, cf. Stade, § 322 c.

more examples: אֵבֶר, אֵבָרִים limbs, parts of the body, Yo. vi. 6 ; דְּשָׁא,
דְּשָׁאִים herbs, Ber. vi. 1 ; זְוָעָה, זְוָעוֹת earthquakes, ib. ix. 2 ; זֶרַע,
זְרָעִים plants, Šab. 95 b ; 31 a ; חוֹל, חוּלִּין common things, Ḥul. v. 1 ;
יָרָק, יְרָקוֹת vegetables, Ber. vi. 1 ; כֶּסֶף, כְּסָפִים money, BM 42 a ;
מָזוֹן, מְזוֹנוֹת maintenance, Sebi. iv. 1 ; קֶמַח, קְמָחוֹת various kinds of
flour, Men. viii. 7 ; רֶמֶשׂ, רְמָשִׂים creeping things ; שֶׁקֶץ, שְׁקָצִים
reptiles, Šebu. iii. 4 ; רַעַם, רְעָמִים thunders, Ber. ix. 2 ; שֶׂה, שְׂיִן
sheep, Bek. 11 a ; שֶׁלֶג, שְׁלָגִים snow, Pes. 94 b ; שֶׁמֶן, שְׁמָנִים oils,
Suk. iv. 4 ; תָּמִיד, תְּמִידִים the daily offerings, sacrifices (Num.
xxviii. 3), Šeq. iv. 1.

292. Conversely, many nouns which in BH appear only in the
plur., are found in MH also in the sing. In addition to those
given in the above lists (e.g. בֵּיצָה, חָנוּת, סַם, &c.) may be mentioned : אַלְמֻג red sandal wood, Kil. xiii. 6 ; בָּצָל onion, Šebi. i. 10 ;
זָוִית corner, Šab. xii. 4 ; סָגָן chief of priests, Pes. i. 6 ; כִּירָה hearth,
Šab. iii. 1 (BH כִּירַיִם) ; שִׁקְמָה sycamore, Kil. i. 8, &c.

5. The Dual.

293. The Dual, which has practically disappeared from Aram.,
is quite common in MH. Not only has MH retained the old BH
duals like עֵינַיִם, רַגְלַיִם, שׁוֹקַיִם, כְּפֵרַיִם, כְּפָלַיִם, מָאתַיִם, &c., but it has
also preserved the absolute form of the dual of nouns which in BH
occur only in the construct or with suffixes, e.g. גַּבַּיִם back, Kel.
xxv. 5 ; עַפְעַפַּיִם eyelids, Šab. 109 a ; קְרָבַיִם intestines, Tam. iv. 2 ;
קַרְסוּלַיִם ankles, Ḥul. iii. 7 ; שׁוּלַיִם skirts, Kel. xv. 1. The following
are new formations : אֲחוֹרַיִם back, Kel. xxv. 1 ; אֶצְבָּעַיִם two fingers,
Oh. iii. 1 ; בֵּינְתַּיִם between, BM x. 6 ; גַּפַּיִם wings. Ḥul. iii. 4 ; [1]
דִּירַיִם shed, t. Ned. i. 3 ; זַרְתַּיִם two spans, t. Men. ix. 3 ; Taʻa. 5 a ;
חֲנִיכַיִם gums, Ḥul. 103 b ; טְלָפַּיִם hooves, Ḥul. ix. 1 ; טְפָחַיִם two

---

[1] i. e. the limbs on which the plumage, כְּנָפַיִם, grows. Hence the Mishnah
says : נִשְׁתַּבְּרוּ גַּפֶּיהָ, but נִמְרְטוּ כְּנָפֶיהָ, ib.

handbreadths, BB i. 1 ; כּוֹרַיִם two *kors*, Kel. xv. 1 ; מְנַפַּיִם greaves, ib. xi. 8 ; מַחֲלָצַיִם windlass, MQ. i. 10 ; (בֵּית) הַמַּטְבְּחַיִם slaughter-house, Ab. v. 5 ; מַסְפָּרַיִם scissors, Kel. xvi. 8 ; קַבַּיִם two *qabs*, 'Ed. i. 2 ; רִבְעָתַיִם two-fourths, Kᵉr. i. 7 ; שִׁירַיִם[1] remainder, 'Er. ii. 6.

IV. PARTICLES

1. Adverbs.

294. MH has lost a considerable number of BH adverbs. Some of these have been replaced by MH formations, or by borrowings from Aram. Others, mostly of a poetical nature, have found no exact substitutes in MH.

The following is a list of BH adverbs not found in MH. The words in brackets represent their MH substitutes.

אוּלָם, (הֵיכָן, אֵיכָן) אֵיפֹה אַיֵּה ; (בְּשָׁעָה זוֹ) אֲנֵי, אָז ; (שֶׁמָּא) אוּלַי ; (אֶלָּא) רַק, אַף ; אָכֵן (common in Aram. in a different sense), אָמְנָם ; (כָּאן) הֵנָּה, הֲלוֹם ; אֵין, לֹא, בִּלְעֲדֵי, בִּלְתִּי, בְּלִי, בַּל, אֶפֶס; (אֱמֶת) תָּמִיד (תָּדִיר) עֵקֶב, (קוֹדֶם שֶׁ, לִפְנֵי שֶׁ) טֶרֶם only of the daily sacrifice, § 291); further, (רֵיקָן) רֵיקָם, פִּתְאֹם (בְּכָל יוֹם, בַּיּוֹם) יוֹמָם, only as adjective, Taʻa. ii. 2.

אֵיכָה, אֵיכָכָה, and כָּכָה are used in shortened forms : אֵיךְ, or with the demonstrative particle הֵי—: הֵיאַךְ, or הֵאֵיךְ, and כָּךְ. So הָלְאָה (also in Aram.) is represented by לְהַלָּן ;[2] כֹּה by כָּן, כָּאן; מֵאַיִן is shortened to מִנַּיִן.

Other new forms peculiar to MH are : כַּיּוֹצֵא בְ־, כִּין, כְּדֵי, בֵּינְתַיִם, עַכְשָׁו (אֱדַיִן),[3] עֲדַיִן (BH עֶדֶן ; Aram. עִדָּן, לְמַפְרֵעַ, כְּלוֹמַר, כְּלוּם (§ 437), כֵּיצַד עַכְשָׁיו (probably = עַד + כְּשֶׁהוּא).

---

[1] This is the traditional pronunciation and the usual spelling. L, however, has always שִׁירִים. Also the construct is pronounced שִׁירֵי, as if from שִׁירִים; cf. above, § 58. שִׁירַיִים silk, σηρικόν, should be pointed שִׁירָיִים, L שִׁירָאִין.

[2] Or, perhaps, לְהַלָּן, viz. לְ +הָל +ן—ַ, cf. § 267, and לְשָׁם for BH שָׁמָּה, § 295.

[3] Krauss's view (*ZDMG.*, 1913, p. 737) that עֲדַיִן is composed of עַד + אֵין

Borrowings from Aram. are: תְּדִיר, (עַל אֲתַר) לְאַלְתַּר, אֶשְׁתָּקֵד; probably also בְּנוֹן, עֲרַאי (= כְּעֵין), and perhaps also לָאו, תֵּכֶף[1]. So also שׁוּב is an Aramaism = תּוּב.

(1) Adverbs of Place.

295. אֵיכָן (אֵי + כָן), commonly הֵיכָן, especially in Babyl. texts, where? Šab. i. 3; Šeq. vi. 1. So in Aram. (cf. Barth, *Pronominalbildung*, p. 81), but very probably indigenous in MH.

With prepositions: לְהֵיכָן whither? Šab. xvi. 1; מֵהֵיכָן whence? Yo. v. 5; עַד הֵיכָן until where? Pes. x. 6.

אֵילָךְ, or הֵילָךְ, הֵלָךְ, only in phrase הֵילָךְ . . . הֵילָךְ, hither and thither, Pes. vii. 13; Zab. iii. 2; or הֵילָךְ וְהֵילָךְ Mak. iii. 12.

אָן where? only with prepos.: לְאָן whither? Ter. iv. 11; Ab. iii. 1 (many texts have לְאָן); מֵאָן whence? Ab. ib.; וּמֵאַיִן וּלְאָן Ḥag. 15 a; more often מְנַיִן: Ber. v. 3; Yo. vi. 8; especially when introducing quotations from Scripture: Šab. ix. 1 ff., &c.

בֵּנְתַּיִם, בֵּנְתַּיִם (especially in L.) between, BM x. 6. Cf. BH בֵּנַיִם 1 Sam. xvii. 4; בֵּנוֹת Ezek. x. 2; perhaps there was a form בֵּינוֹתַיִם Gen. xxvi. 28. So בֵּינַיִם וּבֵינְתַּיִם in the very centre, Gen. R. 4.

הַלָּן there, j. Ket. 28 d; Git. 46 d; usually with לְ: לְהַלָּן beyond, Dam. i. 3. So. vii. 5.

חוּץ outside, with prepositions: בַּחוּץ Zeb. vii. 5; מִבַּחוּץ from outside, 'Er. vii. 9; לַחוּץ outside, after verb of motion, Zeb. viii. 12; מִן הַמּוֹדִיעִית וּלְחוּץ from Modin and outside beyond, as opposed to מִן הַמּוֹדִיעִית וְלִפְנִים Ḥag. iii. 5.

is improbable. Perhaps the Aram. form אֲדַיִן is more original, and is to be equated with the BH אָז. On עַכְשָׁו cf. Dalman, p. 212, foot-note.

[1] From לָא + הוּא, cf. Dalman, § 46. This particle is, however, much more common in MH than in Aram. The traditional pointing לָאו is incorrect, as is shown by the cognate form עַכְשָׁו, עַכְשָׁו; cf. also BH יַחְדָּו, יַחְדָּיו. Some Palest. texts also write לִיו for לָאו above § 39.

כָּא, כָּן in Pal. texts, here, there (BH כֹּה = כֹּא): כָּאן וְכָאן here
and there, 'Er. x. 11; לְכָאן, after a verb of motion, 'Er. 40 b;
מִכָּאן . . . מִכָּאן on the one side, on the other side, Kil. vi. 6;
מִכָּאן וְעַד כָּאן from here to there, Be. iv. 7.

מָה: כַּמָּה how far? Ber. iii. 5.

מַטָּה, or מַטָּן in Palest. texts and also occasionally in others,
especially in passages connected with the Temple and its ritual,
Mid. i. 5, &c. This adverbial termination ‏ָן‎ is a modification of
the BH ‏ָם‎, cf. Ges.-K., § 100 g, h, and above, § 267.

Always with prepositions: לְמַטָּה below, Ḥag. ii. 1; מִלְּמַטָּה from
below, 'Er. viii. 6; מִלְּמַטָּן Šab. 98 b.

מִלְּמַעֲלָה, לְמַעֲלָה, מַעֲלָן, מַעֲלָה above, used exactly as מַטָּה cf. the
passages cited above.

מַפְרֵעַ, only with ל: לְמַפְרֵעַ backwards, Ber. ii. 3.

שָׁם there; after verbs of motion: לְשָׁם (= BH שָׁמָּה, which is
not found in MH) RH ii. 5; Šab. xvi. 4, &c.

(2) Adverbs of Time.

296. אָחוֹר only with prepos. ל: לְאָחוֹר backwards, Ḥag. ii. 1.

מֵעֶוְרָא וְאֵילַךְ, הֵילַךְ, אֵילַךְ further, onwards; מִכָּאן וְאֵילַךְ Ber. i. 2;
Pa. iii. 5.

אֵימָתַי, אֵמָתַי, אֵמְתִּי (L) when, Pea iii. 5; אֵימָתַי שֶׁתִּרְצֶה whenever thou
wishest, BM v. 3; מֵאֵימָתַי from when, Ber. i. 1; עַד אֵימָתַי till when,
ib. viii. 7.

אֶשְׁתָּקַד last year, Šeq. vi. 5 (Aram. compound: שַׁתָּא קָדְמָיָא;
cf. אֶשְׁתְּדָא this year, j. MŠ 35 b).

אֲתַר place (Aram.), with עַל: עַל אֲתַר on the spot, forthwith,
in Pal. texts; contracted in Babyl. texts to לְאַלְתַּר Giṭ. iii. 3; viii. 8.

בֵּינְתַּיִם between, meanwhile; Ṭoh. v. 3, 4.

הֵלָּן, only with ל: לְהֵלָּן further, beyond; מֵחֲצוֹת הַיּוֹם וּלְהֵלָּן from
noon and further, Men. x. 5.

יָד, with the preposition מִן : מִיָּד at once, BB i. 5 ; opposed to עַל יָד gradually, Pa. vii. 7 ; אֵין מְחַיְּבִין אוֹתוֹ לְמְכּוֹר מִיָּד אֶלָּא מוֹכֵר עַל יָד יָד עַל יָד they do not compel him to sell at once, but he may sell very gradually, BQ 80 a. (So perhaps BH, Prov. vi. 5 ; cf. מִן יָד j. Targ. Gen. i. 3, &c. ; BH עַל יָד יָד by degrees, Prov. xiii. 11.)

כָּאן (כָּן) only with מִן : מִכָּאן from now ; מִכָּאן וּלְהַבָּא from now and in the future, Kel. vii. 1 ; לְאַחַר מִכָּאן afterwards, Qid. ii. 6.

כְּבָר already, Yad. iv. 4 ; וּכְבָר a formula introducing a report of an event in confirmation of a previous statement, j. Keᵗ. v. 4.

כָּךְ, only with אַחַר : אַחַר כָּךְ afterwards, Beᵣ. viii. 6 ; לְאַחַר כָּךְ BM viii. 1.

מָה : עַד כַּמָּה how long ? Beᵏ. iv. 1.

מָחָר usually לְמָחָר to-morrow, ʿEr. iii. 9. So וּלְמָחֳרָת San. v. 5.

אֶמֶשׁ yesterday ; אֶמֶשׁ הֲרָגוֹ he slew him yesterday, San. 40 b ; מֵאֶמֶשׁ, opposed to מֵהַיּוֹם Be. i. 6 (BH אֶתְמֹל, which is common in Aram., is never used in MH).

מַפְרֵעַ : לְמַפְרֵעַ before, backwards, Miq. ii. 2.

עוֹד yet, again, Yo. vi. 1 ; with suff. : עוֹדֵהוּ Bik. iii. 6 ; עוֹדָהּ Keᵗ. vii. 8 ; עוֹדְךָ Šab. 151 b ; עוֹדָן ib. 43 b ; מִבְּעוֹד while yet, Šab. i. 5.

עֲדַיִן yet, Neᵈ. xi. 10 (L אֲדַיִן, as in Aram., Dan. ii. 15).

עוֹלָם with prepos. : לְעוֹלָם always, Teᵣ. ii. 4 ; with negative : never, MQ 26 b ; so מֵעוֹלָם, with negative : never, Mak. i. 10 ; עוֹלָמִית for ever, Yeᵇ. iii. 7 ; with negative : never, Šab. xxiii. 4.

עַכְשָׁיו, עַכְשָׁו now, ʿAZ i. 1 ; מֵעַכְשָׁו from now, Giṭ. vii. 3.

עֲרַאי, עֲרָיִי in Palest. texts, irregular, improvised, Ḥal. iii. 1 (opposed to קֶבַע fixed, Suk. 2 a).

פַּעַם : פַּעַם אַחַת once upon a time, ʿEr. iv. 2 , פְּעָמִים sometimes, BB v. 2.

שׁוּב again (Aram. תּוּב), Yeᵇ. xvi. 4, especially common in later literature.

תָּדִיר continually, always, BB iii. 1.

תֵּכֶף immediately, only once in Mishna: Men. ix. 8, but frequent in later literature, e.g. Ber. 42 a, &c.   Cf. the verb, Kil. ix. 10.

297. Other adverbial expressions of time are: בְּרִאשׁוֹנָה at the beginning, formerly, Šebi. iv. 1; תְּחִילָּה first, So. i. 7, בַּתְּחִלָּה (in Babyl. texts always לְבַתְּחִלָּה) as at the beginning, Šab. vi. 5, primarily, מִתְּחִלָּה 'AZ iii. 7, בַּתְּחִלָּה Yeb. v. 6; בָּאֶמְצַע in the middle; בַּסּוֹף in the end, ib.; מִיָּמֵי Zeb. xii. 4, מִיָּמֶיךָ Suk. ii. 7, מִימֵיהֶם Pes. i. 6, with לֹא, never; cf. BH 1 Kings i. 6, &c.

(3) Adverbs of Manner.

298. אֵין not; אֵין אַתָּה בָא thou comest not, Ab. iv. 1; אֵין אַתֶּם 'Er. v. 9; אֵין אָנוּ Šebu. iv. 2 ff. Suffixes are attached in some persons without the so-called *nun epentheticum*, as in BH (Ges.-K., § 100 o, p), thus: 1 sing. אֵינִי Ber. ii. 5; 3 sing. masc. אֵינוֹ; fem. אֵינָהּ So. vi. 3; 3 plur. אֵינָן ib. viii. 3.

Before words beginning with א, אֵין is sometimes shortened to אֵי: אֵי אַתָּה אִם אֵי BM v. 3. So always before אֶפְשָׁר: אֵי אֶפְשָׁר impossible, Šebu. iii. 8, &c.; and אֶפְשִׁי: אֵי אֶפְשִׁי I do not want, Naz. iv. 5.

אַל not, Ab. i. 3, &c.

בַּל = לֹא in quotations of Biblical prohibitions: Pes. iii. 1 (cf. below, § 472).

לְבַד alone, only with suffix: לְבַדָּהּ So. 8 a; or with בְּ: בִּלְבַד, after a negative, Ber. i. 1; or אֶלָּא Dam. iii. 5 (§ 507).

הֵיאַךְ how? BH; אֵיךְ RH ii. 8, &c.

הֵן yes, Gi‍ṭ. vii. 1.

וַדַּי, וַדַּאי certainly (from ודה to confess, agree), Ker. v. 2; וַדַּאי מָעַלְתִּי I have certainly used sacred property; opposed to סָפֵק doubt: סָפֵק אָכַל perhaps he has eaten, ib. iv. 1.

חֲלִילָה round about, over again, Suk. v. 6; Pes. 48 b.

יָכוֹל one might assume, possibly, Ab. iii. 8; כִּבְיָכוֹל as if one

could say (of an anthropomorphic expression applied to the Deity),
San. vi. 5. (Cf. Kohut, iv. 130–2.)

כְּ־, כְּמוֹ, כְּמוֹת, כְּמוּת (with the collective termination ־וֹת, as in BH
סביבות, בינות, &c.) like, followed by the relative שֶׁ־ MŠ v. 2, &c.
With suff.: כְּמוֹתִי BM 59 b; כְּמוֹתָךְ Ned. 4 b; כְּמוֹתוֹ Ber. v. 5;
כְּמוֹתָהּ Qid. iii. 2; כְּמוֹתָן Suk. i. 8.

כְּ־ as prefix: כְּאֶחָד together, t. Neg. i. 1; Ber. vii. 1 (in edd.);
כְּאַחַת Pea i. 4; Ber. ib. (L, of masc.).

כְּגוֹן like the colour of—like, as, for instance, Šebi. viii. 1;
cf. כְּעֵין.

כְּדֵי [1] as much as, Šab. viii. 1.

כְּדֶרֶךְ as Kil. vii. 6; כְּדַרְפּוֹ as his manner, as usual, Ma'a.
iii. 10.

כַּיּוֹצֵא בְ־ like, similarly; כַּיּוֹצֵא בוֹ [2] Pea iv. 8; כַּיּוֹצֵא בָהֶן Šebi.
viii. 2; כַּיּוֹצֵא בְאֵלּוּ Mak. i. 7; כַּיּוֹצֵא בַדָּבָר Sifra (Weiss) 4 a.

כֵּיצַד (צַד+אֵי+כְּ), in Halakic Midrashim כְּאֵיזֶצַד, also (בְּאֵיזֶה צַד)
how? Ber. vi. 1, &c.

כְּלוֹמַר as if to say, San. vi. 4. 6; very common in later MH in
sense of 'that is to say', 'namely'.

כַּמָּה how? Kil. ii. 3; בְּכַמָּה for how much? BM iv. 10;
כַּמָּה נָאִים how beautiful, Šab. 33 b; עַל אַחַת כַּמָּה וְכַמָּה how much
more and more? Mak. i. 7 (in arguments from minor to major).

כְּמִין like the kind of, like, Suk. ii. 2.

כְּנֶגֶד against, Dam. i. 2.

כֵּיוָן straight, immediately, Tam. iii. 6; Pes. 37 a, 54 a.

כָּךְ so, Ber. vii. 3; בְּכָךְ at this, in this, Dam. i. 4; בֵּין כָּךְ וּבֵין כָּךְ

---

[1] Cf., however, Barth, *Etymolog. Stud.*, p. 39, who holds that the כ is a radical
which suffered aphaeresis in BH.

[2] Cf. Sirach xxxviii. 17. It is also found in Aram., no doubt, as an
adaptation from MH., כְּנָפֵּיק בֵּיהּ j. Targ. Gen. ii. 18, 20; Deut. xiv. 18.
The origin of the expression is obscure. Perhaps we may derive it from the
use of יצא בְ־ in such a phrase as יָצָא שְׂכָרוֹ בְּהֶפְסֵדוֹ, &c., Ab. v. 11. 12,
viz. to annul, and hence—to balance, to be equal, like.

whether so or so, Ḥal. i. 8 ; לְכָךְ for this, Ab. ii. 8 ; לְכָךְ וּלְכָךְ Ṭoh. vi. 6, 7 ; עַל כָּךְ for this purpose, 'Ed. viii. 3.

כֵּן so, Bᵉr. 11 b ; וְכֵן likewise, Pea vi. 9 ; כָּל שֶׁכֵּן everything agrees that it is so—how much more so? (in arguments from the minor to the major).

Before אֶלָּא, כֵּן is contracted to כִּי in the phrase לֹא כִּי אֶלָּא it is not so but, Yᵉb. viii. 3 ; BQ iii. 11.[1]

לֹא not, no.

לָאו not, no, particularly in alternatives after אִם, when the verb is omitted, Bᵉr. iii. 2, 5, &c. (§§ 466, 489).

מָה how ? Bᵉr. 10, 2, with preposition : לָמָּה why ? 'AZ ii. 7 ; מִפְּנֵי מָה wherefore ? Šab. xvi. 1 ; בִּשְׁבִיל מָה for which cause, purpose ?

299. Other adverbial expressions of manner are : בְּיִחוּד privately, San. vii. 8 ; with certainty, Šᵉq. vi. 2 ; בַּעֲלִיל clearly, distinctly,[2] RH i. 5 ; בְּטוֹבָה with thanks, i.e. with owner's permission ; שֶׁלֹּא בְטוֹבָה without thanks, against owner's will, Šᵉbi. iv. 2 ; with, without gratuity, 'AZ iv. 3 ; שֶׁלֹּא בְטוֹבָתוֹ against his will, San. vii. 2 ; בְּפֵירוּשׁ distinctly, 'Or. i. 7.

כָּל עִיקָר 'all the root'—altogether, in a negation, Be. iii. 6 ; כָּל צוֹרֶךְ all the need—completely, with suff. : כָּל צָרְכָּן, כָּל צָרְכָּהּ Kil. vii. 7.

עַל כָּרַח perforce, Ab. iv. 22 ; in later MH with בְּ־ : בְּעַל כָּרְחָהּ against her will, So. 19 a, &c.

לוֹכְסָן (λοξόν) across, in a hypotenuse line : שְׁתֵּי שׁוּרוֹת לוֹכְסָן two rows in a cross line, Dam. vii. 8 ; Kel. xviii. 5.

---

[1] Others, following Geiger, *Lehrbuch*, p. 24, point כִּי, and regard the expression as an imitation of the BH לֹא כִּי (1 Sam. viii. 19, &c. ; cf. *BDB.*, p. 475 a), which was misinterpreted by the Rabbis. But such an artificial explanation is most improbable. לֹא כִּי only occurs before א, and is, therefore, parallel to אֵי from אֵין before א, as above.

[2] Cf. RH 21 b from Ps. xii. 7 ; further, Šab. 133 b ; Mᵉn. 64 a ; Gen. R. 23 ; cf. also Barth, *Etymol. Stud.*, p. 65.

סִירוּגִין ('chequer work'), alternately ; קְרָאָהּ סֵירוּגִין he read it in alternate verses, Mᵉg. ii. 2 ; BQ 37 a.

סְתָם ('stopping up '), undefined, unspecified, Dam. iii. 1.

כְּלָל general statement ; לֹא הָיוּ מִתְעַנִּין כְּלָל they did not fast at all, Ta'a. ii. 6.

בְּבַת אַחַת in one *bat* (name of measure, Isa. v. 10)—in one stroke, at once, Ḥul. ii. 3.

2. Prepositions.

300. MH prepositions are all of Heb. origin. They include (*a*) BH prepositions preserved in their old significance ; (*b*) BH nouns or other forms turned by MH into prepositions, e. g. חֵמָה wrath : מֵחֲמַת through the fury of, the energy, or activity of—through, by ; קוֹדֶם לְ preceding, before ; so עַל גַּב ; עוֹבֵר לְ upon the back of, upon ; עַל מְנָת on the portion of, for the advantage of, for the sake of, on condition, in order that ; so שֵׁם name, subject, and its various combinations.

The following BH prepositions have been lost in MH : אֵת (= עִם), בְּנִלָל, בַּעֲבוּר, בְּעַד, מוּל, לְמַעַן and פֶּן (Aram. פּוֹן).

301. אָחוֹר the back, is used as a prepos. in the dual אֲחוֹרַיִים (§ 293), in the sense of ' behind ', corresponding to פָּנִים (below).

אֲחוֹרֵי שְׁתֵּיהֶן behind both, Mid. v. 4 ; אֲחוֹרֵי רַבּוֹ behind his master, opposed to כְּנֶגֶד רַבּוֹ Yo. 37 a. With prefixes : מִ, לְ : לַאֲחוֹרָיו behind him, Kil. v. 7 ; לַאֲחוֹרֵיהֶן behind them, ib. 9 ; מֵאֲחוֹרֵי הַגָּדֵר behind the wall, San. vii. 10 ; מֵאֲחוֹרָיו Giṭ. viii. 2 ; מֵאֲחוֹרֵיהֶם So. viii. 6.

אַחַר, אַחֲרֵי with suffixes. Of time, after : אַחַר חֲצוֹת after midnight, Pes. x. 8 ; אַחֲרָיו שֶׁל מֹשֶׁה after Moses, So. v. 4 ; אַחֲרֵיהֶן after them, Bᵉr. vi. 8. With prefix : לְאַחַר זְמַן after the time, afterwards, 'AZ i. 1 ; לְאַחַר חֲצוֹת after midnight, Zᵉb. ix. 6 ; לְאַחֲרֵיהֶם after them, 'AZ i. 2 ; מִלְאַחֲרֶיהָ after it, opposed to מִלְּפָנֶיהָ before it, 'Er. iii. 6.

Of place, behind; usually with prefix לְ : לְאַחַר הַחַמָּה behind the sun, RH ii. 6 ; שֶׁלְּאַחַר הַקּוֹצְרִים that which is behind the reapers (L שֶׁאַחַר) Pea iv. 11 ; לְאַחֲרֵיהֶם, לְאַחֲרָיו behind him, them, opposed to ; לִפְנֵיהֶם, לְפָנָיו before him, them, ib. vi. 4 ; כְּלְאַחַר יָדוֹ behind, with the back of, his hand (L לְאַחַר), Šab. x. 3.

אֶל rare : אֶל תַּחַת הַמּוֹתָר into the space under the remainder (L omits אל), Kil. vi. 3, 4 ; מִיּוֹם אֶל יוֹם from day to day, Nᵉd. viii. 1 (so L, probably a reminiscence of Num. xxx. 15).[1] With suff. in the plur., as in BH, only in a few exx. : בָּא אֵלַי Naz. 4 b ; חָזַר אֵלָיו it returned to it, Pᵉs. vii. 2 (some texts have עָלָיו) ; לְהַקִּישׁ אֵלֶיהָ to compare to it, BM ii. 6 ; וִידַבְּרוּ אֵלָיו they shall speak to him, Mak. ii. 5. Frequently with prefix מְ and the suff. of the 3rd person in a reflexive sense : מֵאֵלָיו of itself, 'Or. i. 2 ; בָּאוּ מֵאֲלֵיהֶן they came by themselves, BM vii. 9 ; לֹא מֵאֵלַי אֲנִי אוֹמֵר I do not say it from my own authority, Yo. 5 b.

אֵצֶל by the side of, at, to (after verbs of motion—BH אֶל) : בָּאִין זֶה אֵצֶל זֶה they come one to the other, Šᵉq. v. 4 ; מַנִּיחַ טַלִּיתוֹ אֶצְלוֹ he leaves his cloak with him, Šab. xxiii. 1.

בְּ in, as prefix and also with suff. (בִּי, בְּךָ, בִּיךָ, as in Aram., Nid. 58 b, &c.), as in BH. Also in combination with nouns to give them a prepositional character, e.g. בִּשְׁבִיל, בְּצַד, בִּפְנֵי, בִּלְבַד, בְּתוֹךְ, בְּשָׁעַת, בְּשֶׁל, &c.

בֵּין between ; also with suffixes : בֵּינִי, &c. Correlatives ('between . . . and') are expressed by בֵּין . . . לְ : בֵּין יוֹם טוֹב לְשַׁבָּת between a festival and the Sabbath, Mᵉg. i. 5 ff. ; Yo. iii. 5, &c. Also : בֵּין הָאוּלָם וְלַמִּזְבֵּחַ : בֵּין . . . וּלְ Yo. iii. 8 (a standing expression, Hal. i. 9 ; from Joel ii. 17) ; בֵּינוֹ לְבֵין הָעָם between him and the people, ib. 4, 6 ; בֵּינָם לְבֵין עַצְמָם Bik. i. 4 ; בֵּינָם לְבֵין עַצְמָם Ḥul. vi. 2, between him and himself, and themselves—privately ; so בֵּינוֹ לְבֵינוֹ

---

[1] Other scriptural phrases with אֶל are : Yo. v. 6 ; So. vii. 2, 5 ; viii. 1 ; Mak. iii. 2 (L עַל) ; Zᵉb. xiv. 1 ; Pa. xi. 4, 5 (L לְ).

privately, 'AZ ii. 2 ; בֵּינוֹ לְבֵינָהּ Yᵒb. xii. 5. Also as noun : עַל בֵּין
הַבַּדִּים on the space between the staves, Zᵉb. v. 1.

חוּץ, followed by לְ־, outside : חוּץ לַתְּחוּם outside the boundary,
'Er. v. 7 ; also with ה local, but without any special significance :
חוּצָה לָהּ outside it, ib. 6 ; חוּצָה לוֹ Šᵉbi. i. 2 ; especially in the
expression חוּצָה לָאָרֶץ outside the Land (of Israel), as opposed to
הָאָרֶץ Tᵉr. i. 5 ; Ḥal. ii. 1, 2, &c. So בְּחוּצָה לָאָרֶץ Dam. ii. 1.

Followed by מִן except : חוּץ מִן הַפְּתִילָה except the wick, Šab.
ii. 5 ; חוּץ מִזּוֹ בִּלְבַד except this alone, Yo. iii. 3.

כְּ, combines with some nouns to form prepositions : כְּנֶגֶד over
against ; כְּנֶגֶד הַיְסוֹד in front of the foundation, Pᵉs. v. 6 ; זוֹ כְּנֶגֶד זוֹ
one facing the other, Šab. xi. 2 ; תַּלְמוּד תּוֹרָה כְּנֶגֶד כֻּלָּם the
study of the Torah against (= compares, outweighs) them all,
Pea i. 1 ; כְּנֶגְדָּן, כְּנֶגְדּוֹ against (corresponding to) it, them, Šᵉbi.
viii. 8.

כְּדֵי sufficient for : כְּדֵי מְזִיגַת הַכּוֹס sufficient for mixing a cup,
Sab. viii, 1 ff.

כְּלַפֵּי (לְאַפֵּי), cf. כְּ + לְאַפֵּי 1 Sam. xxv. 23) towards : כְּלַפֵּי הָעָם
facing the people ; כְּלַפֵּי הָעֵץ facing the gallows, San. vi. 4 ;
כְּלַפֵּי צָפוֹן towards north, Tam. ii. 5.

לְ־ to, as prefix and with suffixes (לְךָ, לִי fem. לִיךְ Giṭ. iv. 8, &c.),
as in BH. Also prefixed to prepositional nouns : לְבֵין, לְאַחַר.
לְמַעְלָה מִן : לְמַטָּה מִירוּשָׁלַיִם below Jerusalem, Suk. iv. 5 ; לְמַטָּה מִן
זֶה לְמַעְלָה מִזֶּה one above the other, 'Er. i. 9 ; viii. 8 ; לְעִיּפָתָן towards
them (rare), Šᵉq. vi. 3.

לִידֵי to the hands of, to (after verb בָּא): אֵין אַתָּה בָא לִידֵי עֲבֵרָה
thou wilt not come to transgression, Ab. ii. 1 ; לִידֵי סַכָּנָה to danger,
Yo. ii. 2.

לְעִנְיַן to the subject of, in respect to : לְעִנְיַן דְּבָרָיו in respect to his
words, Ya. iv. 3.

לְפִי to the mouth of—according to : לְפִי הָאוֹרְחִין according to the
guests, Šab. xx. 2 ; לְפִי רוֹב הַמַּעֲשֶׂה according to the abundance of

the works, Ab. iii. 15; לְפִי חִיבְּתָן because of the love entertained for them, Ya. iv. 6.

לִפְנֵי before; מִלְּפְנֵי from before; also with suffixes: לְפָנַי, לְפָנֶיךָ, &c., as in BH.

לְשֵׁם to the name of—for the sake of, for the purpose of: לְשֵׁם שָׁמַיִם for the sake of Heaven, Ab. v. 16; לְשֵׁם עֲבוֹדָה זָרָה for the purpose of idolatry, 'AZ. iii. 7.

מִן from, used separately or as prefix; also with suffixes: מִמֶּנִּי, מִמְּךָ, &c., as in BH. Often the demonstrative particle הֵי (= BH הֵא) is prefixed instead of מִ when it has the pronominal suffix: הֵימָךְ from thee, Nᵉd. 5 a; הֵימֶנּוּ from him, Šebi. x. 9; Giṭ. viii. 9; הֵימֶנָּה from her, Pea iv. 3; vii. 8; Kᵉt. 27 b. The texts often waver between these and the older forms: מִמֶּנָּה, מִמֶּנּוּ.

Also in the sense of ' in the power of ': לֹא הֵימָךְ לוֹמַר it is not in thy power to say, Num. R. 4; especially with בָּל־: כָּל הֵימָךְ לוֹמַר Gen. R. 15; לֹא הַבֹּל מִן הָרִאשׁוֹן לְאַבֵּד וְכוּתוֹ שֶׁל שֵׁנִי L.; edd. with anticipation of the genitive (cf. § 389); . . . לֹא כָל הֵימֶנּוּ מִן הָרִאשׁוֹן the first has no power to destroy the right of the second, Giṭ. viii. 8; לֹא כָל הֵימֶנּוּ L.; לֹא הַבֹּל הֵימֶנּוּ edd., he has no power, BQ x. 3; cf. Aram.: אִיהוּ כָל בִּמְיֵנֵיהּ Šebu. 41 a; לָאו כָל בִּמְיֵנָךְ ? BB 154 b.

With לְ־ as correlative: מִבְּנֶגֶד הַחוֹמָה וְלַחוּץ; מִבְּנֶגֶד הַחוֹמָה וְלִפְנִים from the front of the wall and towards within, towards without, MŠ. iii. 7, 8.

Prefixed to prepositional nouns:

מֵחֲמַת because of: מֵחֲמַת הַמַּכָּה because of the wound, BQ viii. 1; מֵחֲמַת חוֹלִי in consequence of the sickness, Giṭ. vii. 3.

מֵעֵין of the colour, appearance, character of: מֵעֵין שְׁמוֹנָה עֶשְׂרֵה an abstract of the eighteen benedictions, Bᵉr. iv. 3 (cf. Bᵉr. 29 a); הַטּוֹבָה מֵעֵין הָרָעָה evil of the nature of good; הָרָעָה מֵעֵין הַטּוֹבָה good of the nature of evil, ib. ix. 3; מֵעֵין מְלָאכָה אַחַת of the nature of, similar to one work, Šab. vii. 1.

מִשֵּׁם ר׳ יִשְׁמָעֵאל in the name of (also often מִשּׁוּם, cf. § 37): מִשֵּׁם ר׳
in the name of Rabbi Ishmael, Kil. iii. 7; because of: אֲסוּרִין
מִשּׁוּם גִּלּוּי forbidden because of uncovering, Ter. viii. 4; נוֹהֵג בּוֹ
מִשּׁוּם אֱלוֹהַּ he behaves to it as to a god, ʿAZ iii. 4.[1] Cf. also on
אֶל, above, and תּוֹךְ, below.

עַד to, as far as; עַד חֲצוֹת up to midnight, Ber. i. 1; עַד בֵּית סָאתַיִם
as far as a space of two *seahs*, ʿEr. ii. 3. עַד is not found with
pronominal suffixes.

עַל upon; also with suffixes: עָלַי, עָלֶיךָ, as in BH; cf. also
below, § 363.

In combination with nouns:

עַל גַּב upon the back of, upon: הַנּוֹתֵן עַל גַּבָּן who puts upon
them, Šab. xi. 2; טָמֵא עַל גַּב עַם הָאָרֶץ unclean upon, because of,
the ʿAm ha-Areṣ, ʿEd. i. 14; עַל גַּב רוּקָּהּ because of her spittle,
Miq. viii. 5. More frequently with the constr. dual (§ 293):
עַל גַּבֵּי הַמִּטָּה upon the bed, Suk. ii. 8; עַל גַּבֵּי רַגְלָיו upon his feet,
ib. iv. 9; Kil. ii. 11; עַל גַּבָּיו upon it, BM x. 4.

עַל יַד by the hand of, through: עַל יָדִי through me, Ber. iv. 2;
עַל יָדוֹ through him, on his behalf, Šebi. vii. 3. More frequently
with the constr. dual: עַל יְדֵי יְחֶזְקֵאל by Ezekiel, Tam. iii. 7;
עַל יְדֵי עוֹרָהּ together with its skin, MŠ. i. 6; iii. 11.

עַל מְנָת on condition; עַל מְנָת כֵּן on this condition, Dam. vi. 3;
Ab. i. 3.

עַל פִּי through: עַל פִּי עֵדִים through witnesses, Šab. xix. 1.

עַל שֵׁם for the name, purpose, of—because of: עַל שֵׁם סוֹפוֹ
because of his end, San. viii. 5, 6.

עִם with; also with suffixes: עִמִּי, עִמְּךָ, &c. (BH עִמָּדִי is not
found in MH).

---

[1] Literally: from the name, category of; cf. אֵינוֹ מִן הַשֵּׁם, it is not of this
name—it does not belong to this category, Ker. iii. 4; so לֹא מִן הַשֵּׁם הוּא,
Šebu. 3 b; מִשֵּׁם אֶחָד מִשְּׁנֵי שֵׁמוֹת, of one category, of two categories,
Kin. i. 3, 4.

Of time: עִם הַשֶּׁמֶשׁ with the sun—while the sun still shines, Šab. i. 8 ; עִם חֲשֵׁכָה while it is getting dark, ib. ii. 7 ; עִם יְצִיאַת נֶפֶשׁ while, before, the soul goes forth, ib. xxiii. 5.

קוֹדֶם preceding, before (properly a participle), followed by the accusative, or by לְ- (indirect object, cf. § 351). The texts waver.

קוֹדֶם לֶעָצֶרֶת before the vintage (L לַבָּצִיר) Pea vii. 7 ; קוֹדֶם הַבָּצִיר (or עֲצֶרֶת), before Pentecost, Ḥal. iv. 10 ; קוֹדֶם אֶת חֲבֵירוֹ precedes its fellow ; קוֹדְמִין לְמוּסָפִין precede the additional sacrifices, Zᵉb. x. 1 ff. Similarly :

עוֹבֵר לַעֲשִׂיָּתָן : עוֹבֵר לְ- before doing them, Pᵉs. 7 b.

תּוֹךְ within ; תּוֹךְ זְמָן within the time, opposed to לִפְנֵי זְמָן before the time, Nid. 45 b, but usually with another preposition prefixed.

בְּתוֹךְ in, at : בְּתוֹךְ הַבַּיִת in the house, Suk. i. 2 ; בְּתוֹךְ חֵיקוֹ within his bosom, Šab. x. 3 ; ii. 7 ; לְתוֹךְ into : יִתֵּן לְתוֹכוֹ מַיִם he will put into it water, Bᵉr. vii. 5 ; מָדַד לְתוֹךְ צְלוֹחִיתוֹ he measured into his flask, ʿAZ v. 7 ; מִתּוֹךְ from : נָטַל מִתּוֹכָה he took from it, Šab. i. 1 ; מִתּוֹךְ שֶׁלּוֹ from his own, Šᵉbi. iii. 6.

תַּחַת under, as in BH : תַּחְתֶּיהָ under it, Kil. vi. 9 ; תַּחַת הַמִּטָּה under the bed, Suk. ii. 1 ; יוֹצֵא מִתַּחַת יָדוֹ comes forth from under his hand, BB 173 a.

3. Conjunctions.

302. Of the old BH conjunctions and conjunctive expressions, MH has lost the following (the words in brackets give the MH substitutes):

אִלּוּ) לוּ ; (אַף-) גַּם ; (שֶׁ-) כִּי ¹ ; (שֶׁ-) אֲשֶׁר ; Qoh. vi. 6 ; Est. vii. 4) ; מִפְּנֵי) יַעַן אֲשֶׁר ; (עַד שֶׁ-) קוֹדֶם שֶׁ- ; טֶרֶם (שֶׁ-) ; Aram. פּוֹן) ; שֶׁמָּא) פֶּן

---

¹ כִּי is common in MH only with וְ as an interrogative particle, וְכִי §§ 303, 462. כִּי alone is preserved only in elevated diction, under the influence of BH, e.g. in the liturgy (cf. Singer, pp. 46, 47, &c.), or in a poetical passage like אוֹי נָא לָהּ . . . כִּי אָבְרָה כְּלִי חֶמְדָּתָהּ woe to her . . . for she has lost her precious jewel, MQ 25 b.

שֶׁ, &c.); כְּדֵי שֶׁ, &c.); עֵקֶב אֲשֶׁר (מִפְּנֵי שֶׁ, &c.; cf.
on Adverbs, § 294).

Of Aram. origin is אֶלָּא (also אִם לֹא—אִן+לָא = אִילָא), and
perhaps also the form בֵּין שֶׁ, which is common in Aram.

The conjunction שֶׁמָּא (= שֶׁלָּמָה, שֶׁלָּמָּה Cant. i. 7; Aram. דִּילְמָא),
was adopted by Aram. from MH. But Aram. influenced its
spelling in MH with final א for ה : שֶׁמָּה.

MH shows some other interesting new formations, such as the
use of the verbal form הוֹאִיל וְ;[1] the compounds אִלְמָלֵא or אִלְמָלֵי
(אִלּוּ+אִם+לֹא), or the Palestinian equivalent אִילוּלֵא, אִילוּלֵי (אִלּוּ+
לֹא); אֲפִילוּ (אַף+אִלּוּ); לְפִיכָךְ; the adaption of a number of other
expressions to conjunctive use : וּבִלְבַד, בִּשְׁבִיל, בִּזְמַן, אַף עַל פִּי,
עַל תְּנַאי, עַל מְנָת, מִתּוֹךְ, מֵחֲמַת, מִשּׁוּם, כְּשֵׁם, &c., all followed by שֶׁ. MH
has also greatly extended and developed the uses of the BH
conjunctions שֶׁ, אֲבָל, אִלּוּ, and וְכִי.

303. We give here a list of the conjunctions and conjunctive
expressions. For examples of their usage and their various
constructions, the reader is referred to the respective sections in
the Syntax.

Co-ordinating : וְ and ; אַף also, moreover, indeed.

Adversative, restrictive, and exceptive : אֲבָל ; אֶלָּא but, except ;
בֶּאֱמֶת of a truth, however.

Disjunctive : אוֹ or ; בֵּין . . . בֵּין whether . . . or.

Conditional : אִם, אִלּוּ, אִלְמָלֵא (אִלְמָלֵי), אִילוּלֵא (אִילוּלֵי) if.

Concessive : אַף, אֲפִילוּ even ; אַף עַל פִּי (שֶׁ) although ; אַף עַל פִּי כֵן
nevertheless.

Interrogative : שֶׁמָּא perhaps ? ; כְּלוּם, וְכִי, וַהֲלֹא, הֲ.

Comparative : כְּ like ; כָּךְ so ; כְּאִילוּ as if.

Consecutive : לְפִיכָךְ therefore.

---

[1] The verb הוֹאִיל is not found otherwise in MH. It is always followed by
וְ as in BH : Joshua vii. 7 ; 2 Sam. vii. 29. Cf. Bacher, *Aelteste Terminologie*,
p. 37.

‫־שֶׁ‬ (‫שֶׁלֹּא‬ ,‫)שֶׁאֵין‬. Its primary function, like BH ‫אֲשֶׁר‬ and ‫כִּי‬, is to
introduce a subordinate clause. Hence like ‫אֲשֶׁר‬, ‫כִּי‬, it assumes
different meanings in accordance with the character of the clause
it introduces, viz. a causal, concessive, conditional, or final meaning.

Like BH ‫אֲשֶׁר‬, ‫שֶׁ‬ combines with prepositional and adverbial
expressions to form the following new conjunctions.

Temporal: ‫כְּשֶׁ־‬, ‫לִכְשֶׁ־‬ as; ‫מִשֶּׁ־‬ after, opposed to ‫עַד שֶׁ־‬ before;
‫לְאַחַר שֶׁ־ ,אַחַר שֶׁ־‬, after; ‫קוֹדֶם שֶׁ־‬ before; ‫אֵימָתַי שֶׁ־‬ when, whenever;
‫כֵּיוָן שֶׁ־‬ as soon as; ‫בִּשְׁעָה שֶׁ־ ,בּוְמַן שֶׁ־‬, ‫כָּל זְמַן שֶׁ־ :‬ when; ‫כָּל שָׁעָה שֶׁ־‬
all the time that; ‫מִשָּׁעָה שֶׁ־‬ from the time that; ‫עַד כְּדֵי שֶׁ־‬ until.

Comparative: ‫כְּעִנְיָן שֶׁ־‬; ‫כְּדֶרֶךְ שֶׁ־‬; ‫כְּשֵׁם שֶׁ־‬; ‫כְּמוֹת שֶׁ־‬; ‫כְּמוֹ שֶׁ־‬ as.

Causal: ‫מִשּׁוּם שֶׁ־‬; ‫מִפְּנֵי שֶׁ־‬; ‫מֵאַחַר שֶׁ־‬; ‫לְפִי שֶׁ־‬; ‫בִּשְׁבִיל שֶׁ־‬;
‫מִתּוֹךְ שֶׁ־‬; ‫עַל שֶׁ־‬; ‫עַל שֵׁם שֶׁ־‬ because.

Final: ‫עַל תְּנַאי שֶׁ־‬; ‫עַל מְנָת שֶׁ־‬; ‫כְּדֵי שֶׁ־‬ in order that.

Restrictive: ‫וּבִלְבַד שֶׁ־‬ only that.

4. Interjections.

304. (1) Pure Interjections.

‫אוֹי לוֹ‬ woe! Yeb. iii. 5 (edd.); xiii. 7 (L); Ber. 28 a, &c.

‫אִי לוֹ‬ woe! Yeb. xiii. 7; iii. 5 (L); 'Ed. iv. 8 (L has ‫אִילוֹ‬ in
one word, as Qoh. iv. 10; cf. x. 16); ‫אִי שָׁמַיִם‬ Oh, heavens!
RH 19 a.

‫הוֹי‬: ‫הוֹי אִישׁ טוֹב וְנֶאֱמָן‬ alas! a good and faithful man, Ber. 16 b.

‫אַלְלַי‬ woe! Ab. deRN. xxv. 3.

‫אָנָא‬ pray, Yo. iii. 8 (only liturgical). So ‫נָא‬ in a poetical passage
MQ 25 b, and in the liturgy.

‫הֵא‬, ‫הָא‬ behold, Mak. iii. 17; ‫הֵא לָךְ‬ (L ‫הֵא לָךְ הֵילָךְ‬) behold, take thee,
Ma'a. ii. 5, 6.

‫הֲרֵי‬ behold, Ber. vii. 5; ‫הֲרֵנִי‬ behold I!

‫וְהַלְוַאי‬ would that! Meg. 14 a; or ‫וּלְוַאי‬ Ber. 28 b (prob. Aram.).

The following BH pure interjections have been lost in MH:
‫אַחֲלֵי ,אָח ,אֲבוֹי‬ (all rare); ‫לוּ ,אֲהָהּ‬.

305. (2) Words and phrases used as Exclamations.

הָאֱלֹהִים by God! Ḥul. 54 a, &c. (late, and mostly in semi-Aram. passages).

בְּרִית by the Covenant! Pᵉs. 38 b; t. Ḥal. 1.

נַפָּה שֶׁל רוֹמִי by the Capitol of Rome, Mᵉn. 44 a (in the mouth of a heathen).

חֲבָל alas! Nᵉd. 74 b; Sifre Deut. xviii. 12 (prob. Aram.).

חַס וְשָׁלוֹם May He have pity and grant peace!—God forbid 'Ed. v. 6; Ya. iii. 5.

הַמָּעוֹן הַזֶּה By this habitation (the Temple)! Kᵉr. i. 7; vi. 3; Kᵉt. ii. 9..

הָעֲבוֹדָה by the worship! Bᵉr. 34 b; Yᵉb. 32 b.

הַשָּׁמַיִם by Heaven, Ab. dᵉRN. xxxviii. 3.

The following BH exclamations have been lost in MH: הָבָה, לְכָה, הִנֵּה.

PART III

SYNTAX

I. THE VERB

1. Tenses and Moods.

306. In the use of the Tenses, MH has attained to a greater precision and exactness than BH. Generally in MH the perfect coincides with the present, the imperfect with the future, and the participle with the present. The perfect and the imperfect (and also the imperative) describe simple acts. Continuous, or repeated, or customary action is expressed by the participle alone for the present, by the participle with the perfect of הָיָה for the past, by the participle with the imperfect of הָיָה for the future, and by the participle with the imperative of הָיָה (= הֱוֵה) for the imperative.

It follows that the use of the perfect for the present in such expressions as זָקַנְתִּי, צָדַקְתִּי, יָדַעְתִּי, אָהַבְתִּי (Ges.-K., § 106 g), or the use of the perfect for actions that lie in the future (*Perfect of Confidence*, &c.; ib., § 106 m–n), is not admissible in MH. Likewise, the use of the imperfect to describe actions, whether simple or continuous, which lie in the past or even in the present (ib., § 107 b–h), is not tolerated in MH.

(1) THE PERFECT.

307. The perfect describes a single act or event that has already taken place, or that is conceived as having taken place. Hence the perfect is the tense of the past, e.g.: יוֹסֵף הַכֹּהֵן הֵבִיא בִּכּוּרִים Joseph the Priest brought first ripe fruits, Ḥal. iv. 2 ; מֹשֶׁה קִבֵּל

תּוֹרָה מִסִּינַי Moses received the Torah from Sinai, Ab. i. 1;
לֹא קָרִינוּ אֶת שְׁמַע we have not read the Šema', Ber. i. 1.

308. In the absence of the imperfect consecutive in MH, the
perfect serves also to describe a series of consecutive acts in the
past: מְסָרוּהוּ ... וְהֶעֱלוּהוּ (הוֹלִיכוּהוּ L) ... הִשְׁבִּיעוּהוּ וְנִפְטְרוּ וְהָלְכוּ לָהֶם
they delivered him ... they brought him up ... they adjured him,
and departed, and went away, Yo. i. 5; הֵבִיאוּ אֶת הָאֲבָנִים וּבָנוּ אֶת
הַמִּזְבֵּחַ וְסָדוּם בַּסִּיד וְכָתְבוּ עֲלֵיהֶם ... וְנָטְלוּ אֶת הָאֲבָנִים וּבָאוּ וְלָנוּ בִמְקוֹמָן
they brought the stones, and built the altar, and plastered them
with plaster, and wrote on them ... and took the stones, and
came and lodged in their place, So. vii. 5.

309. The perf. also expresses an act which is anterior to
another act in the past (pluperfect). Such a pluperfect is usually
placed in a relative clause: רָחַץ בַּלַּיְלָה הָרִאשׁוֹן שֶׁמֵּתָה אִשְׁתּוֹ he
bathed in the first night that his wife had died, Ber. ii. 6; נִתְיַחֵד
עִמָּהּ אַחַר שֶׁכְּתָבוֹ he was alone with her after he had written it,
'Ed. iv. 7; וּכְשֶׁיָּצָא אָמַר and when he had gone forth he said,
'AZ. iii. 4; הֵבִיאוּ כָּל טָהֳרוֹת שֶׁטִּיהַר רַבִּי אֱלִיעֶזֶר they brought all the
things which R. Eliezer had declared to be clean, Ber. 19 a;
וּבָאָה אִשָּׁה ... שֶׁמָּלָה and there came a woman who had circumcised, Šab. 134 a.

310. The perf. is used in hypothetical sentences, with or without
a conjunction, to express a single act conceived as already
performed. English in such cases would often use the present,
e.g. קָרָא וְלֹא דִקְדֵּק בְּאוֹתִיּוֹתֶיהָ ... יָצָא if he has read (the Šema'), but
not pronounced its letters carefully ... he has discharged his
duty; ... קָרָא וְטָעָה יַחֲזוֹר if he has read it, and made an error, let
him return ..., Ber. ii. 3; פָּשַׁט הֶעָנִי אֶת יָדוֹ ... וְנָתַן לְתוֹךְ יָדוֹ שֶׁל
בַּעַל הַבַּיִת אוֹ שֶׁנָּטַל מִתּוֹכָהּ וְהוֹצִיא if the poor man puts forth his
hand ... and puts into the hand of the master of the house, or if
he takes from it and brings forth, Šab. i. 1; אִם הֱבִיאוּהוּ לִידֵי מִיתָה
... לֹא יְבִיאוּהוּ ... if they bring him to death ... should they not

bring him . . ., Kᵉr. iii. 1; אִם בָּאנוּ לִכְתּוֹב אֵין אָנוּ מַסְפִּיקִין if we came to write, we should not be capable, Šab. 13 b; וְאִם כָּבְתָה כָּבְתָה if it is extinguished, let it be extinguished, ib. 120 a; אִם שֶׁלָּנוּ הוּא הַפֶּסַח הַזֶּה יָדֶיךָ מָשׁוּכוֹת מִשֶּׁלָּךְ וְנִמְנֵיתָ עַל שֶׁלָּנוּ if ours be this Paschal lamb, then let thy hands be withdrawn from thine own, and thou art counted for ours, Pᵉs. ix. 10.

311. In descriptions of continuous, or repeated, or customary actions in the past, for which the participle is regularly used, the perf. is sometimes found amidst a series of participles. In such cases the perfect usually has a temporal or hypothetical signifi-cance: הַקְּרוֹבִים מְבִיאִים . . . וְהַשּׁוֹר הוֹלֵךְ עִמָּהֶם . . . וְהֶחָלִיל מַכֶּה לִפְנֵיהֶם עַד שֶׁהֵן מַגִּיעִין קָרוֹב לִירוּשָׁלַיִם הִגִּיעוּ קָרוֹב לִירוּשָׁלַיִם שָׁלְחוּ לִפְנֵיהֶם וְעִטְּרוּ אֶת בִּיכּוּרֵיהֶם וְהַפַּחוֹת יוֹצְאִין לִקְרָאתָם . . . those near bring . . ., and the ox goes with them . . ., and the flute strikes in front of them, until they reach near Jerusalem. When they have reached near Jerusalem, they send (messengers) in front of them, and they crown their first ripe fruits, and the rulers go forth to meet them . . ., Bik. iii. 3; הָיוּ מַכְנִיסִין אֶת הַשֵּׁנִי וּבוֹדְקִין אוֹתוֹ נִמְצְאוּ דִבְרֵיהֶם מְכֻוָּנִים נוֹשְׂאִין וְנוֹתְנִין בַּדָּבָר . . . גָּמְרוּ אֶת הַדָּבָר הָיוּ מַכְנִיסִין they would bring in the second, and examine him. If their words were found to correspond, they discussed the matter . . . When they finished the matter, they would bring in . . ., San. iii. 6–7; v. 4–5; vi. 1. Sometimes the perf. is used in such cases without any apparent hypothetical or temporal significance: פּוֹשְׁטִים וּמְקַפְּלִים וּמַנִּיחִים וּמִתְכַּסִּים . . . אֵירַע קְרִי לְאֶחָד מֵהֶם יוֹצֵא וְהוֹלֵךְ לוֹ . . . יָרַד וְטָבַל עָלָה וְנִסְתַּפֵּג וְנִתְחַמֵּם . . . בָּא וְיָשַׁב אֵצֶל אֶחָיו . . . they undress and fold them and put them . . . and cover themselves . . . when an impurity happens to one of them he goes forth and departs . . . and goes down and dips himself, comes up and dries himself and warms himself . . . he comes and sits by the side of his brethren, Tam. i. 1; cf. also Yo. i. 1–5; Suk. iv. 5, 9; Nᵉg. xiv. 1–3; Pa. iii. 2–3, 7–8, f., &c.

312. Sometimes the act described by the perf. has just been performed, in which case English would use the present : עָקַרְתָּ מַה שֶׁכָּתוּב בַּתּוֹרָה thou uprootest what is written in the Torah, Pes. vi. 1 ; מָה רָאִיתָ לְטַמֵּא what (reason) dost thou see to make it unclean? מָצִינוּ we find, 'Ed. vi. 3 ; קִיַּמְתָּ thou hast fulfilled, BQ iii. 9 ; נֵר שֶׁכָּבָה וְהוֹלֶכֶת מַנִּיחַ אָדָם אֶצְבָּעוֹ עָלֶיהָ מִיַּד כָּבְתָה a lamp which is gradually going out, when a man lays his hand upon it, immediately it is extinguished, Šab. 151 b. So also of single acts that may be performed at any time : נִכְנַס יַיִן יָצָא סוֹד when wine goes in, the secret goes out, 'Er. 65 a ; הַכֹּל יוֹדְעִין כַּלָּה לְמָּה נִכְנְסָה לְחֻפָּה every body knows for what purpose a bride enters the bridal chamber, Ket. 8 b.

313. Finally, the perf. is found, though very rarely, also of a future act conceived as already performed : כְּשֵׁם שֶׁקִּבַּלְתִּי שָׂכָר עַל הַדְּרִישָׁה כָּךְ קִבַּלְתִּי שָׂכָר עַל הַפְּרִישָׁה just as I shall receive reward for expounding, so shall I receive reward for withdrawing (from expounding), Qid. 57 a.[1] So sometimes in a conditional sentence, as a *futurum exactum*, for which usually the participle or imperfect is used (cf. §§ 321, 486): אִם אֵחַרְתִּי שַׁחֲטוּ עָלַי if I shall have delayed, slay on my behalf, Pes. ix. 10 ; זֶה גִטֵּךְ אִם מַתִּי . . . אִם לֹא בָאתִי this is thy bill of divorcement if I shall have died ... if I shall not have come, Giṭ. vii. 3, 7–9.

(2) The Imperfect.

314. The imperf. describes a single act or event which has not yet taken place. It is, therefore, the tense of the future : אֲנִי אַחֲזִיר אֶת הַדִּינָר (L.) I shall restore the *dinar*, Ket. xi. 4 ; נִכְתּוֹב גֵּט let us write a bill of divorcement, Giṭ. vii. 1, 2. So in dependent clauses pointing to the future : עַד שֶׁיַּעֲלֶה עַמּוּד הַשַּׁחַר until dawn

---

[1] So in BQ 41 b. In Pes. 22 b; Bᵉk. 6 b, the apodosis has a participle אֲנִי מְקַבֵּל.

rise, Ber. i. 1; אֶלָּא כְּדֵי שֶׁיִּשׁוֹרוּ; כְּדֵי שֶׁיַּחֲבִילוּ, &c., except there be sufficient time that they be soaked, heated, &c., Šab. i. 5, 6; בַּקֵּשׁ עָלָיו רַחֲמִים וְיִחְיֶה seek for him (God's) mercy that he live, Ber. 32 a. Also in questions: מַה יַּעֲשׂוּ what shall they do? Šab. 26 a; כַּמָּה יַרְחִיקוּ how far shall they go? Toh. x. 2; וְלֹא אֶבְכֶּה shall I not weep? Ber. 28 b; וְלֹא אֲקַיְּמֶנּוּ shall I not fulfil it? Yo. 19 b. So even of a past act: מָה אֶעֱשֶׂה וְרַבּוּ עָלַי what can (could) I do, when they were a majority against me? (L, edd.: שֶׁחֲבֵרַי רַבּוּ עָלַי).

315. The futurity of an act is sometimes emphasized by periphrasis with עָתִיד שֶׁ, especially in the later Agadic style: עֲתִידָה אִשָּׁה שֶׁתֵּלֵד a woman will bear; עֲתִידָה אֶרֶץ יִשְׂרָאֵל שֶׁתּוֹצִיא the land of Israel will bring forth, Šab. 30 b; עֲתִידָה תוֹרָה שֶׁתִּשְׁתַּכַּח the Torah will be forgotten, ib. 138 b.

316. The imperf. is used to describe a series of consecutive acts in the future, where BH would use the perf. consecutive: תָּחוּבוּ חוֹבַת גָּלוּת וְתִגְלוּ לִמְקוֹם הַמַּיִם הָרָעִים וְיִשְׁתּוּ הַתַּלְמִידִים וְיָמוּתוּ... you will incur the guilt of exile and you will be exiled to the place of the evil waters, and the disciples will drink and die, Ab. i. 9; אֵלֵךְ לְבֵיתִי וְאוֹכַל... וְאֶשְׁתֶּה... וְאִישַׁן וְאַחַר כָּךְ אֶקְרָא... וְאֶתְפַּלֵּל I shall go home and eat . . . and drink . . . and sleep and after that I shall read Šema' and pray, Ber. 4 b.

317. The imperf. is used of hypothetical acts, the performance of which lies in the future: לִכְשֶׁתָּבוֹא אֶצְלִי אֲזוּנֶהָ I shall feed her when she comes to me, Ket. xii. 1; אִם יִרְצֶה יִשְׂרָאֵל if the Israelite should wish, 'AZ. iv. 12; אִם תַּקְנִיטֵנִי if thou wilt provoke me, Šab. 17 a.

318. As a subjunctive: וְלֹא זָכִיתִי שֶׁתֵּאָמֵר I was not able to prove that it should be said, Ber. i. 5; לֹא יִדְחוּ; לֹא תִדְחֶה should it not, should they not push away (override)? Pes. vi. 2; מַה יַּעֲשֶׂה הַבֵּן שֶׁלֹּא יֶחֱטָא what can that son do that he might not sin? (he cannot hel committing sin), Ber. 32 a.

319. The imperf. is used to express a wish or a prayer (Optative or Precative): מִי יְגַלֶּה עָפָר מֵעֵינֶיךָ Oh, who would uncover the dust from thine eyes, So. v. 2; יִכְבְּשׁוּ רַחֲמַי אֶת כַּעֲסִי וְיִגּוֹלּוּ רַחֲמַי עַל כַּעֲסִי; וְאֶתְנַהֵג עִם בָּנַי בְּמִדַּת רַחֲמִים וְאֶכָּנֵס לָהֶם may my mercies suppress mine anger, and may my mercies roll themselves against mine anger, and may I conduct myself towards my children with the attribute of mercy, and may I enter for them . . ., Ber. 7 a; cf. ib. 16 b; 29 a; 60 b, &c. (§ 467).

320. To express a command that some act should or should not be performed (Jussive): תֵּדְעוּ כָּל בָּעֶרֶב know ye! Ber. 288; אָדָם יַטּוּ וְיִקְרוּ וּבַבֹּקֶר יַעֲמֹדוּ in the evening all men should incline and read, but in the morning they should stand, Ber. i. 3; אַל תְּרַצֶּה אֶת חֲבֵרְךָ . . . וְאַל תְּנַחֲמֶנּוּ . . . וְאַל תִּשְׁאַל לוֹ do not appease thy neighbour . . . and do not comfort him . . ., and do not ask of him . . ., Ab. iv. 18.

321. The imperf. expresses an act which must be performed prior to another act in the future (*Futurum Exactum*). Such an imperf. is put in a dependent clause introduced by שֶׁ: כְּשֶׁאַגִּיע לוֹ אֲלַקְּטֶנּוּ I shall gather it when I shall have reached it, Kil. v. 6; אַל תָּדִין אֶת חֲבֵרְךָ עַד שֶׁתַּגִּיע לִמְקוֹמוֹ do not judge thy neighbour till thou hast reached his place, Ab. ii. 4; מֵאַחַר שֶׁיִּתְלֹשׁוּ after they shall have been plucked, Bik. iii. 1; לֹא יְכַסֶּנּוּ מִשֶּׁתֶּחְשַׁךְ he shall not cover it after it has become dark, Šab. iv. 2; cf. § 513.

(3) The Participle.

322. The participle has retained in MH its twofold character of noun and verb. Its primary function is to describe the subject as being in a state of activity or passivity. By emphasizing the state of the subject, the partic. becomes equivalent to a noun-adjective. By emphasizing the activity or the passivity of the subject, the partic. becomes equivalent to a verb. But as even in the latter case, the activity or passivity of the subject is expressed as a state, the partic. comes to describe an act as in the process of being performed. Hence the partic. becomes in MH the tense of the present. But is by no means confined to the present, even in its verbal character. It is also used, as in BH, of the past and the future to describe acts that are continuous, or repeated, or customary.

323. The partic. as present: עַל שְׁלשָׁה דְּבָרִים הָעוֹלָם עוֹמֵד the world stands on three things, Ab. i. 2; בַּעַל הַבַּיִת דּוֹחֵק the master presses, ib. ii. 15; הַחַזָּן רוֹאֶה הֵיכָן תִּינוֹקוֹת קוֹרְאִים the overseer may see where the children read, Šab. i. 3. With pronouns as subject: יוֹדֵעַ אֲנִי I know; אֵינִי יוֹדֵעַ I do not know, Ned. xi. 7; הוּא רוֹצֶה he is willing, BB vi. 6; קוֹבְלִין אָנוּ we complain, Ya. iv. 7; בְּנֵי אָדָם דּוֹמִים לְעִשְׂבֵי הַשָּׂדֶה הַלָּלוּ נוֹצְצִין וְהַלָּלוּ נוֹבְלִין human beings are like the herbs of the field, some sprout forth, others fade away, 'Er. 54 a.

324. The partic. as past, in a frequentative or iterative sense; usually with the perf. of היה as auxiliary to emphasize the tense: אֲנִי הָיִיתִי בָא בַּדֶּרֶךְ וְהִפְתִּי I was coming by the road, and I inclined, Ber. i. 3; הָיִיתָ נוֹהֵג thou hast conducted thyself, Suk. ii. 7; הָיוּ אוֹמְרִין they used to say, Šebi. iv. 1; גִּילְּתָה אֶת רֹאשָׁהּ וְהָיְתָה מְטַפַּחַת וּמְעַחַת ... she uncovered her head, and kept on gathering it up with her hand and laying it, BQ viii. 6; especially in conditional sentences: אִילּוּ הָיִיתִי יוֹדֵעַ ... לֹא הָיִיתִי נוֹדֵר if I had known it, I would not have vowed, Ned. ix. 2 ff.; אִילּוּ לִפְנֵי מֶלֶךְ בָּשָׂר וָדָם הָיוּ מוֹלִיכִין אוֹתִי ... אַף עַל פִּי כֵן הָיִיתִי בוֹכֶה if they had led me into the presence of a human king ..., I would, nevertheless, have wept, Ber. 28 b; 32 b (§§ 490, 494).

Often, however, the verb היה is omitted, when the context makes it clear that the reference is to the past: מְצָאוֹ שֶׁיּוֹשֵׁב he found that he was sitting, 'Er. 11 b; אִם הָיָה חָכָם דּוֹרֵשׁ וְאִם לָאוּ if he was a scholar, he expounded, but תַּלְמִידֵי חֲכָמִים דּוֹרְשִׁין לְפָנָיו

if not, scholars expounded before him, Yo. i. 6 ; Bik. iii. 1 ; Suk.
iv. 4, and other descriptive passages cited above, § 311.

325. The partic. as future, with or without היה : כְּשֶׁיִּהְיוּ בַּעֲלֵי
הַדִּין עוֹמְדִין ... לְפָנֶיךָ ... וּכְשֶׁנִּפְטָרִין ... when the litigants will be
standing before thee . . . and when they will depart . . ., Ab. i. 8 ;
שֶׁמָּא אַתָּה מַחֲסִיר ... אַתָּה מְיַתֵּר lest thou omit, lest thou add,
'Er. 13 a, for which the parallel passage in So. 20 a has the
imperf. : תְּיַתֵּר, תַּחְסִיר ; מוּבְטָח אֲנִי בָּזֶה שֶׁמּוֹרֶה הוֹרָאָה בְּיִשְׂרָאֵל I am
sure of this one that he will teach doctrine (promulgate decisions)
in Israel, Naz. 29 b ; Git. 58 a ; אֲנִי מֵת I am going to die,
Yᵉb. xvi. 6 ; רָאָה שֶׁהוּא מִתְחַיֵּיב he saw that he was going to be
declared guilty, San. iii. 8. Also of single acts : מַה שֶּׁאַתְּ שׁוֹמַעַת
what thou wilt hear, Bᵉr. 18 b ; אִם אֵין אַתָּה מְלַמְּדֵנִי אֲנִי אוֹמֵר
לְיוֹחָא אַבָּא וּמוֹסֶרְךָ לַמַּלְכוּת if thou wilt not teach me, I shall tell
my father Yoḥa, and he will deliver thee to the (Roman) authority,
Pᵉs. 112 a.

326. The partic. is used with the imperative הוה to command
the performance of a frequentative or iterative act, as contrasted
with the ordinary imperative which signifies the performance of
a simple act : הֱוֵי מִתְאַבֵּק sit in the dust ; הֱוֵי שׁוֹתֶה drink, Ab. i. 4 ;
הֱוֵי מְקַבֵּל receive, ib. 15, viz. regularly and habitually, as opposed
to עֲשֵׂה make ; אֱמוֹר say, ib., which describe single acts.

327. The partic. is similarly used with the infinitive of היה in
a frequentative and iterative sense : הַנּוֹטֵל שְׂכָרוֹ לִהְיוֹת רוֹאֶה he who
takes wages to be examining, Bᵉk. iv. 5 ; הֶחָשׁוּד לִהְיוֹת מוֹכֵר he who
is suspected to be selling, ib. ix ; לִהְיוֹת מַפְרִישׁ to be separating
(tithes), Git. iii. 7 ; הוּחְזְקוּ לִהְיוֹת גּוֹמְרִים they established the rule
to finish, Yᵉb. xii. 6 ; הוּחְזְקוּ לִהְיוֹת מַשִּׂיאִין to allow to marry,
ib. xvi. 7. So with עָתִיד : עָתִיד לִהְיוֹת נָטוּעַ וְעוֹשֶׂה פֵּירוֹת it will be
planted and bear fruit ; עֲתִידִים לִהְיוֹת עוֹשִׂים they will make, Sifra
(Weiss), 110 d ; cf. below, § 349.

328. The auxiliary verb היה is sometimes omitted in the infin.,

as in the perf. and imperf. (§§ 324, 325), but only after certain
expressions.   Thus, after הִתְחִיל (= הֵחֵל) : הִתְחִילוּ כָּל הָעָם שׁוֹרְפִין
all the people began to burn (לִהְיוֹת שׁוֹרְפִין), Pes. i. 5; הִתְחִילוּ
הַיְּחִידִים מִתְעַנִּין individuals began to fast (לִהְיוֹת מִתְעַ') Ta'a. i. 4;
הֵחֵלוּ מַעֲלִין they began to bring up, Tam. ii. 2, 3; הִתְחִיל מְרַדֵּד
he began to spread out, ib. vi. 3.

After דֶּרֶךְ : בְּשָׁעָה שֶׁדֶּרֶךְ בְּנֵי אָדָם שׁוֹכְבִים . . . דֶּרֶךְ בְּנֵי אָדָם עוֹמְדִים
at the hour when it is the custom of men to lie down . . . to rise up,
Bᵉr. i. 3 (לִהְיוֹת שׁוֹ'); BB vi. 6 ; דֶּרֶךְ כָּל הַפּוֹמָתִין מִתְוַדִּין it is the custom
of all those about to be put to death to make a confession, San. vii. 2
(לִהְיוֹת מִתְוַדִּין); נוֹהֲגִין הָיוּ בֵּית אַבָּא נוֹתְנִין the house of father were
accustomed to give, Pea ii. 4; Šab. i. 9 (L); לֹא נִמְנְעוּ עוֹשִׂין they
did not shrink from preparing, Yᵉb. i. 4; 'Ed. iv. 8 (var.:
לֹא נֶחְשְׁדוּ חֲבֵרִים תּוֹרְמִין); (לִהְיוֹת עוֹשִׂין associates are not suspected of giving tithes . . ., t. Ma'a. ii. 5 (but var. לִתְרוֹם; so
Ḥul. 7 a).

329. The partic. also expresses an act which is customary,
without any reference to a particular time : הַכֹּהֲנִים נִכְנָסִין לֶאֱכוֹל
the priests enter to eat, Bᵉr. i. 1 ; יוֹרֵד אָדָם לְתוֹךְ שָׂדֵהוּ וְרוֹאֶה . . .
a man goes down to his field and sees . . ., Bik. iii. 1 ; כְּשֶׁחוֹתְכִין
. . . אֵין חוֹתְכִין אֶלָּא עַל גַּב הַשֻּׁלְחָן כְּשֶׁנּוֹשְׁקִין אֵין נוֹשְׁקִין אֶלָּא עַל גַּב הַיָּד
וּכְשֶׁיּוֹעֲצִין אֵין יוֹעֲצִין אֶלָּא בַשָּׂדֶה when they cut . . ., they do not cut
but upon the table ; when they kiss, they do not kiss but upon the
hand ; when they hold counsel they do not hold counsel but upon
the field, Bᵉr. 8 b.   The subject is often omitted, and then the
partic. has the force of an impersonal verb, which may usually
be rendered in English by a passive : הַקּוֹרֵא אֶת שְׁמַע Bᵉr. ii. 3.
This is especially common in the plur. : כֵּיצַד מַפְרִישִׁין אֶת הַבִּכּוּרִים
how are the first-ripe fruits separated? Bik. iii. 1 ; עַכְשָׁיו שֶׁמּוֹלִיכִים
אוֹתִי now that I am led, Bᵉr. 28 b ; מִיָּד יוֹעֲצִים בַּאֲחִיתוֹפֶל וְנִמְלָכִים
בְּסַנְהֶדְרִין וְשׁוֹאֲלִים בָּאוּרִים וְתוּמִּים immediately they take counsel with
Ahitophel, and consult the Sanhedrin, and inquire of the oracle,

ib. 3 b ; מְבִיאִין לוֹ עֲרֵיבָה מְלֵאָה מַיִם a tub full of water was brought to him, Sab. 25 b.   Cf. below, § 439.

330. Such participles often assume a somewhat jussive sense : מֵאֵימָתַי קוֹרִין אֶת שְׁמַע from when may the Šᵉmaʻ be read? Bᵉr. i. 1 ; כָּל אָדָם קוֹרֵא כְּדַרְכּוֹ one may read in one's own way, as opposed to the preceding, יַטּוּ וְיִקְרָאוּ one must read in a bent position, ib. 3 ; מַשְׁאֶלֶת אִשָּׁה . . . ; מֵשִׁיב שׁוֹאֵל one may ask, answer, ib. ii. 1 ; וּבוֹרֶרֶת וְטוֹחֶנֶת וּמַרְקֶדֶת a woman may lend . . . and pick and grind and sift . . . , Šᵉbi. v. 9.   The transition from this usage to a real jussive or imperative is easy : בּוֹדְקִין אֶת הֶחָמֵץ leaven must be searched, Pᵉs. i. 1 ; הִתְקִינוּ שֶׁיְּהוּ אוֹמְרִין it was ordained that they should say ; שֶׁיְּהֵא אָדָם שׁוֹאֵל that one must ask, Bᵉr. ix. 5.   Particularly with a negative : אֵין עוֹמְדִין לְהִתְפַּלֵּל one must not stand up to pray, ib. v. 1 ; בַּמֶּה מַדְלִיקִין וּבַמָּה אֵין מַדְלִיקִין wherewith may one light, and wherewith may not one light ? Sab. ii. 1 ; הִתְקִין רַבָּן גַּמְלִיאֵל שֶׁלֹּא יְהוּ עוֹשִׂין כֵּן Rabban Gamaliel ordained that one must not do so, Giṭ. iv. 2.

331. The partic. retains its verbal character even when it is apparently used as a noun : הַקּוֹרֵא אֶת שְׁמַע וְלֹא הִשְׁמִיעַ לְאָזְנָיו if one reads the Šᵉmaʻ, but has not made it audible to his ears, Bᵉr. ii. 3.   Here the partic. takes the article like a noun, yet it also takes a direct object and is co-ordinated with a finite verb. Other examples are הַמִּתְפַּלֵּל וְטָעָה one who prays and makes a mistake, ib. v. 5 ; Šᵉbi. x. 2 ; Tᵉr. iii. 1, and often ; cf. also § 374.

332. As already stated in the treatment of the Verb (§§ 113, 127), in the passive forms the static significance of the partic. is predominant.   The passive partic. of the Qal, and the participles Puʻal and Hophʻal are practically equivalent to adjectives.   Thus, (לוּלָב) הַגָּזוּל that has been obtained by robbery, is parallel to הַיָּבֵשׁ a dry one, Suk. iv. 1 ; תָּלוּשׁ plucked from the ground ; מְחוּבָּר joined to the ground, are parallel to חָדָשׁ new ; יָשָׁן old, MŠ. v. 11 ; מְלוּבָּן whitened, washed, parallel to צוֹאִי dirty, Ḥul. xi. 2.   So רָכוּב

BM i. 3 ; מְעוּפָּד, מְיוּשָׁב Meg. 21 a, in a riding, standing, sitting posture, contrasted with the active forms רוֹכֵב, עוֹמֵד, יוֹשֵׁב.

333. These participles, viz. the passive of Qal, and the participles of Puʻal and Hophʻal, describe a more or less permanent state as the result of a verbal action. They thus differ from the participles of the corresponding reflexive-passive stems, which describe the verbal action as in the process of being performed. Thus פָּטוּר free, Šab. ii. 5 ; הַנִּפְטָר who frees himself—departs, MQ 29 a ; שָׁחוּף consumptive ; נִשְׁחָף wasting away, Sifra 111 c ; מְבוּעָר cleared away ; מִתְבַּעֲרִים being cleared away, MŠ. v. 6 ; מְעוּשָּׁרִין tithed (adjective) ; מִתְעַשְּׂרִין are tithed, Dam. iv. 1 ; ii. 1 ; מְחוּיָב having an obligation, RH iv. 8 ; מִתְחַיֵּב incurring guilt, Ab. iii. 9 ; מְעוּנֶּה and מִתְעַנֶּה t. Taʻa. ii. 7.

334. The passive partic. sometimes has the significance of the Latin gerundive (cf. Ges.-K., § 116 e): שׁוֹר הַנִּסְקָל an ox that is to be stoned, Qid. ii. 9 ; שָׂעִיר הַמִּשְׁתַּלֵּחַ the goat that is to be sent away, Yo. vi. 1 ; זֵתִים הַנִּכְתָּשִׁין olives that are to be crushed ; עֲנָבִים הַנִּדְרָכוֹת grapes that are to be trodden, Ter. i. 8 ; פָּרִים הַנִּשְׂרָפִים bulls that are to be burnt, Yo. vi. 7 ; כָּל הַמּוּמָתִין all that are to be put to death, San. vi. 2.[1]

335. The active partic. Qal is sometimes found in a middle sense which is equivalent to an English passive : חֲמוֹר טוֹעֶנֶת a loading—loaded ass, BM v. 4 ; פּוֹרֶקֶת unloading—unloaded, ib. vii. 4 ; קוֹטְעִין cut (ears of corn), Maʻa. i. 6 ; שׁוֹפְכִין pouring out—to be poured out, i. e. ill-smelling liquid, Šab. viii. 1.

336. The passive partic. Qal, being almost equivalent to an adjective, is found in an active sense in a few intransitive and transitive verbs. So already in BH, Ges.-K., § 50 f ; also in Aram., and especially in Syriac, Nöldeke, *Syr. Gr.*, § 280 ; *Mand. Gr.*, § 380.

---

[1] The other examples cited by Albrecht, § 107 m, do not belong to this category.

The following is a fairly exhaustive list of such cases in MH.

(i) Intrans.: אֲבוּדָה lost, BM 22 b; מָתוּן cautious, Ab. i. 1;
יָרוּד lowly, j. BM iv. 1; נְטוּפָה dripping, Pea vii. 1; סָבוּר thinking,
Qid. iii. 5 (an Aramaism—סְבִיר); עֲסוּקִים occupied, Pa. iv 4 (L);
רְבוּצִים lying down, Bᵉk. ix. 7; רָכוּב riding, BM i. 3 (edd.; so
BM 9 a, &c.); שָׁקוּד watchful, Ab. ii. 14; שְׁרוּיָה dwelling, ib. iii. 2.

(ii) Transitive: אֲחוּזַת הַדָּם holding in the blood, Ḥul. 58 b;
אָרוּס betrothed male, masc. of אֲרוּסָה Kᵉt. 13 b; זָכוּר remembering,
Kᵉt. ii. 10; חֲשׂוּכֵי בְגָדִים lacking garments, Kel. i. 2; טְבוּל יוֹם
one who bathed by day, TY ii. 1; כְּפוּיֵי טוֹבָה repressing thanks,
ungrateful, ʿAZ 5 a; נָדוּר having vowed, t. Dam. ii. 23; נָשׂוּי שְׁתֵּי
נָשִׁים married to two wives,[1] Kᵉt. x. 1, 2; שֶׁלֹּא רָחוּץ יָדַיִם וְרַגְלַיִם
not having washed the hands and feet,[2] Kel. i. 9; Pa. iv. 1;
תְּפוּסֵי מַעֲשֵׂי אֲבוֹתֵיהֶם holding the acts of their fathers, Sifra 112 b.[3]

The following are only apparently active: חֲלוּצָה a woman that
has received ḥaliṣa,[4] Yᵉb. ii. 3; טְעוּנָה burdened with—requiring,
So. ii. 1; סָמוּךְ leaning on—near, Yo. i. 8 (cf. BH נִשְׁעָן); שָׁחוּל
suspended—falling, Bᵉk. vi. 7; שְׁלוּחִין stripped—olives dropping
their kernels, ʿAZ ii. 7; שָׁקוּל balanced—even, So. ix. 2; תָּלוּי
hanged—hanging, ib.[5]

[1] As opposed to פְּנוּי unmarried, t. Qid. i. 1. Cf. the active and passive
forms side by side: הַנְּשׂוּאִין אֶת הָאֲחָיוֹת נוֹשְׂאִין, those who are married to the
sisters may marry . . ., t. ʿEd. ii. 9, the first expressing a state or condition,
the second expressing an act.

[2] A standing phrase, derived from Exod. xxx. 21. Cf. t. Yo. i. 18;
San. xiv. 6.

[3] Contrast אוֹחֲזִין מַעֲשֵׂי אֲבוֹתֵיהֶם, Bᵉr. 7 a; San. 27 b.

[4] In Deut. xxv. 7-10 the woman is conceived as active (וְחָלְצָה, ver. 9), and
the man as passive (חֲלוּץ הַנַּעַל, ver. 10); so also in MH: לֹא תַחֲלוֹץ,
Yᵉb. iv. 10; חָלְצָה, ib. xii. 3. More often, however, the condition is reversed:
the man is active, הַחוֹלֵץ, Yᵉb. iv. 1, 7; חֲלוֹץ, 5, 6; חָלַץ, v. 2 ff., and the
woman is passive, חֲלוּצָה.

[5] The forms כְּתִיב written, Ab. vi. 10; שְׁכִיב מְרַע lying with disease, Pea
iii. 7, &c., are pure Aramaisms.

337. In spite of the strong development of the verbal character of the participle in MH, the idiom has also retained in full the substantival usages of the partic. found in BH. Thus, the partic. is widely used as a noun, especially when determined by the article, e. g. הָעוֹמֵד what is standing; הַפָּרוּץ what is broken, Kil. iv. 4; הַנּוֹלָד what is born = the result of a action, Ab. ii. 9, &c. As an attribute, the partic. with the article often has the force of a relative clause, as in BH; cf. שׁוֹר הַנִּסְקָל and the other exx. in § 376.

338. The partic. often stands in the construct state: נְקוּבַת הַוֵּשֶׁט having a hole in the gullet; פְּסוּקַת הַגַּרְגֶּרֶת cut in the windpipe, Ḥul. iii. 1; מוּכַּת שְׁחִין struck with leprosy, Ket. iii. 5; חוֹתְמֵי בְרָכוֹת those who conclude the benedictions, Ber. ix. 5; cf. § 380.

339. In accordance with its substantival character, the partic. is regularly negatived by אֵין: אֵין מַדְלִיקִין Šab. ii. 1; cf. exx. above, §§ 329–30. Frequently, however, it is negatived by לֹא, but as a rule only when it is intended to impart a certain emphasis to the negation. This happens either when the negative follows immediately upon an affirmative, or when two or more negatives follow each other. In the first case, וְלֹא has the force of 'but not', in the second case לֹא . . . וְלֹא means 'neither . . . nor'. The participial clause negatived by לֹא contains, as a rule, no other words but the participle.

Exx. (i) יֵשׁ מְבִיאִין בְּכּוּרִים וְקוֹרִין מְבִיאִין וְלֹא קוֹרִין there are some who bring first-fruits and recite, some who bring but do not recite, Bik. i. 1, 3, 4; נִשְׁבָּעִין וְלֹא מְשַׁלְּמִין they take an oath, but do not pay, Šebu. vii. 1; cf. further, Šab. xi. 2; Yeb. iii. 1 f.; vi. 1; vii. 4; x. 8, 9; xi. 4, 6; So. 1, 2; San. vii. 5; Ḥul. i. 7.

(ii) תּוֹלִין לֹא אוֹכְלִין וְלֹא שׂוֹרְפִין they are in suspense: neither may they eat (the leavened bread), nor need they burn it, Pes. i. 5; Be. ii. 8; v. 2; Yeb. vii. 5; viii. 4, 5; לֹא חוֹלְצִים וְלֹא מְיַבְּמִים

neither do they give *ḥaliṣa*, nor do they marry (the deceased brother's childless wife), xi. 2. Contrast with 5, 7, where in similar cases the negative is אֵין, because the clauses are longer, and there is no particular emphasis on the negative ; So. iv. 1 f. ; Mak. iii. 13 ; 'Ed. v. 2 ; Ḥul. viii. 1 ; Tᵉm. iv. 1 ; M'il. iii. 1 ff. (contrast with 3) ; Nᵉg. x. 4 : Nid. vi. 1.

(iii) The two cases side by side : כֹּהֵן גָּדוֹל מַקְרִיב אוֹנֵן וְלֹא אוֹכֵל וְהַהֶדְיוֹט לֹא מַקְרִיב וְלֹא אוֹכֵל the High Priest may offer sacrifices on the day of the death of a near kinsman, but may not eat of a sacrifice, while an ordinary priest may neither offer a sacrifice, nor eat of one, Hor. iii. 5 ; BB viii. 1 ; 'Ar. vii. 1 ; Oho. viii. 1 ; Miq. vii. 1 ; 'Uq. v. 5.

In longer clauses the partic. is negatived by אֵין, even in such cases as described above : אֵין מוֹעֲלִים בָּהֶם וְאֵין חַיָּבִים עֲלֵיהֶם מִשֵּׁם . . . one does not incur *mᵉ'ila* by using them, nor is one guilty in their case of . . . Mᵉ'il. i. 3 ; 'Ar. ii. 6 ; Kᵉt. v. 5.

340. There are, however, exceptions to the above rules, when the partic. is negatived by לֹא, where we would expect אֵין, especially in later texts ; cf. Kᵉt. vii. 6 ; 'Ar. ii. 3 ; vii. 1, &c. But we also find in BH numerous examples of such an irregular construction,[1] e.g. Deut. xxviii. 61 ; Hab. i. 14 ; Job xii. 3 ; xxix. 12. Further, 2 Sam. iii. 34 ; Ezek. iv. 14, where the partic. is parallel to a finite verb.

341. The subject of a participial predicate is often placed after the partic., as in BH,[2] but as a rule only when a certain emphasis is intended on the predicate : בַּמֶּה בְהֵמָה יוֹצְאָה וּבַמֶּה אֵינָהּ יוֹצְאָה יוֹצֵא הַגָּמָל wherewith may an animal go out, and wherewith may it

---

[1] All the examples in BH are collected and classified by E. Sellin, *Ueber die verbal-nominale Doppelnatur d. hebr. Participien u. Infinitive*, p. 27, and by J. Kahan in his dissertation with the same title, p. 19. Cf. also Ges.-K., § 152 d.

[2] Cf. Driver, *Tenses*, § 135 (4). So also in Phoenician : פֹּעֵל קְרָא אנך, אנך, Cooke, op. cit., No. 3, ll. 2, 3, and the note p. 21 f.

not go out? The camel may go out, Šab. v. 1. Contrast with 2 :
מִתְיַחֵד אָדָם, וּכָרִים יוֹצְאִין, חֲמוֹר יוֹצֵא, &c.; a man may be alone,
opposed to the preceding לֹא יִתְיַחֵד Qid. iv. 12; אוֹכֵל פּוֹעֵל a work-
man may eat, opposed to the following לֹא יֹאכַל פּוֹעֵל BM vii. 5, 6.
So also with pronoun as subject : לֹא יִתֵּן לְתוֹכוֹ צוֹנֵן אֲבָל נוֹתֵן הוּא לְתוֹכוֹ
one may not put into it cold water, but one may put into it . . . ,
Šab. iii. 5; מָה אָנוּ לְיָרֵד . . . מוּתָּרִים אַתֶּם what are we in respect to
going down? . . . you are permitted, 'Er. iv. 2.

Often, however, the emphasis is hardly noticeable : יוֹדֵעַ אֲנִי
I know, Bᵉr. v. 5 (so Qoh. viii. 12); רוֹאֶה אֲנִי I prefer, Ab. ii. 9
(so Gen. xxxi. 5); זָכוּר אֲנִי I remember, Kᵉt. ii. 10 וְזְכוּרַנִי, in Aram.
fashion, Šab. 115 a, and often);[1] קוֹבֵעַ אַתָּה you rob, Yad. iv. 3;
קוֹבְלִין אָנוּ we complain, ib. 6.

342. Similarly the auxiliary verb הָיָה sometimes follows the
partic.: נוֹהֲגִין הָיוּ . . . . my father's house were accustomed, Pea ii. 4,
modifying the preceding statement; צוֹפֶה הָיִיתִי I was watching,
Suk. iii. 9; אֲבָל אֲנוּסִים הָיִינוּ but we were forced, Kᵉt. ii. 3:
פּוֹטְרוֹ הָיָה רַבִּי יְהוֹשֻׁעַ אַף . . . . R. Joshua acquitted him even . . . ,
Kᵉr. iv. 2. So also in BH for the sake of emphasis : Exod. xxvii. 1;
xxviii. 16; Deut. ix. 7, 22, 24; Joshua v. 5, &c. So in Aram. :
Dan. ii. 31, 34; Ezra iv. 12, 22, &c., and often in the Targumim
and other Aram. dialects.

343. Note. The construction of the partic. with היה in MH
is of native origin, and is not borrowed from Aram. It is frequent
in BH even where the partic. has a purely verbal force,[2] e.g. in the

---

[1] This contraction of אֲנִי with the partic., under Aram. influence, is common
in the Midrashim and in late MH generally, but not in the Mishna. Where
such forms occur in some texts of the Mishna they are due to the copyists, cf.
e.g. Nᵉd. i. 1; RH ii. 9; Šab. xxii. 3; Yᵉb. xvi. 7; Ya. iv. 2 in edd. with
L and N. The contraction of אֲנוּ with the partic. is never found even in late
MH, though common in Aram.; cf. Dalman, § 65; Nöldeke, *Syr. Gr.*, § 64;
Mand. Gr., § 175 a.

[2] Cf. Driver, *Tenses*, § 135 (5), and, with fuller lists, Sellin, op. cit., p. 35,
and Kahan, p. 25.

past : Judges i. 7 ; 2 Sam. iii. 7 ; viii. 15; Jer. xxvi. 18, 20 ;
2 Kings xvii. 32, 33 ; of the future : Gen. i. 6 ; Deut. xxviii. 29 ;
Isa. xxx. 20 ; with pass. partic. : Jer. xviii. 23 ; Ezek. xliv. 2 ;
xlvi. 1 ; Zach. xiii. 1 ; especially in the later books : Neh. i. 4 ;
ii. 13, 15 ; iii. 2 ; v. 18 ; vi. 14, 19 ; xiii. 5, 22 ; 2 Chron. xxx. 10 ;
Dan. viii. 5, 7 ; x. 2 ; Esther ii. 7, 15, and with לִהְיוֹת (a genuine
MH construction) : i. 22 ; viii. 13 ; ix. 21.

On the other hand, it is worthy of note that, with perhaps one
doubtful exception (cf. § 184 foot-note), the tenses are never found
in MH combined with היה, as sometimes in the Targumim (e.g.
דהוה חמירת, Gen. iv. 1 (Jer.); הוא נפיק Cant. i. 12), and very
frequently in Syriac (Nöldeke, *Syr. Gr.*, §§ 263, 268), and in
Arabic (Wright, *Arab. Gr.*³, ii. § 3 (c)) : also in Phoenician (כן נדר,
Cooke, *NSI.*, No. 57, l. 5), evidently because there is nothing
approaching such a construction in BH.

(4) THE INFINITIVE.

344. Of the various constructions with the inf. in BH, MH has
preserved only the gerundial use with לְ to express the direction
and purpose of a verb. In its use as a noun, the inf. has been
supplanted in MH by the corresponding verbal nouns which are
so numerous in MH (§ 217). For the BH inf. with the prepositions בְּ, כְּ, MH uses כְּשֶׁ with the finite verb, as often in BH
(כַּאֲשֶׁר), and regularly in Aram. (כְּדִי Dan. vi. 10 ; כַּד).[1] Finally,
the use of the inf. in its absolute form to emphasize a finite
verb is never found in MH,[2] though this construction is very
common in Aram.[3]

---

[1] The infin. with בּ is frequent in the Targumim, e. g. Gen. xii. 4 ; xxiv. 6 ;
xlviii. 7, &c., which proves that the construction was permissible in Aram.

[2] An exception is the liturgical passage : שַׂמֵּחַ תְּשַׂמַּח רֵעִים הָאֲהוּבִים (cf.
Jer. xx. 15) ; שׂוֹשׂ תָּשִׂישׂ וְתָגֵל הָעֲקָרָה (cf. Isa. lxi. 10), Kᵉt. 8 a ; Singer,
op cit., p. 299.

[3] Cf. Nöldeke, *Syr. Gr.*, § 295. In the Targumim the inf. absol. with

The loss of these infinitival constructions in MH is due to natural decay. They are already very scarce in the later books of the Bible. Thus, the combination of the inf. absolute with the finite verb is not found in Qoheleth, Canticles, Ezra, and Daniel, and is rare in Esther, Nehemiah, and Chronicles. So also the inf. with ב, and כ is rare in those books, and where found, it is not always used in a correct way.[1]

345. The use of the inf. with ל coincides generally with the BH inf. construct with ל. The pronominal suffixes attached to this inf. are, however, always of an objective force: לְזָרְעָהּ to sow it, Kil. ii. 3; לְנוֹטְעָהּ to plant it, ib. 4; לִפְדּוֹתוֹ to redeem it, Mš. iv. 6; לְאָכְלָן to eat them, Dam. iii. 3; לְהַחֲיוֹתְכֶם to revive you; לַהֲקִימְכֶם to raise you, Ber. 38 b.

346. After verbs of preventing, restraining, &c., either expressed or understood, the inf. takes the prepos. מִ־ before ־ל: אֲסוּרִין מִלִּזְרוֹעַ וּמִלְּקַיֵּים they are forbidden to be sown and to be kept, Kil. viii. 1; נִמְנְעוּ מִלְהָבִיא they refrained from bringing, Ḥal. i. 7; Pes. i. 6; שַׁבָּת הִיא מִלְּזְעוֹק it is Sabbath, so that one must not cry, Šab. 15 a; נִשְׁתַּהוּ הָעֵדִים מִלָּבוֹא the witnesses delayed to come, RH iv. 4; cf. Ges.-K., § 119 x.

347. The inf. is sometimes used as a verbal noun with the ל in the sense of 'with regard to': מָה אֲנִי לָבוֹא בַּקָּהָל what am I with regard to entering the assembly (of Israel, cf. Deut. xxiii. 4)?—may I enter, &c., Ya. iv. 4; מָה אָנוּ לֵירֵד what are we with regard to going down—may we go down? 'Er. iv. 2; מָהוּ (= מַה+הוּא) לְהַזְכִּיר should one mention? Šab. 24 a.

348. The inf. sometimes expresses necessity, obligation, as in BH (Ges.-K., 114 i–l): הֲרֵי הוּא לְהַסְגִּיר behold, this is to be shut up, Neg. iv. 10; הֲרֵי הוּא לְהַחֲלִיט behold this is to be finally decided

finite verb is used almost always where the Hebrew text has it. Cf. also Winer, *Chald. Gr.* (1882), § 46, 4, 5.

[1] Cf. Driver, *Introd. to the Lit. of the OT.*[6], pp. 506, No. 12; 538, No. 37.

(as impure), ib. 11. The person upon whom the obligation rests is introduced by עַל with the appropriate suffix: הֲרֵי עָלַי לְשַׁלֵּחַ פֶּרַע behold I must let (my hair) grow wild, Naz. i. 1; עָלָיו ... עָלֶיךָ רְאָיָה לְלַמֵּד thou, he must teach (produce) the evidence, Ya. iv. 3.

349. When preceded by the adjective עָתִיד ready, the inf. expresses with certainty and emphasis the occurrence of an act or event in the future (*Periphrastic Future*): אִם עָתִיד לַחֲזוֹר if he is resolved, or going, to return, Meg. ii. 3; גָּמַר מִלִּמְסוֹק אֲבָל עָתִיד לִיקַּח גָּמַר מִלִּיקַּח אֲבָל עָתִיד לִלְווֹת he has finished gathering (the olives), but he is going to buy (more); he has finished buying, but he is going to borrow (more), Ṭoh. ix. 2; Dam. vii. 1; Nᵉd. iii. 1; Šᵉq. vi. 3; Mid. ii. 6, 13 (הם עתידים להיות); Naz. v. 4; So. v. 2; BM iv. 2; San. x. 2; Ab. iii. 1; ʿUq. ii. 12 (a later addition).

These are all the passages in the Mishna where this construction occurs. But it becomes very common in the later Aggadic literature. Sometimes, however, עָתִיד is construed with the imperfect (cf. above, § 315). So also in the Targumim עָתִיד is found in both these constructions (e.g. Gen. iii. 15 in Jerus.; Isa. xl. 2). In Syriac ܚܠܡ is always followed by ܘ with the imperfect. In BH the construction is found only once, and in the primary sense of עָתִיד: הָעֲתִידִים עֹרֵר (לְעוֹרֵר) לִוְיָתָן Job iii. 8; cf. also Esther iii. 14; and עֲתִידֹת the destined future, Deut. xxxii. 35.

350. The inf. expresses the certainty of a future action also when preceded by סוֹף: סוֹפוֹ לְהִשָּׁמֵעַ it will eventually be understood, Ab. ii. 4; סוֹפוֹ לְבַטְּלָהּ: סוֹפוֹ לְקַיְּמָהּ he will eventually fulfil it, neglect it, ib. iv. 9; סוֹפוֹ לִיתֵּן he will eventually give, Mak. i. 1; סוֹפֵינוּ לִבְדּוֹק we shall certainly examine, San. iv. 5. Sometimes, however, the partic. is used, instead of the inf.: סוֹפוֹ יוֹרֵשׁ in the end he will inherit, Ab. i. 5; סוֹפָהּ בְּטֵלָה in the end it will cease, ib. ii. 2.

2. Government of the Verb.

(1) *Subordination of the Noun to the Verb as Accusative.*

351. The method in MH of marking the direct object of a transitive verb is exactly the same as in BH. As a rule, a determinate object is indicated by אֶת, an indeterminate object is left without any mark, e.g. אֵין חוֹפְרִין כּוּכִין ... אֲבָל מְחַנְּכִין אֶת הַכּוּכִין one may not dig (new) sepulchres ... but one may adapt the (old) sepulchres, MQ i. 6 ; קוֹרִין אֶת שְׁמַע read the ' Šema' ', Bᵉr. i. 1, &c. Sometimes, but not more frequently than in BH (Ges.-K., § 117 n), a determinate object is indicated by לְ, instead of אֶת : כַּפֶּר נָא לַעֲוֹנוֹת forgive, I pray, the iniquities, Yo. iii. 8 ; הַמְּקַנֵּא לְאִשְׁתּוֹ one who suspects his wife (cf. Num. v. 14), So. i. 1. Often, however, a determinate object is found without the *nota accusativi*, whether ת or לְ, especially when the object is determined by a possessive suffix : שׁוֹרוֹ he brought in his pots, his fruit, his ox, BQ v. 2, 3 ; תַּרְבֶּה גְּבוּלֵנוּ ... וְתַצְלִיחַ סוֹפֵנוּ ... וְתָשִׂים חֶלְקֵנוּ mayest thou increase our border ... prosper our end ... put our portion, Bᵉr. 16 b. This omission may in many cases be due to scribal negligence, as is shown by the frequent disagreement of the texts : נָטְלוּ כְסוּתוֹ they took his garment, BQ x. 2, L, but edd. את כס' ; הַמַּפְּיר כֵּלָיו if one recognizes his articles, edd., but L את כל' ib. 3, and often.

352. A nominative after a transitive verb is found in the expression יָבִיא הוּא וְלַחְמָהּ let him bring it and its bread, Men. vii. 8 ; יָבִיא הוּא וּנְסָכָיו let him bring it and its drink-offerings, ib. xiii. 7. The phrase may be an invariable technical expression, like אוֹתוֹ וְאֶת בְּנוֹ, § 275.

353. The accusative is found also after a passive verb : נִשְׁבָּר אֶת הַזָּוִיּוֹת gain the corners, 'Er. v. 1 ; לְהִפָּרַע אֶת שֶׁלָּךְ to be paid thine own, Kᵉt. xiii. 18 ; נִזְרַק אֶת דָּמוֹ its blood was sprinkled, Pᵉs. vii. 7 (L, edd. without את) ; cf. Ges.-K., § 121 a, b.

354. The double accusative is somewhat rarer in MH than in BH : לֹא יַעֲשֶׂה אָדָם אֶת סְלָעָיו דִּינְרֵי זָהָב one shall not make (change) his silver sela'im into gold dinars, MŠ. ii. 7 ; לֹא יְמַלֵּא אָדָם קְעָרָה שֶׁמֶן one shall not fill a dish with oil, Šab. ii. 4 ; מוֹצִיא אֶת הָרַבִּים יְדֵי חוֹבָתָן causing the public to discharge their duty, RH iv. 9; אוֹפִין אֶת פִּתָּן גְּרִיצוֹת baking their bread into thick loaves, Be. ii. 6 ; 'Ed. iii. 11.

More frequently the remoter object takes a preposition : הִלְבִּישׁוֹ בָאוּנְקָלִי וַחֲגָרוֹ בְּצִילְצוּל he clothed him with a (woman's) tunic, and girded him with a (woman's) girdle, Men. 109 b. In the passive the verb is followed by the accusative of the remoter object : לָבוּשׁ לְבָנִים וְעָטוּף לְבָנִים clothed in white garments and wrapped in white garments, Yo. 39 b; Men. ib.; טָעוּן פִּשְׁתִּים laden with flax, BM. vi. 8 ; ... טְעוּנָה הַפְשֵׁט requiring flaying, &c., Zeb. v. 4.

355. The accusative, but without the *nota accusativi*,[1] is also used to define the action of the verb in reference to time, especially to express duration of time : נֶאֶסְרָה עָלָיו שָׁעָה אַחַת she was prohibited to him for one hour, Yeb. iii. 7 ; אוֹר לְאַרְבָּעָה עָשָׂר בּוֹדְקִין on the eve of the fourteenth one must search, Pes. i. 1 ; אוֹכְלִין כָּל אַרְבַּע וְתוֹלִים כָּל חָמֵשׁ וְשׂוֹרְפִין בִּתְחִלַּת שֵׁשׁ one may eat all the four (hours), and suspend all the fifth (hour), and burn at the beginning of the sixth (hour), ib. 4 ; עַרְבֵי פְסָחִים ... לֹא יֹאכַל אָדָם on the eve of Passover one must not eat, ib. x. 1 ; נָדְרָה לֵילֵי שַׁבָּת she vowed on the night of the Sabbath, Šab. 157 a (but Ned. x. 8 : נ׳ בְּלֵילֵי שַׁבָּת). More often, the noun is introduced by a preposition, especially when it is intended to express a point of time, and not duration : בְּכָל יוֹם אָדָם מִתְפַּלֵּל every day a man prays, Ber iv. 3 ; וְלַמַּשְׁכִּים הָיָה הַמְמוּנֶה אוֹמֵר early in the morning the director would

---

[1] This accusative of time is found also with אֶת in the liturgical passage : הַחֲלִיצֵנוּ ... אֶת יוֹם רֹאשׁ הַחֹדֶשׁ הַזֶּה fortify us on this day of the New Moon, 'Er. iii. 9.

say, Bik. iii. 2; לְשָׁנָה הָאַחֶרֶת הָלַךְ וְלָן the following year he went and spent the night, Bᵉr. 18 b; cf. § 361 (viii).

356. The accusative also defines a verb as to the place: מָקוֹם שֶׁנָּהֲגוּ לַעֲשׂוֹת in the place where they have been accustomed to do, Pᵉs. iv. 1; מָקוֹם שֶׁהוּא מַתְחִיל the place where he begins, Yo. v. 5; but more frequently with a preposition: נִכְנַס לְמָקוֹם שֶׁנִּכְנַס וְעָמַד בְּמָקוֹם שֶׁעָמַד he entered to the place where he has to enter, and stood in the place where he has to stand, ib. 3.

357. The accus. is often used to describe the mode or manner of a verb: הָעוֹשֶׂה עִיסָּתוֹ קַבִּים if one makes his dough by single qabs, Hal. ii. 4; מַכְנִיסָן זוּג זוּג he brings them in pair by pair; מְצָאָן צְבָתִים he found them in small bundles, 'Er. x. 1; קְרָאָהּ סֵירוּגִין he read it in alternate verses, Mᵉg. ii. 2; לְעוֹלָם יִשְׁנֶה אָדָם לְתַלְמִידוֹ דֶּרֶךְ קְצָרָה one should always teach a disciple in a brief manner, Pᵉs. 3 b; נָטוּעַ עַרְבּוּבְיָה planted in confusion, Kil. v. 1; especially with participles and adjectives: וְקוֹרֵא עוֹמֵד Yo. vii. 1; וְקוֹרֵא יוֹשֵׁב So. vii. 8; he reads standing, sitting; וְקוֹצָה חַלָּתָהּ עֲרוּמָה and she cuts her ḥallah naked, Ḥal. ii. 3; הַבָּא אֶל הַמִּקְדָּשׁ טָמֵא if one comes into the Temple when unclean, Mak. iii. 2; שְׁמָרָהּ עוֹמֶדֶת he watched her as she was standing, BQ viii. 6. Often, however, the partic. takes the prepos. ב (ב essentiae, § 360 (ii)): אוֹרְגִין בֵּין בְּעוֹמְדִין בֵּין בְּיוֹשְׁבִין they may weave whether standing or sitting, Zab. iii. 2; נִכְנַס ר״ט בְּלֹא מִתְכַּוֵּן R. Tarphon entered without intention, 'Er. iv. 4; or it is put in a relative clause with כְּ: אוֹכְלִין אוֹתוֹ כְּשֶׁהוּא חַי they eat it raw, Mᵉn. xi. 7; Qid. ii. 1 (כְּשֶׁהִיא נַעֲרָה, cf. Sirach xxx. 12 a: כְּשֶׁהוּא קָטָן); or, finally, it is put in a circumstantial clause: וְהֵם מְגֻלִּין when they are uncovered, Ma'a. v. 2; cf. below, § 479.

To this usage belongs also the adverbial use of nouns, such as כָּל עִיקָר, סְתָם, תֵּכֶף, מָהָר, אֶמֶשׁ, or with prepositions: לְמַפְרֵעַ, לְמָחָר, בַּעֲלִיל, בַּתְּחִלָּה, בַּתְּחִלָּה, בְּיִחוּד, מֵעוֹלָם, &c. Cf. § 299.

(2) Subordination of the Noun to the Verb by means of Prepositions.

358. As in BH, nouns can be governed by a verb also indirectly, by means of a preposition. Such nouns serve to define the verbal action in its various relations to time, place, manner, &c., but they may also represent the object of the verbal action in the same way as an accusative. The prepositions chiefly used for this purpose are : אֵצֶל, בְּ־, לְ־, מִ־, and עַל. These prepositions have preserved in MH the general characteristics of the meaning and usage which they have in BH. In the following sections some special constructions will be noted. (Cf. Ges.-K., § 119.)

359. אֵצֶל. This prepos. usually takes in MH the place of אֶל is BH (cf. § 301): מִי שֶׁשְּׁלָחַךְ אֶצְלִי he who sent me to thee, Dam. iv. 6 ; גּוֹלְלוֹ אֶצְלוֹ he rolls it up towards himself, 'Er. x. 2 ; נִכְנְסוּ אֶצְלוֹ חַכְמֵי יִשְׂרָאֵל the sages of Israel came in unto him, Ber. 3 b. Also in the old BH sense : מִתְאָרֵחַ אֵצֶל עַם הָאָרֶץ stays as a guest with an *'am ha-ares*, Dam. ii. 2.

360. בְּ־. (i) To introduce the object of a transitive verb :[1] שְׁנַיִם אוֹחֲזִין בְּטַלִּית two hold a cloak, BM i. 1 ; הֶחֱזִיק בָּהּ he took hold of it ; זָכָה בָהּ he acquires it, ib. 2 ; הַחוֹבֵל בַּחֲבֵרוֹ if one injures his neighbour, BQ viii. 1 ; צָרַם בְּאָזְנוֹ he cut (or pulled) his ear ; תָּלַשׁ בִּשְׂעָרוֹ he plucked his hair, ib. 8 ; הִתְרֵיתֶם בּוֹ have you warned him? San. v. 1 ; לָבַשׁ בְּחָלוּק he put on a shirt, Me'il. v. 1. With a partitive sense : לַעֲשׂוֹת בְּצֶמֶר to work at wool, Ket. v. 6 : אוֹכֵל בְּקָדָשִׁים eats of holy things, Naz. viii. 6 ; שׁוֹתֶה בְיַיִן drinks of wine, ib. iv. 3 ; מַרְבֶּה בִּבְדִיקוֹת increases examinations, San. v. 2.

(ii) To describe the character of the subject or object in

---

[1] This use of a preposition to introduce a direct object is exactly parallel to the use of אֶת for the same purpose. In both cases, the preposition or the particle אֶת is dependent on the verb as its accusative, and the noun is dependent on the preposition, or אֶת, as its genitive.

relation to the verb, ב *essentiae*: נָדְרָה בְנָזִיר she vowed as a
Nazirite, Ned. iv. 3; נִכְנַס . . . בְּלֹא מִתְכַּוֵּן he entered without
intention, ʿEr. iv. 4; מַקְרִיב חֵלֶק בְּרֹאשׁ offers a portion as a chief;
נוֹטֵל חֵלֶק בְּרֹאשׁ takes a portion as a chief—offers, takes the first
portion, Yo. i. 2.

(iii) Expressing the instrument or means of an action: מַעֲגִיל
בְּמַעֲגִילָה rolling with a roller; עוֹלֶה בְסוּלָּם; יוֹרֵד בְּסוּלָּם going up,
going down a ladder, Mak. ii. 1; בַּמֶּה מַדְלִיקִין wherewith may one
kindle a light? Šab. ii. 1; or the price: לְשַׁלֵּם . . . בְּמֵיטַב הָאָרֶץ
to pay with the best of his land, BQ i. 1; בְּכַמָּה חֵפֶץ זֶה for how
much is this article, BM iv. 10; מַצִּילִין אוֹתָן בְּנַפְשָׁם one may deliver
them at the cost of their lives, San. viii. 7; or the measure:
הַטֶּבֶל אוֹסֵר . . . בְּנוֹתֵן טַעַם *Tebel* renders a food prohibited when it
is sufficient to add a flavour, Hal. iii. 10; אוֹסֵר בְּכָל שֶׁהוּא prohibits
by any quantity, ʿAZ v. 8; נְקוּבָה בְכוֹנֵס מַשְׁקֶה bored with a hole
large enough to take in liquid, Oh. v. 2; Kel. x. 8; cf. ib. iii. 1, 2.
For BH cf. *BDB*, p. 90 b, iii. 8.

(iv). To define and limit the verb, in the sense of 'in respect
to', 'in the case of': מוּתָּר בְּצָלוּי וּבְשָׁלוּק permitted as regards roast
or seethed food: אָסוּר בְּמַעֲשֵׂה קְדֵרָה prohibited as regards food
prepared in a pot, Ned. vi. 1; מוּתָּרִין בַּאֲכִילָה permitted to eat,
Kil. viii. 1; לָמָּה לֹא אֲסָרוּהָ בַהֲנָאָה why did they not prohibit it as
regards (indirect) profit? ʿAZ ii. 5.

(v) Finally, in a local sense after a verb of motion: שׁוֹלְחִין בְּכָל
הַמְּקוֹמוֹת they send to all places, San. xi. 4; הָיִיתִי בָא בַדֶּרֶךְ I was
coming by the way, Ber. i. 3; הַמְהַלֵּךְ בַּדֶּרֶךְ if one walks by the
way, Ab. iii. 4; הִלֵּךְ בָּהֶן he walked on them, Hul. ix. 2; נְתַתּוֹ
בְּאַנְפּוּלִי [1] thou hast put it into a bag, Šebu. vii. 6.

361. ל. (i) To introduce a direct object, like את; cf. above,
§ 351.

---

[1] Or אַמְפּוּלִי *mappula*; cf. Kohut. i. 124 a.

(ii) To introduce an indirect object, the ל of the dative : נָתְנוּ לוֹ they gave him, 'Er. vi. 3.

(iii) The *dativus ethicus* : בָּא לוֹ he came, Yo. iii. 8 ; נָפַל לוֹ עָלֶיהָ he fell on it, Pe. iv. 2 ; הוֹלֵךְ לוֹ אֵצֶל יוֹחָנָן he goes to Johanan, Šeq. v. 4.

(iv) To introduce the genitive : belonging to, cf. below, § 384.

(v) To introduce the agent after a passive or reflexive verb : וְנֶאֱכָלִין . . . לְכָל אָדָם they are eaten by all men, Zeb. v. 6 ; מִי שֶׁנִּשְׁאַל לְחָכָם if one consults a sage, MQ iii. 2 ; הַמִּשְׁתַּתֵּף לוֹ he who joins him in partnership, Bek. ii. 1 (cf. Ges.-K., § 121 f). So also after an active verb : בּוֹדְקִין . . . לְאוֹר הַנֵּר one searches by the light of a candle, Pes. i. 1 ; שֶׁאֵינִי טוֹעֵם לָךְ, שֶׁאֵינִי אוֹכֵל לָךְ that I will not eat, taste, of thine, Ned. i. 1.

(vi) 'In respect to ' : מְבָרֵךְ לְעַצְמוֹ pronounces a benediction for himself, Ber. vi. 6 ; מוּעָד לְמִינוֹ forewarned in respect to his own kind, BQ iv. 2 ; פָּתִיחַ לָרְוָחָה open wide, Ab. i. 5 ; הַמַּשְׂכִּיר בַּיִת לְשָׁנָה לֶחֳדָשִׁים . . . if one lets a house for a year, for months, BM viii. 8.

(vii) In a local sense, after verbs of motion : 'into'—BH אֶל : הַכּוֹנֵס צֹאן לְדִיר if one gathers sheep into a shed, BQ vi. 1 ; הוֹלַכְתָּם יוֹרְדִין לְשָׁם they go down there, Suk. iv. 5 ; cf. § 295 ; לְתוֹךְ בֵּיתֶךָ thou hast carried them to thine house, Šebu. vii. 6 ; in a figurative sense : אֵין מַעֲלִין לִכְהֻנָּה one does not raise to the priesthood, Ket. ii. 8.

(viii) Of time : לְיָמִים הַרְבֵּה after many days, 'Ed. i. 1 ; לַמַּשְׁכִּים Bik. iii. 2 ; לְכַתְּחִלָּה at the beginning, Šab. 65 a ; לְשַׁחֲרִית מְצָאוֹ ר"ג in the morning R. Gamaliel found him, Pes. 72 b ; cf. §§ 296, 297, 301.

362. מִן. (i) Of place : עָבַר מִכְּנֶגֶד פָּנָיו he passed from before him, Naz. ix. 1 ; מֵחֶצְיוֹ וְלִפְנִים ; מֵחֶצְיוֹ וְלַחוּץ from the half of it and towards outside, inside, BM ii. 3 ; מִן הָאַרְכּוּבָה וּלְמַטָּה from the knee down, Yeb. xii. 1 ; cf. § 301.

(ii) Of time : מוּכָן מִבְּעוֹד יוֹם prepared from day-time, Be. i. 2 ;
מִכָּאן וְעַד ג׳ שָׁנִים from now till three years, BM v. 3.

(iii) Partitive : שָׁמַע מִן הַתִּינוֹקוֹת אוֹמְרִים ; שָׁמַע מִן הַנָּשִׁים אוֹמְרוֹת
he heard some of the women, some of the children, say, Yᵉb. xvi. 5 ;
גְּנַב מִשֶּׁל אָבִיו מִיַּקִּירֵי יְרוּשָׁלַיִם of the notables of Jerusalem, Yo. vi. 6 ;
he stole of his father's, San. viii. 3 ; רָאִיתָ מִיָּמֶיךָ hast thou seen on
any of thy days—ever ? Qid. iv. 14 ; so מִיָּמָיו Suk. v. 1 ; מִיָּמֶיהָ (L) ;
מִימֵיהֶם Pes. v. 7 ; i. 6 (cf. Ges.-K., § 119 w, foot-note 1) ; לְסַפֵּק
סְלָתוֹת מֵאַרְבַּע עָמְדוּ מִשָּׁלֹשׁ to supply flours at four (seaḥs per selaʿ)
they stood at three (seaḥs per selaʿ), Šᵉq. iv. 9 ; so Kel. xvii. 11 ;
Pa. i. 1, &c.

(iv) In a privative sense : 'away from'—not to, after verbs of
preventing, restraining, &c. ; לֹא הָיוּ מוֹנְעִין מִמֶּנּוּ they did not
withhold from him, Yo. i. 4 ; cf. § 346.

(v) Introducing the source, cause, instrument of an action :
לֹא מִפִּיהָ אָנוּ חַיִּין we do not live from her mouth—depend on her
words, Kᵉt. i. 6 ; נֵיאוֹתִין מִמֶּנּוּ make use of it, Šab. iii. 6 ; . . .
שׂוֹרְפִין מֵעֲצֵי עַצְמָן they burn with their own wood, Pᵉs. vii. 8 ;
נָפַל לְפָנָיו מִקּוֹל הַכְּרִיָּיה he fell forward because of the noise of the digging,
BQ v. 8. So with אֶל in a reflexive sense : מְנַגֵּן מֵאֵלָיו plays by
itself, Bᵉr. 3 b ; cf. above, § 301, and below, § 432.

363. עַל. (i) To introduce the object : הִשְׁבִּיעַ עָלָיו he adjured
him (parallel to מַשְׁבִּיעֲךָ), Sᵉbu. v. 2 ; iv. 3 ; מַצִּיל עַל הַכֹּל protects
everything, 'Ed. i. 14 ; כָּבַשׁ עָלָיו לְתוֹךְ הַמַּיִם he pressed him into the
water, San. ix. 1 ; לְלַמֵּד עַל מַעֲשֵׂה הַקְּטֹרֶת to teach the work of
making the incense, Yo. iii. 11.[1]

(ii) After verbs of going, standing, &c. : מְהַלְּכִין עַל כָּל הָאַחִין
they go over all the brothers, Yᵉb. iv. 5 ; הָלְכָה לָהּ עַל לִבּוֹ it went

---

[1] Further examples of this unusual construction are : לְהַעֲבִיר עַל הַכֶּתֶם
to remove a stain, Šab. ix. 5 (L and j.) ; edd. 'אֶת הכ) ; אֵין מְשַׁנִּין עַל הַמִּנְהָג,
one should not change the custom, j. BM vi. 4. So, perhaps, in BH : חוֹלֵשׁ
עַל גּוֹיִם Isa. xiv. 12 ; cf. Exod. xvii. 13.

to his heart, San. ix. 2 ; יְחַזְרוּ עַל הַפְּתָחִים (L וְיִשְׁאֲלוּ), let them go about (beg) at the doors, Kᵉt. xiii. 3 ; עוֹמֵד עַל דְּבָרָיו stand on his words, refuse to change one's opinion, ʿEd. i. 4 ;[1] יָדוֹ עַל הָעֶלְיוֹנָה (L לְעֵלָּ׳) to have an advantage, Šᵉq. iv. 9 ; עַל הַתַּחְתּוֹנָה (L לַתַּחְ׳) to have a disadvantage, BM vi. 2 ; ג׳ עַל ג׳ עַל רוּם ג׳ three (cubits) by three by three high, Šᵉbi. iii. 5 ; אֶחָד יוֹשֵׁב עַל פֶּתַח one sits at the door . . . , San. xi. 2.

(iii) In the sense of ' in addition to ': נוֹשְׂאִין עַל הָאֲנוּסָה וְעַל הַמְּפוּתָּה one may marry in addition to the woman that has been forced or seduced, Yᵉb. xi. 1 ; מוֹסִיף עָלָיו it adds unto it, Kᵉt. iii. 5 ; יְתֵרוֹת עַל הָרִאשׁוֹנוֹת exceed the first, Taʿa. i. 6 ; and so often to express the comparative degree of adjectives, § 391. So עַל יַד : יִקָּבֵר עַל יַד עוֹרוֹ let it be buried together with its skin, MŠ. i. 6 ; iii. 11 ; . . . , מְמַעֶטֶת עַל יַד reduces by the side of . . . , Nⁱd. i. 1 ; cf. *BDB*, p. 755, 4.

(iv) ' In respect to ', ' concerning ' : אָמְרוּ לָהּ עַל בִּתָּהּ they told her about her daughter, Naz. vi. 11 ; הַשּׁוֹמֵעַ עַל מֵתוֹ if one hears concerning his dead, Pᵉs. 92 b ; נִמְלַךְ עֲלֵיהֶן he changed his mind concerning them, BM. i. 7 ; שָׁחַט עָלֶיהָ he slew on her behalf, Pᵉs. viii. 1 ; cf. *BDB*, p. 754 b (g).

(v) To express the agent or cause : שֶׁלֹּא יִמָּחֶה עַל הַמַּיִם that it might not be blotted out by the water, So. i. 4 ; הַבָּנוֹת נִזּוֹנוֹת עַל הַבָּנִים the daughters are maintained by the sons, BB. viii. 8 ; נוֹמֵל לֹא יִשְׁחוֹט עָלָיו he shall not slay (it) through it, Bᵉk. v. 2 ff. ; קְרָאָהּ נַפְשׁוֹ עָלֶיהָ his life is taken because of it, Mak. iii. 15 ; so : הַמְחַלֵּק נְכָסָיו עַל פִּיו עַל פֶּה he read it by mouth—by heart, Mᵉg. ii. 2 ; if one divides his property by word of mouth, BB ix. 7.

(3) *Co-ordination of a Verb to another Verb as Auxiliary*

364. Certain verbs are used in an auxiliary character to give an adverbial definition to another verb with which they are

---

[1] Contrast עוֹמֵד בְּדִיבּוּרוֹ keeping his word, BM 47 b.

co-ordinated. Some of these, as in BH (Ges.-K., § 120 d), stand before the principal verb which they serve to define. Others stand after the principal verb.

(i) Before the principal verb.

דחק to press : דָּחַק וְנִכְנַס he entered by force, Ber. 31 b ; Naz. 49 b ; וַאֲנִי דָחַקְתִּי וְנִכְנַסְתִּי and I entered by pressing, San. 70 b.

חזר to return : חוֹזֵר וּמְחַלְלָם he changes them again, MŠ ii. 6 ; חָזַר וְהוֹסִיף he added again ; יַחֲזוֹר וְיִתְרוֹם let him tithe again, Tᵉr. iv. 3.   But also with inf. : חָזְרוּ לוֹמַר they said again, Giṭ. vi. 5, &c.

מהר to hasten : מַהֲרוּ וְהוֹצִיאוּ bring forth quickly ; מַהֲרוּ וַעֲשׂוּ do quickly, 'Er. vi. 1.

הִשְׁכִּים to rise early : מַשְׁכִּימִים וּבָאִין they come early in the morning, Suk. iii. 13 ; מַשְׁכִּים וְטוֹבֵל he immerses himself early, Tam. i. 2 ; הִשְׁכִּים וּמָצָא he found early, Ḥul. ii. 6 ; הַשְׁכֵּם וְצֵא הַעֲרֵב וְצֵא go forth early in the morning, go forth late in the evening, Bᵉr. 62 a.

שׁנה to repeat : שׁוֹנִין וְאוֹמְרִין they say a second time (L שׁוֹנִין לוֹמַר), Suk. v. 4 ; שָׁנָה וְלִימֵּד he taught a second time, San. xi. 2.

שׁקד to be diligent ; כָּל אוּמּוֹת שׁוֹקְדוֹת וּבָאוֹת all nations come diligently, Bᵉr. 58 a.

365. (ii) After the principal verb.

בא to come : לֹא יְהֵא זוֹרֵעַ וּבָא he shall not sow on, Kil. ii. 5 ; אֲנִי מְרַקֵּד וּבָא I come on dancing, Ber. 51 a ; הָיָה מוֹדֵד וּבָא he was measuring on, 'Er. 42 b ; נִיזוֹנוֹת וּבָאוֹת נִיזוֹנִין וּבָאִין they are continued to be maintained, t. BB viii. 18, 19.

הלך to go : מוֹסִיף עָלָיו וְהוֹלֵךְ he goes on adding to it, Šebi. iii. 3 ; מִתְנַוְנָה וְהוֹלֶכֶת she goes on decaying more and more, So. iii. 5 ; הָיְתָה דוֹלֶקֶת וְהוֹלֶכֶת מְסַפֵּר וְהוֹלֵךְ he goes on relating, Bᵉr. 13 a ; כָּל הַיּוֹם כּוּלּוֹ it was burning continually for the whole day, Šab. 23 a ; מִתְמַעֲטִין וְהוֹלְכִין they may go on becoming fewer and fewer, Pᵉs. 99 a ; אוֹכֵל וְהוֹלֵךְ he may go on eating, ib. 99 b ; 105 a.

ירד to go down : הִתְחִיל מְחַטֵּא וְיוֹרֵד he began to purify down-

wards, Yo. v. 5 ; מִתְגַּלְגֵּל וְיוֹרֵד it rolls downwards, ib. vi. 6 ;
הָיָה חוֹתֵךְ וְיוֹרֵד he would cut downwards, Tam. iv. 3.

עלה to go up : הָיוּ הַמַּיִם צָפִין וְעוֹלִין לִקְרָאתוֹ the waters were floating
upwards towards him, Ab. deRN. xx ; הָיָה מִתַּמֵּר וְעוֹלֶה (the smoke)
was going straight upwards (palm-like), ib. xxxv. 7 ; טוּמְאָה בּוֹקַעַת
וְעוֹלָה בּוֹקַעַת וְיוֹרֶדֶת the impurity breaks through upwards, downwards, Oh. vi. 6 ; מְטַפֵּס וְעוֹלָה מְטַפֵּס וְיוֹרֵד climbing upwards,
downwards, ʿEr. 21 a ; מַשְׁפִּיעַ וְעוֹלָה מַשְׁפִּיעַ וְיוֹרֵד sloping upwards,
downwards, ib. 43 b.

יצא to go forth : הָיָה מוֹשְׁכוֹ וְיוֹצֵא he was pulling it out, BQ vii. 6 ;
מְבַצְבֵּץ וְיוֹצֵא bursting outwards, Pes. 13 a ; מְפַכְפְּכִין וְיוֹצְאִין trickling
forth, t. Šeq. iii. 2 ; גְּרָרוּם וְהוֹצִיאוּם they dragged them forth, ib. 1.

ישב to sit : הָיָה הִלֵּל כָּפוּף וְיוֹשֵׁב Hillel was sitting bowed, Šab. 17 a.

עמד to stand : מוּשְׁבָּע וְעוֹמֵד מֵהַר סִינַי he is under oath from Sinai,
Ned. 8 a.

II. THE NOUN

1. Determination of the Gender.[1]

366. In the determination of the gender, MH follows the
principles of BH. Thus, in the case of animate beings the gender
agrees with the sex, whether the two sexes are distinguished by
independent words, as אָב, אֵם ; עֶבֶד, שִׁפְחָה ; חָתָן, כַּלָּה ; or the fem.
is formed from the masc. as חֲמוֹרָה, פִּרְיָה [2] (cf. § 277); טָלֶה (L ;
edd. טַלְיָה) Men. xiii. 6 ; or one word serves for the two sexes, as
נְמָלָה, יוֹנָה, אַרְנֶבֶת, צִפּוֹר, גָּמָל, בָּקָר.

MH shows some new fem. formations from the masc., especially
in late texts. Thus, beside חֲמוֹרָה, טָלֶה we find וְאָבָה Est. R. i. 9 ;
חֲזִירָה ib. iii. 1 ; חֲתוּלָה cat, j. Pea 17 d ; כַּלְבָּה dog, j. San. 26 b ;

---

[1] Cf. Ges.-K., § 122, and H. Rosenberg, *Das Geschlecht d. Hauptwörter in
d. Mischna* (Berlin, 1908), especially pp. 73 ff.

[2] חֲמוֹר is also found as fem. : הָלְכָה חֲמוֹרְךָ thy ass is gone, Dek. iv. 4.
אָתוֹן is not used in MH.

רְחֵלָה ewe, Ḥul. xi. 2 ; also בַּחוּרָה young woman ; בַּחוּרוֹת Gen. R. 71 ; Num. R. 10 ; תְּאוֹמָה twin sister, BB 123 a ; Gen. R. 22.

367. So also in the case of inanimate objects, MH follows generally the rules of BH. The following are construed as fem.

(i) Limbs or parts of the body, especially those in pairs : אֹזֶן, אֶצְבַּע, דּוֹפָן side (and wall) ; חֹפֶן hollow of the hand ; יָד, כַּף palm ; כָּבֵד, כָּנָף, כֶּרֶס (or כָּרֵס) belly ; בֶּרֶע knee ; פָּנִים Ab. i. 13 ; שֵׁן, שׁוֹק, רֶגֶל, קֶרֶן, צִפּוֹרֶן nail (of finger or toe) ; צֵלַע rib ; (For reff. cf. the Lexicons).

The following are of common gender : לְחִי ; לָשׁוֹן, זָנָב and זָקָן are masc.

(ii) Names of tools, utensils, &c. : כַּד, יָתֵד, חֶרֶב, חֵמֶת, אֶבֶן, מַחַט needle ; מַקֵּל, סַיִף sword ; רֵיחַיִם, קֶלַע, סַכִּין Be. ii. 9 (construed as sing. like the Aram. רֵיחְיָא).

(iii) Names of countries, towns, &c. : שָׂדֶה, עִיר, יְרוּשָׁלַיִם, אֶרֶץ BM i. 4.

(iv) Names denoting a circumscribed space : יָצִיעַ, חָצֵר, בְּאֵר, מֶרְחָץ bath, Šᵉbi. viii. 11 ; קֵן. But גַּן, גּוֹרֶן, and דֶּרֶךְ are common.

Fem. are also : דְּיוֹ ink, Ab. iv. 25 ; סוּבִּין bran, Tᵉr. xi. 5 ; פִּשְׁתָּן flax, BQ vi. 6 ; תִּלְתָּן fenugreek, MŠ ii. 3.

The following are common : אוּר fire ; כִּכָּר, חַלּוֹן, Ya. ii. 4 ; מָעוֹת money, small change, MŠ iii. 5 ; iv. 9.

Fem. are names of abstract ideas : גְּדוּלָּה greatness ; שְׂרָרָה dominion ; מַחֲלוֹקֶת controversy ; רַבָּנוּת authority ; also verbal nouns : אֲכִילָה eating ; בַּטָּלָה idling ; הַבְדָּלָה separating, &c. ; cf. §§ 217, 272.

Further, certain collectives : חֲמֶרֶת, גְּמֶלֶת, בַּלֶּשֶׁת (§ 237) ; and most diminutives, § 276.

368. Some nouns change their gender when used in a derived sense : כַּף palm of hand, fem. Ab. ii. 8 ; כַּף spoon, masc. Tam. v. 4 ; סֶלַע rock, masc. BB vii. 1 ; סֶלַע *selaʿ* (weight, or coin), fem. MŠ ii. 10 ; רֶגֶל foot, fem. Oh. x. 2 ; רֶגֶל festival, masc. Pᵉs. viii. 1.

369. The following fem. nouns which form the plur. in ־ִים
are construed in the plur. as masc.: דְּלַעַת pumpkin, דְּלוּעִין Kil. iii. 7 ;
Sᵉbi. i. 7 ; כַּרְשִׁינָה leek, כַּרְשִׁינִין MŠ ii. 4 ; קִישּׁוּת cucumber, קִישּׁוּאִים
Tᵉr. iii. 1 ; Bᵉr. 57 b ; קַשְׂקֶשֶׂת scale (of fish), קַשְׂקַשִּׂין Ḥul. iii. 7 ;
cf. § 289.

370. Certain nouns ending in ת־ are fem., even when the ת is
treated as a radical letter : אוֹת sign, letter of the alphabet, MQ
iii. 4 ; Kil. ix. 10 ; אֱמֶת So. ix. 15 ; נַּת Ma'a. i. 7 ; זֶפֶת Kel. x. 5 ;
עֵת Tam. i. 2 ; דָּת law, Kᵉt. vii. 6 ; חֲבִתִּים wafers, Mᵉn. xi. 3 ;
פַּת Bᵉr. vi. 7 ; צְבַת tongs, Ab. v. 6 ; שַׁבָּת Dam. iv. 2 ; cf. also
Nöldeke, *Syr. Gr.*, § 86.

371. A number of nouns are found both in the masc. and in the
fem. form but with a difference in meaning : נַּן garden ; נַּנָּה (or
גִּינָה) vegetable garden, Kil. ii. 2 ; דִּיר shed for animals, BQ vi. 1 ;
דִּירָה dwelling for human beings, Bᵉr. 77 b ; חוֹב debt, BM i. 7 ;
חוֹבָה duty, Pᵉs. x. 4 ; חוֹל sand, Šab. viii. 5 ; חוֹלָה sand-dune, 'Ar.
iii. 2 ; Sab. 31 a ; חֶרֶב sword, So. viii. 5 ; חַרְבָּה knife, Šᵉbi. viii. 6 ;
צֵל shadow, Pᵉs. 114 a ; צְלָה shade, protection from the sun, Suk.
i. 1 ; קוֹר cold, BM 106 b ; קוֹרָה cooling, satisfaction, Ab. iv. 17.

372. Gender of Greek and Latin nouns.

(i) Nouns ending in ס־ (-ος, -us) are construed as masc. : פָּנָס
φανός, Kel. ii. 4 ; פּוֹלְמוֹס πόλεμος, So. ix. 14 ; פִּנְקָס πίναξ, Ab.
iii. 16 ; סוֹלְיָם *soleas*, Kel. xxvi. 4.

(ii) Nouns ending in ה־ , א־ , ־ (-a, -ια, -εια, -η, -a) are
fem. : טַבְלָה *tabula*, Yo. iii. 10 ; קַצְרָה *castra*, 'Ar. ix. 6 ; קְלוֹסְטְרָא
κλεῖστρα (pl.), Kel. xi. 14 ; דְּיֵיטִי δίαιτα, Šab. xi. 2.

(iii) Nouns ending in וֹן־ , ן־ (-ον), are masc. : סִיקָרִיקוֹן
σικαρικόν, Giṭ. v. 6 ; קָלְבּוֹן κόλλυβος Šeq. i. 6, but קִיטוֹן κοιτών is
construed as fem., Mid. i. 6.[1]

(iv) Nouns ending in ין־ are fem. : אַפּוֹפוֹדִין ὑποπόδιον, Kel.

---

[1] This is not due to the plur. ending (קִיטוֹנוֹת פְּתוּחוֹת) ; cf. קִיטוֹן אַחַד,
Exod. R. 33.

xxiv. 7 ; סַנְהֶדְרִין συνέδριον, San. i 6 ; סוּדָרִין σουδάριον, ib. vii. 2 (L) ; but בִּיבָרִין (*vivarium*) is masc., Šab. xiii. 2 ; cf. further, Krauss, *Lehnwörter*, i, §§ 287–305.

2. The Use of the Article.

373. As in BH, so in MH nouns are either determinate by their nature, such as proper nouns and pronouns, or are rendered determinate by their grammatical connexion, viz. when followed by a determinate noun as genitive, or by a pronominal suffix, or when preceded by the article.

Only in the latter case does MH exhibit certain peculiarities which demand special treatment.

The MH article is identical with the BH article, both in form and in the general characteristics of its usage.

374. (i) The article is used whenever the noun is definite.

Thus with nouns which are definite by themselves : הַחַמָּה the sun ; הָעוֹלָם the world ; הַשַּׁחַר the dawn ; הַשַּׁבָּת the Sabbath. With nouns that have been mentioned before : פּוּכִין, הַפּוּכִין, cf. above, § 351.

With nouns that are known or necessary in connexion with the subject treated : נוֹשְׂאֵי הַמִּטָּה the bearers of the bier, in connexion with a dead body, Ber. iii. 1 ; הַיּוֹם ; הַיַּיִן, &c., in connexion with *Qiddus*, Ber. viii. 1 ff. So also with nouns that are definite in the mind of the speaker : הַצּוֹאָה dirt, Ber. iii. 5 ; הַחֲמוֹר ib. iv. 5 ; הַפֵּירוֹת ib. vi. 1, &c. This last usage is even more common in MH than in BH.[1]

(ii) The article is used with titles : הַמְּמוּנֶּה the overseer, Yo. ii. 1 ; הַסָּגָן the deputy High Priest, ib. vii. 1 ; אַגְרִיפּוֹס הַמֶּלֶךְ King Agrippa, Bik. iii. 4 (but always כֹּהֵן גָּדוֹל the High Priest, even when definite, Yo. i. 1 ; cf. § 378).

---

[1] Cf. Ges.-K., § 126 q–t ; Driver, *Notes on Samuel*, i. 4 ; xix. 13.

(iii) With the vocative : הַמֶּלֶךְ O King! ; הָעֲבוֹדָה ; הַפְּעוֹן הַזֶּה
Sifre Deut. iii. 23 ; cf. § 305.

(iv) With names of material : הַצֶּמֶר wool, Šab. i. 6 ; הָעֵץ wood,
ib. ii. 3 ; הַכֶּסֶף, הַזָּהָב silver, gold, BM iv. 1.

(v) With collectives : הַלּוּף וְהַשּׁוּם lof and garlic, &c., Ter. ix. 6 ;
Kil. i. 1 f.

(vi) With abstracts : הַנּוֹי וְהַכֹּחַ וְהָעוֹשֶׁר וְהַכָּבוֹד beauty, strength,
riches, glory, &c., Ab. vi. 8 ; BM iv. 3.

(vii) The article is used with participles in a somewhat demonstrative sense : he who . . ., she who . . ., &c., especially in
conditional sentences : הַקּוֹרֵא אֶת שְׁמַע he who reads the Šemaʿ,
Ber. ii. 3 ; הַמִּתְפַּלֵּל וְטָעָה he who prays and commits an error,
ib. v. 5 ; הַמּוֹצֵא תְפִלִּין he who finds tephillin, ʿEr. x. 1 ; cf. § 331.

So sometimes in BH : הַנּוֹגֵעַ Gen. xxvi. 11 ; הַמַּקְרִיב Lev. vii. 33 ;
xiv. 46–7 ; xv. 6–10 ; xvi. 28. Contrast : מַכֵּה . . . Exod. xxi. 12 ;
Prov. xv. 32 ; Qoh. x. 8, &c.

(viii) The article is prefixed to adjectives or participles when used
substantivally, i. e. when the nouns to which they refer are omitted.
In such cases the article serves to emphasize the substantival character
of the adjective. When two such adjectives are contrasted, the
article has a demonstrative force : that which. Exx. : טוֹל אַתָּה אֶת
הַלַּח וַאֲנִי אֶת הַיָּבֵשׁ take thou the wet, and I (take) the dry, sc. חִטִּים
mentioned before, or תְּבוּאָה Dam. vi. 9 ; . . . וְלֹא מִן הַתָּלוּשׁ עַל הַמְּחוּבָּר
וְלֹא מִן הֶחָדָשׁ עַל הַיָּשָׁן nor from that which is loose upon that which
is joined (to the soil) . . . nor from the new upon the old . . .,
Ter. i. 5, 7 ; ii. 6 ; iv. 8 ; הַשּׁוֹחֵט הַמְסוּכֶּנֶת if one slays a beast
afflicted with a fatal illness, Ḥul. ii. 6 ; iv. 2, &c.

375. The attribute of a determinate noun regularly takes the
article in MH as in BH : הַיָּם הַגָּדוֹל the great sea, Ber. ix. 2 ;
הַמָּעוֹת הָאֵלּוּ . . . these, those moneys, MŠ iii. 3, 4 ; בְּנוֹ וּבִתּוֹ . . . הָהֵם
הַגְּדוֹלִים his grown-up son and daughter, ib. iv. 4 ; כָּל הַכֵּלִים הַנִּיטָּלִים

all the vessels that may be handled, Šab. xvii. 5 ; שְׁבִיל הַיָחִיד הַקָבוּעַ
a permanent private path, Pea ii. 1.

Where the noun has a preposition prefixed, the preposition may
be pointed with *patah* with the article elided : כְּמַעְיָן הַנּוֹבֵעַ like the
bubbling spring, BB x. 8 ; לַדָּבָר הֶאָסוּר for a thing that is forbidden,
Pe. vi. 5 ; בְּעוֹף הַדַּק in a small bird ; בְּעוֹף הַגַּס in a big bird,
Ḥul. iii. 1.

There are, however, important and numerous exceptions to this
rule.

376. (*a*) The attribute (an adjective, or a participle) is found
with the article, while the noun is without the article.

(i) When one attribute of a substantive is to be distinguished
from another attribute of the same substantive. The article is then
equivalent to a qualifying relative clause.[1]

נֶגֶר הַנִּגְרָר a bolt which is dragged to the ground by a string tied
to the door, opposed to the following : וְהַמּוּנַּח one which lies loose,
'Er. x. 11 ; פֵּירוֹת הַתְּלוּשִׁין fruits which have been plucked, opposed
to הַמְחוּבָּרִין those which are fixed to the ground, Kᵉt. viii. 3.
נְכָסִים הַמְיוּחָדִין property which is the possession of a special owner,
opposed to נִכְסֵי הֶפְקֵר ownerless property, BQ i. 2 ; גִּזֵּי צֶמֶר הַבָּאוֹת
מִמְּדִינָתָן fleece which comes from the country, opposed to הַלְּקוּחוֹת
מִבֵּית הָאוּמָּן fleece which has been taken from the mechanic,
BM ii. 1.

(ii) With one attribute only, where the chief emphasis is to be
laid on the attribute, rather than on the substantive. Here, too,
the article is virtually equivalent to a relative clause : גְּשָׁרִים הַמְפוּלָּשִׁין
covered bridges with an open passage ; מָבוֹי הַמְפוּלָּשׁ a covered
entry with an open passage, 'Er. ix. 4 ; עֵצָה הַהוֹגֶנֶת לוֹ a counsel
which is suitable (profitable) to him, Yᵉb. xii. 6 ; בְּהֵמָה הַמְקַשָּׁה לֵילֵד
a beast which has hard labour in giving birth, Ḥul. ii. 1, 2, 4.

---

[1] The art. is never used in MH as a relative with a finite verb, as sometimes
in BH ; cf. Ges.-K., § 138 i, k.

(iii) With standing expressions which have acquired a technical sense : שַׁעַר הָעֶלְיוֹן the Upper Gate, Šeq. vi. 1; so Ezek. ix. 2; שָׂעִיר הַמִּשְׁתַּלֵּחַ the goat which is to be sent away, as opposed to שְׂעִיר הַחַטָּאת Yo. iv. 2; vi. 2 (cf. Lev. xvi. 10); שׁוֹר הַנִּסְקָל an ox condemned to stoning, Qid. ii. 2 (cf. Exod. xxi. 28); שׁוֹר הַמּוּעָד a goring ox, the owner of which has been forewarned, as opposed to שׁוֹר תָּם BQ i. 4 (cf. Exod. xxi. 29); נַעֲרָה הַמְאוֹרָסָה a betrothed maiden, San. vii. 4 (cf. Deut. xxii. 25, 27); כְּנֶסֶת הַגְּדוֹלָה the Great Synagogue, as distinguished from an ordinary כְּנֶסֶת Ab. i. 1.

(iv) In numerous other cases where no special emphasis can be detected : פּוֹל הַלָּבָן white beans, Ma'a. iv. 6; חוֹמֶץ הָאֲדוֹמִי Idumean vinegar, Pes. iii. 1; מַיִם הָרָעִים evil waters, Ab. i. 11; נֶפֶשׁ הַיָּפָה a good appetite, Ḥul. iv. 7; גָּמָל הָרַכָּה a tender camel, ib. ix. 2, and many more, especially in later texts. Many of these are, indeed, due to the negligence of copyists, as shown by a comparison of different texts. Thus, for שִׁפְחָה הַמְשֻׁחְרֶרֶת a manumitted female slave, L has שִׁ׳ מְשׁוּ׳, 'Ed. v. 6. So K has נַעֲרָה מְאוֹרָסָה for המא נ׳ Ned. x. 1; שׁוֹר נִסְקָל for הנ׳ ש׳ San. i. 4, &c.[1] There still remain, however, a large number of genuine cases which exhibit a looseness in the observance of this rule. But this irregularity is also found in BH; cf. Ges.-K., § 126 w, x; Driver, *Tenses*, § 209. It was probably peculiar to popular speech even in the Biblical period.

377. (*b*) Conversely, cases are found where the substantive has the article, but not the attribute. In some of these cases the attribute has the force of a circumstantial clause : הַמַּאֲכִיל אֶת בָּנָיו קְטַנִּים וְאֶת עֲבָדָיו בֵּין גְּדוֹלִים וּבֵין קְטַנִּים one who gives to eat his sons when small, and his slaves whether grown up or small, Ter. vii. 3; הִכְנִיס רֹאשׁוֹ לַאֲוִיר הַתַּנּוּר טָהוֹר טִמְּאָהוּ if he caused his head to enter into an oven which is clean, he has defiled it; הִכְנִיס רֹאשׁוֹ לַאֲוִיר הַתַּנּוּר טָמֵא נִטְמָא . . . an oven which is unclean, he becomes unclean, Kel. viii. 10. So also : נֶאֱמָנִין עַל הַיֶּרֶק חַי וְאֵין נֶאֱמָנִין

[1] Cf. Krauss, *MGWJ.*, li, p. 452.

עַל הַמְּבוּשָׁל they are believed in the case of vegetables when raw, but they are not believed in the case of cooked (vegetables), Pea vii. 4.[1]

Other exx. do not allow of such an explanation, e. g. הַמַּעֲרָכָה גְדוֹלָה the great pile, Tam. ii. 4; but for הַמַּעֲרָכָה שְׁנִיָּה ib. 5, L has הם' השנ'. So other cases rest on a textual error: הֶחָבִית מְרוּתַּחַת the foaming jar, L has חב' מר', while M reads הח' המר' 'AZ iv. 10; הַמַּיִם שְׁאוּבִים drawn water, L שא' מים. N הם' הש' Tᵉm. i. 4; הַשֵּׂעָר צָהוֹב yellow hair, Nᵉg. x. 3, L; שער צהוב, and so elsewhere.

The article is sometimes omitted with a demonstrative attribute: הַכְּרִי זֶה this heap, Tᵉr. iii. 5; הַכִּיס זֶה this bag, Mᵉʿil. vi. 6.

For such irregularities in BH, cf. Ges.-K., § 126 y, and especially Koenig, *Syntax*, § 334 m, s.[2]

378. The article is always omitted with a number of common expressions, especially compounds, which are considered definite in themselves: תַּלְמוּד תּוֹרָה the study of the Torah, Pea i. 1; דֶּרֶךְ אֶרֶץ good manners, Ab. ii. 2; בַּעַל קְרִי one with an issue, Miq. iii. 4; בַּעַל מוּם one with a blemish, 'Ed. iv. 1; יוֹם טוֹב a festival, 'Er. vi. 6; כֹּהֵן גָּדוֹל High Priest, Yo. i. 1; יֵצֶר טוֹב the good inclination, Bᵉr. 5 a. Conversely, other nouns of the same character are only found with the article: בַּעַל הַבַּיִת the master of the house, Šab. i. 1; בֵּית הַמִּדְרָשׁ house of study, Šab. xvi. 1; בֵּית הַכְּנֶסֶת a synagogue, Mᵉg. iii. 1; but plur. is without the article: בַּעֲלֵי בָתִּים Kel. xvii. 1; בָּתֵּי כְנֵסִיּוֹת, בָּתֵּי מִדְרָשׁוֹת Tᵉr. xi. 10. Further, עַם הָאָרֶץ Dam. i. 3; plur. עַמֵּי הָאָרֶץ Ab. iii. 10

---

[1] L actually reads in the second clause עָלָיו מְבוּשָׁל, which shows that חַי is an accusative of state, like הַזֶּרַע בְּשֵׁלָה, Num. vi. 19; cf. G. B. Gray's note, *ad loc.* M., however, reads הַחַי.

[2] Cf. also in Moabite and Phoenician, G. A. Cooke, *NSI.*, p. 26; Schroeder, op. cit., §§ 43, 58, and 61. Note also in BH בֵּית חֹרֹן תַּחְתּוֹן 1 Kings ix. 17, contrasted with הַתַּחְתּוֹן ב/ ח' 2 Chron. viii. 5; also ירושלם קדשה on coins of Simon, beside the more usual הקדושה י', Madden, *Coins of the Jews*, p. 67 f. Cf. also Nöldeke, *Syr. Gr.*, §§ 202, B. Rem.; 203.

The article is always omitted with the genitive when introduced by שֶׁל, and preceded by an anticipatory suffix : יָדוֹ שֶׁל עָנִי the hand of the poor man, Šab. i. 1 ; cf. below, § 388.[1]

3. The Expression of the Genitive.

379. The genitive relationship between two nouns is expressed in MH, as in BH, by putting the first noun (*regens*) in the construct state, or by a circumlocution, in which the connexion between the two nouns is indicated by a special particle placed before the second noun (*rectum*). This latter method is much more frequent in MH than in BH. Nevertheless, the construct state still remains in MH the regular and prevailing method. Circumlocution is resorted to, at least in earlier MH, only when the grammatical form of the nouns, or the desire for lucidity makes the use of the construct impracticable. Thus, the use of the circumlocution in MH can be classified under certain logical and grammatical rules.

In Aram., on the other hand, the two constructions are used indiscriminately. Contrast Ezra v. 13 : מלכא די בבל, with vi. 14 : מלך פרס; v. 14 : מאניא די בית with vi. 5 : מאני בית; Dan. ii. 19 with iv. 2, 6 ; ii. 49 with iii. 12 ; iii. 1 with iii. 5, 7, &c. ; v. 5 with v. 24. This is especially the case in the *Targumim* ; cf. Winer, *op. cit.*, § 56. In the non-Jewish dialects of Aram. the construct state has been given up almost entirely, e. g. Syriac (Nöldeke, *Syr. Gr.*, § 205 B), Christian Palestinian Aram. (Nöldeke, *ZDMG.*, p. 507, § 36), and nearly so in Mandaic (Nöldeke, *Mand. Gr.*, § 221 f.).[2]

---

[1] Cf. further, *JQR.*, xx, pp. 653 ff. ; Barth, *Pronominalbildung*, p. 137.

[2] But in the old Aram. of the Zinjirli Inscriptions the constr. state alone is used ; cf. Cooke *NSI.*, Nos. 61-3. In the Aram. papyri of Assuan, however, the constr. is confined to 'the most common words where the relation is a close and natural one' (Cowley, *Introd.*, p. 19).

(1) *The Construct State.*

380. The construct state is especially common in the following cases :

(i) With *nomina actionis* as *regens* : מַגָּע טְרֵפָה touching of *ṭrepha*, Ḥul. iv. 4 ; מַתַּן סָבִיב sprinkling of the blood round about the altar, Zᵉb. xiv. 10 ; שְׁבִירַת הָעֶצֶם breaking the bone, Pᵉs. vii. 12 ; יְדִיעוֹת הַטּוּמְאָה cases of knowledge of uncleanness, Šᵉbu. i. 1 ; בִּיטּוּל בֵּית הַמִּדְרָשׁ the neglect of the house of study, Šab. xvi. 1 ; עֵרוּבֵי תְחוּמִין *'erubim* of limits, 'Er. vii. 11 ; קִלְקוּלֵי הַמַּיִם the damaged receptacles of water, MQ i. 3 ; צִחְצוּחַ חֲרָבוֹת the glistening of swords, So. viii. 1 ; סַכָּנַת נְפָשׁוֹת danger of life, Ḥul. iii. 5 ; הֶפְסֵד מִצְוָה the loss by a commandment, Ab. ii. 1 ; הַדְלָקַת הַגֵּר kindling of the lamp, Šab. ii. 6 ; הוֹרָיַת הַמַּעֲשֵׂר the confession over the tithe, MŠ v. 15.

(ii) With *nomina agentis* as *regens* : חוֹתְמֵי בְרָכוֹת those that close benedictions, Bᵉr. ix. 3 ; עוֹלֵי בָבֶל those that came up from Babylon, Šᵉbi. vi. 1 ; שְׁלוּחֵי מִצְוָה those sent to perform a divine commandment, Suk. ii. 4 ; אֲנוּסַת אָבִיו a woman outraged by her father, Yᵉb. xi. 1 ; חַזַּן הַכְּנֶסֶת beadle of the Synagogue, So. vii. 7 ; חַיָּיבֵי חַטָּאוֹת those bound to bring sin-offerings, Šab. xi. 6. Further, adjectives : נְקִיֵּי הַדַּעַת men pure of mind, Giṭ. ix. 8 ; שְׁחוֹרֵי הָרֹאשׁ black-headed, Nᵉd. iii. 8.

(iii) Nouns of a common type ; קֶשֶׁר מוּכְסִין a knot of tax-gatherers, Šab. viii. 2 ; צָרְכֵי הַמֵּת the requirements of the dead, ib. xxiii. 5 ; וְלַד שִׁפְחָה a child of a female slave, Qid. iii. 12 ; שִׁגְגַת הַמַּעֲשֶׂה error of action, Hor. ii. 3 ; סְעוּדַת אֵירוּסִין a meal of betrothal, Pᵉs. iii. 7 ; תַּנְחוּמֵי אֲבֵלִים consolations of mourners, Mᵉg. iv. 3 ; תַּכְשִׁיטֵי נָשִׁים ornaments of women, Pᵉs. iii. 1 ; רְשׁוּת הָרַבִּים a public place, BQ iii. 1, &c.

381. The formation of the plur. of construct combinations follows the example of BH (cf. Ges.-K., § 124 p-r).

(i) The usual method is to attach the plur. termination to the *regens*: חוּטֵי צֶמֶר woollen threads, Šab. vi. 5; צוֹרְפֵי זָהָב goldsmiths, ib. viii. 4; פְּקִיעֵי עָמִיר bundles of sheaves, ib. xxiv. 2, &c.

(ii) Sometimes both nouns receive the plur. terminations. Thus with בַּיִת: בָּתֵּי כְנֵסִיּוֹת וּבָתֵּי מִדְרָשׁוֹת synagogues and houses of study, Pes. iv. 4; בָּתֵּי הַבַּדִּים wine-presses, MS iii. 7; בָּתֵּי דִינִין courts of law, San. xi. 2; בָּתֵּי נִירִין meshes, Šab. vii. 2; בָּתֵּי דְשָׁנִין receptacles for ashes, Zeb. 104 b. With בַּעַל: בַּעֲלֵי אוּמָּנִיּוֹת artisans, Bik. iii. 3; בַּעֲלֵי דִינִים litigants, Ab. vii. 6; בַּעֲלֵי בָתִּים house-holders, Kel. xvii. 1, בַּעֲלֵי מוּמִים those with a blemish, Bek. vii. 6; בַּעֲלוֹת מוּמִים Tem. iv. 6 (L); בַּעֲלֵי קְרָיִין men with an issue, Miq. viii. 1; בַּעֲלֵי שֵׂיבוֹת greyheads, Ned. iii. 8. With רֹאשׁ: רָאשֵׁי חֳדָשִׁים New Moons, Pes. vii. 4; רָאשֵׁי שָׁנִים New Years, RH i. 1; רָאשֵׁי דְבָרִים chief points, ib. ii. 6. Further, עַרְבֵי פְּסָחִים eves of the Passover, Pes. iv. 1; עַרְבֵי שַׁבָּתוֹת eves of the Sabbath, BM iv. 6; דִּינֵי מָמוֹנוֹת; דִּינֵי נְפָשׁוֹת civil, capital cases, San. iv. 1; עֵדֵי נְפָשׁוֹת witnesses in capital cases, ib. 5; חַיָּיבֵי אֲשָׁמוֹת; חַיָּיבֵי חַטָּאוֹת those bound to bring a sin-offering, a guilt-offering, Ker. vi. 4; חַיָּיבֵי מִיתוֹת men guilty of death, San. vii. 10, but חַיָּיבֵי עוֹלָה Tem. v. 1; גִּטֵּי נָשִׁים bills of divorce; שִׁחֲרוּרֵי עֲבָדִים bills of manumission, Git. i. 4.

(iii) The plur. termination is attached to the *rectum* alone, only with בַּיִת as *regens*: בֵּית הָאֶצְבָּעוֹת (מְהוֹרוֹת) gloves, Kel. xxvi. 3; בֵּית הַבַּדִּין wine-presses, BB iii. 1; בֵּית הַגִּיתּוֹת olive presses, t. Ter. iii. 1; בֵּית הַמִּשְׁתָּאוֹת banqueting houses, So. ix. 11; בֵּית הַטּוּמְאוֹת (מְטַמְּאִין) houses for menstruous women, Nid. vii. 4; בֵּית הַסְּתָרִים וּבֵית הַקְּמָטִים (אֵינָן) folds and hidden parts (of the body), Miq. viii. 5; בֵּית פְּרָסוֹת fields rendered unclean by dead bones from a ploughed grave, Oh. xviii. 2; בֵּית הַשְּׁוָוקִים market places, Makš. vi. 2.

382. A *nomen rectum* can itself become a *regens* to another *rectum*, but it can take only one *regens*. When one *rectum* has more than one *regens*, the second *regens* follows the *rectum*, and takes the appropriate possessive suffix, as in BH (Ges.-K., § 128 a): וְלַד תּוֹדָה וּתְמוּרָתָהּ the child and the exchange of a thank-offering, Men. vii. 4 ; זוֹמְמֵי בַת כֹּהֵן וּבוֹעֲלָהּ the false witnesses against, and the paramour of, the daughter of a priest, San. xi. 1 ; מִבְּלָאֵי מִכְנְסֵי כֹּהֲנִים וּמֵהֶמְיָנֵיהֶן from the worn-out breeches and girdles of the priests, Suk. v. 3.

383. The construct is not found in MH before a relative clause, except in stereotyped conjunctional expressions like כְּדֵי שֶׁ־, מִפְּנֵי שֶׁ־, כִּלְפֵי שֶׁ־, &c. (§ 303). Also with חֲזָקָה state, assumption, which is very common in the constr. state before nouns (e.g. Ket. i. 6, 7 ; Naz. ix. 2 ; BB iii. 1 &c.): בְּחֶזְקַת שֶׁהוּא קַיָּים on the assumption that he is alive, Git. iii. 3, 7, 8 (cf. 4); בְּחֶזְקַת שֶׁלֹּא נָתַן, בְּחֶזְקַת שֶׁנָּתַן, on the assumption that he has given . . . that he has not given, BB i. 4 ; בְּחֶזְקַת שֶׁנִּפְדָּה in the state of having been redeemed, Bek. viii. 6.

(2) Simple Circumlocution of the Genitive.

384. In addition to the constr. state, BH also indicates the genitival connexion between two nouns by the preposition לְ, prefixed to the *rectum* in apposition to the *regens* which remains in the absolute state (e.g. בֵּן לְיִשַׁי); or, further, by placing the *rectum* with this לְ in a relative clause אֲשֶׁר לְ־, so as to specify more clearly the subordinate relation of the *rectum* to the *regens* (e.g. הַצֹּאן אֲשֶׁר לְאָבִיהָ Ges.-K., § 129 a f.). This אֲשֶׁר לְ־ would become in colloquial speech שֶׁלְּ־, cf. § 77 f.

In MH circumlocution of the genitive by means of לְ alone is extremely rare, and generally only when the לְ may also be construed as a לְ of the dative or of reference.[1] Exx. : הֲלָכָה לְמֹשֶׁה מִסִּינַי a law of Moses from Sinai (sc. שֶׁנִּיתְּנָה, Pea ii. 6) ; אוּר לי"ד the eve of the fourteenth, Pes. i. 1 ; so אוּר לפ"א Ker. i. 6, but

---

[1] So in Ethiopic; cf. Dillmann, *Aethiop. Gr.*, § 145, 6.

אוּר עִבּוּרוֹ the eve of its intercalation (the 30th day of the month), RH 22 b; רֹאשׁ הַשָּׁנָה לִמְלָכִים the New Year of Kings, RH. i. 1; וְנָב לָאֲרָיוֹת a tail of lions, Ab. iv. 15; אַלְפָּא לְסֹלֶת ἄλφα (the first, best) of fine flour, Mᵉn. viii. 1 ; and a few more.[1]

385. Much more common is the use of the relative clause in its colloquial form שֶׁל־. This particle is merely a prefix of the *rectum*, as in BH (Cant. iii. 7) and in older texts of MH. But it was gradually detached from its noun and given the appearance of an independent particle.

It follows from what has been said that the use of שֶׁל in MH is a genuine Hebraic construction derived from the BH use of אֲשֶׁר לְ. שֶׁל is not an adaptation of the Aram. דִּי, ־דְּ which is merely equivalent to אֲשֶׁר, שֶׁ־ alone. On the contrary, the frequent use of דְּל־, דִּיל־ in Jewish Aram., instead of the more regular דִּי, or דִּיד (דְּיָד), must be ascribed to MH influence.[2]

386. The use of של for the genitive may be classified as follows.

(i) To express the material.[3]

סָדִין שֶׁל בּוּץ a sheet of fine linen, Yo. iii. 4 ; חָבִית שֶׁל זָהָב a jar of gold, Suk. iv. 10 ; also to express a quality : יָרָק שֶׁל תְּרוּמָה vegetables of *tᵉruma*, 'Ed. ii. 2 and often. But the constr. is also common : בֶּן הַזָּהָב base of gold, Yo. v. 2 ; Pᵉs. v. 5 ; Tam. i. 4.

(ii) When more than one *regens* govern one *rectum* : תְּאֵנִים

---

[1] Cf further, *JQR.*, xx, pp. 725–6.

[2] In Phoenician the genitive is expressed by prefixing to the *rectum* לְ, then by אשל, and finally by של. In late Phoenician, however, שׁ takes the place of של, evidently under Aram. influence. In MH we never find the use of שֶׁ־ for שֶׁל־. For possible cases in BH of אֲשֶׁר expressing the genitive, cf. *BDB.*, p. 83, and Koenig, *Syntax*, § 283.

[3] This construction is not found in BH, except, perhaps, Lev. xiii. 48 ; Ezra i. 11. It is regular in the Targum; cf. Gen. xxiv. 21, 53 ; Exod. ii. 2, 4 (but contrast vers. 21, 22, &c.), also Dan. v. 7 ; cf. Kautzsch, *Gr. d. Bib. Aram.*, § 81 c.

וַעֲנָבִים שֶׁל טֶבֶל figs and grapes of untithed produce, Maʻa. i. 7;
זִכְרוֹן מַלְכוּת וְשׁוֹפָר שֶׁל פֻּרְעָנוּת verses of retribution containing the
words 'remembering', 'king', and 'shofar', RH iv. 6; Tᵉr. xi. 4;
BM x. 1, &c. So in BH: Gen. xl. 5; Exod. xiv. 28; 2 Kings
xi. 10; cf. Ges.-K., § 129 h.

(iii) When the *regens* consists of a construct combination : תְּרוּמַת
פַּר עֲבוֹדַת Dam. iv. 1; מַעֲשֵׂר עָנִי שֶׁל דְּמַאי ib. 3, 4; מַעֲשֵׂר שֶׁל דְּמַאי
הָעוֹלָם דָּבָר שֶׁל מָשִׁיחַ Sifre Num. viii. 3.

When the *rectum* is made up of such a compound expression :
נְכָסִים שֶׁל מַכְבֵּשׁ שֶׁל בַּעֲלֵי בָתִּים a press of householders, Šab. xx. 5;
בְּנֵי בְרִית property of sons of the Covenant, BQ i. 2; or both *regens*
and *rectum* consist of compound expressions ; תְּפִיסַת יָד שֶׁל בַּעַל הַבַּיִת
holding of hand (right of access) by the householder, ʻEr. viii. 4;
כָּל יְדוֹת הַכֵּלִים שֶׁל יוֹם הַכִּפּוּרִים all the handles of the vessels of the
Day of Atonement, Yo. iii. 10.

The constr. is also found in such cases, e. g. שִׂמְחַת בֵּית הַשּׁוֹאֵבָה
the joy of the (celebration of) drawing of water, beside הֶחָלִיל שֶׁל
בֵּית הַשּׁוֹאֵבָה the flute of . . . , Suk. v. 1. So in BH: Gen. xxv. 6;
Num. xvi. 22; xxxi. 48, &c; Ges.-K., § 129 d, 2; cf. also Koenig,
Syntax, § 281 l–m; § 282 e, f.

(iv) When an adjective intervenes between the *regens* and the
rectum : יְסוֹד מַעֲרָבִי שֶׁל מִזְבֵּחַ the western base of the altar, Yo.
v. 6; כּוֹר אֶחָד שֶׁל חִטִּים one *cor* of wheat, Nᵉd. viii. 7; שׁוּרָה שֶׁל
עֶבֶד שֶׁל שְׁנֵי שׁוּתָּפִים חֲמִשָּׁה גְּפָנִים a row of five vines, Kil. iv. 5;
a slave of two partners, Pᵉs. viii. 1. So in BH: 1 Sam. xxii. 20;
Ezek. xl. 40 b.

(v) Circumlocution is generally used with nouns borrowed from
other languages, including Aram., which the language could not
assimilate so thoroughly as to inflect them like native words:
פּוּנְדְּקָאוֹת שֶׁל עכו״ם אִיסְטְרַטְיָא שֶׁל מֶלֶךְ the King's στρατιά, Qid. iv. 5;
the πανδοκεῖα of the heathen, ʻAZ ii. 1.

(vi) Generally when for one reason or another the *regens* or the *rectum* is to be emphasized, as when a noun is used in a secondary or derived sense : זוּג שֶׁל סַפָּרִים shears of barbers, Kel. xiii. 1 (זוּג סַפָּרִים may mean a pair of barbers); הַשֵּׁן שֶׁל מַעְדֵּר the tooth of a mattock, ib. 2 ; or in enumerating different cases which either agree with or differ from one another ; טַבַּעַת שֶׁל מַתֶּכֶת טַבַּעַת שֶׁל אַלְמוּג ..., a ring of metal ... a ring of sandal wood, ib. 6 ; מַסְרֵק שֶׁל פִּשְׁתָּן וְשֶׁל צֶמֶר ..., a comb for flax ... and for wool, 8 ; xiv. 8 ; xv. 2, &c. Cf. in BH 2 Sam. iii. 2, 3.

Circumlocution is found also in many other cases which cannot be well brought under the above rules, especially in later MH under Aram. influence.

(3) *Circumlocution of the Genitive with Anticipation.*

387. The circumlocutory genitive is often anticipated in MH by a possessive suffix attached to the *regens*, e. g. יָדוֹ שֶׁל עָנִי the hand of the poor man, Šab. i. 1. The construction is only employed when the *regens* is a flexible noun, which is elsewhere found in the constr. state, as otherwise it could not take the suffix.

388. The *rectum* is almost always determinate, either by a suffix (תְּבוּאָתוֹ שֶׁל חֲבֵרוֹ his neighbour's produce, Kil. vii. 4) or by being a proper noun (תַּלְמִידָיו שֶׁל אַהֲרֹן Aaron's disciples, Ab. i. 12): a demonstrative pronoun (הֶפְשֵׁיטָן וְנִתּוּחָן שֶׁל אֵלּוּ the flaying and cutting up of these, Yo. vii. 2) ; by having been mentioned before ; or, finally, by being well known generally, or only in connexion with the subject treated in the context. Nevertheless, this determinate *rectum* never takes the article, except in such stereotyped expressions as הַקָּדוֹשׁ בָּרוּךְ הוּא, בַּעַל הַבַּיִת, and עַם הָאָרֶץ, which are never found without the article (cf. § 378). Cf. the following passages in which the *rectum* is mentioned previously with the article, but the article is dropped when the *rectum* stands in our construction : הֶעָנִי, but יָדוֹ שֶׁל עָנִי Šab. i. 1 ; הָעוּבָּר the embryo, but חֶלְקוֹ שֶׁל עוּבָּר the share of the embryo, Yᵉb. vii. 3 ;

הָעִיר but תְּחוּמָהּ שֶׁל עִיר the boundary of the city, Nᵉd. vii. 5; הֶחָצֵר
but אַוֵּירָהּ שֶׁל חָצֵר the air of the courtyard, BB iv. 3; So. viii. 8
(עָם); Šebu. i. 7 (פָּר); Mᵉn. xi. 5 (שֻׁלְחָן); Oh. ii. 1 (מֵת); Nᵉg.
xiv. 1 (מְצוֹרָע).

Evidently, the *rectum* is regarded as having been determinated
by the suffix of the *regens*, and, therefore, can as little take the
article, as if the suffix had been attached to itself. Hence in
Ethiopic, which has no article, this construction is regularly used
for rendering a noun definite.[1]

In Aram., however, the *rectum* when standing in this construction is always in the emphatic state; cf. Dan. ii. 20, 44;
iii. 26, and so in the *Targumim*.

389. This construction of anticipating the noun by a preceding
pronominal suffix is widely used in MH to express the genitive.
But it occurs also in other cases when the noun is introduced by
a preposition.

With בְּ, only in the phrase בּוֹ בְיוֹם Ya. iv. 1, &c. Cf. in Aram.:
Dan. iii. 6–8, 15; v. 11; Ezra v. 3.

With לְ: אָמְרוּ לוֹ לְרֹ"ג 'Er. iv. 2; הָיוּ לוֹ לְשַׁעַר Mid. iv. 2; so
usually with דִּי: דַּיּוֹ לְיָחִיד sufficient for the private person, Mᵉn.
xii. 4; דַּיָּהּ לְקוֹרָה sufficient for the beam, 'Er. i. 3; so also to
express an object: אֵין מְקָרְבִין לוֹ לְאָדָם they do not draw a man
near, Ab. ii. 3

With מִן (הֵימֶ", cf. § 301), only in the expression: לֹא כָל הֵימֶנּוּ מִן
הָרִאשׁוֹן everything does not depend on him, even on the first,
Giṭ. viii. 8; cf. BQ x. 3.

With עַל: אָמְרוּ עָלָיו עַל רחב"ד they said of him, of R. Ḥanina . . .;
Bᵉr. v. 5; מָה עָלָיו עַל אָדָם what is there on a man, t. Ḥag. ii. 6.

390. This construction is, of course, very common in Aram.,
but it is also extensively used in Assyrian (Delitzsch, *Assyr. Gr.*,
§ 166), and in Ethiopic (Dillmann, *Aeth. Gr.*, § 172). It is also

---

[1] Cf. Dillmann, *Aeth. Gr.*, § 172 c.

found in BH. Thus, before the construct state : Jer. lii. 20 (בְּבֹאָם הַכֹּהֲנִים) ; Ezek. x. 3 (בְּבֹאוֹ הָאִישׁ) ; xlii. 14 (לְנֶחְשְׁתָּם כָּל הַכֵּלִים); xlvi. 22 ; Prov. xiii. 4 (נַפְשׁוֹ עָצֵל) ; Job xxix. 3 (בְּהִלּוֹ נֵרוֹ) ; Ezra ii. 62 (כְּתָבָם הַמִּתְיַחֲשִׂים) ; iii. 12 (בְּיָסְדוֹ זֶה הַבַּיִת). With circum-locution, Cant. iii. 7 (מִטָּתוֹ שֶׁלִּשְׁלֹמֹה). With לְ alone : Num. i. 21–43 (פְּקֻדֵיהֶם לְמַטֵּה) ; Ezra ix. 1 (כְּתוֹעֲבוֹתֵיהֶם לַכְּנַעֲנִי), &c. With the object : Exod. ii. 6 (וַתִּרְאֵהוּ אֶת) ; Deut. iii. 14 (וַיִּקְרָא וַיְעִירֵהוּ . . . אֹתָם) ; 1 Kings xix. 21 (בִּשָּׁלֵם הַבָּשָׂר) ; xxi. 13 (. . . אֶת) ; 2 Kings xvi. 15 (אֶת . . . וַיְצַוֵּהוּ Kᵉthib) ; 1 Sam. xxi. 14 (וַיִּשַׁנּוֹ אֶת) ; Jer. ix. 14 (מַאֲכִילָם אֶת) ; Ps. lxxxiii. 12 ; Num. xxxii. 33 (וָאֹמְרָה אֲלֵיהֶם לָרֹעִים) ; Ezek. xxxiv. 2 (וַיִּתֵּן לָהֶם . . . לִבְנֵי) ; 1 Chron. v. 26 ; xxiii. 6 ; 2 Chron. xxv. 5, 10. Cf. further, Driver, *Tenses*, § 201 ; also Ges.-K., § 131 m, n.

It is, therefore, clear that the construction in MH is of native origin, but its somewhat extensive use, especially in late MH, may be due to Aram. influence.

4. Comparison of Adjectives.

391. The Comparative degree is expressed, as in BH, by מִן or ־מִ, following the adject. : עָמֹק מִזֶּה deeper than this, Nid. ii. 7 ; חַמָּתָהּ מְרוּבָּה מִצִּילָתָהּ its sun is greater than its shade, Suk. i. 1 ; יְתֵרָה מְבַעֲרָשָׂהּ מְשׁוּנָּה מֵחַבְרוֹתֶיהָ different from its fellows, Šᵉq. vi. 2 ; more than the measure of a lentil, Nᵉg. vi. 4.

Very often יָתֵר is followed by עַל : יָתֵר עַל נ' סֶלַע more than 50 *selaʿ*, ʿAr. ii. 1 ; יְתֵרוֹת עַל הַבִּנְיָן exceeding the building, ʿEr. i. 8, 9 ; יְתֵרוֹת עַל בְּנוֹת ג' . . . more than 3 years old, Kᵉt. i. 4. Cf. in BH הָעוֹדְפִים עַל . . . Num. iii. 46 ; also Gen. xlviii. 22. See further above, § 363 (iii).

יוֹתֵר more, and פָּחוּת less, are often used adverbially to emphasize the comparison : עָנִי יוֹתֵר מֵהִלֵּל poorer than Hillel ; עָשִׁיר יוֹתֵר מֵר״א richer than R. Elʿazer, Yo. 35 b ; פָּחוּת מִבַּגְּרוֹגֶרֶת less than a dried fig, Šab. ix. 7. So after a verb יוֹתֵר is sometimes omitted :

O

יִתְמַעֵט פָּחוּת מִשָּׁוֶוה פְּרוּטָה it will become less than the value of a *pᵉruṭa*, BQ ix. 7 ; רוֹאֶה אֲנִי אֶת דִּבְרֵי רַאב"ע מִדִּבְרֵיכֶם I approve the words of . . . more than your words, Ab. ii. 13, 14.

392. The Superlative degree is expressed when the adjective is followed by a determinate noun, or by a pronoun, with the partitive בּ prefixed, and introduced by the relative שֶׁ. The adjective may take the article or not : הַיָּפָה שֶׁבָּהֶן the fairest (best) of them, Pᵉs. ix. 8 ; הַגָּדוֹל שֶׁבַּדַּיָּנִין the greatest of the judges, San. iii. 7 ; קְטַנָּה שֶׁבַּבָּנוֹת the smallest of girls, Šab. viii. 4 ; גְּדוֹלָה שֶׁבַּגְּדוֹלוֹת the lightest of eggs, ib. 5 ; בֵּיצָה קַלָּה שֶׁבַּבֵּיצִים the oldest of the big ones; קְטַנָּה שֶׁבַּקְּטַנּוֹת the youngest of the little ones, Qid. iii. 8 ; טוֹב שֶׁבָּרוֹפְאִים the best of physicians ; הַכָּשֵׁר שֶׁבַּטַּבָּחִים the worthiest of butchers, ib. iv. 14. Cf. in BH הַיָּפָה בַּנָּשִׁים Cant. vi. 1 ; Ges.-K., § 133 g.

393. The superlative idea is also expressed by the repetition of the adjective or the noun in the construct state, or, rarely, in the comparative : דַּקָּה מִן הַדַּקָּה thinnest, Yo. iv. 4 ; חַמֵּי חַמִּין exceedingly hot, Bᵉr. 16 a ; דַּלֵּי דַלּוּת the greatest poverty, Kᵉr. 10 b ; so חַדְרֵי חֲדָרִים the innermost chamber, Šab. 64 b (cf. 1 Kings xx. 30 ; xxii. 25 : חֶדֶר בְּחָדֶר) ; עֲדִי עֲדָיִים greatest ornament, 'AZ 24 b (cf. Ezek. xvi. 7); further, לִפְנִים וְלִפְנַי וְלִפְנִים within and right within, BM 16 a ; Zᵉb. 52 a ; 57 a (cf. 1 Kings vi. 17, 29). So also in BH ; cf. קֹדֶשׁ הַקֳּדָשִׁים Exod. xxvi. 33 ; Ges.-K., § 133 i.

5. Numerals.

(1) CARDINALS.

394. אַחַת, אֶחָד, follow the noun : פֵּאָה אַחַת ; מִין אֶחָד Pea ii. 5 ; sometimes, with אַחַת יָד, precedes the noun : מֵאַחַת יָד from one place, Pea iii. 3 ; בְּאַחַת יָד Šᵉbi. iii. 9 ; Pa. vii. 2, 3 (cf. Neh. iv. 11 ; Dan. viii. 13). All the other numerals when used as cardinals always precede the noun. שְׁתַּיִם, שְׁנַיִם are always in the construct state to the noun. The other numerals are usually in the absolute state, and in apposition to the noun. Sometimes, however, they are in the constr. state, thus: אַרְבַּעַת BB ii. 5; vi. 7; חֲמֵשֶׁת Ned. vii. 2; שִׁבְעַת Bik. i. 3; Yo. i. 1; עֲשֶׂרֶת San. **x**. 3, but the texts differ. The constr. is especially common in L: שְׁלֹשֶׁת, תִּשְׁעַת BM iii. 7; שְׁמוֹנַת iv. 3, &c.

Some of the units take the pronominal suffixes. In addition to the BH שְׁנֵיהֶם שְׁתֵּיהֶם שְׁלָשְׁתָּם, and אַרְבַּעְתָּם, we also find חֲמִשְׁתָּן Men. xiii. 2; שִׁשְׁתָּן Mak. ii. 4; שִׁבְעָתָן Nid. ix. 8 (L, and so in citations, San. 49 b; Zeb. 95 b).

The number 2 is often expressed by the dual: קַבַּיִם two *qabs*, 'Ed. i. 2 (cf. § 293), but the dual is also found with the number, no doubt for the sake of emphasis שְׁתֵּי כִירַיִם Toh. v. 6; שְׁנֵי כְבָרִים Kel. vi. 3.

395. With the numerals 2–10, the object numbered takes the plur. In שְׁמוֹנָה כֶסֶף, אַרְבָּעָה כֶסֶף, שְׁתֵּי כֶסֶף BM iv. 3, 7, the name of a coin in the plur. (מָעוֹת) must be understood. So שְׁתֵּי הַלֶּחֶם, *sc.* חַלּוֹת Men. v. 1; xi. 1.

396. The numerals 11–19 also take the object numbered in the plur.: י״ב שְׁבָטִים, י״ב פָּרִים Hor. i. 5; י״ד כְּבָשִׂים Suk. v. 6; י״ד סְעוּדוֹת ib. ii. 6; ט״ו מַעֲלוֹת v. 4, &c. Certain nouns, however, that are in frequent use, remain in the sing.: י״ב מָנֶה BM v. **2**, י״ב זָהָב ib. viii. 8; י״ב חֹדֶשׁ Git vii. 8; י״ד חֹדֶשׁ BB iii. 1; י״ד שָׁנָה Naz. iii. 6; ט״ו מָנֶה Ket. vi. 3; ט״ז אַמָּה Kil. iv. 1; י״ח חֹדֶשׁ Git. vii. 6.

397. Tens (20–90) and hundreds take the noun in the sing.: עֶשְׂרִים עִשָּׂרוֹן Men. vii. 1; ל׳ קַב ib. vii. 1; מ׳ זוּג RH i. 6; נ׳ זוּז BQ iv. 1 (but also נ׳ דִּיּוּרִים 50 dwellings, 'Er. v. 6); ס׳ לֹג Men. ix. 3; ע׳ לָשׁוֹן Šeq. v. 1; פ׳ מַעֲשֵׂר Dam. vii. 7; צ׳ רִים Yo. vi. 4; ק׳ סְאָה Ter. iv. 11. (In מֵאָה חוּלִּין Dam. vii. 7, the noun has no sing. in that special technical sense), ק׳ שִׁפְחָה Ket. v. 5 (L; edd. שְׁפָחוֹת); but ק׳ עוֹפוֹת; ק׳ חַיָּיה (L חַיָּיוֹת) Hul. vi. 4; ק״ב לֹג Suk. v. 2;

300 times ג׳ מֵאוֹת שִׁיפָה BQ viii. 6; ד׳ מֵאוֹת זוּ Ket. iv. 7; מָאתַיִם זוּ rubbing; 500 times kicking (with the fist), ה׳ מֵאוֹת בְּעִיטָה Men. vi. 5; ז׳ מֵאוֹת זוּ BM ix. 10; but ג׳ מֵאוֹת כֹּהֲנִים Šeq. viii. 5; אַרְבַּעַת אֲלָפִים אַמָּה 'Er. iv. 3; אַלְפַּיִם אַמָּה Ket. vi. 3; אֶלֶף דִּינָר ib. iv. 7.

But when units are added, the plur. is used: עֶשְׂרִים וְאַרְבָּעָה כ״ד חוּטִין Men. vi. 6; עֶשְׂרוֹנִים מכ״ד סְאִין Kil. iv. 1; כ״ד אַמּוֹת Šeq. viii. 5; כ״ח קָנִים Ket. xii. 4; כ״ז אֲבָנִים Šebi. iii. 5; כ״ה שָׁנִים Men. xi. 6; מ״ה גְּפָנִים Kil. v. 5; ע״ב נִימִין 72 cords, Šeq. viii. 5 [1]: מֵאָה וּשְׁנֵי חֲצָאִים 102 halves, Ter. iv. 13.

(2) ORDINALS.

398. רִאשׁוֹן Yo. ii. 2; רִאשׁוֹנָה ib. i. 8; שֵׁנִי ii. 3; שְׁנִיָּה iv. 2 (with פַּעַם understood), Pea viii. 1; שְׁנַיִם Hag. ii. 2; שְׁנִיּוֹת Ta'a. ii. 9; שְׁלִישִׁי Yo. ii. 4; שְׁלִישִׁית Kil. viii. 3; רְבִיעִי Yo. ii. 4; רְבִיעִית Ber. v. 2. Also with secondary forms: שְׁלִישִׁית רְבָעִי Pa. i. 1; חֲמִישִׁי Suk. v. 6; חֲמִישִׁית Meg. iii. 4, &c., as in BH.

399. Ordinals above ten are expressed by the corresponding cardinals, but with a noun always before the numeral, to distinguish them from the cardinals: לְיוֹם שְׁלֹשִׁים on the 30th day, Naz. iii. 1; יוֹם שְׁלֹשִׁים וְאֶחָד the 31st day, ib.; יוֹם שִׁשִּׁים the 60th; יוֹם שִׁשִּׁים וְאֶחָד the 61st; יוֹם שִׁשִּׁים חָסֵר אֶחָד the 60th less one—the 59th, ib. 2; יוֹם מֵאָה the 100th; יוֹם מֵאָה וְאֶחָד the 101st, ib. 4. Contrast this with the position of nouns with cardinals and ordinals in BH, Ges.-K., § 134 c, o, in which the difference between the two is not clear.

400. In counting the days of the month יוֹם is omitted: בְּעֶשְׂרִים וַחֲמִשָּׁה, בט״ו בּוֹ, בְּאֶחָד בַּאֲדָר the 1st, 15th, 25th of Adar,

---

[1] In שִׁבְעִים וּשְׁנַיִם זָקֵן Zeb. i. 3, the sing. is explained as indicating the complete unanimity of the assembled elders; cf. Zeb. 12 b with Rashi, *ad loc.* Some texts have also here the plur. זְקֵנִים.

Šeq. i. 1, 2 ; בִּשְׁנַיִם בַּחֹדֶשׁ the 2nd of the month, San. v. 3 ;
בי"ז בְּתַמּוּז the 17th of Tammuz ; בַּחֲמִשָּׁה עָשָׂר בְּאָב ,בט׳ בְּאָב 9th,
15th of Ab, Ta'a. iv. 6, 8 ; Šeq. iii. 1, &c. In giving the time of
the day שָׁעוֹת may be expressed or omitted : בִּשְׁתֵּי שָׁעוֹת,
בְּחָמֵשׁ ,בְּשָׁלֹשׁ שָׁעוֹת at 2, 3, 5 o'clock, San. v. 3 ; Pes. i. 4.

(3) Distributives.

401. The distributive is expressed by the repetition of the
number without the copula :[1] אַחַת אַחַת, אֶחָד אֶחָד one by one, one
at a time, Ma'a. iii. 2, 3 ; שְׁתֵּי חֲצֵרוֹת שֶׁל שְׁנֵי שְׁנֵי בָתִּים two courts
with two houses each, 'Ar. ix. 7 ; שְׁנַיִם שְׁנַיִם Yo. ii. 6 ; שְׁלֹשָׁה שְׁלֹשָׁה
ib. 7 ; שָׁלֹשׁ שָׁלֹשׁ Šebi. iii. 3 ; Kil. v. 5 ; עֶשֶׂר עָשֶׂר שֶׁל שׁוּרוֹת עֶשֶׂר
שֵׁשׁ עֶשָׂרָה ; Dam. vii. 8 ; כַּדֵּי יַיִן ten rows of ten jars of wine each
שֵׁשׁ עֶשְׂרֵה אַפֶּה Kil. iv. 9.

(4) Fractions.

402. מֶחֱצָה half, Pea v. 5 ; חֲצִי קַב half a *qab* ; קַב וָחֵצִי a *qab*
and a half, ib. viii. 5 ; שְׁנֵי חֲצָאֵי זֵיתִים Oh. iii. 1 ; שְׁלִישׁ a third,
Pea v. 5 ; שְׁנֵי שְׁלִישִׁים 'Er. 10 b ; רָבִיעַ a quarter, Pea ib. ; רְבִיעִית
ib. viii. 5 ; רוֹבַע a quarter, Kil. ii. 1 ; רְבָעַתַיִם two quarters,
Ker. i. 7 ; חֲמִשָּׁה רְבִיעִים קֶמַח Ḥal. ii. 6 ; חוֹמֶשׁ a fifth, Pea vii. 6 ;
חֲמִשִׁיּוֹת fifths, BQ 65 b ; שְׁתוּת[2] a sixth, Ter. iv. 7 ; שְׁמִין 1/8 of
a *ma'ah*, j. Qid. i. 1 ; שְׁמִינִין Qid. 12ᵃ ; שְׁמִינִית an eighth, Pea viii. 5 ;
תִּישׁוּעַ a ninth, j. Dam. vii, and עִישׂוּר a tenth, MŠ v. 9 ; אֶחָד מכ"ד
1/24, Kil. ii. 2 ; אֶחָד מִשְּׁלֹשִׁים וְשָׁלֹשׁ וְשָׁלִישׁ 1/33-1/3, Dam. v. 2 ;
אֶחָד ממ"ח 1/48, Ḥal. ii. 7 ; אֶחָד מִמֵּאָה 1/100 Dam. v. 2 ; אֶחָד
מֵרִבּוֹא 1/10,000, Pea iii. 8.

---

[1] But with כָּל, the copula is used : כָּל אֶחָד וְאֶחָד, כָּל אַחַת וְאַחַת,
Pea iii. 1, 2.

[2] ת receives *dagesh* after שׁ to prevent the concurrence of two similar sounds ;
so in BH שְׁתַּיִם.

Sometimes אֶחָד is omitted : אֵין פּוֹחֲתִין . . . מִשִּׁשִּׁים one must not give less than 1/60, Pea i. 2 ; בְּמָאתַיִם by 1/200 Kil. v. 6.

403. (5) The following numerals are found in verbal forms : שְׁלֹשָׁה : שָׁנוּ Pes. v. 2 ; שׁוֹנִין Suk. v. 4 ; נִשְׁנֵית San. 59 a ; לְהִשְׁתַּלֵּשׁ Pes. ib. ; יְשַׁלֵּשׁוּ : מְשׁוּלָּשִׁים BB x. 7 ; הִשְׁלִישׁ ib. 5 ; Mak. iii. 11 ; לְרַבְּעָה : אַרְבָּעָה t. ʿEr. ii. 1 ; vi. 10 ; מְרַבֵּעַ ʿEr. 56 b ; מְתַעֲשֵּׂר Oh. xii. 8 ; מְרוּבַּעַת, מְרוּבָּע : חֲמִשָּׁה : מְחוּמָּשׁוֹת BB 150 a ; תִּשְׁעָה : j. Šebi. 33 b ; עֲשָׂרָה : יַעֲשֵׂר ; מְעַשֵּׂר Dam. iii. 1, 2 ; מְתַעַשְּׂעִים Maʿa. iv. 3.

III. THE PRONOUN

1. The Personal Pronoun.

404. The personal pronoun is expressed with a finite verb, whenever it is desired to emphasize the subject : נָגַח הוּא if he gored, BQ v. 3 ; אֲבָל הוּא לֹא יִקְרָא but he himself must not read, Šab. i. 3 ; הֵם אָמְרוּ they said, Ab. i. 2 ; קְרָא אַתָּה read thou, Yo. i. 3 ; לְכִי אַתְּ go thou, Bʿr. 18 b ; אֲנִי הָיִיתִי בָא I was coming, Bʿr. i. 6 ; אִלּוּ אֲנִי פָסַקְתִּי לְעַצְמִי if I had assigned by myself, Ket. xiii. 5. The emphasis is often strengthened by the addition of the particle אַף : אַף הוּא הֵעִיד he also testified, ʿEd. ii. 3 ; אַף הִיא עָשְׂתָה ; אַף הוּא עָשָׂה he, she also made, Yo. iii. 10 ; אַף הֵם אָמְרוּ they said, Suk. ii. 7 ; אַף אֲנִי לֹא אָמַרְתִּי Taʿa. i. 1 ; הָבֵא לְךָ אַף אַתָּה bring for thyself, Pes. iv. 2 ; אַף אַתָּה אַל תִּתְמַהּ neither shouldst thou be surprised, ib. vi. 2.

On the whole, MH uses the pronoun more sparingly than BH. It is omitted even with participles when the subject is understood : רוֹצָה הִיא . . . וּבוֹשָׁה מֵחֲתָנָהּ she desires . . . and is ashamed of her son-in-law, Dam. iii. 6.

405. The pronoun of the third person is regularly employed in noun clauses as the copula between subject and predicate : אַתָּה הוּא הִלֵּל art thou Hillel ? Šab. 31 a ; לֹא שָׂרָה הִיא זוֹ is not this

a field ? 'Er. 53 a; אֵלּוּ הֵן הַמְמֻנִּים these are the overseers, Šᵉq. v. 1 ;
הַפֶּה שֶׁאָסַר הוּא הַפֶּה שֶׁהִתִּיר the mouth that declared it forbidden is
the mouth that declared it permitted, Dam. vi. 1; אֲנִי הוּא הַטָּמֵא
I am the unclean, Naz. viii. 1.   The pronoun is sometimes placed
at the end for emphasis : אָדָם חָלוּל הוּא a man is hollow, Oh. xi. 3 ;
הַיָּדַיִם עַסְקָנִיּוֹת הֵן the hands are busy, Šab. 14 a.   Sometimes the
pronoun stands before the subject in anticipation : שֶׁלָּנוּ הוּא הַפֶּסַח
ours is the paschal sacrifice, &c., Pᵉs. ix. 10; מְעוּבֶּרֶת הִיא צָרָתָהּ
her rival is pregnant, Yᵉb. xvi. 1 ; עוֹמֵד הוּא הַטָּהוֹר the clean one
may stand, Pa. x. 5 ; xii. 5.   Cf. in BH Cant. vi. 9, and Driver's
Tenses, § 201.

2. The Possessive Pronoun.

406. Possession is expressed by the pronominal suffixes attached
to the noun in exactly the same way as in BH.   MH, however,
also makes wide use of the relative שֶׁ with the preposition לְ (שֶׁלְּ)
as an independent possessive pronoun (cf. §§ 79, 385).   It is used
both in substantival and adjectival constructions.

(i) Substantival : שֶׁלִּי שֶׁלְּךָ וְשֶׁלָּךְ שֶׁלִּי mine is mine and thine
is mine, Ab. v. 10 ; הַכֹּל שֶׁלּוֹ everything is his, ib. iv. 22 ; מֵפֵר אֶת
שֶׁלָּהּ וְשֶׁלּוֹ קַיָּים he annuls hers but his remains in force, Naz. iv. 1 ;
אֵלּוּ שֶׁלָּהֶן these are theirs, BM i. 5.

407. (ii) Adjectival, taking the place of the pronominal suffix.

This construction is used, at least in earlier MH works, only in
the following cases.

(*a*) On grounds of grammar :

(1) With compound expressions which have become standing
phrases are thus inseparable : מַעֲשֵׂר שֵׁנִי שֶׁלָּהֶם their Second Tithe,
MŠ iii. 6 ; בֵּית קִיבּוּל שֶׁלָּהּ its receptacle, 'Ed. iii. 5 ; 'לֹא הוֹדַע' שֶׁעָנָהּ
(cf. Lev. iv. 28) Kᵉr. i. 2.

(2) With a composite subject : כִּפֵּא וּסְמוּכוֹת שֶׁלּוֹ his seat and
supports, Šab. vi. 8 ; הַפַּת וְהַשֶּׁמֶן שֶׁלָּהֶם their bread and oil, 'AZ ii. 6.

(3) With indeclinable nouns : בַּשֵּׁנִי שֶׁלּוֹ ; בַּשְּׁמִינִי שֶׁלּוֹ Pes. viii. 5 ;
רֵחַיִם שֶׁלָּהֶן their mill, 'Ed. iii. 12 ; חַמִּין שֶׁלּוֹ his hot water, t. Šab.
iii. 3 ; שַׁעֲוָה שֶׁלָּהּ her wax, t. ib. xviii. 8 ; הָאַלְיָה שֶׁלָּהֶן their tail,
Šab. v. 4 ; especially foreign nouns : הָאוּנְקְלִי שֶׁלָּהּ ἀγκύλη Kel.
xiii. 7 ; מוּכְנִי שֶׁלָּהּ μηχανή, ib. xviii. 2 ; הַפִּיטְמָה שֶׁלָּהֶן their flower,
'Uq. i. 2.

408. (*b*) On grounds of style.

(i) With nouns used in a secondary or derived sense : הַתַּחְתּוֹן שֶׁלָּהּ
its lower part, Šab. i. 10 (to distinguish from תַּחְתּוֹנָה, adjective) ;
קַב שֶׁלּוֹ his artificial foot, ib. vi. 8 (not *qab*, measure) ; הַבֵּיצִים שֶׁלּוֹ
testes, Yeb. viii. 4 ; הָאֵם שֶׁלָּהּ the matrix, Bek. iv. 4 ; הַפֶּרַח שֶׁלָּהּ the
calyx of a candlestick, 'Oh. iv. 8.

Sometimes to emphasize specially the noun, rather than the
possessor : אֲפִילּוּ הַחֶלְמוֹן שֶׁלָּהּ even its yolk, Ter. x. 12 ; חַפִּין שֶׁלָּהּ
its teeth (of a key) ; חוֹתָם שֶׁלָּהּ its seal (of a ring), Kel. xiii. 6, in
antithetical cases.

409. This construction is also frequent in BH, cf. מְעָרַת הַמַּכְפֵּלָה
אֲשֶׁר לוֹ Gen. xxiii. 9 ; xli. 43 ; Exod. xxxviii. 30 ; Lev. ix. 8 ;
xvi. 6, 11 ; הַנַּעַר אֲשֶׁר לוֹ 1 Sam. xx. 40 ; 2 Sam. xiv. 31 ; 1 Kings
i. 33 ; iv. 2 ; Ruth ii. 21 ; כְּרֵעַ כְּאָח לִי Ps. xxxv. 14 ; cxx. 1 ;
לְכִסֵּא לָךְ cxxxii. 11, 12 ; Lam. i. 10, &c. ; cf. Koenig, *Syntax*,
§ 28 i, o.

So also in Phoenician (Punic), Schröder, § 69, and in modern
Arabic, Spitta, §§ 77 c, 119 a, 120 c.

3. The Demonstrative Pronoun.

410. The demonstratives זֶה, זוֹ, אֵלּוּ, are used both substantively
and adjectivally : זֶה אוֹמֵר ... וְזֶה אוֹמֵר this one says ... and this
one says, BM i. 1 ; מַעְשְׂרוֹת זוֹ בְזוֹ the tithes of this one are in this
one, Dam. vii. 6 ; אֵלּוּ וָאֵלּוּ מִתְעָרְבִין both these and these mingle, Yo.
v. 6 ; or the noun follows as a predicate which is further defined

by a relative clause : אֵלּוּ דְבָרִים שֶׁאֵין לָהֶם שִׁעוּר these are the things which have no measure, Pea i. 1 ; Bᵉr. vii. 1.

411. When used adjectivally the pronoun follows the noun : כִּכָּר זוֹ this loaf, Šᵉbu. iii. 7 ; שׁוֹר זֶה this ox, Mᵉn. xiii. 9 ; הַמָּעוֹת הָאֵלּוּ this money, MŠ iii. 3. Sometimes, however, the pronoun precedes the noun in Aram. fashion : זֶה מִדְרָשׁ דָּרַשׁ ר"א this exposition, R. El'azar ... expounded, Kᵉt. iv. 6 ; זוֹ עֵדוּת הֵעִיד ר"פ R. Papias bore this testimony, Naz. iii. 2 ; v. 4 (but cf. below, § 477) ; עַל אֵלּוּ טוּמְאוֹת over these cases of uncleanness, ib. vii. 2. Cf. in BH, Ges.-K., § 136 d, foot-note 1.

412. Similarly, the stronger demonstratives הַלָּז, הַלָּלוּ, are used in both these ways : לַמָּקוֹם הַלָּז to that place, Ṭoh. iv. 3 ; vi. 5 ; בַּפֶּתַח הַזֶּה ... בַּפֶּתַח הַלָּז in this entrance ... in that entrance, ib. vi. 8 ; הַמּוּמִין הַלָּלוּ those blemishes, Kᵉt. vii. 8 ; ג' דְּבָרִים הַלָּלוּ those three things, Ab. v. 19. On the other hand : הוֹצִיא הַלָּז וְתֵצֵא הַלָּזוֹ אֶת רֹאשׁוֹ that one brought forth his head, Mak. ii. 2 ; and that one should go forth, Yᵉb. xiii. 7 ; הַלָּלוּ נוֹצְצִין, הַלָּלוּ נוֹבְלִין these sprout forth, these fade, 'Er. 54 a.

413. The shortened form הַלָּה is found only substantivally : וְהַלָּה אוֹמֵר and that one says, Šᵉbu. vi. 7 ; הַלָּה מוּתָּר that one is permitted, Nᵉd. iv. 8 ; v. 6 ; כֵּיצַד הַלָּה עוֹשֶׂה סְחוֹרָה how can that one make a business, BM iii. 2 ; San. vi. 1.

414. The pronoun of the third person is also used as a demonstrative : בִּזְמַן שֶׁאֵין לָהֶם אוּמָּנוּת אֶלָּא הִיא (L ; ed. הוּא) when they have no other trade but that one, San. iii. 3 ; so especially in contrast to the nearer demonstrative : חֲמוֹרְךָ זֶה ... חֲמוֹרְךָ הוּא this ass, that ass, of thine, BB v. 2 ; הַפֵּירוֹת הָאֵלּוּ ... הַפֵּירוֹת הָהֵם this fruit ... that fruit ; הַמָּעוֹת הָאֵלּוּ ... הַמָּעוֹת הָהֵם this, that money, MŠ iii. 4 ; but more frequently הַלָּה is found : ... זֶה אוֹכֵל ... וְהַלָּה עוֹשֶׂה this one eats ... and that one does ..., ib. 3. Cf. also the exx. above, § 74. הַלָּה is used also in contrast with הוּא : הוּא אוֹמֵר לוֹ ... וְהַלָּה אוֹמֵר לוֹ San. vii. 10 ; Šᵉbu, vii. 1.

415. The interrogative pronoun אֵיזֶה, אֵיזוֹ is used as a demonstrative to specify one out of a number of objects : מְבָרֵךְ עַל אֵיזֶה מֵהֶן שֶׁיִּרְצֶה he pronounces the benediction on whichever he likes, Bᵉr. vi. 4 ; Yᵉb. ii. 2 ; יָבִיא אֵיזוֹ שֶׁיִּרְצֶה he brings that one which he likes, Mᵉn. xiii. 1 ; אֵיזֶה שֶׁלָּקַח רִאשׁוֹן that one (of the two) who took first, Ḥul. v. 3.

416. MH also uses the particle אֶת as a demonstrative. The particle stands alone when introducing a clause : אֶת שֶׁיַּבֶּלֶת בְּעֵינוֹ the one which has a wart in its eye, Bᵉk. vi. 10 ; אֶת שֶׁהַגּוֹלֵל נִשְׁעָן עָלָיו that one on which the *golel* (the stone cover of a grave) is supported, Oh. ii. 4 ; Giṭ. ix. 5–7 ; Makš. i. 2 ; v. 2. So especially to introduce two alternate cases : אֶת שֶׁלִּפְנֵי הַמִּטָּה וְאֶת שֶׁלְּאַחַר הַמִּטָּה אֶת שֶׁלַּמִּטָּה צוֹרֶךְ בָּהֶן פְּטוּרִין אֶת שֶׁאֵין לַמִּטָּה צוֹרֶךְ בָּהֶן חַיָּיבִין both of those before the bier, and of those behind the bier : those of whom the bier has need are absolved, but those of whom the bier has no need are bound (to read the *Šᵉma‘*), Bᵉr. iii. 1 ; ʿEr. viii. 11 ; Šᵉq. viii. 7 ; BQ iv. 2, &c. Sometimes the particle is omitted before the second case : Nᵉd. x. 7 ; ṬY iii. 1 ; Ya. iii. 1.

417. When introducing a noun, אֶת takes the appropriate pronominal suffix of the third person : אוֹתוֹ הַיּוֹם וְאוֹתוֹ הָאִישׁ that day and that man, ʿAZ i. 3 ; אַנְשֵׁי אוֹתָהּ הָעִיר the men of that city, Be. v. 5 ; לְאוֹתוֹ הַמָּקוֹם to that place, ʿAZ i. 4 ; בְּאוֹתָהּ שָׁעָה in that moment, Bᵉr. v. 3 ; אוֹתָן הַחוּלִּין those common things, Tᵉr. v. 1 ; אוֹתָן הַיָּמִים those days, Nᵉd. ix. 6 ; אוֹתָן שְׁתֵּי רוּחוֹת those two spirits, Bᵉr. 18 b.

The origin of this demonstrative use of אֶת is to be found in the BH use of אֶת before the nominative, in order to emphasize the noun, cf. Ges.-K., § 117 i ; Koenig, *Syntax*, § 279 f. ; *BDB.*, p. 85, 3. An analogy to the MH use of אֶת . . . אֶת may be found in Ezek. xxxv. 10. Cf. also Barth, *Pronominalbildung*, p. 125.[1]

---

[1] This use of אֶת (= יָת) is not found in Jewish Aram., or in the other

4. The Interrogative Pronoun.

418. מִי is only used substantivally : מִי יְגַלֶּה who would uncover ?
So, v. 2 ; לְמִי מְשַׁלֵּם to whom does he pay ? BM iii. 1 ; מָה occurs
in both the substantival and adjectival use : מָה הִפְסִיד what has he
lost ? ib. v ; מַה מְטַמֵּא לוֹ what defiles him ? Neg. xii. 5 ; מָה הַלָּשׁוֹן
אוֹמְרִים what expression do men say ? ib. x. 1 ; מַה קוֹל שָׁמַעְתָּ what
voice hast thou heard ? Ber. 3 a ; מָה אֲנִי what am I ? Ya. iv. 4.

L often has מִי in a neuter sense in the frequent phrase בְּמִי דְבָרִים
אֲמוּרִים in what case does the statement apply, e. g. Šebi. iii. 7 ;
Šab. xvii. 8 ; 'Er. vii. 9, 11 ; x. 1. Conversely, מָה is found
in L of persons : חוּץ מִמַּה שֶׁיֵּשׁ לוֹ except one whom he has, Yeb.
ii. 5. Cf. in BH מִי שְׁמֶךָ Judges xiii. 17 ; *BDB.*, p. 566 a (a).

מִי is but rarely used to introduce an interrogative clause, e. g.
מִי כָאן הִלֵּל is Hillel here ? Šab. 31 a.

419. אֵיזוֹ, אֵיזֶה, can be used both substantivally and adjectivally,
e. g. בְּאֵיזֶה יוֹם ; בְּאֵיזוֹ שָׁעָה San. v. 1. When used substantivally,
they are followed by the enclitic הוּא, הִיא, often spelt in one word,
and without the final א : אֵיזֶהוּ דָבָר which is a thing that . . . ?
Ter. ix. 6 ; אֵיזֶהוּ הוּא בֶן זוּגוֹ which is its pair ? Šab. xii. 3 ; אֵיזוֹ הִיא
שִׁכְחָה what is a forgotten sheaf ? Pea vii. 8, 4 ; בְּאֵיזֶה ; בְּאֵיזוֹ שָׁנָה
שָׁבוּעַ in which week, year, San. v. 1, &c.

So also the rare plur. form אֵילוּ can be used in both ways :
אֵלּוּ הָאֲבָנִים which stones ? BM אֵלּוּ שֶׁהֻפְכוּ וְאֵלּוּ שֶׁקָּדְמוּ t. Neg. ii. 7 ;
x. 1 ; cf. above, § 81.

Aram. dialects, except in Christian Palestinian Aram., and in Samaritan.
Nöldeke's view that MH borrowed this usage from these two Aram. dialects
(*ZDMG.*, xxii, p. 471) is improbable, in view of the great frequency of this
usage in MH and its complete absence in Jewish Aram. It is more probable
that Christian Palestinian Aram. and Samaritan borrowed this usage from MH.
For other borrowings by the first-named dialect from MH, cf. Nöldeke,
ib., pp. 513, 522.

5. The Relative Pronoun. The use of שֶׁ.

420. The particle שֶׁ is used to introduce a clause which
serves to define a preceding noun or pronoun. It is then equivalent to the English relative 'who, which'. Thus, in the nominative:
שׁוֹר שֶׁנָּגַח an ox which has gored, BQ iv. 1; אֵלּוּ שֶׁהֵם צְרִיכִים;
אֵלּוּ שֶׁאֵינָם צְרִיכִים these that require, that do not require, Miq. x. 3, 4;
חַטָּאת שֶׁקִּבֵּל דָּמָהּ a sin-offering, the blood of which he received,
Zeb. viii. 12. Accusative: שָׂדֶה שֶׁקְּצָרוּהָ גוֹיִם a field which Gentiles
have reaped, Pea ii. 7; אֲבָנִים שֶׁזְּעֲזָעָתָן הַמַּחֲרֵישָׁה stones which the
plough has moved, Šebi. iii. 7. Usually, however, the retrospective
pronominal suffix is omitted, as in BH (Ges.-K., § 138 b):
שׁוֹרִי שֶׁגְּנַבְתָּ my ox which thou hast stolen, Šebu. viii. 4; דֶּרֶךְ יְשָׁרָה
שֶׁיָּבוֹר לוֹ הָאָדָם a straight road which a man should choose for
himself, Ab. ii. 1; כָּל טָהֳרוֹת שֶׁטִּיהַר ר"א all things which R. Eli'ezer
had declared clean, Ber. 19 b.

421. Similarly, with nouns indicating place or time, when there
is no risk of ambiguity, the retrospective preposition is omitted:
מָקוֹם שֶׁנָּהֲגוּ לַעֲשׂוֹת a place where they are accustomed to do, Pes.
iv. 1; מִשָּׁעָה שֶׁהַכֹּהֲנִים נִכְנָסִין from the time when the priests enter;
לְמָקוֹם שֶׁמַּיִם אַחֲרוֹנִים חוֹזְרִין to the place where the water for washing
the hands after a meal returns, Ber. 46 b. But more often the
preposition is expressed: מָקוֹם שֶׁנַּעֲשׂוּ בוֹ נִסִּים a place where
miracles were wrought; מָקוֹם שֶׁנֶּעֶקְרָה מִמֶּנּוּ a place from which idols
have been uprooted, Ber. ix. 1; הַמָּקוֹם שֶׁיָּצָא מִשָּׁם whence he came
forth; הַמָּקוֹם שֶׁהָלַךְ לְשָׁם whither he went, Pes. iv. 1; דְּבָרִים שֶׁאָדָם
יוֹצֵא בָהֶן things with which one discharges one's duty, ib. ii. 4, 5;
דְּבָרִים שֶׁאֵין נִשְׁבָּעִין עֲלֵיהֶם things on which one does not take an oath,
Šebu. vi. 5; מִי שֶׁהַפִּקָּדוֹן אֶצְלוֹ he with whom is the deposited article,
ib. 7; כָּל שֶׁאֵין הַכֶּלֶב יָכוֹל לְחַפֵּשׂ אַחֲרָיו everything that a dog cannot
search out, Pes. ii. 2.

422. The original demonstrative significance of שֶׁ is still

apparent in cases where the indefinite מִי, מָה stands as its antecedent (cf. § 436): מִי שֶׁהוֹצִיאוּהוּ ; מִי שֶׁיָּצָא anyone whom they
brought forth; who went forth, 'Er. iv. 1, 3, 4, 5; מַה שֶׁעָשָׂה עָשׂוּי
what he has done is done, BB viii. 5. In BH אֲשֶׁר can stand in
such cases without an antecedent, cf. Num. xxii. 6, &c.; Ges.-K.,
§ 138 e. In MH שֶׁ must always have an antecedent.

Sometimes, however, שֶׁ is omitted after מִי, מָה: אֵין לוֹ מִי יַתִּירֶנּוּ
he has no one who would make it permissible = שֶׁיַּתִּירֶנּוּ Men. iv. 3;
אֵין לִי מָה אָשִׁיב I have nothing to reply = שֶׁאָשִׁיב Kel. xiii. 7. Cf.
also § 477.

Likewise, the particle אֵת can stand as antecedent to שֶׁ, whether
in the accusative or the nominative: מְעַשֵּׂר אֶת שֶׁהוּא אוֹכֵל וְאֶת
שֶׁהוּא מוֹכֵר וְאֶת שֶׁהוּא לוֹקֵחַ he tithes what he eats, sells, buys, Dam.
ii. 2; אֶת שֶׁהָעֵדִים נִקְרָאִין עִמּוֹ that one with which the witnesses can
be read (i.e. their signatures following immediately), Giṭ. ix. 5–7;
cf. above, § 416.

423. Like אֲשֶׁר, and especially כִּי in BH (Ges.-K., § 157),
שֶׁ also introduces a clause which serves as the object of a verb.
שֶׁ is then equivalent to a conjunction: לֹא לְמַדְתָּנוּ . . . שֶׁחָתָן פָּטוּר
didst thou not teach us that a bridegroom is absolved . . . ,
Ber. ii. 5; יוֹדֵעַ אֲנִי שֶׁהוּא מְקוּבָּל I know that he is accepted, ib. v. 5;
סָבוּר שֶׁנָּדְרָה he thought that she had vowed, Ned. xi. 5; . . . לֵידַע
שֶׁהוּא אֵל to know that He is God, AB iv. 22.

שֶׁ often has as its antecedent a conjunction or a preposition:
אַחַר שֶׁ, מִשֶּׁ, כְּשֶׁ, &c.; cf. § 303. So אשר in BH, Ges.-K.,
§ 104 b.

424. The use of שֶׁ to introduce direct narration is rare and
doubtful: הִיא כוֹתֶבֶת שֶׁנִּתְקַבַּלְתִּי she writes: I have received, Ket.
v. 1 (L; edd. 'נתק) אָמַר לָהֶם שֶׁהַטְּהוֹרָה he said to them: the clean
one, Ned. iv. 3; אָמַר לָהֶם שֶׁהַזָּהָב Men. ii. 1 (but שֶׁ in these cases
may stand for מִפְּנֵי שֶׁ because); after an oath: שְׁבוּעָה שֶׁאֵינִי יָשֵׁן
שֶׁאֵינִי מְדַבֵּר an oath, that I will not sleep, speak, Ned. ii. 1, 2;

cf. below, §§ 456, 458 f. For similar use of אֲשֶׁר in BH, cf. Ges.-K., § 157 c.

425. שֶׁ־ is regularly used in adverbial expressions before לֹא : בְּטוֹבָה וְשֶׁלֹּא בְטוֹבָה with, and without thanks, Šᵉbi. iv. 2 ; בְּפָנָיו וְשֶׁלֹּא בְבֵית דִּין at a court of law, and not at a court of law : בְּפָנָיו וְשֶׁלֹּא בְפָנָיו in his presence, and not in his presence, Yᵉb. xiii. 1 ; שֶׁלֹּא בִכְתוּבָּה without the marriage settlement, Kᵉt. vii. 6. Rarely without שֶׁ־, as in BH בְּלֹא : בְּלֹא מִתְכַּוֵּן בְּלֹא מִסְפָּר 'Er. iv. 4 ; Suk. v. 4.

426. שֶׁ־ is also often found before a verb introduced by אוֹ : שֶׁהָיוּ אוֹ שֶׁנָּתַן or put, Šab. i. 1 ; שֶׁנָּטַל אוֹ or he took ; שֶׁהָיוּ אוֹ or they were, Suk. iii. 2 ; שֶׁהוּזְלוּ אוֹ הוּקְרוּ they became dear or cheap, BB v. 8. Contrast, however, אוֹ מֵיאֵנוּ, &c. or repudiated, Yᵉb. i. 1, and often.

427. שֶׁ־ is also attached to a verb to lend it special emphasis in an antithesis : אָמַר לוֹ מֵת וְהוּא שֶׁנִּשְׁבַּר he said to him : it was dead, but it was really broken (injured) ; וְהוּא שֶׁמֵּת it was really dead, Šᵉbu. viii. 2, 3, 5, 6 ; so in L וְהֵם שֶׁיּוֹדְעִין and they did really know, ib. iv. 11.

6. Reflexive and Reciprocal.

428. The expression of the reflexive by the simple pronominal suffix is rare in MH. Examples are : גּוֹלְלוֹ אֶצְלוֹ he rolls it up to himself, 'Er. x. 3 ; הָאִישׁ מְקַדֵּשׁ בּוֹ וּבִשְׁלוּחוֹ a man can betroth by himself or by his messenger ; הָאִשָּׁה מִתְקַדֶּשֶׁת בָּהּ a woman can be betrothed by herself . . ., Qid. ii. 1 ; הָאִשָּׁה כּוֹתֶבֶת אֶת גִּטָּהּ a woman may write her own *Get*, Giṭ. ii. 5 ; אֲבֵידָתוֹ וַאֲבֵידַת אָבִיו his own lost property and his father's lost property, &c., BM ii. 11.

429. Usually, a periphrasis is employed to express the reflexive idea. The most common noun used for this purpose is עֶצֶם with the appropriate suffix.

Nomin. : (הַתְּמִיד) עַצְמוֹ הַפְּרִי the fruit itself, Šebi. viii. 7 ; עַצְמוֹ בְּתִשְׁעָה itself by nine, Yo. ii. 5 ; הָאִשָּׁה עַצְמָהּ the woman herself, Giṭ. ii. 7 ; תְּמַהּ עַצְמְךָ wonder thyself, Makš. i. 3.

Genit. : עֲצֵי עַצְמָן their own wood, opposed to עֲצֵי הַמַּעֲרָכָה the wood of the pile, Pes. vii. 8 ; מַעֲשֵׂה עַצְמוֹ his own act, opposed to מַעֲשֵׂה שׁוֹרוֹ BQ iii. 9 ; דְּבָרִים שֶׁל עַצְמוֹ his own words, opposed to דְּבָרִים שֶׁל אֲחֵרִים Šebu. iii. 5 ; אֵין אָדָם מֵעִיד עַל יְדֵי עַצְמוֹ a man cannot give evidence for himself, Keṭ. ii. 9 ; כְּסוּת עַצְמָן their own garment, Tam. i. 1 ; בֵּינוֹ לְבֵין עַצְמוֹ privately, Bik. i. 4.

Accus., after transitive verbs, as a periphrasis of the reflexive stem : קוֹנָה אֶת עַצְמָהּ acquires herself, Qid. i. 1 ; אַל תַּעַשׂ עַצְמְךָ do not make thyself, Ab. i. 8 ; יָזֹמּוּ אֶת עַצְמָן refute themselves, Mak. i. 4 (L) ; אֵין אָדָם מֵשִׂים אֶת עַצְמוֹ רָשָׁע a man cannot make himself guilty, Yeb. 25 b.

With a preposition : זֶה בְעַצְמוֹ וְזֶה בְעַצְמוֹ this by itself and this by itself, Šab. xix. 2 ; לָחוֹב בְּעַצְמְךָ to be guilty against thyself, Ber. i. 3 ; בְּעַצְמוֹ שֶׁל כֹּהֵן by the priest himself, Sifra, 8 d ; זוֹ לְעַצְמָהּ וְזוֹ לְעַצְמָהּ this for itself and this for itself, Pes. i. 2 ; אִם יָצְאוּ מֵעַצְמָן if they went forth of themselves, Šab. 143 b.

430. Sometimes, עֶצֶם is preceded by כָּל, for the sake of emphasis : כָּל עַצְמוֹ אֵינוֹ כוֹתֵב altogether he only writes, So. ii. 3 ; כָּל עַצְמָן אָסוּר לְקַיֵּם they are altogether forbidden to preserve, t. Šab. iv. 9 ; כָּל עַצְמָהּ אֵינָה נַעֲשֵׂית the whole of it is not done, Sifra, 8 d ; כָּל עַצְמָם שֶׁל מְלָכִים the kings themselves, Sifre, Deut. i. 1.

431. The use of עֶצֶם is peculiar to MH. The similar use of גֶּרֶם in late Aram. must be an imitation of MH.[1] In BH עֶצֶם is found in an analogous sense, but only in the construct state, and of things, not of persons : בְּעֶצֶם הַיּוֹם הַזֶּה Gen. vii. 13, and frequently ; כְּעֶצֶם הַשָּׁמַיִם Exod. xxiv. 11 ; בְּעֶצֶם תֻּמּוֹ Job xxi. 23

---

[1] So perhaps also in BH : גֶּרֶם הַמַּעֲלוֹת 2 Kings ix. 13.

(Ges.-K., § 139 g). But it is obvious that a word meaning 'bone' must have been applied first to animate beings, and then only figuratively to inanimate objects. It is, therefore, clear that the expression must have been more commonly used in colloquial speech than appears in the literary remains of BH.

432. The BH נֶפֶשׁ is used rarely as a reflexive: תְּמַהּ נַפְשֶׁךְ wonder thyself; מִתְחַיֵּב בְּנַפְשׁוֹ becomes guilty against himself, Ab. iii. 4.

So גּוּף: גּוּפָהּ שֶׁל מִנְחָה the meal offering itself, Sifra 25 b; גּוּפוֹ his own person, Ab. iv. 8.

Finally, the compound preposition מֵאֵל with the appropriate suffix sometimes expresses the reflexive idea: הָעוֹלָה מֵאֵלָיו what springs up of itself, 'Or. i. 2; בָּאוּ מֵאֲלֵיהֶן they came of themselves, BM vii. 9; cf. § 301.

433. Reciprocity is expressed by such circumlocutions as the repetition of the demonstrative: שֶׁחִרְרוּ זֶה אֶת זֶה they liberated each other, Yeb. xi. 5; רוֹאִין אֵלּוּ אֶת אֵלּוּ they see one another, Mak. i. 9; rarely רֵעַ ... אִישׁ: לֹא יַכּוּ אִישׁ אֶת רֵעֵהוּ they should not strike one another, Pea iv. 4. Note also the use of חָבֵר, חֲבֵרֵת with inanimate objects: בֵּין פַּצִּים לַחֲבֵרוֹ between one beam and its fellow, Šab. viii. 7; מִסְּפִינָה לַחֲבֶרְתָּהּ from one ship to the other, ib. xi. 5; בֵּין שׁוּרָה לַחֲבֶרְתָּהּ between one row and the other, Kil. iii. 6; iv. 8; cf. § 139.

7. Indefinite.

434. Like BH, MH possesses no special indefinite pronouns. It employs certain nouns, and pronouns, and certain parts of the verb to express the indefinite subject, or object.

(i) אָדָם: שׁוֹאֵל אָדָם one may ask, Šab. xxiii. 1; מוֹנֶה אָדָם one may count, ib. 2; לֹא יִקּוֹב אָדָם one may not bore, ib. ii. 4; שֶׁיָּבוֹר לוֹ הָאָדָם which one should choose for oneself, Ab. ii. 1; יְכַוֵּין אָדָם אֶת דַּעְתּוֹ לַשָּׁמַיִם one should direct one's mind towards

heaven, Mᵉn. xiii. 11. אָדָם is often strengthened by כָּל: כָּל אָדָם
יַטּוּ anyone must recline; כָּל אָדָם קוֹרֵא anyone may read ...,
Bᵉr. i. 5; כָּל אָדָם מִיִּשְׂרָאֵל anyone in Israel, 'Ed. v. 6.

435. (ii) כָּל alone followed by a participle, or by ־שֶׁ: כָּל הַשּׁוֹכֵחַ
anyone who forgets, Šab. vii. 1, 5; כָּל הַמִּסְתַּכֵּל anyone who gazes,
Ḥag. ii. 1; כָּל שֶׁאֵינוֹ יָכוֹל one who is not able, ib. i. 1; כָּל שֶׁעָשָׂאָהּ
one which he made, Suk. i. 1; ... כָּל שֶׁיִּנָּטֵל one which when the
tree be removed, ib. ii. 3; אָכַל כָּל מַאֲכָל he ate any food; שָׁתָה כָל
מַשְׁקִין he drank any drink, Zab. ii. 2. So especially with the
pronoun of the third person: כָּל שֶׁהֵן, כָּל שֶׁהִיא, כָּל שֶׁהוּא somewhat,
something, anything, Šab. i. 14; ix. 6; 'Er. ii. 2, &c.

This use of כָּל is also very frequent in BH; cf. *BDB.*,
p. 482 a (e).

436. (iii) מִי: מִי לָחָשַׁךְ if anyone whispers to thee, Sifre, Deut.
xi. 27; but usually with ־שֶׁ and a relative clause, when מִי has
a somewhat demonstrative force: מִי שֶׁאָכַל וְשָׁכַח if anyone ate and
forgot, Bᵉr. viii. 7; זָכָה מִי שֶׁנִּצְּבָה he wins whoever wins, Tam. v. 2;
מִי שֶׁלֹּא שָׁהֲתָה any woman who has not waited, Yᵉb. xi. 6; מִי
שֶׁנִּתְחָרֵשׁ בַּעְלָהּ anyone whose husband became deaf mute, So. iv. 5.
So in BH: מִי אֲשֶׁר Exod. xxxii. 33; 2 Sam. xx. 11; cf. *BDB.*,
p. 567 a (g).

מִי is often strengthened by כָּל: כָּל מִי שֶׁלֹּא רָאָה whoever has not
seen, Suk. v. 1; כָּל מִי שֶׁאֵינוֹ צָרִיךְ whoever is not in need, Pea
viii. 8; מַאֲכִיל לְכָל מִי שֶׁיִּרְצֶה he gives to eat to whomever he wishes,
BB viii. 7.

So with מָה: מַה שֶּׁנָּתַן נָתַן whatever he gave, he gave, ib. vi. 7;
טוֹל מַה שֶׁהֵבֵאתָ take whatever thou hast brought, Ḥul. iv. 4;
עַל מַה שֶׁלֹּא שָׁמַע about what he has not heard, Ab. v. 7; מַה שֶׁאַתְּ
שׁוֹמַעַת whatever thou hearest, Bᵉr. 18 b; cf. § 422. This usage
is common in Qohelet, *e.g.* i. 9; iii. 15, 22, &c.; cf. *BDB.*,
p. 553 a (e(b)); also col. b, 3; Ges.-K., § 137 c.

So especially with הוּא, הִיא, often written without א: מַשֶּׁהוּ,

מַשֶּׁהִי something, anything; אָדָם טוֹעֶה מַשֶּׁהוּ one errs somewhat,
Pes. 11 b; אֶחָד עָשָׂר וּמַשֶּׁהוּ eleven and something·over, 'Er. 87 a;
נָתַן מַשֶּׁהוּ שֶׁמֶן he gave a little oil, Mᵉn. 60 a.

437. (iv) כְּלוּם anything, equivalent to BH מְאוּמָה (from which it
seems to be derived with the addition of כָּל, like the other indefinite
nouns described above = מְאוּם + כָּל ¹), used as indefinite pronoun
only with negatives: לֹא עָשָׂה כְלוּם he did nothing, Yo. v. 7;
לֹא נִשְׁתַּיֵּיר הֵימֶנָּה כְּלוּם nothing was left of it, Ḥul. iii. 1; the negative is sometimes strengthened by the addition of וְלֹא: לֹא עָשָׂה
וְלֹא כְלוּם he did nothing at all, Pᵉs. 89 b. So מאומה in BH is
usually found with negatives, Gen. xxii. 12; xxx. 31, &c.

(v) מִקְצָת some: נָטַל מִקְצָת פֵּיאָה he took some of the *Pea*,
Pea iv. 2; מִקְצָתָן רוֹאִין some of them see, Bᵉr. vii. 5; הָיוּ מִקְצָת הֶעָלִין
some of the leaves were, Kil. i. 9.

(vi) פְּלוֹנִי, פְּלוֹנִית so and so, an unnamed one; אִישׁ פְּלוֹנִי בֶּן אִישׁ
פְּלוֹנִי מִמָּקוֹם פְּלוֹנִית Yᵉb. xvi. 6; אֵינִי נוֹשֵׂא אֶת פְּלוֹנִית מֵת I will not
marry so-and-so, Nᵉd. ix. 3; עֲבֵרָה פְּלוֹנִית a certain transgression,
San. vi. 1. So also שְׁנַת כָּךְ וְכָךְ: כָּךְ וְכָךְ, the year so-and-so,
RH 18 b; כָּךְ וְכָךְ פּוֹעֲלִים so many labourers, Šab. 150 b.

438. (vii) An indefinite subject is also expressed by the cognate
participle: מֵת לוֹ מֵת, if anyone died to him, San. ii. 3; סִילֵק הַמְּסַלֵּק
וְהַטּוֹמֵן הַטּוֹמְנִין וְהַדְּלִיק הַמַּדְלִיק he that has to remove removes, that
has to hide hides, that has to light lights, Šab. 35 b; הַנִּכְנָס יִכָּנֵס
וְהַיּוֹצֵא אַל יֵצֵא anyone may enter, but no one may go out, ib. 60 a;
cf. BH Isa. xvi. 10; xxviii. 4, 24, &c.

439. (viii) More often the subject is omitted altogether, and the
verb alone, in the third person, whether in the sing. or the plur.,
expresses the indefinite subject. Thus the participle שׁוֹאֵל . . . וּמֵשִׁיב
one asks . . . one answers, Bᵉr. ii. 1; especially with the article,
used with a demonstrative force: הַקּוֹרֵא if one reads, ib. ii. 3;

---

¹ But it may, perhaps. be connected with the Arab. كلم, and equivalent to
דְּבָר anything.

הַשּׁוֹחֵט if one slays, Šᵉbi. x. 2 ; cf. above, §§ 329, 374 (vii). So in
the plur., but without the article : קוֹרִין Bᵉr. i. 1 ; מַזְפִּירִין ib. 8. So,
particularly, when the subject is the Divine power : נִפְרָעִין מִמֶּנּוּ
retribution is taken from him, Ab. iv. 5 ; מַסְפִּיקִין בְּיָדוֹ they enable
him, ib. 6 ; הַבָּא לִיטַּהֵר מְסַיְּעִין לוֹ הַבָּא לִיטַּמֵּא פּוֹתְחִין לוֹ if one comes
to purify himself, they assist him ; if one comes to defile himself,
they open to him (an opportunity), Šab. 104 a.

So with the perfect : וִימֵּן לְבָנִים וּמָצָא שְׁחוֹרִים if one prepared white
ones, and found black ones, Be. i. 5 ; מָזְגוּ לוֹ they poured out to
him, Pᵉs. x. 2 ; הֵבִיאוּ לְפָנָיו they brought before him, ib. 3 ;
בִּירָה שֶׁהִסִּיקוּהָ ... נוֹתְנִין עָלֶיהָ a hearth which has been heated ...
one may put on it ..., Šab. iii. 1.

With the imperf. : לֹא יִתֵּן עַד שֶׁיִּגְרוֹף אוֹ עַד שֶׁיִּתֵּן אֶת הָאֵפֶר one
may not put until one removes the coals, or until one puts on
ashes, ib., &c. Cf. in BH, Ges.-K., § 144 d, g, i.

IV. SENTENCES AND CLAUSES

1. The Nominative Absolute.

440. The Nominative Absolute is very common in MH, as in
BH and Aram.[1] In this construction the noun is placed at
the head of the sentence for emphasis, and its proper grammatical
relation is expressed later in the sentence by a resumptive pronoun.

441. (i) With a definite subject : פֵּאָה אֵין קוֹצְרִין אוֹתָהּ בְּמַגָּלוֹת וְאֵין
עוֹקְרִין אוֹתָהּ בְּקַרְדּוּמוֹת Pea[2]—they may not reap it with sickles,
nor uproot it with axes, *Pea* iv. 4 ; הַנַּחְתּוֹמִין לֹא חִיְּיבוּ אוֹתָם חֲכָמִים
the bakers—the sages have not laid on them the obligation,
Dam. ii. 4 ; הַתְּרוּמָה מֶה הָיוּ עוֹשִׂין בָּהּ the heave offering (of the

---

[1] Cf. Ges.-K., § 143 ; Nöldeke, *Syr. Gr.*, § 317 ; *Mand. Gr.*, § 275.

[2] The corn in the corner of a field which had to be left for the poor,
Lev. xxiii. 22.

shekels)—what did they do with it, Šeq. iv. 1, 3 f.; הַדַּמַּאי אֵין לּוֹ חוֹמֶשׁ *Dammai*[1]—it has not the law of the fifth, Dam. i. 2 ; אַמַּת הַמַּיִם . . . אֵין מְמַלְּאִים הֵימֶנָּה a pool of water—one may not fill from it, 'Er. viii. 7 ff.

442. (ii) With an indefinite subject (cf. §§ 435 f., 439). Such sentences are usually equivalent to a conditional sentence in English : הָאוֹמֵר . . . מְשַׁתְּקִין אוֹתוֹ if one says . . . they silence him, Ber. v. 3 ; הַקּוֹצֵר בַּלַּיְלָה וְהַמְעַמֵּר וְהַסּוּמָא יֵשׁ לָהֶם שִׁכְחָה if one reaps or binds sheaves by night, and the blind man—to them applies the law of a forgotten sheaf (Deut. xxiv. 19), Pea vi. 11 ; מִי שֶׁאֲחָזוֹ בּוּלְמוֹס מַאֲכִילִין אוֹתוֹ he whom faintness has seized—they make him eat, Yo. viii. 6, 7 ; מִי שֶׁאָבַד חוֹתָמוֹ מַמְתִּינִין לוֹ if anyone has lost his seal—they wait for him, Šeq. v. 5 ; מַה שֶּׁהוּא מְשַׁיֵּר יַנִּיחֶנּוּ whatever he leaves—he must put it away, Pes. i. 3 ; . . . כָּל שֶׁבָּא בְחַמִּין שׁוֹרִין אוֹתוֹ whatever came into hot water—they may soak it, Šab. xxii. 2 ; כָּל הַמְקַבֵּל עָלָיו . . . מַעֲבִירִין מִמֶּנּוּ whoever receives upon himself . . . they remove from him, Ab. iii. 6.

443. To this construction belongs the frequent resumption of the subject by the graphic particle הֲרֵי with the demonstrative pronoun : הַחוֹלֵץ לִיבִמְתּוֹ הֲרֵי הוּא כְּאֶחָד מִן הָאַחִים if one grants *ḥaliṣa* to the childless widow of his deceased brother—lo, he is like one of the (other) brothers, Yeb. iv. 7. This happens, especially, when the subject is described by a more or less lengthy intervening clause, or when the subject is compound : מִי שֶׁיֵּשׁ לוֹ נ' זוּז וְהוּא נוֹשֵׂא וְנוֹתֵן בָּהֶם הֲרֵי זֶה לֹא יִטּוֹל if anyone has 50 *zuzim* with which he trades—lo, this one must not take, Pea viii. 9. Contrast with : הֲרֵי . . . מִי שֶׁיֵּשׁ לוֹ מָאתַיִם זוּז לֹא יִטּוֹל ib. 8 ; הָיָה עוֹשֶׂה בְיָדָיו אֲבָל זֶה אוֹכֵל if he worked with his hands, but not with his feet : . . lo, this one may eat, BM vii. 3. Contrast with the following : הָיָה עוֹשֶׂה בַתְּאֵנִים לֹא יֹאכַל בָּעֲנָבִים if he worked at figs, he must not

---

[1] Fruit about which there is a doubt whether it has been tithed or not.

eat of grapes. ‏נ׳ אִילָנוֹת שֶׁל ג׳ בְּנֵי אָדָם הֲרֵי אֵלּוּ מִצְטָרְפִין‎ 3 trees
of 3 men—lo, these combine, Šᵉbi. i. 5; ‏אֲבָנִים שֶׁזְּעֲזָעָתָן הַמַּחֲרֵישָׁה אוֹ‎
‏הֲרֵי אֵלּוּ יִנָּטֵלוּ . . . שֶׁהָיוּ מְכוּסּוֹת וְנִתְגַּלּוּ . . .‎ stones which the plough has
moved, or if they were covered and became uncovered . . .—lo,
these may be taken away, ib. iii. 7; ‏הַחִטִּים וְהַשְּׂעוֹרִים . . . הֲרֵי אֵלּוּ‎
‏חַיָּבִין בְּחַלָּה‎ wheat, barley . . .—lo, these are liable to the law of
Ḥalla (Num. xv. 20).

444. Such a nom. abs. often consists of a subject, qualified
by a relative clause, which has been removed from a subordinate
object clause, and placed before the principal sentence. ⸱This
happens usually in the case of an object clause dependent on
the verb ‏אמר‎, where two or more opposing views are expressed
by different sages. The position of the nom. abs. serves to direct
attention to it as the subject of the discussion that follows. Exx.:
‏בֵּיצָה שֶׁנּוֹלְדָה בְּיוֹם טוֹב בֵּית שַׁמַּאי אוֹמְרִים תֵּאָכֵל וּבֵית הִלֵּל אוֹמְרִים‎
an egg born on a festival—the House of Šammai say, it may be
eaten; but the House of Hillel say, it may not be eaten. This
is equivalent to: ‏בֵּית שַׁמַּאי אוֹמְרִים בֵּיצָה שֶׁנּוֹלְדָה בְּי״ט תֵּאָכֵל‎ Be. i. 1;
so ib. 2, 8. Contrast ib. 3–7, &c.: ‏הַשּׁוּתָּפִין שֶׁתָּרְמוּ זֶה אַחַר זֶה ר׳‎
‏עֲקִיבָא אוֹמֵר תְּרוּמַת שְׁנֵיהֶם תְּרוּמָה וַחֲכָמִים אוֹמְרִים תְּרוּמַת הָרִאשׁוֹן . . .‎
‏. . . ר׳י אוֹמֵר‎ partners who tithed one after the other = R. Akiba
says: the tithing of both is tithes; the sages say: the tithing
of the first (alone) is tithes; R. Jose says . . .—‏ר׳ע אוֹמֵר הַשּׁוּתָּפִין‎
‏שֶׁתָּרְמוּ . . .‎ Tᵉr. iii. 3; so ib. 5; viii. 8, 9 (with the verb ‏מוֹדֶה‎);
‏מִי שֶׁלִּיקֵּט אֶת הַפֵּאָה וְאָמַר הֲרֵי זוֹ לְאִישׁ פְּלוֹנִי עָנִי ר׳ אֱלִיעֶזֶר אוֹמֵר זָכָה לוֹ‎
‏וַחֲכָמִים אוֹמְרִים‎ if anyone gathers *pea*, and says: lo, this shall be
for a certain poor man—R. Eliezer says: he acquires it for
him; but the sages say . . ., Pea iv. 9; BM iii. 12; Yᵉb. iv. 3
(with ‏מוֹדִים‎).

445. Frequently, a nom. abs. is left suspended, and is not
resumed again at all, but the predicate is attached to another
implicit subject, whether mentioned expressly before, but in a

dependent relation, or not mentioned expressly, but understood from the context. Here, again, the position of the nom. abs. is designed to give special emphasis to a particular circumstance in the case under discussion. This construction is very common in the Mishna and Tosefta, and is characteristic of their Halakic diction. Exx.: מָעוֹת חֻלִּין וּמָעוֹת מַעֲשֵׂר שֵׁנִי שֶׁנִּתְפַּזְּרוּ מַה שֶׁלִּיקֵּט (viz. הַמְלַקֵּט) לִיקֵּט לְמַעֲשֵׂר שֵׁנִי common money and money of the second tithe which have been scattered together—whatever he picks up, he picks it up for the second tithe, MŠ ii. 5; עוֹבֵד כּוֹכָבִים שֶׁשָּׁלַח עוֹלָתוֹ מִמְּדִינַת הַיָּם וְשָׁלַח עִמָּהּ נְסָכִים קְרֵיבִין (viz. הַנְּסָכִים) מִשֶּׁלּוֹ if a heathen has sent from the country across the sea his burnt-offering, and has (also) sent with it libations,—then they (the libations) are offered of his own; so further: גֵּר שֶׁמֵּת . . . Šeq. vii. 6. With indefinite subject: הַמְּקָרֶה סֻכָּתוֹ בְּשַׁפּוּדִין . . . כְּשֵׁרָה (viz. הַסּוּכָּה) if anyone covers his tabernacle with spits . . . it (the tabernacle) is fit, Suk. i. 8, 9, 11 (implicit object); ii. 2–4; הָאוֹמֵר לִשְׁלוּחוֹ צֵא וּתְרוֹם תּוֹרֵם (הַשָּׁלִיחַ viz.) כְּדַעְתּוֹ שֶׁל בַּעַל הַבַּיִת if anyone says to his messenger: go out and tithe—then he (the messenger) tithes in accordance with the mind of the house-holder (the sender), Ter. iv. 4; מִי שֶׁזִּימֵּן אֶצְלוֹ אוֹרְחִים לֹא יוֹלִיכוּ הָאוֹרְחִים) בְּיָדָם מָנוֹת viz.) if anyone invited to himself guests—then they (the guests) may not carry with them gifts, Be. v. 7, 6; Yeb. x. 4; Ket. xiii. 2.

446. The nom. abs. may consist even of a grammatically complete sentence (i. e. with a finite verb), which is yet dependent upon a following predicate, as is shown by the context: הָיָה רוֹכֵב עַל גַּבֵּי בְהֵמָה וְרָאָה אֶת הַמְּצִיאָה וְאָמַר לַחֲבֵרוֹ תְּנָה לִי נְטָלָהּ (חֲבֵרוֹ viz.) וְאָמַר (if) he rode upon an animal and saw a lost article and said to his neighbour: give it to me—he (the neighbour) took it and said . . ., BM i. 3.

447. Sometimes, the new subject is expressly referred to by a demonstrative, especially with הֲרֵי: הֲרֵי זֶה לֹא הָיְתָה בֵּין הַקְּבָרוֹת

(הַמּוֹצֵא .viz) יִטַּמָּא לָהּ if it was among the graves—lo, he (the finder, if a priest) should not defile himself for it, BM ii. 10 ; כֹּהֶנֶת שֶׁנִּתְעָרֵב וְלָדָהּ בּוֹלַד שִׁפְחָתָהּ הֲרֵי אֵלּוּ אוֹכְלִין בִּתְרוּמָה the wife of a priest, whose child was mixed up with the child of her female slave—lo, these (the two children) eat of *teruma* (priestly tithes), Yᵉb. xi. 5, iii. 4, &c.

2. Agreement between Subject and Predicate.

448. Collective nouns as subject sometimes take the predicate in the sing., sometimes in the plur.: שֶׁיְּהֵא הַבָּקָר עוֹבֵר בְּכֵלָיו that the oxen may pass with their harness, Šebi. i. 5 ; נִטְמָא קָהָל the congregation became unclean, Pᵉs. vii. 6 ; בַּלֶּשֶׁת שֶׁנִּכְנְסָה a troop that has entered, ʿAZ v. 6 ; בָּקִי . . . לֹא הָיָה בֵּית דִּין the court of law was not expert, San. vii. 2 ; but : הוֹרוּ בֵּית דִּין the court of law taught, Ho. i. 1 ; הִתְקִינוּ . . . כְּשֶׁרָאוּ בֵּית דִּין when the court of law saw . . . they ordained . . . , Yo. ii. 2. The two constructions may be found side by side, the sing. preceding the subject : וּנְצָחוּם . . . כְּשֶׁגָּבְרָה מַלְכוּת when the kingdom of the house of Hasmonai prevailed, and conquered them, Šab. 21 b ; מִשְׁפָּחָה אַחַת הָיְתָה בִּירוּשָׁלַיִם שֶׁהָיוּ פְּסִיעוֹתֵיהֶן נַּסּוֹת there was a certain family in Jerusalem whose steps were big, ib. 63 b ; further . . . מַחֲנֶה הַיּוֹצֵאת מוּתָּרִין a troop that goes forth . . . are permitted, ʿEr. 17 a.

449. So with a construct expression as subject ; הָיוּ מְקְצָת הֶעָלִין מְגוּלִּין if a portion of the leaves were uncovered, Kil. i. 9 ; שְׁאָר נְכָסִים יִפְּלוּ the remainder of the property shall fall, Šᵉq. iv. 81 ; קִבְּלוּ רוֹב הַצִּבּוּר the majority of the public have received, ib. v. 2 ; but נִטְמָא מְעוּט הַקָּהָל the minority of the congregation became unclean, Pᵉs. vii. 6 ; אֵין כָּל אָדָם חַיָּבִין no man is guilty, Mak. ii. 7 ; sometimes the texts differ : כָּל אָדָם יַטֶּה וְיִקְרָא every man must incline and read ; כָּל אָדָם קוֹרֵא כְּדַרְכּוֹ reads according to his own way, Bᵉr. ii. 3 edd., but L : קוֹרִין ; יַטּוּ וְיִקְרוּ כְּדַרְכָּן ; so Sifre, Deut. vii. 7 ; San. vi. 2, edd., but L : אוֹמְרִין . . . יְהוּא יְהֵא כָּל אָדָם אוֹמֵר.

450. A compound subject, consisting of a masc. and a fem. noun, takes the predicate in the masc.: הַסֹּלֶת וְהַשֶּׁמֶן מְעַכְּבִין זֶה אֶת זֶה the fine flour and the oil keep back each other, Mᵉn. iii. 5. The masc. is used even with fem. nouns: אֵין אֲכִילָה וְהַקְטָרָה מִצְטָרְפִים eating and burning incense do not combine, Zᵉb. vi. 7 (end); מַחַט אוֹ טַבַּעַת ... נִרְאִין ... יוֹצְאִין a needle or a ring ... are seen but do not protrude, Kel. ix. 1.

451. Sometimes the gender agrees strictly with the grammatical form of the noun, rather than with the sense: בַּלֶּשֶׁת שֶׁנִּכְנְסָה 'AZ v. 6; שְׁתֵּי כִתֵּי עֵדִים מְעִידוֹת two groups of witnesses, Naz. iii. 7; אוּמָּנִיּוֹת שׁוֹקְדוֹת handicrafts labour diligently, t. Bᵉr. vii. 2. Sometimes the gender agrees with the sense, and not with the grammatical form; especially when removed from the noun: כָּל הָעֲיָירוֹת מִתְכַּנְּסוֹת ... וְלָנִים ... נִכְנָסִים all the towns assemble ... and spend the night ... enter ..., Bik. iii. 2; עֲיָירוֹת גְּדוֹלוֹת קוֹרִין big towns read (sc. אַנְשֵׁי), Mᵉg. i. 2; שָׁלֹשׁ אוּמָּנִיּוֹת עוֹשִׂין ... הַחַיָּיטִין ... three handicrafts may work ... tailors ..., Pᵉs. iv. 6; בֵּית הַפַּרְוָוה וּבַקֹּדֶשׁ הָיְתָה the house of Parva, and it was in the holy precincts (sc. לִשְׁכַּת), Yo. iii. 6.

452. When the verb precedes the noun it may, sometimes, be used in an impersonal sense without reference to the gender and number of the following subject: הוּתַּר מִקְצָתוֹ its portion was made permissible, Nᵉd. ix. 6; הִגִּיעַ עֵת the time has reached, Ta. i. 4; הָיָה לָהּ שְׁעַת הַבּשֶׁר it had a time when it was fit, Zᵉb. xi. 2; but Ḥul. iv. 7: יִלְקַח בּוֹ עוֹלוֹת הָיְתָה לָהּ שְׁעַת burnt-offerings shall be bought with it, Šᵉq. vi. 6; נָפַל לְתוֹכוֹ מַשְׁקִין there נָפַל לְתוֹכוֹ מַיִם fell into it water, liquids, &c.; Pa. ix. 1.

3. Sentences expressing an Oath or a Vow.

453. Sentences expressing an oath are introduced by an imprecation followed by אִם, which then assumes a negative force, and by אִם לֹא with an affirmative force, as in BH (Ges.-K.,

§ 149 d). The tense used is the perf. for the past, and the imperf. for the future.

Exx. יֵהָנֶה סַם הַמָּוֶת בְּאַחַד בָּנֶיהָ שֶׁל אוֹתָהּ אִשָּׁה אִם נֶהֱנֵיתִי מִדִּינָרְךָ כְּלוּם *may poison have enjoyment of one of the children of that woman (the speaker's), if I have enjoyed anything of thy dinar,* Giṭ. 35 a = I have not, &c.; ¹אֲקַפֵּחַ אֶת בָּנַי אִם לֹא רָאִיתִי אֶת שִׁמְעוֹן *may I cut down my children if I have not seen Simeon,* j. Yo. i. 1 (end)= I did see, &c. יָבוֹא עָלַי אִם רָאוּ קוֹרוֹת בֵּיתִי שַׂעֲרוֹת רֹאשִׁי *may (some evil) come upon me if the rafters of my house have ever seen the hair of my head,* j. Meg. i. 12 = they have never seen, &c.; יָבוֹא עָלַי אִם נִתְכַּוַּונְתִּי לְכָךְ . . . . *if I intended this,* j. So. iii. 3 = I did not intend this. So even after a prayer for a blessing אִם לֹא still has an affirmative force, though really the opposite is meant by the speaker: אֶרְאֶה בְנֶחָמָה אִם לֹא הָרַגְתִּי עֵד זוֹמֵם *may I behold the consolation (of Israel)! I have slain a false witness* ²; אֶרְאֶה בְנֶחָמָה אִם לֹא שָׁפַכְתָּ דָּם נָקִי *may I behold the consolation! thou hast shed innocent blood,* Mak. 5 b; San. 37 b; j. Mak. vii. 11.

454. So with the formula ³קוֹנָם: קוֹנָם אִם אָכַלְתִּי, אִם שָׁתִיתִי *qonam, I have not eaten, I have not drunk;* . . . . קוֹנָם אִם לֹא רָאִיתִי *q., I have seen . . . ,* Ned. iii. 2; ⁴(קוֹנָם) אִם אֶרְחַץ אִם לֹא אֶרְחַץ אִם אֶתְקַשֵּׁט אִם לֹא אֶתְקַשֵּׁט *q., I will not wash, I will wash; I will not adorn myself, I will adorn myself,* ib. xi. 1. So ק' אִי (אִם =) אַתָּה נֶהֱנֶה לִי *q., thou wilt not benefit of mine,* BQ ix. 10.⁵

¹ This particular oath was peculiar to R. Tarphon. Later generations disapproved of this form of oath, cf. BM 85ᵃ.

² This is probably a euphemism for a curse = לֹא אראה בנחמה; cf. above, בניה של אותה אשה, for בָּנֶי; so איבי דוד 1 Sam. xx. 16; xxv. 22; see Driver's notes, ad loc.

³ The origin and exact meaning of this word are obscure; cf. the Lexicons and Cooke, *N. Sem. Inscriptions,* pp. 33–4. Perhaps it is a popular word for curse.

⁴ קוֹנָם is to be understood; cf. the paraphrase in the Talmud babli, Ned. 79 b.

⁵ L has ק' שֶׁאַתְּ, so also in citation, Ned. 42 a: שֶׁאַתָּה. The emendation of Albrecht, § 15 a, is unnecessary.

455. So with the formula שְׁבוּעָה expressed or understood: מַשְׁבִּיעַ אֲנִי (שְׁבוּעָה) (an oath), I have seen, Šᵉbu. iii. 8; עֲלֵיכֶם אִם לֹא תָבוֹאוּ וּתְעִידוּנִי I adjure you to come and give evidence for me, ib. iv. 5 ff.

456. Often, however, such sentences are introduced by שֶׁ־, preceded by various formulae, and construed regularly (like כִּי in BH, e. g. 1 Sam. xiv. 44).

Exx.: נִשְׁבַּע אֲנִי בְשִׁמְךָ הַגָּדוֹל שֶׁאֵינִי זָז I swear by thy great name: I will not move, Taʻa. iii. 10; נִשְׁבַּע הַקָּדוֹשׁ בָּרוּךְ הוּא שֶׁאֲנִי גוֹאֵל אֶתְכֶם the Holy One, blessed be He, swore I will redeem you, So. 13 a; מַשְׁבִּיעִין אָנוּ עָלֶיךָ . . . שֶׁלֹּא תְשַׁנֶּה דָבָר we adjure thee . . . that thou shalt not change anything, Yo. i. 3; אָמֵן שֶׁלֹּא נִטְמֵאתִי אָמֵן שֶׁלֹּא סָטִיתִי Amen, I have not been defiled; Amen, I have not gone astray, So. ii. 6; אֲקַפַּח אֶת בָּנַי שֶׁזּוֹ הֲלָכָה מְקוּפַּחַת may I cut down my children: this is a mutilated *halaka*, Oh. xvi. 1; Šab. 116a; with לֹא j. Yo. i. 1; הָעֲבוֹדָה שֶׁאֲגַלַּחְךָ לַשָּׁמַיִם by the Service I will shave thee for heaven, Nᵉd. 9 b; but more frequently הָעֲבוֹדָה is used as an exclamation in apposition, and without שֶׁ־: הָעֲבוֹדָה . . . לֹא חִסַּרְתֶּם וְלֹא הוֹתַרְתֶּם you have made it neither less nor more, Bᵉr. 34 b; הָעֲבוֹדָה כָּךְ שְׁמַעְתִּי מֵרַבִּי . . . thus I heard from Rabbi, Yᵉb. 32 b.

457. So also are other formulae used in an asseveration as exclamations: הַמָּעוֹן הַזֶּה לֹא זָזָה יָדָהּ by this habitation (the Temple)! her hand did not move, Kᵉt. ii. 9; בְּרִית הֵן הֵן הַדְּבָרִים שֶׁנֶּאֶמְרוּ לְמשֶׁה בְּסִינַי by the Covenant! these are the very words which were told to Moses on Sinai, Pᵉs. 38 b; נַפָּהּ שֶׁל רוֹמִי אֵינִי מַנִּיחֲתָךְ by the Capitol of Rome! I will not leave thee, Mᵉn. 41 a; cf. § 305 חַיֶּיךָ וְחַיֵּי רֹאשְׁךָ לֹא שָׁעָה זוֹ בִלְבַד by thy life and by the life of thy head! not this hour alone . . . Bᵉr. 3 a.

458. Likewise, שְׁבוּעָה may be followed by שֶׁ־ with the regular construction: שְׁבוּעָה שֶׁאוֹכַל וְשֶׁלֹּא אוֹכַל וְשֶׁאָכַלְתִּי וְשֶׁלֹּא אָכַלְתִּי an oath. I will eat, I will not eat; I have eaten, I have not eaten, Šᵉbu.

iii. 1 ff.; but also without ‑שֶׁ: שְׁבוּעָה לֹא אוֹכַל לָךְ, beside שְׁבוּעָה
שֶׁאוֹכַל לָךְ Nᵉd. ii. 2.   An affirmative after שְׁבוּעָה שֶׁ‑ can, however,
also be intended to have a negative force: שֶׁאוֹכַל לָךְ /ש an oath,
I will *not* eat of thine, ib. Cf. the explanation of Abbaye, Nᵉd. 16 a;
Šᵉbu. 19 b, f.   So ... שֶׁאֲנִי יָשֵׁן שֶׁאֲנִי מְדַבֵּר /ש ... that I will not
sleep, that I will not speak, ib. 1, in L.   In edd. שֶׁאֵינִי is probably
a correction, cf. the comment of R. Nissim on this passage,
Nᵉd. 14 b.

So with the formula שֶׁ קָרְבָּן, an affirmative is equivalent to
a negative: קָרְבָּן שֶׁאוֹכַל לָךְ what I will eat of thine be *qorban* =
I will not eat ..., Nᵉd. i. 4.

459. In expressing a vow, קוֹנָם, followed by an affirmative
is equivalent to a negative.   It is construed with a participial verb
with the meaning of a future tense, and if the subject is a pronoun,
it takes the introductory particle ‑שֶׁ: קוֹנָם שֶׁאֲנִי יָשֵׁן שֶׁאֲנִי מְדַבֵּר שֶׁאֲנִי
מְהַלֵּךְ *qonam*, I will not sleep, speak, walk, Nᵉd. ii. 1; [1] קוֹנָם שֶׁאַתָּה
נֶהֱנֶה לִי *q.*, thou wilt not benefit of me, ib. viii. 7.   The object is
placed first, as usual in emphatic speech: קוֹנָם סוּכָּה שֶׁאֲנִי עוֹשֶׂה
לוּלָב שֶׁאֲנִי נוֹטֵל *q.*, I will not make a tabernacle; I will not take
a *lulab*, ii. 2; קוֹנָם יַיִן זֶה שֶׁאֲנִי טוֹעֵם *q.*, this wine that I will not
taste, iv. 10; קוֹנָם לְבֵיתְךָ שֶׁאֲנִי נִכְנָס שָׂדְךָ שֶׁאֲנִי לוֹקֵחַ *q.*, that I will
not enter thy house; that I will not buy thy field, v. 3.   But
without ‑שֶׁ when the subject is a noun: קוֹנָם פִּי מְדַבֵּר עִמָּךְ יָדִי
עוֹשֶׂה עִמָּךְ *q.*, that my mouth will not speak with thee, that my hand
will not work with thee, i. 4; קוֹנָם אִשְׁתִּי וּבָנַי נֶהֱנִים לִי *q.*, that my
wife and children will not benefit of me, iii. 5.

4. Interrogative Sentences.

460. A question is often expressed in MH, as in BH (Ges.-K.,
§ 150 a), merely by the emphasis of the voice, and without any

---

[1] The reading in edd. שֶׁאֵינִי is an erroneous correction, as shown by the
citation from viii. 7. Cf. also H. Laible, שׁאני *oder* שׁאיני, *MGWJ*. vol. lx,
pp. 29-40.

special introductory particle: עַד שֶׁבְּחֶבְרוֹן as far as those in
Hebron? Yo. iii. 1; הִתְרֵיתֶם בּוֹ did you warn him? San. v. 1;
הָיִיתָ מַחֲזִיר לוֹ would'st thou have returned to him? Ber. 32 b;
so with copulative וְ: וְלֹא אֶבְכֶּה shall I not weep? ib. 28 b.
Especially in long argumentative questions: . . . אִם הֶעֱלוּ חוּלִּים
. . . תַּעֲלֶה תְרוּמָה if common things raised . . . should *teruma*
raise . . .? Ter. v. 4; . . . אִם אָמַרְתָּ בַּפֶּסַח . . . תֹּאמַר בִּזְבָחִים if thou
didst say it in case of the paschal offering . . . wilt thou say . . .?
Pes. vi. 5.

461. More frequently the interrogative sentence is introduced
by a particle. The BH interrogative הֲ is rare in MH, e.g.
הֲתַחֲמִיר זוֹ מִן הַגֶּפֶן wilt thou make this more grave than the vine?
Kil. iii. 7; הֲכָזֶה רָאִיתָ did you see like this? RH ii. 8. It is,
however, common with לֹא, which is further strengthened by the
copulative וְ used in an interrogative force (cf. last §; Ges.-K.,
§ 150 a): וַהֲלֹא יֵשׁ שֶׁאֵינָן מוֹסְקִין but are not there some who do not
gather their olives . . .? Pea viii. 1; וַהֲלֹא מִסֵּפֶר כְּתוּבָּתָהּ נִלְמוֹד
but do we not learn from the text of her marriage settlement?
Yeb. xvi. 3; וַהֲלֹא ר׳ יְהוֹשׁוּעַ אָמַר but did not R. Joshua say?
Ber. 27 b. But frequently the interrogative particle is omitted:
לֹא יַעֲלֶה וְיִטְּלֶנָּה לֹא לִמַּדְתָּנוּ didst thou not teach us? Ber. ii. 5;
should he not go up and take it? Ber. 53 b; לֹא שָׂדֶה הִיא זוֹ is not
this a field? 'Er. 53 b.

462. The particle וְכִי, which is rare in BH as an interrogative
(Isa. xxxvi. 19; Job xxxix. 27) is very common in MH as introducing
a lively question: וְכִי יָדָיו שֶׁל מֹשֶׁה עוֹשׂוֹת מִלְחָמָה but was it the hands
of Moses that made war? RH iii. 8; וְכִי מִפְּנֵי שֶׁהִיא אַחֲרוֹנָה נִשְׂכֶּרֶת
but should she gain because she is last? Ket. x. 5; וְכִי כָל הָעֵצִים
כְּשֵׁרִים but are all woods fit . . .? Ta. ii. 3. Frequently וְכִי stands
even before another interrogative particle to give it greater
emphasis: וְכִי הֵיאַךְ הֶעָנִי הַזֶּה מַחֲלִיף but how can this poor man
exchange? Pea v. 2; וְכִי מִפְּנֵי מָה אֵין מְמִירִים but wherefore may

they not exchange . . . ? T^{em}. i. 1 ; וְכִי בְּאֵיזוֹ שָׁעָה הַמְמוּנֶּה בָא but at what hour does the overseer come ? Tam. i. 2.

463. The interrogative adverb מָה is often used as an introductory particle in long argumentative questions (קַל וָחוֹמֶר) : מָה אִם הַפֶּסַח . . . חַיָּב הַזְּבָחִים . . . אֵינוֹ דִין שֶׁיְּהֵא חַיָּב what ! if the Passover offering . . . is it not justice that he should be liable . . . ? Pes. vi. 5 ; מָה אִם עֶצֶם כִּשְׂעוֹרָה . . . אֵינוֹ דִין שֶׁיְּהֵא נָזִיר מְגַלֵּחַ what ! if a bone like a barley . . ., is it not justice that the Nazirite should shave . . . ? Naz. vii. 4 ; וּמָה אִילּוּ טָעָה . . . שֶׁמָּא עָשָׂה כְלוּם and what ! if he had erred . . . has he done anything ? ib. v. 3, &c.

464. In later MH (not in the Mishna), a question can also be introduced by כְּלוּם (§ 437) : כְּלוּם שָׁתִינוּ have we drunk . . . ? כְּלוּם הִכִּירְךָ ר' גַּמְלִיאֵל מֵעוֹלָם has Rabban Gamaliel ever known thee ? 'Er. 64 b ; כְּלוּם יֵשׁ אָדָם שֶׁיּוֹדֵעַ is there anyone who controverts . . . ? B^{er}. 27 b ; כְּלוּם חָסֵר לְבֵית הַמֶּלֶךְ is anything needed for the king's house ? כְּלוּם יֵשׁ סְעוּדָה בְּלֹא טוֹרַח is there a feast without effort ? Šab. 153 a ; 89 a ; P^{es}. 66 a ; 118 b ; B^{er}. 10 a ; 'Ar. 15 a, &c.

Further, שֶׁמָּא ('perhaps') : שֶׁמָּא אֵינוֹ צָרִיךְ לוֹמַר is it unnecessary to say ? j. Giṭ. i. 1 ; שֶׁמָּא מְגוֹרֶשֶׁת הִיא is she perhaps divorced ? ib. viii. 5 ; שֶׁמָּא כְלוּם הוּא is it anything ? j. So. i. 1.

465. An indirect question is construed just like a direct question : הַחַזָּן רוֹאֶה הֵיכָן הַתִּינוֹקוֹת קוֹרִין the beadle sees where the children read, Šab. i. 3 ; . . . בּוֹאוּ וְהָפִיסוּ מִי מַעֲלֶה come and cast lots who should bring up . . ., Tam. v. 2 ; שָׁמִין אוֹתָהּ כַּמָּה הִיא רְאוּיָה לַעֲשׂוֹת they value it how much is it capable of producing, BM ix. 3

466. In a disjunctive question, the first is formed like an ordinary question, the second is introduced by אוֹ : וְכִי מֵרוֹב הָעֳמָרִים יֻפִּי כֹחוֹ שֶׁל בַּעַל הַבַּיִת אוֹ הוּרַע כֹּחוֹ is the power of the owner improved because of the multitude of the sheaves, or is it worsened ? Pea vi. 6 ; הֲכָזֶה רָאִיתָ אוֹ כָזֶה hast thou seen like this, or like this? RH ii. 8 (L has הַכְוָה after אוֹ); תְּפִלַּת עַרְבִית רְשׁוּת אוֹ חוֹבָה is evening prayer optional, or obligatory? Bᵉr. 27 b.

An indirect disjunctive question is introduced by אִם in both clauses: אֵינִי יוֹדֵעַ אִם הֶחֱזַרְתִּי לָךְ אִם (L) וְאִם) לֹא הֶחֱזַרְתִּי לָךְ I do not know whether I have restored to thee, or not, BQ x. 7; v. 1 וְאֵין יָדוּעַ אִם בֶּן ט׳ לָרִאשׁוֹן אִם (L) וְאִם) בֶּן ז׳ לָאַחֲרוֹן (אִם ... וְאִם : L) it is not known whether it is a child of nine months of the first, or of seven months of the last, Yᵉb. xi. 6; נִיכַּר אִם תַּלְמִיד חָכָם הוּא אִם לָאו it is recognized whether he is a scholar, or not, Bᵉr. 50 a; Pᵉs. 61 a; 9 b. Rarely by אוֹ ... אִם : אֵינוּ יָדוּעַ אִם בְּלוּלוֹת הֵן אוֹ לְאַיִן נָפְלָה it is not known whether they are mixed, or where it fell, Tᵉr. iv. 11.

5. Desiderative Sentences.

467. A wish may be expressed by the simple imperfect (§ 319): יַנִּיחַ לָנוּ ר׳ט let R. Tarphon leave us alone, BM iv. 3; especially in prayers: וְנִהְיֶה כֻּלָּנוּ יוֹדְעֵי תוֹרָתֶךָ let us all be skilled in thy law, Bᵉr. 11 b; הַמָּקוֹם יְמַלֵּא חֶסְרוֹנָךְ may the Omnipresent make good thy loss, ib. 16 b; בַּעַל הַגְּמוּל יְשַׁלֵּם לָכֶם may the Lord of requital pay you, Kᵉt. 8 b.

468. More frequently the imperf. is preceded by the formula: יְהִי רָצוֹן שֶׁתֵּלֵד יְהִי רָצוֹן שֶׁ- may it be the (divine) will that . . . ; יְהִי רָצוֹן שֶׁלֹּא יְהוּ אֵלּוּ בְתוֹךְ בֵּיתִי אִשְׁתִּי זָכָר may my wife bear a male; may these not be in my house, Bᵉr. ix. 3; or with the full formula: יְהִי רָצוֹן מִלְּפָנֶיךָ ה׳ אֱלֹהֵינוּ ... שֶׁ- Ab. v. 20; Bᵉr. 16 b; 17 a, &c.; Singer, pp. 7, 14, &c.

469. A wish can also be expressed by מִי with the imperf., as in BH (Ges.-K., § 151 a, b): מִי יְגַלֶּה עָפָר מֵעֵינֶיךָ oh, that the dust may be removed from thine eyes, So. v. 2; מִי יִתֶּן לִי תֵּל זֶה; מִי יִתֶּן לִי חָרִיץ זֶה oh, that one would give me this heap, this trench, Mᵉg. 14 a. It may be noted that מִי יִתֶּן is used in its literal

sense. It is never found in MH in the derived BH sense:
oh, would! (Ges.-K., § 151 b).

470. In later Aggadic diction a wish is also expressed by הַלְוַאי
(= BH לֹא, § 304) : הַלְוַאי אוֹתִי עָזְבוּ וְאֶת תּוֹרָתִי שָׁמָרוּ would, they had
forsaken Me, and kept My Torah, j. Ḥag. i ; הַלְוַאי יְהֵא חֶלְקִי בָּאָרֶץ
הַזֹּאת oh, would that my portion were in this land, Gen. R. 39 ;
הַלְוַאי תְּהֵא מַעֲלַת חֵן לְפָנַי oh, would that she were graceful before me,
ib. 89. הַלְוַאי also stands at the end of the sentence as an
exclamation : טוֹל אוֹתָהּ בְּחִנָּם וְהַלְוַאי take it for nothing, oh do!
Mᵉg. 14 a.

6. Negative Sentences.

471. The uses of the negative adverbs אַל, אֵין, לֹא follow the
same rules as in BH. לֹא is used to negative verbal clauses, while
אֵין is used to negative noun clauses. Sometimes, however, participles are negatived by לֹא ; cf. above, §§ 339–40. אַל is only used
with the imperfect to express a negative wish, an exhortation, or
a mild prohibition. With ordinary prohibitions, as well as in
negative statements with the perfect and imperfect, לֹא is used :
אַל תִּהְיוּ כַעֲבָדִים be not like servants, Ab. i. 3 ; אַל תַּעַשׂ עַצְמָךְ make
not thyself, ib. 8 ; לֹא יָקֵל אָדָם אֶת רֹאשׁוֹ one must not be light-
headed (i.e. guilty of levity), Bᵉr. ix. 5.

472. The form בַּל is found for לֹא in citations of Biblical
prohibitions : הוּא עוֹבֵר עַל בַּל תִּגְרַע he transgresses (the command)
'thou shalt not diminish'; . . . הוּא עוֹבֵר עַל בַּל תּוֹסִיף 'thou shalt
not add' (Deut. xiii. 1) ; לֹא נֶאֱמַר בַּל תּוֹסִיף לֹא נֶאֱמַר בַּל תִּגְרַע 'thou
shalt not add', 'thou shalt not diminish' was not said, Zᵉb.
viii. 10 ; כָּל שֶׁהוּא בְּבַל תָּשׁוּב all that is in (the category of) 'thou
shalt not return' (Deut. xxiv. 19), Pea vi. 4 (L has בל for בבל);
שְׁמוּזְהָרִים עָלָיו בְּבַל יֵרָאֶה וּבְבַל יִמָּצֵא about which one is prohibited :
'it shall not be seen', and 'it shall not be found' (Exod. xiii. 7 ;
xii. 19); Pᵉs. iii. 3 (L has וּבַל . . . בַּל); אָסוּר בְּבַל יֵרָאֶה וּבְבַל יִמָּצֵא

prohibited by (the command) 'thou . . .', ib. ix. 3. Contrast:
הוּא בְּלֹא יָבוֹא he is in (the category of) 'he shall not come'),
(Deut. xxiii. 3); Yeb. iv. 13; הֲרֵי זֶה בְּלֹא יַחֵל דְּבָרוֹ lo, this one is
in (the category of) 'he shall not profane his word' (Num.
xxx. 3); Ned. ii. 1 (L has בל for בלא). Perhaps בל, בבל is not
a genuine grammatical form, but merely a scribal contraction for
בל׳ = בלא .

473. The negative is sometimes repeated to add emphasis:
אֵין לָהֶם לֹא כָּךְ וְלֹא כָּךְ they have not, either so or so, Šab. 26 a;
לֹא עָשָׂה וְלֹא כְלוּם he has done nothing at all, Pes. 89 b; Ned. 7 b.
Emphasis is also expressed by כָּל עִיקָּר at the end of the clause;
אֵינוֹ מְעָרֵב כָּל עִיקָּר he does not make an 'erub at all, 'Er. iii. 6;
אֵין מַשְׁגִּיחִין . . . כָּל עִיקָּר one must not observe . . . at all, Be. iii. 6.

474. In a series of parallel verbs, the negative is sometimes
expressed only with the first verb, but its force is extended also
to the following verbs, as in BH (cf. Ges.-K., § 152 z): לֹא יָקוֹב
אָדָם . . . וִימַלְאֶנָּה . . . וְיִתְּנֶנָּה one must not perforate . . . and fill it
. . . and place it . . ., Šab. ii. 4; לֹא יִקְשׁוֹר . . . וְיִמְשׁוֹךְ one must not
bind . . . and draw, ib. v. 3; 'Er. x. 5, 6, 9; אֵין מַשְׁקִין וְשׁוֹחֲטִין one
may not give to drink nor slay . . ., Be. v. 7.

475. שֶׁמָּא is used, like פֶּן in BH, to introduce a clause after
a verb of fear or caution, expressed or implied, and is then
equivalent to a negative: הָיָה יָרֵא שֶׁמָּא תִתְעַבֵּר he was afraid, lest it
be intercalated (= שֶׁלֹּא), 'Er. iii. 7; הֱוֵי זָהִיר . . . שֶׁמָּא . . . יִלְמְדוּ לְשַׁקֵּר
be careful . . . that they should not learn . . . to lie, Ab. i. 9, 11;
הִזָּהֲרוּ שֶׁמָּא תִגְּעוּ take care that you touch not, Ḥag. iii. 8 (L;
edd. שֶׁלֹּא); שֶׁמָּא יְקַלְקְלוּ (for fear) lest they spoil, Ḥul. i. 1;
שֶׁמָּא יַקְדִּים קָנֶה לְוֵשֶׁט (for fear) lest the windpipe come before the
gullet, Ta'a. 5 b.

476. Note.—In colloquial speech, viz. in vows, לֹא was sometimes joined with the following noun almost like a preposition:
לֹא חוּלִּין = לְחוּלִּין Ned. i. 3; לֹא קָרְבָּן = לְקָרְבָּן ib. 4 (L has

לֹא קָרְבָּן, לֹא חוּלִּין; but cf. the discussion in Nᵉd. 11 a, b; 13 b, and
the comment of R. Nissim on Nᵉd. i. 3. In ii. 1, L also has
(לֹא חוּלִּין = לְחוּלִּין).

7. Relative Clauses.

477. The construction of relative clauses has already been
described in the treatment of שֶׁ־ (§ 420 f.). Here we may add that
sometimes a relative clause stands in apposition to the noun it
qualifies, and without שֶׁ־: לֹא זוֹ הִיא דֶרֶךְ מוֹצִיאַתּוּ מִידֵי עֲבֵרָה this
is not the way that brings him out of the power of a transgression,
Yᵉb. xv. 6, 7; יֵשׁ בּוֹ דְרָכִים שָׁוֶה לְחַיָּה it has ways in which it is like
a (wild) animal, Bik. ii. 8; אֵין לוֹ מִי יַתִּירֶנּוּ it has none that will
make it permissible, Mᵉn. iv. 3 (cf. § 422). Perhaps here belong
also cases with the demonstrative before the noun when followed
by a verb: שֶׁהֵעִיד = זוֹ עֵדוּת הֵעִיד הָעִיר; שֶׁדָּרַשׁ = זֶה מִדְרָשׁ דָּרַשׁ, cf.
above, § 411.

8. Circumstantial Clauses.

478. The circumstances attending an action, or the subject
or object of an action, are usually expressed by a dependent
clause. Such a clause may be a simple relative clause, or, more
frequently, a relative or other clause under the government of
a preposition. Exx.: יוֹשְׁבִים שֶׁלֹּא מְסוּמָּכִים sitting without being
supported, Kel. ii. 2; אֵין טוֹמְנִים ... בָּעֲשָׂבִים בִּזְכַן שֶׁהֵם לַחִים one
may not hide ... in grass when it is moist, Šᵃb. iv. 1; נוֹלַד כְּשֶׁהוּא
מָהוּל he was born circumcised, Šab. 135 a; נִכְנַס ר"ט בְּלֹא מִתְכַּוֵּן
R. Tarphon entered without intention, 'Er. iv. 4; חוֹלֵץ תְּפִלִּין בְּרָחוֹק
ד' אַמּוֹת he removes the *tephillin* at a distance of four cubits,
Bᵉr. 23 a.

Sometimes a participle or adjective in apposition will express
a circumstance: קוֹצָה חַלָּתָהּ עֲרוּמָה; קוֹרֵא עוֹמֵד, cf. § 357.

479. More frequently, however, the circumstantial clause is

co-ordinated with the principal clause either with the copulative וְ,
or without.

(i) Without the copula: שְׁאוֹר ... שֶׁנָּפְלוּ ... לֹא בָזֶה כְּדֵי לְחַמֵּץ
leaven ... that fell ... there not being sufficient to leaven,
Or. ii. 11, 14, 15; הָיָה רָחוֹק ... יֵשׁ אֵמוּת אוֹמְרִים לוֹ when he was
10 cubits distant ... they would say to him, San. vi. 3; יָלְדָה עוֹדָהּ
שִׁפְחָה ... בָּא לוֹ she gave birth while still a slave, viii. 1; הַסְּגָן ... בָּא לוֹ
בְּיָמִינוֹ he came ... the deputy at his right, Yo. iii. 9; so Šab. i. 1;
Pes. viii. 1, &c.

(ii) With copula: בָּא לוֹ אֵצֶל פָּרוֹ וּפָרוֹ הָיָה עוֹמֵד he came to his
bullock, the bullock standing, Yo. iii. 8; בֵּית הַפַּרְוֹוה וּבַקֹּדֶשׁ הָיְתָה
ib. 6; מְמָאֶנֶת וְהִיא קְטַנָּה she can repudiate while a minor, Yeb.
xiii. 1; נָפְלָה עֲלֵיהֶם מַפּוֹלֶת וְהֵם מְגוּלִים earth fell upon them while
(the leaves) were bare, Ma'a. v. 2; מְכַסֶּה וְעוֹדָהּ בְּבֵית אָבִיהָ he covers
her while she is still in her father's house, Ket. vi. 5; vii. 8;
Nid. x. 1; נוֹטֵל אָדָם אֶת בְּנוֹ וְהָאֶבֶן בְּיָדוֹ one may carry his son with
a stone in his (the son's) hand, Šab. xxi. 1; חָלָב שֶׁחֲלָבוֹ גוֹי וְאֵין
יִשְׂרָאֵל רוֹאֵהוּ milk which a heathen has milked without an Israelite
watching him, 'AZ ii. 9, 10.

480. For the sake of emphasis, a circumstantial clause can
precede its principal clause: עוֹדֵהוּ הַסַּל עַל כְּתֵפוֹ קוֹרֵא he reads while
the basket is still on his shoulder, Bik. iii. 6; מַטָּה עַל צִדָּהּ וְהִיא
נוֹפֶלֶת it falls off as he tilts it on its side, Šab. xxi. 2; iv. 2;
הוּא נוֹטֵל אֶת הַגְּלָלִים וְהַחֲרָסִים נוֹפְלִים the potsherds fall, when he takes
away the dung, Kel. iii. 4. Cf. in BH, Ges.-K., §§ 116 v, 142 e;
Driver, *Tenses*, § 166 ff.

9. Causal Clauses.

481. A clause giving the reason of a preceding or following
sentence can be introduced by a variety of conjunctions.

By the fossilized verb הוֹאִיל, followed by the copula (§ 302, note):
הוֹאִיל וְנִרְאָה כְתַבְנִית הַכְּרָמִים הֲרֵי זֶה כֶּרֶם because it looks like the

shape of a vineyard, it is a vineyard, Kil. v. 1; הוֹאִיל וְלֹא הָיְתָה כַּוָּנָתוֹ לְכָךְ since his intention was not for this, 'Er. iv. 4.

482. By שֶׁ, שֶׁאֵין, שֶׁלֹּא: עַל הַיַּין הוּא אוֹמֵר for on wine he says, Ber. vi. 1; שֶׁלֹּא נֶחְשְׁדוּ because they are not suspected, Šebi. ix. 1; שֶׁאֵינוֹ יָכוֹל לוֹמַר for he cannot say, Bik. i. 4; לֹא שֶׁהָיוּ צְרִיכִים לָהֶם not because they needed them, RH ii. 6.

By שֶׁ combined with other conjunctions: מִפְּנֵי שֶׁהוּא מְכַבֶּה because he extinguishes, Šab. iii. 6; מִפְּנֵי שֶׁהֵן לִירוֹקָה because they are for jaundice, ib. xiv. 3; מִפְּנֵי שֶׁלֹּא שָׁווּ because they are not equal, ib. vii. 4. Before a noun מִפְּנֵי stands as regens without שֶׁ: מִפְּנֵי בִּטּוּל בֵּית הַמִּדְרָשׁ because of the neglect of the house of study, ib. xvi. 1; מִפְּנֵי הַכָּתוּב בַּתּוֹרָה because of what is written in the Torah, Bik. i. 3.

לְפִי שֶׁ: לְפִי שֶׁאֵינוֹ מִן הַמּוּכָן because it is not prepared, Šab. iii. 6; לְפִי שֶׁאֵינוֹ מַאֲכַל בְּרִיאִים because it is not the food of healthy persons, ib. xiv. 3.

מֵאַחַר שֶׁ: מֵאַחַר שֶׁשְּׁנֵיהֶם יְכוֹלִים because both are able, BM x. 6; מֵאַחַר שֶׁהֵעַדְתָּ לָנוּ since thou hast testified to us, Yeb. vii. 3.

בִּשְׁבִיל שֶׁ: בִּשְׁבִיל שֶׁאֲנִי זָכָר הִפְסַדְתִּי because I am a male should I lose! BB ix. 1; בִּשְׁבִיל שֶׁבְּנָעֲנִי זֶה הֶרְאָה בְּאֶצְבָּעוֹ because this Canaanite has shown with his finger, So. 46 a.

עַל שֶׁ: עַל שֶׁהָרַג אֶת הַנֶּפֶשׁ because he slew a person, 'Ed. vi. 1.

עַל שֵׁם שֶׁ: עַל שֵׁם שֶׁפָּסַח הקב״ה because the Holy One, blessed be He, passed over, Pes. x. 5; עַל שֵׁם שֶׁמֵּרְרוּ; עַל שֵׁם שֶׁנִּגְאֲלוּ because they were redeemed, they embittered, ib.

מִשּׁוּם שֶׁ: מִשּׁוּם שֶׁנֶּאֱמַר because it is said, Bik. i. 2.

10. Conditional Sentences.

483. The construction of conditional sentences in MH follows in the main the principles of similar sentences in BH (Ges.-K., § 159).

The great variety of these sentences may be classified under two heads: those without an introductory particle, and those with an introductory particle.

484. (i) Without an introductory particle.

The relation between the protasis and the apodosis can be expressed by mere juxtaposition. This happens only when the condition is conceived as already fulfilled. The verb in the protasis is always the perfect; in the apodosis it is usually a participle, but sometimes a perfect. But when a command or prohibition is implied, the apodosis takes the imperfect (cf. above, § 310).

Exx.: נִמְצָא הַגַּנָּב מְשַׁלֵּם תַּשְׁלוּמֵי כֶפֶל, טָבַח וּמָכַר מְשַׁלֵּם ד' וה' if the thief has been found, he pays a double payment; if he slew it, or sold it, he pays four- or five-fold, BM iii. 1; נִגְמַר הַדִּין מוֹצִיאִין אוֹתוֹ when the case is finished, they lead him forth, San. vi. 1; קָרָא וְלֹא דִקְדֵּק בְּאוֹתִיּוֹתֶיהָ ... יָצָא if he read, but was not careful in (the enunciation of) its letters ... he has discharged his duty, Ber. ii. 3; קָרָא וְטָעָה יַחֲזוֹר if he read and made a mistake, he must return ..., ib.; נִזְכַּר שֶׁהוּא בַעַל קְרִי לֹא יַפְסִיק if he recollected that he had an issue, he should not stop, ib. iii. 5; לֹא כִיסָּהוּ מִבְּעוֹד יוֹם לֹא יְכַסֶּנּוּ מִשֶּׁתֶּחְשַׁךְ if he did not cover it while it was day, he must not cover it after it has become dark, Šab. iv. 2.

Here may be mentioned the sentences with an indefinite subject, such as a determinate participle, or מִי שֶׁ־, especially with Nominative Absolute, which are equivalent to a conditional sentence in English; cf. §§ 436, 442.

485. (ii) With an introductory particle.

אִם. אִם introduces a condition that has already been fulfilled in the past or that is capable of fulfilment in the present or future. In the first case, the protasis always takes the perfect, since the condition has already been fulfilled. The apodosis takes the perfect, if its act lies in the past; the participle, if the act lies

in the present or the future, and the imperfect, if a command
is implied.

Exx.: אִם כִּוֵּן לִבּוֹ יָצָא if he directed his attention, he has discharged his duty, Bᵉʳ. ii. 1 ; אִם נִתְרַפֵּא נִתְרַפֵּא if he was healed, he
was healed (then it does not matter), Šab. xxii. 6 ; אִם מֵיאֲנָה מֵיאָנָה
if she has repudiated (her marriage), then it is a repudiation,
Yᵉb. xiii. 7 ; אִם בָּא לְהוֹסִיף מוֹסִיף if he has come to add, he may
add, Šab. 51 a ; אִם לֹא עָלָה עַמּוּד הַשַּׁחַר חַיָּיבִין אַתֶּם if dawn has not
risen, you are bound to . . . Bᵉʳ. i. 1 ; with the apodosis first:
חָתָן פָּטוּר . . . אִם לֹא עָשָׂה מַעֲשֶׂה a bridegroom is absolved . . . if he
has not performed the act, ib. ii. 5 ; אִם לֹא הֵבִיא כְּלִי מֵעֶרֶב שַׁבָּת
מְבִיאוֹ בַּשַּׁבָּת if he has not brought the instrument on the eve of the
Sabbath, he may bring it on the Sabbath, Šab. xix. 1 ; אִם מֵת
יַנִּיחוּהוּ if dead, they must leave him, Yo. viii. 7 ; אִם רָאִיתָ תַּלְמִיד
. . . אַל תְּהַרְהֵר . . . חָכָם שֶׁעָבַר עֲבֵרָה if thou hast seen a scholar
commit a transgression . . . do not think . . . , Bᵉʳ. 19 a.

486. When the condition has not been fulfilled, but is capable
of fulfilment in the present or the future, the protasis takes the
participle, or, less frequently, an imperfect, or even a perfect in
the sense of a *futurum exactum* (cf. § 313).   The apodosis takes
a participle, or an imperfect when a command is implied, or even
an imperative.

Exx.: אִם רָצָה לִקְרוֹת קוֹרֵא if he wishes to read . . . , he may
read, Bᵉʳ. ii. 8 ; אִם יְכוֹלִין לְהַתְחִיל . . . יַתְחִילוּ if they are able to
begin . . . let them begin, ib. iii. 2 ; אִם אֵינוֹ יָכוֹל לֵירֵד יַחֲזִיר אֶת פָּנָיו
if he cannot go down, then he should turn his face, ib. iv. 5 ;
אִם תַּקְנִיטֵנִי גּוֹזְרַנִי if thou wilt provoke me, I shall decree . . . ,
Šab. 17 a ; אִם אֶחַרְתִּי צְאוּ וְשַׁחֲטוּ עָלַי if I shall have been late, go
forth and slay for me, Pᵉs. ix. 9.

487. Both protasis and apodosis can consist of a noun clause,
as in some of the examples above ; further : אִם תָּרְמוּ אֵין תְּרוּמָתָם
תְּרוּמָה if they did tithe, it is not *teruma*, Tᵉr. i. 1 ; אִם אֵין רְצוֹנוֹ

בַּעֲבוֹדָה זָרָה מִפְּנֵי מָה אֵינוֹ מְבַטְּלָהּ if his wish is against idolatry, why does he not abolish it, 'AZ iv. 7.

488. The subject of the apodosis is sometimes resumed by הֲרֵי with the demonstrative (cf. § 443): אִם יֵשׁ לָהֶם עָלָיו מְזוֹנוֹת הֲרֵי אֵלּוּ לֹא יֹאכֵלוּ if they have (to receive) from him food, lo, these shall not eat, Ma'a. iii. 1; וְאִם מִתְחַשֵּׁב הוּא הֲרֵי זֶה לֹא יִרְחוֹץ if he claims importance, lo, this one shall not wash, Šebi. viii. 11.

489. An alternative condition in the negative is expressed by וְאִם לָאו but if not, without the repetition of the verb: אִם כֵּיוָן לִבּוֹ[1] אִם יְכוֹלִין לְהַתְחִיל . . . וְאִם לָאו לֹא יַתְחִילוּ Ber. ii. 1; יָצָא וְאִם לָאו לֹא יָצָא ib. iii. 2; אִם שְׁגוּרָה תְפִלָּתִי בְּפִי . . . וְאִם לָאו יוֹדֵעַ אֲנִי if my prayer is fluent in my mouth . . . but if not, I know . . . , ib. v. 5.

490. אִילּוּ, אִילּוּ לֹא, if the condition is represented as not fulfilled. The protasis takes the perfect, the apodosis takes the perfect if the consequence lies in the past, and the imperfect, if the consequence lies in the future: אִילּוּ הָיִיתִי יוֹדֵעַ . . . לֹא הָיִיתִי נוֹדֵר if I had known . . . I would not have vowed, Ned. ix. 2, 4, 5; אִילּוּ הָיִיתָ עוֹמֵד . . . הָיִיתָ מַחֲזִיר לוֹ if thou hast been standing . . . wouldst thou have returned . . . ? Ber. 32 b; אִילּוּ לֹא הָיְתָה שְׂרֵפָה חֲמוּרָה לֹא נִתְּנָה if burning had not been heavier, it would not have been given . . . , San. ix. 3; אִילּוּ אֲנִי פָּסַקְתִּי לְעַצְמִי אֲשֵׁב עַד שֶׁיַּלְבִּין רֹאשִׁי if I had fixed it for myself, then I would sit till my head has become white, Ket. xiii. 5.

491. אִילּוּלֵי; אִלְמָלֵא, אִלְמָלֵא לֹא (or אִלְמָלֵי), אִלְמָלֵא in Palestinian texts (cf. § 302). Like אִילּוּ, these conjunctions introduce a condition that has not been fulfilled. The verb is in the perfect, both in the protasis and apodosis: אִלְמָלֵא הִטִּיחַ בֶּן זַכַּאי אֶת רֹאשׁוֹ . . . לֹא הָיוּ מַשְׁגִּיחִין בּוֹ if the son of Zakkai had shot his head . . . , they would have taken no notice of him, Ber. 34 b; אִלְמָלֵא לֹא נִתְּנָה תּוֹרָה הָיִינוּ לְמֵדִין צְנִיעוּת if the Torah had not been given, we would have learnt

---

[1] Cf. BH וְאִם לֹא Gen. xxiv. 39; 1 Sam. ii. 16; וְאִם אַיִן Gen. xxx. 1; Exod. xxxii. 32.

chastity, &c., ʿEr. 100 b ; אִלְמָלֵא כָּעַסְתִּי לֹא נִשְׁתַּיֵּיר if I had been
angry, there would not have remained . . . , Ber. 19 a ; אִלְמָלֵא לֹא
דַּיֵּינוּ . . . עָלֵינוּ אֶלָּא לֶאֱכוֹל if we had come up only to eat . . . it
would have been sufficient for us, Pes. 8 b. When introducing a
noun clause, אִלְמָלֵא (or אִלְמָלֵי) has the sense of ' if not ' : אִלְמָלֵא
אֵילוּלֵי L) מוֹרָאָהּ אִישׁ אֶת רֵעֵהוּ חַיִּים בְּלָעוֹ) if not the fear of it, they
would have swallowed each other alive, Ab. ii. 2 ; אִלְמָלֵא אוֹהֲבִי זֶה
הֲרַגְתִּיךָ . . . if not this my friend . . . I would have killed thee,
Ber. 32 a ; 58 b ; אִלְמָלֵא חוֹנִי אַתָּה גּוֹזְרַנִי עָלֶיךָ if thou wert not Ḥoni
I would have decreed against thee, Taʿa. 19 a ; Pes. 53 a ; אִלְמָלֵא
הוּא נִגְנַז סֵפֶר יְחֶזְקֵאל if not for him, the book of Ezekiel would
have been hidden away, Šab. 13 b ; Yo. 20 b ; Meg. 12 b ; 24 b ;
אִלְמָלֵא הִיא לֹא בָרָא (אֵילוּלֵי L) . . . but for it, he would not have
created . . . , Ned. iii. 11 (end); San. 49 a ; 63 a.[1]

492. Hypothetical sentences can also be introduced by other
conjunctions. Thus, בְּזְמַן שֶׁאֵין לָהֶם עָלָיו מְזוֹנוֹת : בְּזְמַן שֶׁ when (if)
they have not to receive from him food, Maʿa. iii. 1 ; בְּזְמַן שֶׁהֵם
לַחִים when (if) they are moist, Šab. iv. 1 ; כְּשׁ : כְּשֶׁיִּהְיוּ בַּעֲלֵי הַדִּין
עוֹמְדִים לְפָנֶיךָ יִהְיוּ when litigants stand before thee, let them be,
Ab. i. 8 ; הֲרֵינִי נָזִיר כְּשֶׁיִּהְיֶה לִי בֵּן lo, I am a Nazirite if I shall have
a son, Naz. ii. 7 ; with אַף : אַף כְּשֶׁאָמְרוּ even when they said, ib. 1 ;
אֲפִילוּ : יָכוֹל אֲפִילוּ תָּקְפָה עָלָיו מִשְׁנָתוֹ even if his study was too hard
for him, Ab. iii. 8 ; אֲפִילוּ צ"ט אוֹמְרִים even if 99 say to divide,
Pea iv. 1.

11. Concessive Clauses.

493. A concessive clause can be introduced by the simple
copula : נִשְׁבֵּתִי וּטְהוֹרָה אֲנִי I was taken captive, nevertheless I am
pure, Ket. ii. 6 , וְהֵן מִתְחַפְּרִנְסִין . . . רָאִיתָ מִיָּמֶיךָ hast ever seen . . . yet

---

[1] Against Tossaphot, Meg. 21 a, Kohut i, p. 98 f., who make a distinction
between אִלְמָלֵא and אִלְמָלֵי. Cf. also Lambert, RÉJ., ix, p. 273 ff. ; Jastrow,
ibid, xi, p. 151 f. ; Ben Yehuda, Thesaurus, i, p. 250 f.

they maintain themselves, Qid. iv. 14 ; כַּמָּה תְהֵא הַסֶּלַע חֲסֵרָה וְלֹא
יְהֵא בָהּ אוֹנָאָה by how much may the *sela'* be deficient, and yet there
may be no deceit in its use, BM iv. 5.

494. More commonly, concessive clauses are introduced by
special conjunctions. These consist of combinations with אַף :
אֲפִילוּ הַמֶּלֶךְ : אַף עַל פִּי כֵן, אַף עַל פִּי, אַף כְּשֶׁ־, (אַף+אִילוּ =) אֲפִילוּ
שׁוֹאֵל בִּשְׁלוֹמוֹ לֹא יְשִׁיבֶנּוּ even though a king greets him, he must not
answer him, Ber. v. 1 ; אֲפִילוּ נוֹטֵל אֶת נַפְשֶׁךְ even though he takes
thy life, ib. ix. 5 ; אַף כְּשֶׁאָמְרוּ even when they said, Naz. ii. 1, 2 ;
אַף עַל פִּי שֶׁאֵין מְבִיאִין מוּגְמָר although perfumes are not brought in,
Ber. vi. 6 ; אַף עַל פִּי שֶׁאָמְרוּ although they have said, Pea i. 2 ;
so before a participle, but without שֶׁ־ : סִילוֹנוֹת אַף עַל פִּי כְפוּפִין אַף
עַל פִּי מְקַבְּלִין pipes, though bent, though receiving, Kel. ii. 3 ;
אַף עַל פִּי כֵן חוֹזֵר וְקוֹרֵא אוֹתָם nevertheless, he calls them again,
Bik. iii. 1 ; אַף עַל פִּי כֵן יַד כּוּלָּן שָׁוָה nevertheless, they are all equal,
Šeq. ii. 4 ; אַף עַל פִּי כֵן הָיִיתִי בוֹכֶה nevertheless, I would have wept,
Ber. 28 b.

12. Comparative Clauses.

495. As in BH, comparison is expressed by כְּ־. From the
nature of its substantival origin, כְּ־ alone can stand only before a
noun as its *regens*, e.g. תֶּבֶן כִּמְלֹא פִּי פָרָה straw like the mouthful
of a cow, Šab. vii. 4 ; דָּמוֹ טָעוּן כִּיסּוּי כְּדַם חַיָּה its blood requires
covering like the blood of a beast, Bik. ii. 9 ; שׁוֹאֵל כְּעִנְיָן וּמֵשִׁיב
כַּהֲלָכָה he asks according to the subject, and answers according to
the law, Ab. v. 10. To introduce a clause, כְּ־ must combine with
another word to form a conjunction. Thus, כְּאִילוּ עָשָׂה : כְּאִילוּ
בְּתוֹךְ הַבַּיִת as if he made it within the house, Suk. i. 2 ; כְּאִילוּ הִיא
מְרוּבַּעַת ; פְּשׁוּטָה כְּאִילוּ הִיא מְרוּבַּעַת as if it was straight, square, 'Er. i. 5 ;
כַּיּוֹצֵא בוֹ, to introduce a new case similar to the preceding one ;
כַּיּוֹצֵא בוֹ הַמַּשְׂכִּיר בַּיִת לַחֲבֵרוֹ likewise, if one lets a house to his
fellow, Šebi. ix. 7 ; כַּיּוֹצֵא בוֹ רוֹצֵחַ שֶׁגָּלָה similarly, a murderer who
went into exile, ib. x. 8 ; Hal. iii. 9.

496. A comparative clause is also introduced by שְׁ כְּמוֹת
כְּמוֹת (כְּמוֹ שֶׁ־): כְּמוֹת שֶׁהוּא לָמוּד as he is accustomed, Ter. iv. 3;
שֶׁהַחֶנְוָנִי לוֹקֵחַ וְלֹא כְמוֹת שֶׁהוּא מוֹכֵר as the shop-keeper buys, and not
as he sells, MŠ iv. 2. By וְכֵן: וְכֵן חָבִית שֶׁל שֶׁמֶן שֶׁנִּשְׁפְּכָה likewise,
a jar of oil that was spilled, Ter. xi. 7; וְכֵן כַּיּוֹצֵא בָהֶם בִּשְׁאָר שְׁנֵי שָׁבִיעַ
and similarly in the other years of the Seven, Šebi. iv. 8, 9.

497. A more complete agreement is expressed when the two
members of the comparison are both introduced by correlative
conjunctions. The following correlatives are found:

כְּ ... כָּךְ: כְּזֵירוּדָהּ וּכְפִיסוּלָהּ שֶׁל חֲמִשִׁית כָּךְ שֶׁל שִׁשִּׁית just like the
thinning and trimming of the fifth, so of the sixth, Šebi. ii. 3;
כְּעוֹנָתָן לְמַעְשְׂרוֹת כָּךְ עוֹנָתָן לִשְׁבִיעִית as their season for tithes, so their
season for the seventh year, ib. iv. 9. These correlatives are used
with nouns only.

כְּשֵׁם שֶׁ ... כָּךְ: כְּשֵׁם שֶׁאָמְרוּ לְהַחֲמִיר כָּךְ אָמְרוּ לְהָקֵל as they said to
make it heavy, so they said to make it light, Kil. ii. 2; כְּשֵׁם שֶׁחוֹלְקִין
בַּתְּבוּאָה כָּךְ חוֹלְקִין בְּתֶבֶן just as they divide the produce, so do they
divide the straw, BM ix. 1; כְּשֵׁם שֶׁהוֹצֵאתַנִי ... כָּךְ תַּכְנִיסֵנִי just as
thou hast brought me forth ... so shalt thou bring me in,
Ber. 48 b. Sometimes כָּךְ is omitted: כְּשֵׁם שֶׁדַּנְתַּנִי ... הַמָּקוֹם יָדִין
אוֹתְךָ as thou hast judged me ... may the Almighty judge thee;
כְּשֵׁם שֶׁדַּנְתּוּנִי ... הַמָּקוֹם יָדִין אֶתְכֶם Šab. 127 b.

כְּשֵׁם שֶׁ ... כֵּן: כְּשֵׁם שֶׁהוּא מֵדֵל בְּתוֹךְ שֶׁלּוֹ כֵּן הוּא מֵדֵל בְּשֶׁל עֲנִיִּים
just as he thins out among his own, so he thins out of the poor,
Pea vii. 5. After a long protasis, the comparison is resumed by
means of the copula: וְכֵן, ... כְּשֵׁם שֶׁאָמְרוּ הַפּוֹגֶמֶת כְּתוּבָּתָהּ לֹא תִפָּרַע
יְתוֹמִים לֹא יִפָּרֵעוּ just as they said (that) she who damages the bill
of her marriage settlement shall not be paid ... so orphans shall
not be paid ..., Šebu. vii. 7.

כְּדֶרֶךְ שֶׁ ... כָּךְ: כְּדֶרֶךְ שֶׁאֵין מְקַלְקְלִין בִּרְשׁוּת הָרַבִּים כָּךְ לֹא יְתַקֵּן
just as one must not cause damage in a public thoroughfare, so
must not one repair therein, Šebi. iii 10.

כְּעִנְיָן שֶׁהוּא מְבָרֵךְ כָּךְ עוֹנִין אַחֲרָיו : כְּעִנְיָן שֶׁ־ ... כָּךְ according as he pronounces the benediction, so they respond after him, Bᵉr. vii. 3.

498. The apodosis may come first for special emphasis, and then the protasis alone has the conjunction : חַיָּב אָדָם לְבָרֵךְ עַל הָרָעָה כְּשֵׁם שֶׁהוּא מְבָרֵךְ עַל הַטּוֹבָה one is bound to bless (God) for evil, as one blesses Him for good, Bᵉr. ix. 5 ; נוֹהֵג בִּתְרוּמָה כְּדֶרֶךְ שֶׁהוּא נוֹהֵג בְּחֻלִּין one behaves towards *teruma*, just as one behaves towards common things, Tᵉr. xi. 5 ; Šebi. iv. 1.

499. An argument to prove a similarity between two cases is introduced by the exclamatory מָה in the protasis, and אַף in the apodosis : מָה הַטְּהוֹרָה עוֹלָה אַף הַטְּמֵאָה תַעֲלֶה what ! the pure rises, also the impure shall rise = just as ... so ..., Tᵉr. v. 4 ; מָה הַנִּדָּה מְטַמְּאָה בְמַשָּׂא אַף עֲבוֹדָה זָרָה מְטַמְּאָה בְמַשָּׂא what ! the menstruous defiles by carrying, also the idol defiles by carrying, AZ iii. 6.

500. In an argument from the minor to the major (קַל וָחֹמֶר), the protasis is introduced by מָה אִם, the apodosis by דִּין הוּא : מָה אִם ... מָקוֹם שֶׁאֵין כֹּהֵן הֶדְיוֹט מִטַּמֵּא ... דִּין הוּא שֶׁלֹּא יְהֵא כֹהֵן גָּדוֹל מִטַּמֵּא what ! if ... where a private priest may not defile himself ... it is justice that the High Priest should not defile himself, Sifre Num. vi. 6. But more often the apodosis is put in a rhetorical question in the negative : מָה אִם שְׁחִיטָה ... דּוֹחָה אֶת הַשַּׁבָּת אֵלּוּ ... לֹא יִדְחוּ אֶת הַשַּׁבָּת what ! if slaughtering ... overrides the Sabbath, these ..., should they not override the Sabbath ? Pᵉs. vi. 2 ; especially with מָה אִם הַפֶּסַח ... חַיָּב הַזְּבָחִים ... אֵינוֹ דִין שֶׁיְּהֵא חַיָּב : אֵינוֹ דִין what ! if the Passover sacrifice ... he is liable, the sacrifices ..., is it not justice that he should be liable ? ib. 5 ; Nᵉd. x. 6 ; Naz. vii. 4 ; So. vi. 3, &c. The apodosis may also take the phrase עַל אַחַת כַּמָּה וְכַמָּה before the predicate : מָה אִם הָעוֹבֵר עֲבֵרָה ... אַחַת what ! הָעוֹשֶׂה מִצְוָה אַחַת עַל אַחַת כַּמָּה וְכַמָּה שֶׁתִּנָּתֵן לוֹ נַפְשׁוֹ if one who commits one transgression ..., one who performs one command, how much more so should his life be given to him ?

Mak. iii. 15 ; וּמַה אִם הַדָּם . . . גֵּזֶל וַעֲרָיוֹת . . . עַל אַחַת כַּמָּה וְכַמָּה שֶׁיִּזְכֶּה
what! if blood ... robbery and incest ..., how much more so
should he secure merit ..., ib.; ib. i. 7; Ab. vi. 3, &c.; or,
finally in later diction, by the rhetorical negative question, placed
at the end as a predicate, לֹא כָל שֶׁכֵּן is not everything (in its
favour) that it should be so? : כְּשֶׁהוּא שָׂבֵעַ מְבָרֵךְ כְּשֶׁהוּא רָעֵב לֹא
כָל שֶׁכֵּן if he blesses when he is full, when he is hungry all the
more so, B^er. 48 b, &c.[1]

13. Disjunctive Clauses.

501. A clause giving an alternative case is co-ordinated with the
preceding clause with or without the copula, but only in the case
of very short clauses : נִקְלַף נִסְדַּק נִיקַּב וְחָסֵר כָּל שֶׁהוּא if it was
peeled, or cracked, or perforated, or had something missing,
Suk. iii. 6, 1, 2 ; גְּזַלְתִּיךְ וְהִלְוִיתַנִי וְהִפְקַדְתָּ אֶצְלִי I robbed thee, or
thou didst lend me, or thou didst deposit with me, BQ x. 7 ;
so with adjectives : בָּשָׂר צָלוּי שָׁלוּק וּמְבוּשָּׁל roast, or seethed, or
cooked meat, P^es. x. 4. But a longer clause is introduced by אוֹ :
הָיוּ שְׁנַיִם רוֹכְבִין . . . אוֹ שֶׁהָיָה אֶחָד רוֹכֵב וְאֶחָד מַנְהִיג two were riding ...,
or one was riding and one leading, BM i. 2.

502. Two or more alternative cases may be introduced by
correlative conjunctions, as follows :

אוֹ . . . אוֹ either . . . or ; אוֹ חוֹלֶצֶת אוֹ מִתְיַבֶּמֶת she either takes
ḥaliṣa, or she is married to her deceased husband's brother,
Y^eb. iii. 3 ; iv. 5, 6 ; אוֹ מְעָרֵב . . . אוֹ אֵינוֹ מְעָרֵב he either makes an
'erub ... or he does not make an 'erub, 'Er. iii. 9 ; אוֹ לֶחִי אוֹ קוֹרָה
either a board or a beam, ib. i. 2.

לֹא . . . וְלֹא neither . . . nor ; לֹא אוֹכְלִין וְלֹא שׂוֹרְפִין they neither
eat, nor burn, P^es. i. 5 ; Y^eb. xi. 2 ; cf. § 339 (ii).

אִם . . . אִם whether . . . or ; cf. § 466. אִם הַיּוֹם אִם לְמָחָר whether
to-day or to-morrow, 'Er. iii. 9.

[1] Cf. Bacher, *Aelteste Terminologie*, p. 172 f.

אֶחָד שֶׁהֵן כֶּסֶף וְאֶחָד שֶׁהֵן ‏... ‏אֶחָד שֶׁ whether ‏... or: ‏וְאֶחָד שֶׁ
פֵּירוֹת whether they are silver or whether they are fruit, MŠ v. 7.
This is especially common before nominal forms without ‏שֶׁ:
אֶחָד שׁוֹגֵג וְאֶחָד מֵזִיד whether in error or intentionally, Ab. iv. 4;
אֶחָד הָאוֹכֵל וְאֶחָד הַשּׁוֹתֶה וְאֶחָד הַסָּךְ whether one eats, or drinks, or
anoints, Tᵉr. vi. 1. Sometimes אֶחָד is expressed before the first
case only: אֶחָד הַחוֹפֵר בּוֹר שִׁיחַ וּמְעָרָה whether one digs a pit, or
a ditch, or a cave, BQ v. 5.

בֵּין שֶׁיֵּשׁ בּוֹ ‏... whether it has in
it ‏... or it has not in it ‏... 'Or. ii. 6, 7; בֵּין שֶׁנִּרְאָה בַעֲלִיל וּבֵין שֶׁלֹּא
נִרְאָה בַעֲלִיל whether it was seen clearly, or not, RH i. 5; with
nominal forms without ‏שֶׁ, except before a negative (cf. § 425):
בֵּין מִתּוֹכוֹ בֵּין מֵעַל גַּבָּיו whether within, or above, Šab. iii. 2; בֵּין עוֹשִׂין
בֵּין שֶׁאֵינָן עוֹשִׂין whether they produce, or not, Šᵉbi. i. 4.

פְּעָמִים שֶׁ ‏... וּפְעָמִים שֶׁ sometimes ‏... sometimes: פְּעָמִים שֶׁהוּא
פְּעָמִים שֶׁאַתָּה מִתְעַלֵּם וּפְעָמִים שֶׁאֵין Bik. iv. 5; אִישׁ וּפְעָמִים שֶׁהוּא אִשָּׁה
אַתָּה מִתְעַלֵּם sometimes thou mayest hide thyself, and sometimes
not, BM 30 a. Before nominal forms without ‏שֶׁ: פְּעָמִים מְכוּרִים
וּפְעָמִים אֵינָן מְכוּרִים sometimes they are sold, sometimes not, BB
v. 2. Also ‏... אוֹ: פְּעָמִים שֶׁ פְּעָמִים שֶׁהוּא בָא מִקְרִיאַת הַגֶּבֶר אוֹ סָמוּךְ לוֹ
sometimes he comes with the crowing of the cock, sometimes
near it, Tam. i. 2.

14. Adversative, Exceptive, and Restrictive Clauses.

503. A clause expressing the antithesis to a preceding clause
can be introduced by the simple copula: מֵת וְהוּא שֶׁנִּשְׁבַּר (he said)
it had died, but really it was broken, Šᵉbu. viii. 2 f., 6 ff.; הָעוֹף
עוֹלֶה עִם הַגְּבִינָה ‏... וְאֵינוֹ נֶאֱכָל the bird goes up with the cheese ‏...
but is not eaten, 'Ed. v. 2; מוּתָּרִין ‏... וְהַשּׁוֹחֵט ‏... חַיָּב they are
permitted ‏..., but he who slays ‏... is liable, Pᵉs. vi. 5.

More frequently, an antithesis is introduced by אֲבָל or אֶלָּא.

אֲבָל introduces a co-ordinated sentence which contains a new

case in opposition to the foregoing : לֹא יַתִּיר אֶת סֻכָּתוֹ אֲבָל מוֹרִיד
הוּא אֶת הַכֵּלִים he must not undo his tabernacle, but he may take
down the things, Suk. iv. 8 ; אֵין נוֹתְנִין לְתָלוּיָה בְּשַׁבָּת אֲבָל נוֹתְנִין
לְתָלוּיָה בְּיוֹם טוֹב one may not put (wine) into a hanging (strainer)
on the Sabbath, but one may put . . . on the Festival, Šab. xx. 1 ;
יוֹדֵעַ אֲנִי שֶׁיֵּשׁ נְזִירוּת אֲבָל אֵינִי יוֹדֵעַ שֶׁהַנָּזִיר אָסוּר בְּיַיִן I know that there
is the state of the Nazirite, but I do not know that the Nazirite is
forbidden the use of wine, Naz. ii. 4 ; MŠ iii. 1 ; Bᵉr. iii. 5 ;
'Er. ii. 3, &c.

504. אֶלָּא is but rarely used like אֲבָל to introduce an adversative
sentence : כָּל כֹּהֵן שֶׁאֵינוֹ שׁוֹקֵל חוֹטֵא אֶלָּא שֶׁהַכֹּהֲנִים דָּרְשׁוּ . . . any priest
that does not pay the shekel is a sinner ; however, the priests
expound . . ., Šᵉq. i. 4 ; הָיָה כִדְבָרֶיךָ אֶלָּא אָמְרוּ חֲכָמִים it would be
as thou sayest, but the sages have said, Bᵉk. iii. 1 ; with a mild
adversative (like וְ) : עַל הַחֲדָשִׁים אָנוּ בוֹשִׁין אֶלָּא שֶׁאַתֶּם מְגַלְגְּלִין עָלֵינוּ אֶת
הַיְשָׁנִים we are ashamed of the new ones, and you roll upon us also
the old ones, Kᵉt. viii. 1 ; BB ix. 10.

505. More often אֶלָּא introduces an exceptive or restrictive
clause : כָּל הַזְּבָחִים . . . כְּשֵׁרִים אֶלָּא שֶׁלֹּא עָלוּ לַבְּעָלִים לְשֵׁם חוֹבָה all
sacrifices . . . are proper, except that they do not rise for the
owner to the category of a duty (discharged, &c.), Zᵉb. i. 1 ;
Mᵉn. i. 1 ; הַמּוּרָם מֵהֶם כַּיּוֹצֵא בָהֶם אֶלָּא שֶׁהַמּוּרָם נֶאֱכָל what is lifted
from them (for the priests) is like them, except that what is lifted
may be eaten, Zᵉb. v. 6, 7 ; הֲרֵי אַתְּ מֻתֶּרֶת לְכָל אָדָם אֶלָּא לְאִישׁ פְּלוֹנִי
lo, thou art free to marry any man, except so and so, Giṭ. ix. 1, 2.

506. In this exceptive or restrictive sense, אֶלָּא is very widely
used after a negative (as in Aram. and כִּי אִם in BH, Ges.-K.,
§ 163 a, f.).[1] The negative with אֶלָּא may usually be rendered in
English by an affirmative with ' only ' : לֹא הָיוּ אֶלָּא שְׁנַיִם they had

---

[1] This use of אֶלָּא after a negative is already found in BH with אִם לֹא, the
equivalent of אֶלָּא (§ 302), Gen. xxiv. 37–8 ; Ps. cxxxi. 1–2. Cf. also
the French ne . . . que.

been only two, Yo. iii. 10; לֹא נְעְנְעוּ אֶלָּא בְּ they only shook at ...,
Suk. iii. 9; אַף הִיא לֹא תִפָּרַע אֶלָּא בִשְׁבוּעָה she, too, shall be paid
only by oath, Ket. x. 5; אֵין ... אֵין נוֹשְׁקִין אֶלָּא ... , אֵין חוֹתְכִין אֶלָּא
יוֹעֲצִין אֶלָּא ... they only cut ...; they only kiss ...; they only
consult ..., Ber. 8 b (§ 329).

507. אֶלָּא is sometimes strengthened by בִּלְבַד placed at the end
of the sentence : אֵין מַדְלִיקִין אֶלָּא בְשֶׁמֶן זַיִת בִּלְבַד one may light only
with olive oil alone, Šab. ii. 2 ; לֹא הָיוּ תוֹקְעִין אֶלָּא בְבֵית דִּין בִּלְבַד they
only blew (the *shofar*) at the *Beth Din* alone, RH iv. 2.

508. אֶלָּא introduces a complete antithesis in the idiomatic
expression לֹא כִי אֶלָּא not so, but : לֹא כִי אֶלָּא בְסֶלַע לָקָה not so, but
he struck against a stone, BQ iii. 11 ; Šeq. i. 4 ; Yeb. viii. 3, 4 ;
Šebu. vi. 7 ; Men. iv. 3. Cf. § 298.

So with כְּלוּם which is equivalent to a negative : כְּלוּם אָמַרְתָּ אֶלָּא
מִפְּנֵי כְבוֹדִי thou only saidst it for my honour, Ned. viii. 7 ; כְּלוּם
נָתַתִּי לְךָ גְדוּלָה אֶלָּא בִשְׁבִיל יִשְׂרָאֵל I have only given thee greatness
for the sake of Israel, Ber. 32 a.

509. Such a clause following אֶלָּא may have a conditional force :
אֵין שׁוֹרִין אֶלָּא כְדֵי שֶׁיִּשּׁוֹרוּ one may not soak ... unless they can
be soaked ..., Šab. i. 5–8, 10. If such a condition is introduced
by אִם, the conditional particle is usually strengthened by כֵּן :
אֵינוֹ מַפְסִיק אֶלָּא אִם כֵּן חָרַשׁ it does not separate, unless he
ploughed it, Pea ii. 1 ; אֵין נוֹעֲלִים בָּהֶם אֶלָּא אִם כֵּן גְּבוֹהִים מִן הָאָרֶץ
one must not shut with them, unless they are high above the
ground, 'Er. x. 8 ; לֹא יִטּוֹל אֶלָּא אִם כֵּן נִעֲנַע מִבְּעוֹד יוֹם he must
not take unless he shook it while it was still day, Be. i. 3, 5 ;
ii. 5 ; iii. 2.

510. The same construction is found with clauses introduced
by עַד ' after '—viz. until the condition named has been fulfilled.
The verb used is the imperfect (§ 321) : אֵין מְעִידִין אֶלָּא עַד שֶׁתֵּצֵא
נַפְשׁוֹ no evidence must be given, except after his soul is gone forth,
Yeb. xvi. 3. But, usually, אֶלָּא is omitted in such a construction :

אֵינוֹ מֵת עַד שֶׁיִּצְטָרֵךְ לַבְּרִיּוֹת he will not die, until after he has become dependent on his fellow creatures = אֶלָּא עַד, Pea vii. 8;

עַד שֶׁיְּפַרְנֵס אֲחֵרִים ... until after he has fed others = אֶלָּא עַד ib.;

אֵינוֹ חַיָּב עַד שֶׁיִּכְתּוֹב he is not liable until after he has written = אֶלָּא עַד, Mak. ii. 7. Sometimes the negative also is omitted: וַחֲכָמִים אוֹמְרִים עַד שֶׁיִּרְשׁוֹם ... (No, except) if he mark, Be. iv. 7; עַד שֶׁתִּפַּרְכֵּס (not, except) if it has moved convulsively, Ḥul. ii. 6.

511. The negative is also omitted before אֶלָּא in answer to a question: לָמָּה נֶאֱמַר ... אֶלָּא בְּשָׁעָה שֶׁדֶּרֶךְ why is it said ...? (not) except when it is the custom ... (= לֹא נֶאֱמַר אֶלָּא), Ber. i. 3; וּמִי שׁוֹמֵעַ לוֹ שֶׁיִּדּוֹר בְּנָזִיר אֶלָּא מֵבִיא but who will listen to him to vow as a Nazirite? (no), but he brings ..., Naz. viii. 1; מַה בֵּין שָׂדֶה אֲחוּזָה לְשָׂדֶה מִקְנָה אֶלָּא שֶׁבְּשָׂדֵה אֲחוּזָה what is the difference between an inherited field and a purchased field? (none) except that in a purchased field ... (= אֵין בֵּין ... אֶלָּא), 'Ar. iii. 2; מַה בֵּין נְדָרִים לִנְדָבוֹת אֶלָּא שֶׁהַנְּדָרִים what is the difference between vows and free-will offerings? (none) except that, Qin. i. 1. Cf. אֵין בֵּין שַׁבָּת לְיוֹם טוֹב אֶלָּא אֹכֶל נֶפֶשׁ בִּלְבָד there is no difference between the Sabbath and the Festival except in the matter of food alone, Meg. i. 5–11.

Cf. the omission of the negative before כִּי אִם in BH, 1 Sam. xxvi. 10, &c., *BDB.*, p. 475 a.

512. Exceptive clauses are also introduced by וּבִלְבַד שֶׁ־: וּבִלְבַד שֶׁיּוֹרִיעֶנּוּ but only if he will make it known to him, Dam. iii. 3; וּבִלְבַד שֶׁיְּהֵא מַמָּשׁ בִּדְבָרָיו but only when there will be something real in his words, San. vi. 1; וּבִלְבַד שֶׁיִּתֵּן כְּנֶגֶד הַיְסוֹד but only if he will put it against the base, Zeb. v. 8.

By חוּץ מִ־ outside of: חוּץ מִשֶּׁנִּטְמְאָה except that which was defiled, MŠ. iii. 9; or without שֶׁ־ before nominal forms: חוּץ מֵאֶחָד מֵהֶם; חוּץ מִן הַפַּת; מִן הַיַּיִן except wine, bread, Ber. vi. 1; חוּץ מֵאֶחָד מֵהֶם except one of them, Zeb. viii. 8. Sometimes strengthened by

חוּץ מִלֵּילֵי . . . הָרִאשׁוֹן בִּלְבַד : בִּלְבַד except the first night . . . alone, Suk ii. 6 ; חוּץ מִזּוֹ בִלְבַד except this alone, Yo. iii. 3.

15. Temporal Clauses.

513. The relation of time between two verbs is expressed by various conjunctions followed by ‑שֶׁ.

כְּשֶׁ‑ when : כְּשֶׁהָיוּ יִשְׂרָאֵל בַּמִּדְבָּר when the Israelites were in the wilderness, Mᵉn. iv. 3 ; כְּשֶׁיָּצָא אָמַר when he had gone forth, he said (pluperfect, § 309), 'AZ. iii. 4 ; כְּשֶׁאַגִּיעַ לוֹ אֲלַקְּטֶנּוּ I shall gather it when I shall have reached it (*fut. exactum*, § 321), Kil. v. 6. In later MH often with ‑ל prefixed : . . . לִכְשֶׁיִּבָּנֶה בֵּית הַמִּקְדָּשׁ when the Temple will be re-built, I will bring, Šab. 12 b. Cf. in BH, Ges.-K., § 164 d ; *BDB.*, p. 455.

מִשֶּׁ‑ after : מוֹכֵר הוּא מִשֶּׁיֵּגַּץ he may sell after he has cut down, 'AZ. i. 8 ; מִשֶּׁתֶּחְשַׁךְ after it has become dark, Šab. iv. 2 ; with pleonastic ‑כְּ : מִכְּשֶׁיָּצָאת הָאֶבֶן after the stone had gone forth, Mak. ii. 2. מִשֶּׁ‑ with the perfect is usually found only as correlative to עַד שֶׁ‑, see next section. In BH this temporal use of מִן is only found with nouns : כְּמִשְׁלֹשׁ חֳדָשִׁים Gen. xxxviii. 24 ; cf. *BDB.*, p. 581, 4 b.

עַד שֶׁ‑ until, before : עַד שֶׁיַּעֲלֶה עַמּוּד הַשַּׁחַר until dawn will rise, Bᵉr. i. 1. After a negative, with אֶלָּא understood (§ 510) : אַל תָּדִין אֶת חֲבֵרְךָ עַד שֶׁתַּגִּיעַ לִמְקוֹמוֹ judge not thy neighbour before thou shalt have reached his place, Ab. ii. 4 (§ 321) ; לֹא הָיָה מַגִּיעַ . . . עַד שֶׁנַּעֲשָׂה he did not reach . . . before he became, Yo. vi. 6 (cf. Aram. : לֹא מְטוֹ . . . עַד דִּי שַׁלִּיטוּ Dan. vi. 25). Cf. BH : עַד שֶׁתֶּחְפָּץ Cant. ii. 7, עַד שֶׁיָּפוּחַ 17, &c. ; *BDB.*, p. 724 f.

עַד שֶׁלֹּא : עַד שֶׁלֹּא נִבְחֲרוּ before they had been chosen, Mak. ii. 4 ; so in BH עַד אֲשֶׁר לֹא יָבֹאוּ before they will come, Qoh. xii. 1, 2, 6.

So, especially, as correlative to מִשֶּׁ‑ : . . . עַד שֶׁלֹּא בָא לְעוֹנַת נְדָרִים מִשֶּׁבָּא before he had reached the season of vows . . . after he had

reached ... Tᵉr. i. 3 ; ... מִשֶּׁהִגְרִיל ... עַד שֶׁלֹּא הִגְרִיל before he had cast lots ... after he had cast lots ..., Yo. vi. 1 ; עַד שֶׁ א.
נְגָחָהּ ... מִשֶּׁנְּגָחָהּ before he had gored her ... after he had gored her, BQ v. 1.

עַד כְּדֵי שֶׁ until : עַד כְּדֵי שֶׁיִתְאַכֵּל הַמָּזוֹן until the food will be digested, Bᵉr. viii. 7 ; עַד כְּדֵי שֶׁיֵדְעוּ בוֹ שְׁכֵנָיו until his neighbours will know of it, BM ii. 6. (But L has : עד שישמעו שכינים.)

בְּשָׁעָה שֶׁ when (a point of time) : בְּשָׁעָה שֶׁהַמְּלָכִים עוֹבְרִים when kings pass, 'AZ iv. 6 ; כָּל שָׁעָה שֶׁ when (duration of time) : כָּל שָׁעָה שֶׁמּוּתָּר לֶאֱכוֹל when, as long as, he is allowed to eat, Pᵉs. ii. 1.

מִשָּׁעָה שֶׁ : מִשָּׁעָה שֶׁהַכֹּהֲנִים נִכְנָסִין from the time when the priests enter, Bᵉr. i. 1 ; מִשָּׁעָה שֶׁנִּפְסְקָה 'Or. i. 5.

בִּזְמַן שֶׁ when, usually with a hypothetical force : בִּזְמַן שֶׁקָּנָה קַרְקַע אֲבָל בִּזְמַן שֶׁלֹּא קָנָה קַרְקַע when he bought land, but when he did not buy land, Ma'a. v. 5 ; cf. § 492.

כָּל זְמַן שֶׁ when, while (duration of time) : כָּל זְמַן שֶׁבְּנֵי אָדָם חוֹרְשִׁין while men plough, Šᵉbi. ii. 1 ; כָּל זְמַן שֶׁבִּכְּרוּ when they have ripened, ib. ix. 4.

אֵימָתַי שֶׁ whenever ; אֵימָתַי שֶׁתִּרְצֶה whenever thou wishest, BM v. 3 ; אֵימָתַי שֶׁיִּבָּנֶה בֵית הַמִּקְדָּשׁ whenever the Temple will be re-built, MŠ v. 2.

כֵּיוָן שֶׁ as soon as : כֵּיוָן שֶׁהִגִּיעַ הַשָּׂעִיר as soon as the goat reached, Yo. vi. 8 ; כֵּיוָן שֶׁהִיא נוֹתֶנֶת אֶת הַמַּיִם as soon as she puts in the water, Hal. iii. 1.

קוֹדֶם שֶׁ before : קוֹדֶם שֶׁתִּתְאָרֵס before she was betrothed, So. ii. 6.

אַחַר שֶׁ after : אַחַר שֶׁכְּתָבוֹ לָהּ after he had written it for her, 'Ed. iv. 7 ; or with ל : לְאַחַר שֶׁהוֹדוּ after they had agreed, Tᵉr. v. 4.

עֵת שֶׁ when (rare) : עֵת שֶׁבָּאוּ אֲבוֹתֵינוּ when our fathers came, 'Or. i. 2.

מִיָּד immediately : מִיָּד הָיָה עוֹמֵד וְעוֹסֵק בַּתּוֹרָה immediately he

would arise and study the Torah; מִיַד יוֹעֲצִים בַּאֲחִיתוֹפֶל immediately
they would consult Ahitophel, B^{er}. 3 b; מִיַד כָּבְתָה immediately it
is extinguished, Šab. 151 b.

16. Final Clauses.

514. The purpose or aim of an action may be expressed by
the infinitive with -לְ: נִכְנָסִין לֶאֱכוֹל they enter to eat, B^{er}. i. 1 ;
הִפֵּיתִי לִקְרוֹת I inclined to read, ib. 3. In the negative: שֶׁלֹּא לְהַבְעִית
not to frighten, Yo. v. 2 ; שֶׁלֹּא לְבַיֵּישׁ not to shame, Ta'a. iv. 8.
After verbs of preventing, &c., the inf. takes מִן: לֹא נִמְנְעוּ
מִלְּשָׂרוֹף . . . מִלְהַדְלִיק they refrained not from burning . . . from
kindling, P^{es}. i. 6 ; cf. § 346. The infin. can also be introduced
by כְּדֵי: אָמְרוּ . . . כְּדֵי לְהַרְחִיק they said . . . in order to remove,
B^{er}. i. 1 (L אֶלָּא לְהַרְחִיק). By עַל מְנָת: הַקּוֹרֵעַ עַל מְנָת לִתְפּוֹר if one
tears in order to sew ; הַמְקַלְקֵל עַל מְנָת לְתַקֵּן if one damages, in
order to repair, Šab. xiii. 2, 3.

515. Clauses expressing purpose are introduced by שֶׁ-, שֶׁלֹּא:
לֹא שֶׁיַּעֲלֶה אֶלָּא שֶׁלֹּא יוֹסִיף not that it may rise, but that it may not
increase, Šab. xxiii. 5 ; שֶׁלֹּא יְהִיוּ מֵימָיו נִפְסָלִין that its water may not
be disqualified, Yo. iii. 10.

כְּדֵי שֶׁ-, כְּדֵי שֶׁלֹּא: כְּדֵי שֶׁיְּהוּ רוֹאִין זֶה אֶת זֶה that they may see one
another, San. iv. 3 ; כְּדֵי שֶׁלֹּא לְשַׁבֵּחַ אֶת הַתִּינוֹקוֹת not to make the
children forget, 'Er. vii. 9.

בִּשְׁבִיל שֶׁ-, בִּשְׁבִיל שֶׁלֹּא: בִּשְׁבִיל שֶׁיֵּחַמּוּ ; בִּשְׁבִיל שֶׁיֵּצַנּוּ in order that
they may be cold, hot, Šab. xxii. 4 ; בִּשְׁבִיל שֶׁיַּמְתִּין that he may last,
ib. xxiii. 5 ; בִּשְׁבִיל שֶׁלֹּא תֵצֵא that it should not go out, ib. xv. 2 ;
בִּשְׁבִיל שֶׁלֹּא יִמּוֹקוּ that they may not melt, Ta'a. iii. 8.

עַל מְנָת שֶׁ-: עַל מְנָת שֶׁיִּלְקוֹט בְּנוֹ on condition that his son may
gather, Pea v. 6.

17. Consecutive Clauses.

516. Clauses expressing the consequence of an action may be
introduced by the simple copula, especially in questions: בַּמֶּה

יִבְנֶה וִיהֵא חַיָּיב how much should he build, so as to be liable? Šab. xxii. 1 ; כַּמָּה יִשְׁהוּ וְיִהְיוּ אֲסוּרִים how long should they abide, so as to become prohibited? Ter. viii. 4 ; Šebi. iv. 10 ; Oh. xii. 8 ; מָתַי יָבוֹא לְיָדִי וַאֲקַיִּמֶנָּה when will it come to my hand that I may fulfil it? Ber. 61 b ; שֶׁלֹּא יְהֵא רַעַבְתָן וִיהֵא סוֹתֵם אֶת הַפֶּתַח בְּפָנָיו that he may not be a glutton, and so shut the door in his own face, BM vii. 5.

More often, consecutive clauses are introduced by ‑שֶׁ כְּדֵי , כְּדֵי שֶׁלֹּא : נוֹתֵן . . . כְּדֵי שֶׁיִּטּוֹל מִן הַמּוּקָּף he gives . . . so that he may take from the nearest, Hal. ii. 8 ; קוֹצֵץ כְּדֵי שֶׁיְּהֵא גָמָל עוֹבֵר וְרוֹכְבוֹ he cuts off, so that a camel may pass with its rider, BB ii. 14; כְּדֵי . . . יִתְחַלָּקוּ שֶׁלֹּא יְהֵא בְּמָקוֹם אֶחָד כַּבֵּיצָה they shall be divided, so that there be not in one place as much as an egg, Ter. v. 1.

517. Consecutive sentences, as distinguished from consecutive clauses, are introduced by לְפִיכָךְ : לְפִיכָךְ אִם אֵירַע בָּהֶן פְּסוּל therefore, if a disqualification occurred in them, Pes. viii. 6; לְפִיכָךְ אָנוּ חַיָּיבִין therefore, we are bound to, ib. x. 4 ; לְפִיכָךְ נִבְרָא אָדָם therefore, was man created, San. iv. 5.

INDEX OF BIBLICAL PASSAGES

(The references are to sections. n. = foot-note.)

PRINTED IN GREAT BRITAIN
AT THE UNIVERSITY PRESS, OXFORD
BY CHARLES BATEY, PRINTER TO THE UNIVERSITY